Basic Nuclear Engineering

This book is a part of the

ALLYN AND BACON SERIES IN MECHANICAL
ENGINEERING AND APPLIED MECHANICS

Consulting Editor: FRANK KREITH
University of Colorado

BASIC
NUCLEAR ENGINEERING
Second Edition

ARTHUR R. FOSTER

Chairman, Department of Mechanical Engineering
Northeastern University

ROBERT L. WRIGHT, JR.
Mechanical Engineering Specialist
Postal Service, Management Institute

Allyn and Bacon, Inc.
Boston • London • Sydney

LIBRARY OF CONGRESS CATALOG CARD NUMBER: 72-89618

PRINTED IN THE UNITED STATES OF AMERICA

ISBN: 0-205-03653-8

Fourth printing . . . February, 1975

Contents

Preface

BASIC NUCLEAR ENGINEERING is designed as a text to be used by advanced undergraduate engineering students. It treats the broad spectrum of nuclear activity. Nuclear physics, radiation detection, health physics, and radioisotope applications are among the topics treated. However, much of the emphasis is centered about the power reactor, the major nuclear application from the point of view of manpower involved and dollars invested.

Although the book was intended primarily for undergraduates in the various engineering disciplines, it also should prove helpful to practicing engineers who may find themselves thrust into a nuclear environment. In most chapters there are solutions of typical problems, numerous illustrations, problems for the student to solve, and references for further study.

The book is designed to be flexible. Complete coverage of the material would require a full year course. A single term course for students having an adequate nuclear physics background might omit Chapters 2, 3, and 4. Other special topics such as radiation detection, nuclear materials, or heat transfer might appropriately be omitted by the instructor to allow the course to conform to the time available and the desired depth of coverage.

After an introduction to the broad spectrum of nuclear activity in Chapter 1 the necessary background in nuclear physics is developed in Chapters 2, 3, and 4. Fusion reactors and the strange particles produced by high energy particle accelerators are included in Chapter 4. Chapter 5 deals with radiation detection. Chapter 6 covers health physics and biological radiation detection with an introduction to some of the problems of shielding. A wide variety of radioisotope applications are discussed in Chapter 7.

The next three chapters center more specifically about the nuclear reactor and the development of power from the controlled fission process. Chapter 8 covers the fission process and the interaction of neutrons with matter. Chapter 9 is devoted to the steady state reactor core. The principles allowing critical size determination, the calculation of power level, and the effect of reflectors are considered. One-group theory, modified one-group theory, and two-group theory are discussed in some detail. Chapter 10 treats the control of reactors and their transient behavior. The reactivity effects of temperature, fission product accumulation, and conversion are considered.

Radiation damage and reactor materials problems are covered in Chapter 11. The effects of various types of radiation on materials are discussed with particular emphasis on the effects of fast neutron damage to structural and cladding materials and fuels, and, in the case of fuels, to the damage caused by fission fragments. The properties of uranium and plutonium are discussed, and a survey of their use in alloys, dispersion type fuels and ceramic fuels is given. Graphite is discussed, both as a moderator and as a matrix material for high temperature carbide fuels.

Chapter 12 considers a number of areas in heat transfer which are peculiar to reactors. These include the temperature distribution in fuel elements, the temperature distribution and heat flow along a fission heated coolant channel, boiling heat transfer with the application of DNB data to design, and nuclear superheat. Chapter 13 treats the economics of nuclear power generation, discusses typical reactor plants which are in operation or are being considered for future applications, and dual purpose plants accomplishing electrical power generation and desalination using multistage flash evaporators.

We have received assistance and suggestions from many sources during the preparation of this volume. The various ASEE-AEC summer institutes which have been attended by the authors were invaluable. We acknowledge gratefully the contributions of our students and we wish particularly to express indebtedness to Mr. Robert Bowker, Professor Thomas C. Coleman, Jr., Professor Frank Kreith, and Professor Leslie Wilbur for their constructive suggestions and encouragement.

ARTHUR R. FOSTER
ROBERT L. WRIGHT, JR.

Preface to the 2nd Edition

The pace of development in the nuclear engineering field has led to the introduction of material to be included in an introductory text of this nature. The basic approach used in the first edition remains unchanged, but the following specific objectives are sought in the new edition:

1. to reflect current thinking and interest in topics which were only touched upon in the first edition, such as breeder and fast reactors,
2. to take advantage of the teaching experience with the previous edition and suggestions received from others,
3. to update the book with the latest applications and developments in the nuclear field, and
4. to incorporate concepts reflecting increased concern for our environment and usage of natural resources.

The reorganization and rewriting of material has led to a modest increase in the length of the book. However, we believe it still can be completely covered in a full year course. This edition retains the modular concept of the first edition.

Treatment of radiation damage mechanisms, fuel cycles and the economics of nuclear power, molten salt reactors, gas cooled reactors, and fast reactor systems have been substantially expanded. Sections have been added on one group theory for fast reactors, control of fast reactors, thermal discharges and their ecological impact, loss of coolant accidents, and engineering problems related to the development of fusion reactors. New problems have been added.

During the preparation of this edition, assistance and suggestions have been received from numerous sources. We wish especially to express our appreciation and thanks to Mr. Richard Muranaka, Mrs. Tamels Unger, Professor H. Frederick Bowman, and Professor Ralph Buonopane.

Chapter 1

Introduction

The utilization of energy for the performance of tasks has always been integral with man's standard of living. This utilization can be traced all the way from the first use of the wheel, to the great works of the ancient Egyptians, through the power producing devices of Newcomen and Watt, up to the present advanced state of our technology and standard of living. The great wars of history provide examples of vast amounts of energy expended.

Historically, except for the last few hundred years, man's primary energy source has been wood. In fact, in many parts of the world today wood is still one of the chief sources of power. In the middle 1800's fossil fuels replaced wood, now oil seems to be replacing coal, and in the future nuclear fuels will undoubtedly replace fossil fuels.

Most forecasts of energy requirements for the immediate future are based on an analysis of population growth and per capita energy consumption. Two of the more interesting forecasts have been made by P. Putnam and H. Brown. Their predictions are shown in Fig. 1.1.

Meeting these tremendous demands will require diverse sources of energy. The present practical sources of energy are: a) fossil fuels, b) flowing water, c) winds, d) ocean tides, e) solar energy, f) geothermal

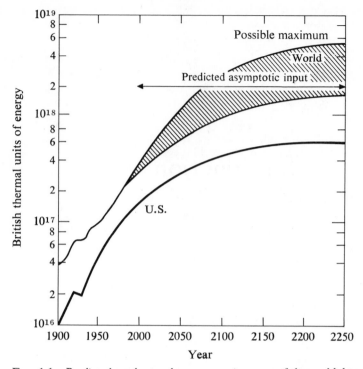

Fɪɢ. 1.1 *Predicted total annual energy requirements of the world, based on population growth predictions of References 1 and 2 and per capita energy requirement predictions of the U. S. Atomic Energy Commission.*

energy, g) fissionable nuclei, and h) fusionable nuclei (questionable as to its practicability).   At some time all fossil fuels will be used up and energy will be derived solely from the remaining sources and the nuclear fuels.   Various estimates have been made of the time when the supply of fossil fuels will be exhausted.   They range from twenty-five to two hundred years.   The important point, however, is that the world's energy requirements will outstrip the economically recoverable fossil fuels.   Another source of energy must then be developed to meet the world's energy demands.

The contributions of wind, ocean, tides, solar and geothermal energy, and flowing water are too limited and costly ever to become a large percentage of the total energy produced.   This leaves nuclear fuels as the only economical source for the energy requirements shown in Fig. 1.1. The forecasts made concerning future nuclear capacity are summarized in Fig. 1.2.

This book concerns the applications of nuclear fission to power production and isotope technology.   Nuclear fusion, while theoretically a possible source of energy, has presented formidable problems. Until these problems (described in some detail in Chapters 4 and 13) are solved, fusion reactions will not be a useful source of energy.

There is a vast amount of energy available from fission (and fusion). Various estimates place the amount of fissionable ore reserves at about 16 million tons (excluding Communist countries). If one pound of uranium underwent complete fission it would produce about 30,000,000,000 Btu of energy. It is believed that the earth's crust contains about 40×10^7 million tons of uranium and thorium compounds. The challenge is to recover this fissionable material economically and convert it into energy.

NUCLEAR FUELS

In a chemical combustion reaction there is a rearrangement in the atoms of fuel and oxygen to form molecules of combustion products.

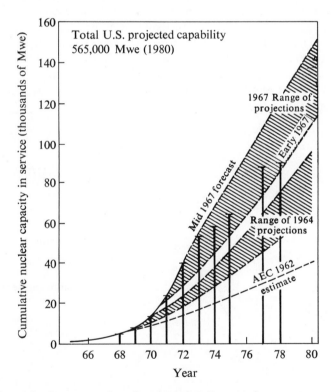

FIG. 1.2 *Forecasts of nuclear growth. Bar graphs represent actual capacity of ordered and announced plants in service based on plans as of April, 1971.* [*From* Nuclear News, **10**, *No. 9 (September, 1967).*]

During this combustion an insignificant amount of mass is converted into energy. However, in fission reactions a larger proportion of the mass is converted into energy, and the fissioning nuclei split into different elements.

There are, presently, four radioactive materials which are suitable for fission. They are ^{233}U, ^{235}U, ^{239}Pu, and ^{241}Pu. The isotopes ^{238}U and ^{232}Th are fissionable by what are termed fast neutrons, as opposed to thermal neutrons used with ^{233}U, ^{235}U, ^{239}Pu, and ^{241}Pu. A detailed discussion of neutron interactions is found in Chapter 8.

FISSION

Fission (illustrated schematically in Fig. 1.3) occurs when a fissionable nucleus captures a neutron. Capture upsets the internal force balance between neutrons and protons in the nucleus. The nucleus splits into two lighter nuclei, and an average of two or three neutrons is emitted. The resulting mass of products is less than that of the original nucleus plus neutron. The difference in masses appears as energy in an amount determined according to Einstein's formula, $E = mc^2$. If one of the neutrons emitted is captured by another fissionable nucleus a second fission occurs similar to the first, another neutron may produce a third fission, and so on. When the reaction becomes self-sustaining so that one fission triggers at

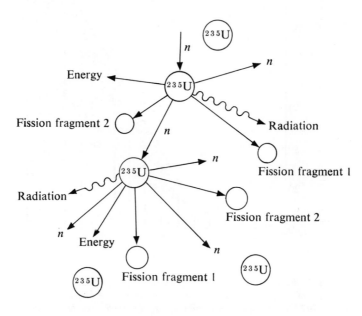

FIG. 1.3 *Schematic of* ^{235}U *fission.*

least one more fission, the phenomenon is termed a chain reaction. The device in which this chain reaction is initiated, maintained, and controlled is called a nuclear reactor.

Three results of a fission chain reaction are important. The first is the energy released. About 80 percent of this energy appears as kinetic energy of the product nuclei (fission fragments) and neutrons. Through numerous collisions among fission fragments, neutrons, structural material, and fuel their kinetic energy is removed and released in the form of heat.

The second important result is the radiation emitted during the reaction. Succeeding chapters treat radiation in more detail. It suffices to say here that the radiation appears either in the form of electrons, helium nuclei, or pure electromagnetic radiation. The radiation from a nuclear reactor comes directly from fission and from the decay of fission fragments. Radioactive isotopes, that is, isotopes which are unstable and emit radiation, can be formed by placing stable nuclei in a reactor. In the reactor they are bombarded by neutrons, and their nuclear structure is altered. The radiation is potentially harmful to living organisms and to materials. With proper application, however, the radiation can also be extremely useful to materials and living organisms. The branch of nuclear engineering which treats radiation and its uses is termed radioisotope technology.

Finally, the neutrons released during fission are important in the overall fission process. In order for a fission reaction to be self-sustaining (a chain reaction) at least one neutron released per fission must be captured and cause fission in another nucleus. Depending on the fate of the neutrons released, the reaction becomes subcritical, critical, or supercritical. Critical describes a chain reaction in which fission is maintained at a constant rate per unit time. A reactor in which the rate of fissioning is decreasing is subcritical, and one in which the rate of fissioning is increasing is supercritical. An atomic bomb, obviously, is super-super-critical.

The problem in nuclear engineering appears to be how to harness and control the nuclear chain reaction. After this is done one must find a way to convert the released energy to a useful form or utilize the radiation emitted. Figure 1.4 illustrates how a nuclear reactor might be designed. It is readily observed that the reactor takes the place of the combustion device in a conventional power cycle.

REACTOR USE AND CLASSIFICATION

The uses for nuclear reactors are varied. The major application, however, is for the production of electric power. Here the objective is to

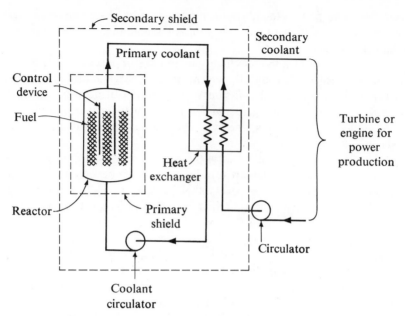

FIG. 1.4 *Schematic of a nuclear reactor power plant. The primary coolant might also be used as working substance in the power plant.*

have a high rate of energy release at a high enough temperature for the attainment of a high thermal efficiency in the associated power cycle. Research reactors supply a large quantity of neutrons for irradiation of various materials in the core or to be allowed to stream from the reactor through a beam port. The temperatures in most research reactors are relatively low when compared with power reactors and disposal of the heat generated may be a nuisance. University research reactors are often used as training reactors in addition to performing their research mission. A medical reactor is designed to facilitate the treatment of patients by radiation from beam ports. Hospital facilities must be associated with such an installation. Other reactors may be used for the irradiation of stable isotopes to produce useful radioisotopes. Reactors also contribute to our space effort. Small compact units generate auxiliary power aboard space vehicles and larger units provide propulsion, as in the Rover project. Under study and development are in-pile thermoelectric and thermionic reactors.

Reactors may be classified in a number of ways: the use to which the neutrons produced by fission are put, the energy spectrum of the neutron population, the degree of conversion of fertile material, the dispersion of the core materials, and by the types of materials selected for fuel, moderator, cladding and control. Table 1.1 lists some materials of thermal reactor components and their function. These classifications are not mutually exclusive.

In all reactors there must be some means of controlling the neutron population. The removal of all neutrons not required for a critical reaction is accomplished with control rods. A control rod regulates the reaction rate by absorbing neutrons. The control rods may be moved in or out of the reactor core to present more or less absorbing material to the neutrons. Control rods are usually made from cadmium or boron compounds, but sometimes they are made from fertile material (such as ^{238}U) to utilize the neutrons released by fissioning. A fertile material is a substance which can be converted into fissionable material by neutron absorption and subsequent decay to a fissionable species.

TABLE 1.1

REACTOR COMPONENTS AND MATERIALS

Component	Material	Function
Fuel	^{233}U, ^{235}U, ^{239}Pu, ^{241}Pu	Fission reaction
Moderator	light water, heavy water, carbon, beryllium	To reduce energy of fast neutrons to thermal neutrons
Coolant	light water, heavy water, air, CO_2, He, sodium, bismuth, sodium potassium, organic	To remove heat
Reflector	same as moderator	To minimize neutron leakage
Shielding	concrete, water, steel, lead, polyethylene	To provide protection from radiation
Control rods	cadmium, boron, hafnium	To control neutron production rate
Structure	aluminum, steel, zirconium, stainless steel	To provide physical support of reactor structure and components, containment of fuel elements

The *energy of the neutrons inducing fission* constitutes one of the major classes of nuclear reactors. Thus, a thermal reactor is one in which fission is induced by neutrons in thermal equilibrium with the reactor core material. Most of today's reactors are thermal. The neutron produced in the ^{235}U fission of Fig. 1.3 has much energy and a very small probability of interacting with another ^{235}U atom. The probability of an interaction of a neutron with a bombarded nucleus is referred to as *neutron cross section*. A moderator is put into the reactor core to slow the neutron to thermal energies by collision (called scattering). A good moderator reduces the energy (speed) of neutrons in a small number of collisions (possesses a high scattering cross section).

Fast reactors make no attempt to slow neutrons and thus, contain no moderator. The average neutron energy is of the order of 0.5 to 1.0 MeV. At these energies it is easier to convert a larger fraction of any fertile ^{238}U and ^{232}Th to fissionable ^{239}Pu and ^{233}U. Today's thermal reactors convert much less fertile material to fissionable material than they consume and would be called burner reactors. Perhaps a conversion ratio of 50% is reasonable for today's power reactors. If this conversion ratio exceeds 100% the reactor is a breeder. A fast neutron spectrum favors breeding and opens the possibility of converting our vast supplies of ^{232}Th and ^{238}U to nuclear fuel. Fast breeder reactors would be designed to produce large blocks of power, as well as a surplus of fuel. EBR-II, shown in Fig. 1.7, is an experimental prototype of a breeder which produces 20 Mwe, as well as plutonium. An intermediate reactor would have the average energy of its neutrons in the epithermal (above thermal) region. Reactors with this type of energy spectrum have been investigated, but the results have not justified active development.

Materials consisting of low mass number atoms usually make the best moderators. In this respect hydrogen makes an ideal moderator (except that hydrogen absorbs some neutrons). Light water is desirable because it is cheap and plentiful. Furthermore, the light water can be used as both moderator and coolant; however, the water must be completely free from impurities in order to avoid neutron absorption and possible radioactivity. Water also has a relatively low boiling point; thus pressures must be high if high temperatures are desired. Heavy water, D_2O, is also an excellent moderator and coolant. Heavy water has a smaller probability for neutron absorption than light water, but it is not quite as effective as light water in slowing down the neutrons. Its chief disadvantage is its high cost. Carbon is another good moderator because it does not absorb many neutrons and does scatter neutrons well. Carbon is readily available in the form of graphite. One disadvantage is that graphite may oxidize at high temperatures. Beryllium is one of the best solid moderators and is used either as metallic beryllium or as beryllium oxide. Beryllium has a low absorption cross section, a high scattering cross section, and a high melting point, 1158°K.

The reactor coolant removes the heat released by fission from the reactor. To do this efficiently the coolant should have a high specific heat, high conductivity, good stability, good pumping characteristics, and low neutron absorption cross section. Coolants can be either liquid or gaseous. The popularity of light and heavy water as coolants was mentioned in the preceding paragraph.

Liquid metals such as sodium, sodium-potassium (NaK), and bismuth make desirable coolants. They have a high boiling point and therefore can be used at low pressures. The heat transfer and nuclear properties are good, but the metals must be preheated before reactor startup. Some organic substances (diphenyl, $C_{12}H_{10}$) have been tried experimentally as reactor coolants, but they have not yet had commercial application. Their chief disadvantage has been a tendency to decompose.

The motion of neutrons in a reactor is completely random. Unless the reactor core is surrounded by a reflector, neutrons may leak out. The amount of fissionable material in a reactor may be reduced by placing this reflector around the core to "reflect" the neutrons back into the core. A good reflector normally has the same characteristics as a good moderator.

A shield is necessary to prevent or reduce passage of radiation to the outside of the reactor. All types of radiation are dangerous to personnel and must be reduced to tolerable levels. Neutrons and gamma radiation are the most penetrating radiations; if these two are stopped the other radiations and fission products will be stopped as well. Shielding is dependent on the purpose of the reactor. For example, a zero power reactor requires very little or no shielding. In general the best shield for neutrons is a low atomic weight material and for gamma rays a high atomic weight material. Frequently, a shield is made of layers of heavy and light material such as concrete and polyethylene or concrete and water.

As previously mentioned, control materials are used to regulate the neutron density in the reactor. The reactor power is directly proportional to the neutron density; removing neutrons from the reactor core, therefore, will decrease the power and reaction rate. Conversely, not removing as many neutrons will increase the power. The control materials are usually in the form of rods. The rod material must have a huge neutron absorption cross section. Control rods are made from cadmium, boron, or hafnium.

Three types of control rods are used:

(1) Shim rods are used for making occasional coarse adjustments in neutron density.
(2) Regulating rods are used for fine adjustments and to maintain the desired power output.
(3) Safety rods are capable of shutting down the entire reactor in case of failure of the normal control system. The control rods are normally suspended above the reactor core by a magnetic clutch. In the case of shutdown they drop by gravity into the reactor core, absorb neutrons, and stop the chain reaction.

The reactor structural materials must have high structural impact and tensile strength, high corrosion resistance, high rupture strength, low neutron absorption, little interaction with radiation, and ease of fabrication.   Aluminum, stainless steel, zirconium, nickel, magnesium, concrete, and many others are used as reactor structural materials.

All the components are assembled into the complete nuclear reactor, whether it be for power, irradiation, production of fissile material, research, or other purposes.

It is enlightening to examine reactors according to the major class of *nuclear configuration*.   Based on nuclear configuration a reactor is either homogeneous or heterogeneous.   In a homogeneous reactor the core materials are distributed in such a manner that the neutron characteristics can be accurately described by the assumption of homogeneous distribution of materials throughout the core.   In a heterogeneous reactor the core materials are segregated to such an extent that the neutron characteristics cannot be accurately described by the assumption of homogeneous distribution of materials throughout the core.

From the standpoint of neutron economy a spherical core is best. A spherical core, however, is only economical in a homogeneous reactor. Since the coolant-fuel mixture becomes heated in the reactor core, it must be circulated through a heat exchanger to remove this heat.

Analytically, it is simplest to treat a homogeneous reactor and, for the most part, the theoretical and design considerations of this book are for homogeneous reactors.   (Heterogeneous reactors with small fuel elements may often be treated as being homogeneous without introducing serious errors.)   A homogeneous reactor uses a uranium salt mixed with coolant.

A homogeneous reactor is not practical for power production purposes because the radioactive fission products in the fuel-coolant mixture must be circulated through the heat exchanger.   The whole plant must then be shielded; the mass of circulating mixture will be enormous, and maintenance will be extremely difficult and expensive.

A heterogeneous reactor is much more practical from the standpoints of both power and economy.   The solid fuel heterogeneous reactor is usually cubical or cylindrical.   The fuel is uniformly spaced throughout the moderator while the coolant circulates through passages between fuel elements.   As mentioned previously, the coolant and moderator are frequently one and the same.   For economy, effective heat transfer, and ease of refueling, fuel elements have been fabricated as thin rods, plates, and small diameter pins.   These are assembled into bundles of parallel elements.

In the case of a pressurized water or organic cooled reactor, the heated coolant, after passing from the fuel element passages, gives up its heat in a heat exchanger.   Figure 1.5 is a cutaway view of the Connecticut Yankee Atomic Electric Company's pressurized water power reactor core. If the coolant is gas (GCR) or steam as in a boiling water reactor (BWR),

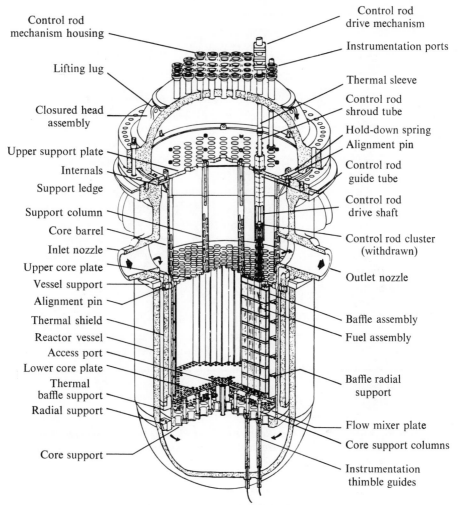

Control rod
mechanism housing

Lifting lug

Closured head
assembly

Upper support plate

Internals

Support ledge

Support column

Core barrel

Inlet nozzle

Upper core plate

Vessel support

Alignment pin

Thermal shield

Reactor vessel

Access port

Lower core plate

Thermal
baffle support

Radial support

Core support

Control rod
drive mechanism

Instrumentation ports

Thermal sleeve

Control rod
shroud tube

Hold-down spring

Alignment pin

Control rod
guide tube

Control rod
drive shaft

Control rod cluster
(withdrawn)

Outlet nozzle

Baffle assembly

Fuel assembly

Baffle radial
support

Flow mixer plate

Core support columns

Instrumentation
thimble guides

FIG. 1.5 *Connecticut Yankee Pressurized Water Reactor Core.*
[*Courtesy Westinghouse Electric Corporation.*]

the coolant may pass directly to a turbine for the production of useful
work.   In this type of reactor, heat exchangers and pumps may be eliminated, reducing the total plant equipment necessary.   Figure 1.6 is a cutaway view of a boiling water reactor.

In any of the heterogeneous reactor configurations, heavy shielding
is put around the reactor.   Lighter shielding is used around the coolant
piping, heat exchangers, and pumps.   By judicious selection of coolant
almost 100 percent of the radioactivity present is confined inside the

FIG. 1.6 *Boiling Water Reactor building showing pressure suppression containment.* [*Courtesy General Electric Company.*]

heavy, or primary, shield. As indicated in Table 1.1, heavy materials make the best radiation shields. It is this factor which has severely handicapped the development of a nuclear aircraft engine.

Finally, research and irradiation reactors are another important major class of reactors. Irradiation reactors take several forms, but essentially they all use either neutrons or gamma radiation from the fission reaction for food irradiation, biomedical irradiation, material processing and testing, or isotope production for industrial uses.

Practically a separate industry has grown from the field of radioisotope technology. Neutron bombardment of certain stable isotopes produces radioactive isotopes. New uses of these radioisotopes are constantly being developed. Some commercially available radioactive isotopes produced in reactors are ^{60}Co, ^{131}I, ^{3}H, ^{59}Fe, ^{90}Sr, ^{65}Zn, and ^{206}Tl.

^{60}Co is used in cancer irradiation. Other isotopes are used as tracers in medical research. Industrially, radioisotopes have a wide variety of uses. They serve as thickness gages, tracers, level gages, and sources of energy. They are used for promotion of chemical reactions and for

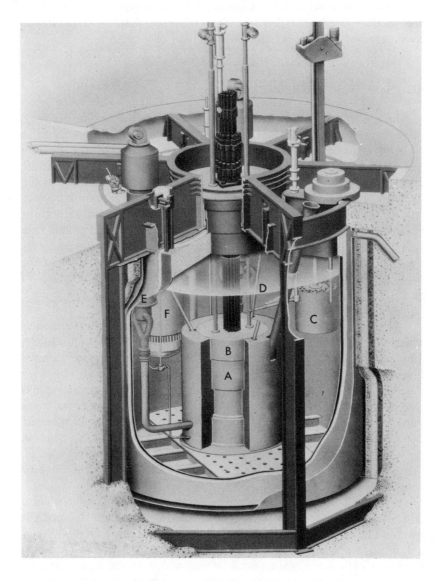

FIG. 1.7 *Cutaway drawing showing the major reactor components of Argonne National Laboratory's Experimental Breeder Reactor II. [Courtesy Argonne National Laboratory.]*

radiographic inspections. The field of radioisotope technology requires not only a knowledge of interactions of radiation with matter, but knowledge of detection and production of isotopes as well as an understanding of the design and operation of reactors.

Only a few general remarks concerning general types of reactors have been made. A more detailed description of some reactor types and design considerations is found in Chapter 13.

REACTOR DESIGN PROBLEMS

In a heterogeneous reactor the fuel and moderator are lumped throughout the reactor. Since the heat is produced in the fuel elements, it is desirable to have a uniform heat and neutron flux. To do this the fuel elements are sometimes spaced closer together near the edge of the reactor. This levels off the heat flux somewhat and causes most of the fuel elements to operate near their maximum temperature limits. Theoretically, a reactor is a source of energy at unlimited temperature, and the higher the temperature at which heat is supplied to the working fluid of a cycle the higher the thermal efficiency of the cycle will be. However, considering the hydraulic, nuclear, and heat transfer characteristics of the core, the temperature must be kept below melting point temperatures of metals in the core and below boiling point temperatures for the coolant, in the case of a liquid-cooled reactor.

When a reactor is designed care must be exercised to select materials which will not become excessively radioactive. Manganese, for example, a component of many steels, becomes radioactive on exposure to neutrons. Some electrical insulation loses its strength upon exposure to radiation. The strength characteristics of metals change and some lubricating oils turn heavy and gummy after exposure. These and many other problems must be accounted for and solved before a reactor is successfully operated.

Care must be taken to ensure that pipes will not make a "hole" in the shield. The piping and the material in it are not good shields; therefore, shielding must be built over the pipes, or the pipes must be bent inside the shield, or both.

Eventually the fuel in a reactor becomes used to a point when a critical chain reaction can no longer be sustained. When this point is reached the reactor must be refueled. The reactor now contains a valuable amount of usable fuel, radioactive fission products, and stable fission products. The fuel elements must be removed from the reactor and reprocessed. Since they are radioactive they must be handled remotely after they have "cooled" somewhat, usually by being stored under water for about ninety days. After the cladding material is removed the uranium is reclaimed by a solvent extraction process.   The Atomic Energy Commission has built a large plant on the Savannah River in South Carolina to do this reprocessing.   Commercial reprocessing facilities are now also available.

The fission products which remain are radioactive wastes and must be disposed of so as not to endanger persons now or ever.   Contaminated reactor components and materials also come under the category of radioactive wastes.

One last design problem will be posed here.   A reactor that has once been critical always produces some heat from the decay of fission products and spontaneous fission.   This heat must be removed or the reactor will overheat.   A thermal loop is built into the reactor so that this heat, produced after shutdown, will be removed.   This is particularly important if the safety devices cause a sudden or emergency shutdown (called a scram).

ENVIRONMENTAL CONSIDERATIONS

From the beginning it was recognized that nuclear reactors present inherent hazards to the general public.   Furthermore, the nuclear explosions of World War II left an indelible mark on the minds of the public regarding the dangerous capability of nuclear effects.   Unfortunately, there was no such milestone to imprint the beneficial aspects of nuclear energy on the public.

The development of nuclear power has always been characterized by an overriding concern for health and safety.   More attention in the forms of research, debate, legislation, and development has been given to environmental effects of nuclear power than any other technology.

To make the safety problem more difficult, nuclear safety depends on a theoretical potential for conceivable damage.   Other areas of technology have been able to rely on practical experience to demonstrate hazards or lack of safety.   Since nuclear reactor safety requirements must be based on theoretical potentials, an ultra-ultra-conservative approach has been taken.   In many instances the regulatory agencies have insisted on safety precautions which have nearly precluded design or construction of the reactor.

The two basic premises which have been applied in reactor siting are: isolation by distance from inhabited areas, and containment of accidental release of radioactivity by safety devices and design features.   In the past, reactor siting has been made on a combination of these two.   The newest reactors are being located much closer to centers of population than were their predecessors. Despite the outstanding safety record and ultra conservativeness of safety requirements there is little likelihood of changing safety requirements to more practical levels.

As operating experience increases and safe operation is extended, greater knowledge in the characteristics and behavior of reactors is gained; the natural trend is to rely more on engineering safeguards and less on isolation safeguards. This trend is visible for the well-proven reactor designs.

Concern about the discharges of nuclear power plants to the environment continues to be of great interest to a wide spectrum of people including the President, governmental agencies, citizen groups, conservationists, scientists and engineers, and the general public. Concern for the environment is brought to focus for the public almost daily by television and other media. It is not surprising to find opposition to nuclear power plants from people whose attention has been focused on routine releases of radioactive materials to the atmosphere and the polluting aspects of thermal discharges. Many people do not have a thorough understanding of built-in safeguards, of the range of modifications possible, or the need for power plants to meet demands for power.

There is no doubt that nuclear power plants are a potential hazard due to radiation discharges and thermal pollution. Utilities have the responsibility of proving to regulatory agencies, environmentalists and other groups that the power plant will be built and operated safely and without significant effects on the environment. Designers of plants where inadequate cooling water is available are being forced to eliminate the direct release of waste heat by the use of cooling towers.

Every thermal system of converting energy will produce some wasted energy and thermal loss. After all, the second law of thermodynamics guarantees that some energy will be discharged from the system. Because of lower thermal efficiencies, current nuclear power plants discharge about twenty-five to thirty percent greater volume of water than a fossil fuel plant of the same capacity. Also, the size of the plants being installed has increased. The resulting larger discharges are what is leading to the thermal effects problem.

Thermal effects problems are undergoing continued research and are manageable. Better efficiencies for advanced reactors, such as breeder reactors, should reduce the thermal problem as well as conserve natural supplies of fissionable fuels. Solutions to the thermal problems are chiefly economics and siting. The least costly means of discharging waste heat is to dissipate it in large rivers, lakes, or the ocean. The resultant thermal effects may be insignificant, beneficial, or detrimental depending on the use of the water, amount of water available, ecology, etc.

If economics permit or ecology demands, methods other than discharge to bodies of water may be used. Examples are artificial ponds, cooling towers, and use of heat as a by-product.

Other methods will add to the cost of generating power. Unquestionably these costs will be worth it when there will be significant detrimental effects by direct discharge of heat. Unfortunately, not very much is known about environmental effects of the discharge of large amounts of condenser cooling water. Methods for predicting temperature variations must be better developed and checked so that meaningful knowledge on the effects of waste heat on aquatic life can be determined. Studies of both short term and long term effects should be made. The short term information can help determine how individual power plants should be designed while long term information will affect regional power growth and plant siting. The chief concern should be on the water quality criteria, not on numbers of fish killed. Established water temperature standards are well below the lethal temperatures for fish. The fish were apparently killed as a result of mechanical or chemical problems, not thermal or radiation problems. Therefore, improvements in water intake and chemical treatments will have to be made.

It has been suggested that heated water be used for irrigating, thereby extending the growing season for agriculture, to delay freezing of waterways in northern latitudes, and to warm lower depths of the ocean to promote more biological growth. However, any of these alternatives may produce other undesirable environmental effects. Whatever methods of heat removal are used and whatever the power plant—fossil or nuclear—the second law of thermodynamics must be satisfied.

It seems clear, however, that the total environmental effects of nuclear power plants are no worse than those of fossil fuel plants.

Every energy conversion device leaves other waste residue also. Even the good old horse of the horse and buggy left much waste. The internal combustion engine replaced the horse or else the streets would undoubtedly be uninhabitable! Fossil plants produce—ash; nuclear plants—fission products.

The problem of disposing of radioactive waste material produced by nuclear plants is also important. There are two general categories of management of radioactive waste: (1) treatment and disposal of low level radioactive material, and (2) treatment and storage of material with high levels of radioactivity.

The low level radioactive solid wastes are generally separated from the non-radioactive liquids and gases, concentrated, and then encased in concrete or other material.

High level wastes are produced during fuel reprocessing at a few specially selected reprocessing sites. The several ways in which radioactive wastes are disposed of are as follows:

(1) Short-lived isotopes can be diluted and stored in remote locations until their activity is reduced to very low limits. The AEC sets limits of radio-activity which can be released to the environment.

(2) Wastes may be concentrated in tanks and stored on tank farms or buried underground. These methods are dangerous because of leakage and con-tamination problems. Also, aboveground storage requires a very large restricted area.

(3) Wastes may be concentrated and encased in concrete, then dumped at sea. This is dangerous because leakage may be ingested by fish or plants and spread throughout the world.

(4) The radioactive materials may be stored in large caves or deep craters formed by underground explosions. The danger here is that an earth-quake might release contamination.

At present all the above methods are being used for waste disposal. One other proposal has been made, that radioactive wastes be built into rockets and placed in outer space or into orbit. This has not yet been tried be-cause of the obvious problems it presents.

The National Environmental Policy Act of 1969 (NEPA) became effec-tive on January 1, 1970. The NEPA requires that the AEC regulate and assess the impact of nuclear power on the total environment in terms of alternatives and the need for increased electric power. In an interpreta-tion of NEPA, the U. S. Court of Appeals for the District of Columbia in 1971 made a far reaching ruling (commonly referred to as the Calvert Cliffs decision). This ruling resulted in the AEC revising and strengthen-ing its regulations to make a more rigorous implementation of the NEPA. Some of the more significant aspects of this ruling were as follows:

(1) Environmental aspects must be considered at each stage in the licensing process. The environmental reports are circulated to government agencies and other interested persons.

(2) Even if federal or state agencies certify that their environmental standards are satisfied the AEC independently evaluates the total environmental impact. The AEC can, if it chooses, require controls more strict than those of a local agency.

(3) Each nuclear power plant which was under construction but not granted an operating license was required to submit an environmental impact state-ment showing why its construction permit should not be suspended until a complete environmental and impact review was made. This in effect opened the possibility that plants already under construction might have to be redesigned or even abandoned.

The increased review procedures and care which will be taken to pro-tect the environment means that more time will be required to construct and begin operation of nuclear power plants.

One of the most complex problems challenging the ingenuity of the engineering profession is that of air pollution. Any and all forms of combustion yield products which are undesirable in man's environment. Among the pollutants produced by conventional power plants are oxides of sulfur and nitrogen, hydrocarbons, and particulate matter. Air pollution varies from season to season, place to place, and daylight to dark. In addition to the irritating haze, it produces nitrogen oxides which may contribute to respiratory disease. Sunlight combines the hydrocarbons discharged by automobiles and nitrogen oxides to form the infamous photochemical smog. Smog damages crops, trees, materials, causes eyes to smart, and reduces resistance to respiratory disease. Sulfur oxides, on the other hand, corrode stone and metal, and injure plants and animals. Particulate matter produced by combustion dirties the surrounding terrain and reduces visibility. More importantly, however, it acts as a catalyst in formation of other pollutants.

While not all pollutants are caused by discharge from power plants, a significant amount of air pollution can come from these power plants. About ten percent of the heat discharged from a fossil fuel plant is dissipated directly into the atmosphere through the stack. Latest estimates indicate these fossil fuel plants emit approximately 20 million tons of pollutants to the atmosphere, but over ninety percent of pollutants are gases. Until the problem was completely recognized, little effort was made to reduce air pollution. Now the Environmental Protection Agency has extensive programs underway to sample, study, and reduce air pollution. Short of stopping the discharge of pollutants to the atmosphere air pollution can be reduced somewhat, but not eliminated. A nuclear power plant has some inherent environmental advantages over conventional power plants. Since the nuclear reactor replaces the conventional combustion device, there will be no burning of hydrocarbon and oxygen resources and there will be no sulfur or nitrogen oxides and no particulate matter released to the atmosphere. Through careful design and operation there are essentially no radioactive particles released to the atmosphere, either. (In fact, studies have shown that a conventional power plant—and operation of a television set—produce significant radiation.) As nuclear power production replaces conventional power production there should be a reduction in the total number of pollutants introduced into the atmosphere by power plants.

At present, regulations express the maximum allowable concentration of each radioisotope in water or air at the boundary of the plant. The values are taken from National Bureau of Standards Handbook 69 and reduced by a factor of ten. If a group of people live near the boundary the values are further reduced by a factor of 3. The resultant average dose to the population will be no more than 170 millirem per year, approximately equal to the average national background radiation.

In January, 1971, the National Council on Radiation Protection issued a report stating that the above limits provide adequate safety factors. Nevertheless, the AEC in 1971 proposed an amendment to give guidance for lowering the radioactivity below the limits. The guidelines limit maximum exposure to a person living near the boundary of a reactor to 5 millirem per year.

Nuclear power plants (except in a few isolated instances) do not exceed one percent of the allowable limits of radiation exposure for the public. It has been difficult to measure the increase in radioactivity above background levels in bodies of water near nuclear power reactors.

That there is no danger to the population from radioactivity in a nuclear power plant is a testimonial to the Atomic Energy Commission and nuclear power equipment manufacturers. Over 385 reactors have been built in the U. S. since the CP-1 reactor of 1941. In this time period there have been remarkably few significant accidents. Accidents of any type affecting the general public have not occurred in any civilian nuclear power plant in the United States. In fact, through 1969 there had been only four accidents, all extremely minor, in power, production, or propulsion reactors.

HISTORY

The history of the neutron (and, consequently, of atomic energy) dates from 1930. In that year German physicists W. Bothe and H. Becker discovered that when beryllium or boron is bombarded with high energy helium nuclei a highly penetrating radiation is produced. J. Chadwick, in 1932, proved that this radiation is not gamma radiation but an uncharged particle with a mass about the same as a proton. It is called a neutron.

Enrico Fermi used neutrons to bombard several elements. In 1934 he reported that about 40 different target nuclei would become radioactive when bombarded by neutrons. In experiments with uranium he found that different elements were formed with the radioactive isotopes. During the course of his experiments he also suggested that neutron energies were reduced when the neutron passed through water or paraffin. In January, 1939, the German physicists Lise Meitner and Otto Frisch deduced that bombardment of uranium by neutrons causes the uranium to split into two approximately equal parts, each with an enormous amount of energy. This was the discovery of fission. It had been preceded by the work of many experimenters, but none of them individually was able to correctly interpret his results.

On 26 January, 1939, a conference on theoretical physics was convened in Washington, D. C. The theories of fission were discussed and many physicists began experiments to detect the fission products. Within approximately three months the fission process was confirmed by many people and most of the fission products had been identified. The emission of neutrons in the fission process was also discovered. It is, of course, the emission of neutrons that permits the fission process to be self-sustaining and makes possible a nuclear reactor. In October, 1939, President Roosevelt established the "Advisory Committee on Uranium." Six thousand dollars was granted to this committee for the procurement of fifty tons of uranium and four tons of graphite.

By June, 1940, it was known that uranium, thorium, and protactinium could be fissioned. The fragments produced were isotopes of elements with atomic numbers ranging from 34 to 57. These fission fragments have large kinetic energies and are unstable, emitting beta particles through successive elements to a stable isotope. It was known that ^{235}U has a larger probability of fission by low energy neutrons than by high energy neutrons. It was also established that ^{238}U, thorium, and protactinium can be fissioned only by fast neutrons, and that there is a resonance absorption of ^{238}U by neutrons with certain energies between thermal and fast. Finally, it was known that one, two, three, or more neutrons are emitted in each fission. About this time physicists were also investigating the possibility of using uranium in a thermal reactor to make plutonium. The plutonium could then be separated chemically from the uranium and used in a thermal neutron reaction.

The third report of the National Academy of Sciences Committee on Atomic Fission (dated 6 November, 1941) stated that from two kg to one hundred kg of ^{235}U would be required to make a bomb. The report also stated that two methods of separating ^{235}U isotopes from natural uranium were possible (natural uranium is 0.7115 percent by weight ^{235}U). It was estimated that three to four years would be required to produce a significant number of bombs. In August, 1942, President Roosevelt set up the Manhattan Engineer District of the U. S. Army Corps of Engineers to develop an atomic bomb.

By the end of 1941 there were only a few grams of pure metallic uranium available. Experiments indicated that the commercial grade of black uranium oxide available would not sustain a critical reaction. By May, 1942, purer uranium oxide was available, but it was not pure enough to sustain a critical reaction. It was not until July, 1942, that uranium oxide pure enough to sustain a critical reaction was made. It was planned to use graphite as moderator with the natural uranium oxide as fuel for the first critical reaction. By this same time (summer 1942) the problems of purifying graphite were also solved.

In autumn, 1942, enough purified uranium oxide, pure uranium metal, and graphite moderator were assembled in Chicago to build a reactor.

Since the purity of the materials was in doubt, there was concern as to whether or not a self-sustaining reaction could be achieved. There need have been no fear because the pile, as the reactor was called, became critical before it was finished. This first reactor, designed and assembled by Enrico Fermi and his staff, was known as CP-1 and was put into operation on 2 December, 1942. It was constructed in a squash court under the West stands of the University of Chicago's Stagg Field and operated at a power of one-half watt until 12 December when the power was increased to 200 watts. The reactor has since been dismantled, and a bronze sculpture has been erected to commemorate the event. The reactor was made by gradually building up graphite blocks. Uranium metal and uranium oxide were inserted into holes in the graphite blocks. Natural air circulation provided the cooling. Because of its construction methods, the reactor was called a pile. When it was completed it contained about 3,200 uranium metal cylinders and 14,500 uranium oxide lumps for a total weight of about 50 tons of uranium and 470 tons of graphite. There were five cadmium-coated control rods.

Now that it was certain that a chain reaction could be effected, it was decided to use the chain reaction to produce plutonium for atomic bombs. It was necessary to separate the plutonium from the uranium by chemical means. To study reactor operation and isotope separation, a graphite-moderated natural uranium-fueled reactor was built in Oak Ridge, Tennessee. It had forced air cooling and was designed with an initial power of 1000 kW. It was called the X-10 or Clinton pile and subsequently operated at a power of about 4000 kW. It went into operation 4 November, 1943, and was used for extensive production of isotopes and research purposes and the early studies of plutonium production. It was shut down permanently in November, 1963.

Hanford, Washington was selected as the site for large-scale production reactors. Originally the plan was to use helium as the coolant, but because of problems in supplying helium the coolant was changed to water. Construction of the first water-cooled, graphite-moderated reactor was started in June, 1943, and criticality was achieved in September, 1944. Several similar reactors were built at the same location. In the early 1950's more efficient heavy water-moderated plutonium production reactors were built at Savannah River, South Carolina.

There were so many uncertainties in the production of plutonium at Hanford and in the subsequent construction of a bomb that it was decided to undertake the mechanical separation of ^{235}U from ^{238}U. A gaseous diffusion plant was constructed at Oak Ridge, Tennessee. The plant started operation in June, 1945. Its operation is based on the principle that more of the lighter molecules of UF_6 will pass through a porous barrier. The molecules on the far side of the barrier become slightly enriched in the lighter gas ($^{235}UF_6$). It takes approximately 4000 stages of diffusion to produce 99 percent pure ^{235}U. A second plant utilizing a mass spectrograph method was also built at Oak Ridge. The uranium is ionized, collimated, and focused into a magnetic field. Since the ^{235}U ions are lighter, they are deflected more by the magnetic field. Thus, the lighter ^{235}U ions are separated from heavier ^{238}U ions. For more information concerning isotope separation, References 3 and 4 may be consulted.

Nuclear reactor technology and isotope technology are still in their beginning stages. Much more design and development will be done before the full potential of reactor technology is realized. Quantitatively, progress has been very rapid, with the construction of well over 100 reactors within the first 20 years of reactor development. Table 1.2 lists in chronological order some of the early reactors and their significant characteristics. There is a multitude of possible combinations of fuel, moderator, coolant, reflector, etc., for reactor construction. So far no ideal combination has evolved, even though fifty or more combinations have been studied. There are both proponents and opponents of different styles; each country seems to have followed lines determined by its own experience. For example, the United States has favored pressurized water and boiling water reactors using slightly enriched uranium, while the United Kingdom has favored gas-cooled reactors. Canada has concentrated on heavy water-moderated natural uranium-fueled reactors.

THE NUCLEAR INDUSTRY

The nuclear industry is an extremely complex overlapping of many diversified industries and services. It includes applications in every category of science and industry. It is convenient to break the nuclear industry down into three divisions (Ref. 5): (a) output and uses of reactors; (b) fuels and materials; and (c) services and applications.

The useful output of reactors may be power, radiation, steam, or gas. These outputs are used for training, research, testing, production of isotopes, propulsion, public utilities, manufacturing, and in space vehicles.

Nuclear fuels and materials may be the most complex of the three divisions because they involve not only the fissionable and fertile materials, but all materials that are associated with the fission process. This division is composed of exploration, mining, milling, refining and fabrication. In addition there are enrichment, processing, and the development of special materials.

By services and applications are meant fuel reprocessing, reactor

TABLE 1.2

EARLY NUCLEAR REACTORS

Name	Location	Operation	Fuel	Moderator
CP-1	Chicago, Illinois	Dec 1942	50 tons natural U	graphite
X-10	Oak Ridge, Tennessee	Nov 1943	natural U cylinders	graphite
CP-3	Argonne, Illinois	May 1944	natural U rods	D_2O
LOPO	Los Alamos, New Mexico	May 1944	14.6% enrich. ^{235}U, UO_2SO_4 dissolved in H_2O	H_2O
	Hanford, Washington	Sept 1944	natural U slugs	graphite
ZEEP	Chalk River, Canada	Apr 1945	natural U	D_2O
Clementine	Los Alamos, New Mexico	Nov 1946	^{239}Pu rods	—
GLEEP	Harwell, England	Aug 1947	natural U bars	graphite
NRX	Chalk River, Canada	Aug 1947	natural U cylinder rod	D_2O
BSR	Oak Ridge, Tennessee	Nov 1950	enriched sandwich plates	H_2O
JEEP	Kjeller, Norway	Aug 1951	natural U rods	D_2O
EBR-I	NRTS, Arco, Idaho	Dec 1951	90% enriched U rods	—
MTR	NRTS, Arco, Idaho	Mar 1952	enriched ^{235}U sandwich plate	H_2O
APS-I	USSR	1954	5% enriched U rods	graphite
PWR	USS Nautilus	Jan 1955	highly enriched ^{235}U	H_2O
Calder Hall	Cumberland, England	Oct 1956	natural U rods	graphite
EBWR	Argonne, Illinois	Dec 1956	1.5% ^{235}U plates	H_2O
PWR	Shippingport, Pennsylvania	Dec 1957	highly enrich. ^{235}U and nat. U	H_2O

hazards, licensing, and waste disposal, plus the myriad applications of reactor output. Applications of reactor output can be identified in agriculture, medicine, radiation source preparation, explosives, fusion power, industry, and public relations.

It can easily be seen that nearly every industry and service organization in the world can make use of radiation advantageously.

TABLE 1.2

EARLY NUCLEAR REACTORS

Coolant	Reflector	Power	Remarks
free air convection	graphite	200 W	First controlled chain reaction
forced air convection	graphite	4000 kW	Pilot plant for Pu production; used for isotope production and research
D_2O	graphite	300 kW	First D_2O reactor
H_2O	beryllium	1 W	First enriched uranium and first homogeneous water boiler; spherical core
H_2O		100,000 kW (est.)	Plutonium production reactors; no power used
D_2O			First Canadian reactor
Hg	natural U	25 kW	First fast reactor; first ^{239}Pu reactor
air	graphite	100 kW	First English reactor; plutonium production only
H_2O	graphite	40,000 kW	High neutron flux
H_2O	H_2O	100 kW	Free convection cooling; swimming pool type; prototype for research
D_2O	graphite	100 kW	No power used
NaK	natural U	100 kW	First production of electric power; breeder reactor
H_2O	H_2O	40,000 kW	High neutron flux to study effects of radiation on materials
H_2O	graphite	1000 kW elect.	First Russian reactor
H_2O	H_2O		First propulsion reactor; small size high power
CO_2	graphite	4200 kW elect.	First commercial production of power; plutonium production
H_2O	H_2O	5000 kW(e)	First boiling water reactor
H_2O	H_2O	230,000 kW(t) 60,000 kW(e)	First central station nuclear plant in USA

REFERENCES

1. Putnam, Palmer C., *Energy in the Future*. Princeton, N. J.: Van Nostrand Company, 1953.
2. Brown, Harrison, and others, *The Next Hundred Years*. New York: Viking Press, Inc., 1957.

3. Smyth, H. D., *Atomic Energy for Military Purposes*. Princeton, N. J.: Princeton University Press, 1945.

4. Benedict, M., "Separation of Stable Isotopes," TID–5031, U. S. Atomic Energy Commission, 1951.

5. "Nuclear News Panel," *Nuclear News*, **8,** No. 3 (March, 1965).

6. U. S. Bureau of the Census, *Statistical Abstract of the U. S.*, Washington, D. C., 1969.

7. Glasstone, Samuel, *Sourcebook on Atomic Energy*, 2nd ed. Princeton, N. J.: Van Nostrand Company, 1958.

8. Kaufmann, A. R., ed., *Nuclear Reactor Fuel Elements: Metallurgy and Fabrication*. New York: J. Wiley and Sons, 1962.

9. *Nuclear News*, published monthly by American Nuclear Society, Inc., Chicago.

10. *Reactor Handbook*, rev. ed. U. S. Atomic Energy Commission, 1962.

11. "Atomic Energy Facts," U. S. Atomic Energy Commission, 1957.

12. Benedict, M. and A. Pigford, *Nuclear Chemical Engineering*. New York: McGraw-Hill Book Company, 1957.

13. Shoupp, W. E., "The Atom, The Public, and You," *Nuclear News*, **8,** No. 8 (August, 1965), pp. 13–17.

14. Roe, K. A., "What Lies Ahead for Nuclear Power?", *Power*, **109,** No. 7 (July, 1965), pp. 57–59.

15. *Proceedings of the Third United Nations International Conference on the Peaceful Uses of Atomic Energy*, Geneva, Switzerland, 1965.

16. *Thermal Effects and U. S. Nuclear Power Stations*, U. S. Atomic Energy Commission, 1971.

17. Jordan, W. H., "The Issues Concerning Nuclear Power," *Nuclear News*, **14,** No. 10 (October, 1971), pp. 43–49.

18. Weinberg, A. M., "The Moral Imperatives of Nuclear Energy," *Nuclear News*, **14,** No. 12 (December, 1971), pp. 33–37.

19. *Plan for the Management of AEC—Generated Radioactive Wastes*, U. S. Atomic Energy Commission, 1972.

Chapter 2

Atomic Structure

THE ATOM

The atom is an assemblage of neutrons and protons tightly clustered in a nucleus and surrounded by electrons whirling in a variety of orbits. The protons are positively charged particles, each having a unit charge exactly opposite that of a negatively charged electron. The mass of the proton is 1836 times that of an electron. Neutrons have no electrical charge and a mass just slightly larger than that of a proton. Outside the nucleus a neutron cannot exist alone; it is unstable and will decay into a proton and an electron. Figure 2.1 shows a schematic arrangement of a

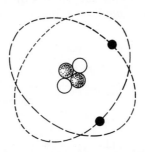

FIG. 2.1 *Helium atom containing two neutrons and two protons in the nucleus. Two electrons are in orbit outside the nucleus.*

helium atom with two protons and two neutrons in the nucleus, plus two orbiting electrons.

A particular atom may be designated by its atomic number, Z, which represents the number of protons present, and by its mass number, A, which is equal to the number of neutrons, N, plus the number of protons.

$$A = N + Z \qquad (2.1)$$

It is possible for an element to have various values of the mass number, A, for a given number of protons, Z. These differing atoms of the same element are known as isotopes. Although they may behave similarly in chemical reactions, their nuclear characteristics may differ markedly. An example of this is found in natural uranium whose three naturally occurring isotopes are listed below with their abundances (abundance is the atom percentage of an isotope present in a mixture).

$$_{92}^{234}U - 0.006\%$$
$$_{92}^{235}U - 0.714\%$$
$$_{92}^{208}U - 99.28\%$$

Note that an isotope may be designated by its chemical symbol with the Z value as a presubscript and the mass number, A, as a presuperscript, $_{Z}^{A}X$.

The difference in nuclear characteristics of two isotopes is illustrated by ^{238}U which will not fission by absorption of a slow (thermal) neutron, whereas, ^{235}U fissions readily when a thermal neutron is absorbed.

Some elements have only a single stable isotope, such as, ^{23}Na, ^{27}Al, and ^{9}Be. Other elements have many stable isotopes. For example, molybdenum has 7, cadmium has 8, and tin has 9. It is interesting to observe that nuclei with even numbers of protons and neutrons have a better probability of stability, as is indicated by Table 2.1.

Hydrogen and its isotopes are of particular interest since $_{1}^{1}H$, light hydrogen, is a common reactor moderating material either in water or an organic compound. Deuterium is heavy hydrogen formed when a neutron joins the proton in the nucleus to form $_{1}^{2}H$. It is also designated as $_{1}^{2}D$. A second neutron addition produces tritium, $_{1}^{3}H$ (or $_{1}^{3}T$). Deute-

TABLE 2.1

STABLE ISOTOPES

		Number of Neutrons	
		Odd	Even
Number of Protons	Odd	8	52
	Even	56	167

rium has much less probability of neutron absorption than light hydrogen, thus making heavy water an effective moderating medium. Tritium becomes important when fusion reactions are considered.

Two other terms are used to describe related nuclear species (nuclides): (1) *Isobars* are nuclides having the same mass number (*A*), but different numbers of protons (*Z*). In radioactive decay the ejection of an electron from the nucleus forms an isobar of the parent. (2) *Isotones* are nuclides with like numbers of neutrons.

The physical atomic mass unit (*u*) is equal to one-twelfth of the mass of a $_6^{12}C$ atom. This is equal to 1.660438×10^{-24} grams. (The chemical atomic mass system assigns a mass of 16 to the naturally occurring mixture ^{16}O, ^{17}O, and ^{18}O.) Formerly the physical atomic mass unit was based on one-sixteenth of the mass of an atom of the $_8^{16}O$ isotope. The change to the carbon base gives values for the physical and chemical atomic mass units which are quite nearly equal for any isotope. In selection of data from different sources caution must be exercised that ^{12}C and ^{16}O based data are not mixed inadvertently.

The masses for the three types of atomic particles based on the carbon system are listed below.

$$\text{Proton} \quad - \quad 1.007277 \ u$$
$$\text{Neutron} \quad - \quad 1.008665 \ u$$
$$\text{Electron} \quad - \quad 0.000548597 \ u$$

Avogadro's hypothesis states that equal volumes of gases at the same pressure and temperature contain equal numbers of molecules. This permits the determination of the relative weights of various molecules. Thus, when the molecular weight of a particular type of molecule is expressed in grams, it represents a definite number of molecules (or atoms of a monatomic substance). This is known as Avogadro's number, which is 6.02252×10^{23} molecules per gram mole (or atoms per gram atom).

The number density, *N*, of atoms (or molecules) may be found by using the density of the material, ρ, its atomic (or molecular) weight, and Avogadro's number

$$N = \frac{\rho \times 6.023 \times 10^{23}}{\text{atomic weight}} \tag{2.2}$$

Example 1a. If natural uranium has a density of 19.0 gr/cm³, find the number density of ^{235}U atoms present.

$$N_{235} = \frac{19.0(\text{gr U/cm}^3) \times 6.023 \times 10^{23}(\text{atoms U/gr atom U})}{238(\text{gr U/gr atom U})}$$

$$\times 0.00714(\text{atoms } ^{235}U/\text{atom U})$$
$$= 3.43 \times 10^{20} \text{ atoms } ^{235}U/\text{cm}^3$$

Example 1b. If an uranium-aluminum alloy contains 10 w/o U and 90 w/o Al and has a density of 3.0 gr/cm³, compute the number density of aluminum atoms present.

$$N_{Al} = 3.0(\text{gr alloy/cm}^3) \times 0.9(\text{gr Al/gr alloy})$$

$$\times \frac{6.023 \times 10^{23}(\text{atoms Al/gr atom Al})}{27(\text{gr Al/gr atom Al})}$$

$$= 6.023 \times 10^{22} \text{ atoms Al/cm}^3$$

Note that in the previous example where the number density of the uranium as a whole has been multiplied by the abundance of ^{235}U, the mass number used is for the composite material. When a weight percent is given, the density is multiplied by the weight percent of the particular element and the atomic weight used is for that element, as illustrated by Example 1b.

BINDING ENERGIES

If the masses of the neutrons and the protons making up the nucleus of an atom are added, the total will exceed the experimentally determined mass for that nucleus. This loss in mass is due to its conversion to binding energy in accordance with Einstein's famous equation

$$\Delta E = \Delta mc^2 \qquad (2.3)$$

where ΔE represents the binding energy and Δm is the loss in mass, or so-called mass defect, and c is the speed of light. This same amount of energy would need to be supplied to the nucleus to separate all of the nucleons.

In evaluating the mass defect, note that the isotopic masses given in Appendix A are given for the complete atom. To obtain the mass of the nucleus, the electron masses must be subtracted from the isotopic mass, M_x.

$$\Delta m = Z(m_p) + N(m_n) - (M_x - Zm_e) \qquad (2.4a)$$

If the electron and proton masses are combined, the mass of the hydrogen atom is approximately correct in the following alternate relation. It is in error only by the amount of the electron binding energy of a few electron volts.

$$\Delta m = Z(m_H) + N(m_n) - M_x \qquad (2.4b)$$

Example 2. Compute the mass defect and the binding energy per nucleon for $_3^7Li$.

From Appendix A the isotopic mass of ^7Li is 7.01601 u. Using Eq. (2.4a)

$$\Delta m = 3 \times 1.007277 + 4 \times 1.008665 - (7.01601 - 3 \times 0.000549)$$
$$= 0.04213 \, u$$

From this mass defect the total binding energy is determined using Eq. (2.3).

$$\Delta E = \Delta mc^2 = 0.04213 \, u \times 1.660438 \times 10^{-24} \, gr/u$$
$$\times (3.0 \times 10^{10})^2 \, cm^2/sec^2 \times (1/1.60210 \times 10^{-6})$$
$$MeV/(gr \, cm^2/sec^2) = 39.3 \, MeV$$

The binding energy per nucleon is then

$$BE/\text{nucleon} = \frac{39.3}{7} = 5.61 \text{ MeV/nucleon}$$

Figure 2.2 shows the variation in binding energy per nucleon with mass number. The magnitude of the binding energy per nucleon increases somewhat erratically from zero for $_1^1H$ to a rather flat peak in the vicinity of A = 56 (iron) where the value is approximately 8.7 MeV/nucleon. It then falls slowly to a value of about 7.5 MeV/nucleon for the uranium isotopes.

Both the fission process, where a heavy nucleus splits into two fragments, and the fusion process, where two light nuclei are joined to form a heavier nucleus, tend to move the elements formed toward the region of greater stability. The resultant energy release of these processes accounts

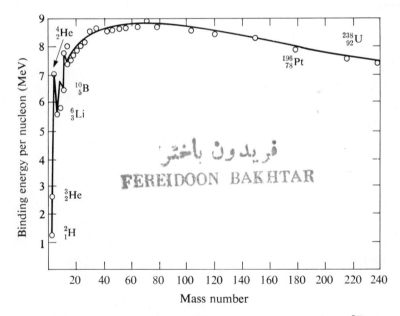

FIG. 2.2 *Binding energy per nucleon versus mass number.* [*From Cahen, G. and P. Treille,* Nuclear Engineering, *trans. G. B. Melese. Boston: Allyn and Bacon, Inc., 1961.*]

for the development of nuclear power as a reality and the harnessing of fusion energy as a hope for the future.

As mass numbers become larger, the ratio of neutrons to protons in the nucleus becomes larger. For ^{4}He and ^{16}O this ratio is unity. For ^{115}In it has increased to a value of 1.35 and for ^{238}U it is 1.59. This variation is shown by Fig. 2.3. When the heavy uranium nucleus splits into two fission fragments each will have an excess of neutrons, accounting for the intense radioactivity of these species in irradiated nuclear fuels. Radioactive decay will be discussed in detail in Chapter 3.

RELATIVISTIC VELOCITIES

Einstein's theory of relativity further indicates that as the velocity of a body increases toward the speed of light, its mass increases toward infinity. Unless the velocity is greater than 0.1 c the correction is not important to engineering calculations.

$$m = \frac{m_0}{\sqrt{1 - (v^2/c^2)}} \tag{2.5}$$

where m is the relativistic mass and m_0 is the rest mass in a given reference system. Thus, the total energy, E, for the mass is

$$E = mc^2 = \frac{m_0 c^2}{\sqrt{1 - (v^2/c^2)}} \tag{2.6}$$

The kinetic energy is determined by subtracting the rest mass energy from the total energy.

$$KE = (m - m_0) c^2 = m_0 c^2 \left[\frac{1}{\sqrt{1 - (v^2/c^2)}} - 1 \right] \tag{2.7a}$$

When $v \ll c$ the first two terms of the binomial expansion

$$\left(1 + \frac{1}{2} \frac{v^2}{c^2} + \cdots \right)$$

may be used for $1/\sqrt{1 - (v^2/c^2)}$.

$$\frac{1}{\sqrt{1 - (v^2/c^2)}} = 1 + \frac{1}{2} \frac{v^2}{c^2} + \cdots \tag{2.7b}$$

Substituting into Eq. (2.7a) gives the familiar expression for nonrelativistic kinetic energy.

$$KE_{\text{nonrel}} = m_0 c^2 \left[1 + \frac{1}{2} \frac{v^2}{c^2} - 1 \right]$$

$$= \frac{m_0 v^2}{2} \tag{2.7c}$$

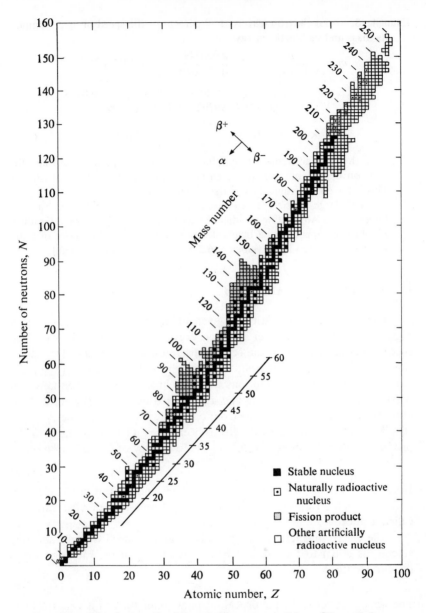

FIG. 2.3 *Distribution of stable and radioactive nuclides.* [*From Cahen, G. and P. Treille*, Nuclear Engineering, *trans. G. B. Melese.   Boston: Allyn and Bacon, Inc., 1961.*]

Example 3. If an electron travels at 90 percent of the speed of light, compute its mass and its kinetic energy.

$$m = \frac{m_0}{\sqrt{1 - (v^2/c^2)}} = \frac{0.000549}{\sqrt{1 - (0.9)^2}} = 0.001263 \; u$$

$$KE = (m - m_0)c^2 = (0.001263 - 0.000549)u \times 1.660438$$
$$\times 10^{-24} \; \text{gr}/u \times (2.997925 \times 10^{10})^2 \; \text{cm}^2/\text{sec}^2$$

$$\times 6.242 \times 10^6 \frac{\text{MeV}}{\text{gr cm}^2/\text{sec}^2} = 0.660 \; \text{MeV}$$

Note that it is convenient to combine the constant speed of light and the two conversion constants just used into a single constant 931.482 MeV/u. This is the energy equivalent of the atomic mass unit.

The large particle accelerators, such as the Brookhaven National Laboratory's Alternating Gradient Synchrotron and ANL's/Zero Gradient Synchrotron, produce particle velocities approaching the speed of light. A 2.5 GeV proton has a velocity 96.2 percent of the speed of light.

ENERGY LEVELS IN AN ATOM

Electromagnetic radiation is given off as an electron drops from a higher energy level to a lower atomic energy level. The first theory which successfully accounted for the certain discrete energy levels of this radiation was proposed by Nils Bohr. Although the Bohr theory of the atom has been supplanted by solutions to the Schroedinger wave equation, it is still useful in understanding and approximating the energy emitted (or absorbed) as an electron jumps from one energy level to another.

The energy emitted as an electron changes its state is equal to the product of Planck's constant, h, and the frequency of the radiation, ν.

$$E_2 - E_1 = h\nu \tag{2.8}$$

Here E_2 represents the final electron energy and E_1 the initial electron energy. Such an amount of discrete energy emission (or absorption) is called a photon.

The electromagnetic radiation travels at the speed of light and this velocity is equal to the product of the frequency of the radiation times its wavelength, λ.

$$c = \nu\lambda \tag{2.9}$$

The wave number is the reciprocal of the wavelength and is denoted by $\bar{\nu}$.

$$\bar{\nu} = \frac{1}{\lambda} = \frac{\nu}{c} \tag{2.10}$$

The force of attraction between the electron and the positively charged nucleus is balanced by the centrifugal force of the electron as it whirls in an orbit about the nucleus

$$\frac{Ze^2}{r^2} = \frac{m_e V^2}{r} \tag{2.11}$$

Z represents the number of protons in the nucleus, e is the unit electronic charge, and r is the orbital radius. m_e is the mass of the electron and V represents its velocity.

The angular momentum $(m_e Vr)$ of an electron must be an integral multiple of $h/2\pi$. This in effect fixes the radii at which the electron may travel.

$$m_e Vr_n = \frac{nh}{2\pi} \tag{2.12}$$

where r_n is the radius of an allowable orbit and $n = 1, 2, 3, \cdots$. Eliminating first the radius and then the velocity by combining (2.11) and (2.12) allows one to solve for the orbital velocity and radius of an electron's orbit.

$$V = \frac{2\pi Z e^2}{nh} \tag{2.13}$$

$$r_n = \frac{n^2 h^2}{4\pi^2 m_e Z e^2} \tag{2.14}$$

Figure 2.4 shows the allowable electron orbits for the hydrogen atom. The electron in the hydrogen atom is shown as having just dropped from the third shell to the first with the emission of a photon. Since it drops from the third, rather than from the second orbit, to the first, the frequency is higher.

To determine the energy of an electron in a given orbit, its kinetic and potential energies must be added.

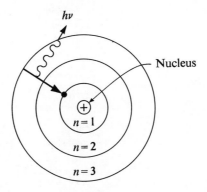

FIG. 2.4   *Bohr's model of the hydrogen atom showing allowable electron orbits.*

Consider first that an electron completely divorced from a nucleus has zero potential energy.   As a free electron at an infinite radius falls into an allowable orbit of radius r_n it will lose potential energy.   At radius r the force of attraction between the nucleus and the electron is

$$F = \frac{Ze^2}{r^2} \tag{2.15a}$$

It will acquire a differential amount of potential energy dPE as it moves a differential distance dr.   Integrating between ∞ and r_n gives the potential energy for the electron.

$$\int_0^{PE_n} dPE = \int_\infty^{r_n} \frac{Ze^2}{r^2} \, dr$$

$$PE_n = -\frac{Ze^2}{r_n} \tag{2.15b}$$

From Eq. (2.11)

$$v_n^2 = \frac{Ze^2}{r_n m_e}$$

and thus,

$$KE_n = \frac{m_e v_n^2}{2} = \frac{Ze^2}{2r_n} \tag{2.15c}$$

The total electron energy in the nth allowable orbit is then

$$E_n = PE_n + KE_n$$

$$= -\frac{Ze^2}{r_n} + \frac{Ze^2}{2r_n} = -\frac{Ze^2}{2r_n} \tag{2.15d}$$

combining with Eq. (2.14) this becomes

$$E_n = -\frac{2\pi^2 Z^2 m_e e^4}{n^2 h^2} \tag{2.15e}$$

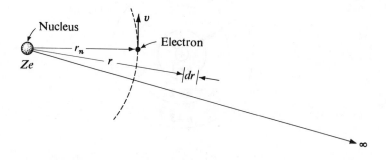

FIG. 2.5 *Sketch showing relation of an electron in the nth allowable orbit to the nucleus of an atom.*

The change in energy from one orbit, n_1, to another, n_2, is

$$\Delta E = [(1/n_1^2) - (1/n_2^2)] \frac{2\pi^2 Z^2 m_e e^4}{h^2} \tag{2.16}$$

When an electron falls from an outer orbit to an inner one, ΔE is negative and energy is released as a photon. If it jumps to a higher orbit, energy is absorbed.

Example 4. Compute the radius of the innermost electron orbit in a carbon atom. What will be the energy of the photon given off if a free electron ($n = \infty$) falls into the innermost orbit?

$$r_1 = \frac{n^2 h^2}{4\pi^2 m_e Z e^2}$$

$$= \frac{1^2 \times (6.625 \times 10^{-27})^2 \text{ erg}^2 \text{ sec}^2 \times 1 \text{ gr}^2 \text{ cm}^4 \text{ sec}^{-4} \text{ erg}^{-2}}{4 \times \pi^2 \times 9.1085 \times 10^{-28} \text{ gr} \times 6 \times (4.80 \times 10^{-10})^2 \text{ esu}^2}$$

$$\times \frac{1}{1 \dfrac{\text{gr cm}^3}{\text{sec}^2 \text{ esu}^2}} = .0791 \times 10^{-8} \text{ cm}$$

$$\Delta E = [(1/n_1^2) - (1/n_2^2)] \frac{2\pi^2 Z^2 m_e e^4}{h^2}$$

$$= [(1/\infty^2) - (1/1^2)] \frac{2\pi^2 \times 6^2 \times 9.1085 \times 10^{-28} \text{ gr}}{(6.6252 \times 10^{-27})^2 \text{ gr}^2 \text{ cm}^4 \text{ sec}^{-2}}$$

$$\times \frac{(4.80 \times 10^{-10})^4 \text{ esu}^4 \times 1 \text{ gr}^2 \text{ cm}^6 \text{ sec}^{-4} \text{ esu}^{-4}}{1.60210 \times 10^{-12} \text{ gr cm}^2 \text{ sec}^{-2} \text{ ev}^{-1}}$$

$$= -489 \text{ eV}$$

Wave mechanics shows that electrons are not always at a fixed distance from the nucleus, as predicted for the Bohr atom. Their location may be more properly described by a position probability curve. For an electron in a particular energy state, this plots the probability of being at a given radius versus distance from the center of the nucleus. Figure 2.6 shows such curves for the hydrogen atom.

In order to completely describe the energy state of an electron, four quantum numbers are required, rather than just the one used in Bohr theory. The principal quantum number, n, indicates the most probable radius of an electron orbit. It may have any integral value from 1 to ∞. The orbital quantum numbler, l, indicates the angular momentum of the electron and the eccentricity of the orbit. It may have values from 0 to $(n - 1)$. The magnetic orbital quantum number, m, indicates the "plane" of the electron's orbit about the nucleus. It may have values from $-l$ to $+l$. The spin number, s, has only two possible values for an electron, $\pm 1/2$.

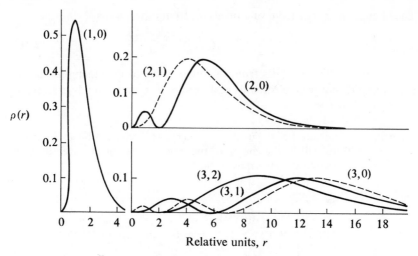

FIG. 2.6   *Hydrogen atom-probability densities.   The scale is the same for all curves.*   [*From Pitzer, K. S.,* Quantum Chemistry.   *Englewood Cliffs, N. J.: Prentice-Hall, Inc., 1953.   Reprinted by permission.*]

Figure 2.6 shows for $_1^1$H the probability of finding an electron at a given radius for values of the principal quantum number $n = 1$, 2, or 3 and for the orbital quantum number $l = 0$, 1, or 2.   From this figure it may be observed that the most probable radius is related to n.   Electrons with a particular value of the principal quantum number are said to be in the same shell.   The Pauli exclusion principle stipulates that no two electrons in a given atom may have the same set of quantum numbers.   Therefore, the maximum number of electrons in a given shell is $2n^2$.   A shell containing this maximum number of electrons is said to be filled.   The electrons in an unfilled outer shell are the valence electrons.   Thus, magnesium with its twelve electrons has two in the first shell, eight in the second, and two valence electrons in the third shell.   Elements with all shells filled, such as helium and neon, are inert.   In heavier elements, if there are eight electrons in the outer shell, the configuration is very stable and valence may be figured as the difference between the electrons in the outer shell and eight.

In stable atoms, as protons are added to the nucleus, corresponding electrons are added in order of decreasing binding energies.   Starting with the lightest elements, electrons fill first the energy states in the innermost shell and then those in the second shell, etc.   This takes the elements from an atomic number of 1 for hydrogen up to argon with an $A = 18$ (3,1 state).   After this point the 4,0 state will have a lower binding energy than the 3,2 state; thus, the transition elements will have the 4,0 state filled before electrons complete the third shell. Many important metals are included in these transition elements. Included are V, Cr, Mn, Fe, Co, and Ni. There is a similar premature filling of the outer shells in many of the heavier elements.

X-RAYS AND BREMSSTRAHLUNG

X-rays are electromagnetic radiation produced when energetic electrons interact with matter. In an X-ray tube, the electrons are emitted by a heated cathode whose potential may be the order of 30,000 to 50,000 volts above the target which is made of a material such as tungsten or molybdenum. X-rays are emitted by the target which stops the electrons. They form a continuous spectrum with wavelengths longer than a minimum value dictated by the energy of the electrons as they strike the target. Superimposed on the continuous spectrum may be several sharp spikes. The continuous spectrum is due to *bremsstrahlung* or braking radiation. It is radiation emitted as electrons decelerate in the Coulomb fields of the target nuclei. The sharp peaks are caused by the electronic rearrangement which takes place when atoms are struck by energetic electrons. These characteristic X-rays are produced as electrons fall from excited energy states to lower energy levels. Figure 2.7 shows the X-ray spectrum for a molybdenum target operated with a 35,000 volt potential. Two sharp peaks are superimposed on the continuous spectrum.

The X-ray spectrum for a tungsten target operated with a 35 kV potential would show no sharp peaks. It would have only a continuous spectrum since the electrons striking the target would lack the energy to raise the tungsten atoms to the lowest excited state. It would be necessary to double the operating voltage of the tube to produce the first two characteristic peaks for tungsten.

ATOMIC BONDING

The atomic bonding which holds molecules together and provides for the rigidity of solids may be one or a combination of the following:

(1) *Ionic bonding* occurs when there is an exchange of electrons where the donor becomes positively charged and the recipient is negatively charged. The bond is then electrostatic in nature. A simple example is found in magnesia (MgO), an effective moderator for nuclear reactors. The magnesium (Z = 12) has two electrons in the third shell which it gives up to an oxygen atom (Z = 8) which lacks two electrons to complete the second shell.

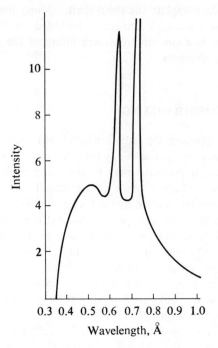

FIG. 2.7   *X-ray spectrum for a molybdenum target operated at 35,000 volts.*

(2)   *Covalent bonding* takes place when electrons are shared by the bound nuclei. The hydrogen molecule (H_2) illustrates this type of bond. The electrons are shared by the two nuclei, in effect filling both inner shells.

(3)   *Metallic bonding* leaves the valence electrons relatively free to wander through the lattice structure acting much like a gas. The negative charge of the free electrons and the net positive charge of the nucleus with its firmly bound electrons cause a mutual attraction binding the structure together.

(4)   *Van der Waal bonds* are relatively weak bonds due to the nonsymmetrical distribution of electrons in atoms or molecules. This produces polarization and attraction of unlike charges. This accounts for the forces of attraction when an inert material such as helium or argon is solidified at cryogenic temperatures.

In many cases the bonding is not a simple matter of being merely one of the preceding types. A case in point is graphite where in the basal planes of the hexagonal lattice the bonding is covalent, but where Van der Waal bonds exist between the planes.

NUCLEAR STRUCTURE AND BINDING FORCES

The exact nature of nuclear binding forces is not known.   However, they must be short-range (2×10^{-13} cm) and stronger than the electrostatic forces which tend to drive apart the protons of like charge.   They also must be of such a nature that the particles are not drawn together into a fused mass.   Further, the uncharged neutrons must be tightly bound.

The key to understanding the "strong" force holding the atomic nucleus together may lie in the internal structure of neutrons and protons. Both neutrons and protons respond to electromagnetic forces and the scattering patterns for high energy electrons has indicated that nucleons may have an internal structure consisting of point particles which have been named partons.   They will be discussed further in Chapter 4 along with antimatter and strange particles (hyperons, mesons, etc.).

To describe the state of the nucleus, a set of four quantum numbers is required for the protons and another set of four for the neutrons. One may infer from the previous discussion of the atom that when one of the nucleons drops to a lower energy state, electromagnetic radiation carries the energy away.   This energy is transmitted by gamma rays which are similar to X-rays except for their source.   Gamma rays originate from the nucleus, while characteristic X-rays are due to a change in electronic configuration.

Figure 2.8 shows the energy levels for a ^{15}O nucleus.   The lowest

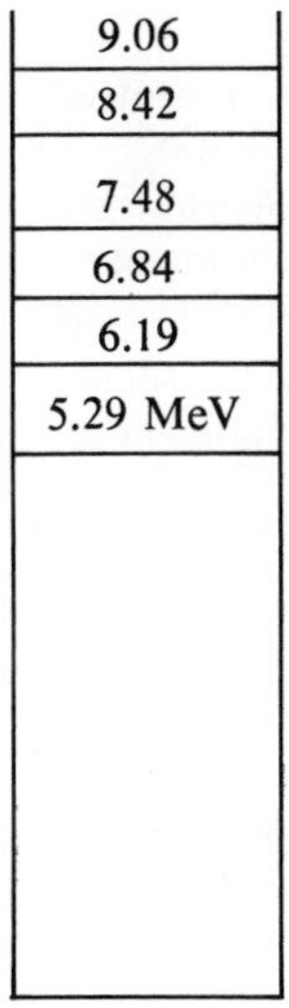

| 9.06 |
| 8.42 |
| 7.48 |
| 6.84 |
| 6.19 |
| 5.29 MeV |

FIG. 2.8   *Energy level diagram for a ^{15}O nucleus.*

energy level is at 5.29 MeV. If the nucleus has a scattering collision with a neutron of less than 5.29 MeV, the process is elastic. However, if more than 5.29 MeV is imparted to the nucleus on the collision, a 5.29 MeV gamma will be given off. The remaining energy would be shared by the recoiling nucleus and the scattered neutron in such an inelastic scattering process.

For light elements the first excited state is normally several MeV above ground level. The interval between levels decreases to a few keV above 8 MeV and becomes nearly continuous above 15 MeV. Since the slowing down of neutrons is accomplished primarily by light atoms in the moderator of a thermal reactor, scattering may be considered elastic. This is so because the average energy of a fission neutron is only 2 MeV.

For heavy elements inelastic scatter is more prevalent, since their energy levels are only about 0.1 MeV apart near ground level. The differences in energy levels decrease to a few eV at 8 MeV.

PROBLEMS

1. Compute the number density of atoms in the following cases:
   (a) Pure aluminum
   (b) ^{17}O in the atmosphere at 14.7 psia and 60°F.
   (c) Aluminum in a 90 w/o Al − 10 w/o Mg alloy which has a density of 2.55 gm/cm³.

2. Determine the binding energy per nucleon and the mass defect (u) for $_{90}^{232}$Th and for $_{27}^{59}$Co.

3. The average KE of a fission neutron is 2 MeV. What is its velocity? Must it be considered relativistic?

4. Calculate the ratio of a particle's mass to its rest mass when the particle travels at the following fractions of the speed of light: 0.1, 0.5, 0.9, 0.999.

5. Compute the kinetic energy of the particle (MeV) in the preceding problem for each of the velocities if it is (a) an electron (b) a deuteron.*

6. Show that the relativistic momentum of a particle may be expressed as

$$p = (1/c)\sqrt{(KE)^2 + 2m_0c^2(KE)}$$

7. Show the wave number for an X-ray may be expressed as

$$\bar{\nu} = RZ^2 \left[\frac{1}{n_1^2} - \frac{1}{n_2^2} \right]$$

where R represents the Rydberg constant.

$$R = \frac{2\pi^2 m_e e^4}{ch^3}$$

8. When a free electron ($n = \infty$) falls into the innermost shell of a chlorine atom, what will be the energy of the X-ray emitted and its wave length?

*A deuteron is the nucleus of a deuterium atom.

9. Compute the velocity of an electron in the first shell (ground state) of a hydrogen atom. What would it be if it were in an excited state in the third shell? What would be the orbital radius for each of these shells and the energy of an X-ray emitted when the excited electron drops back to the ground state?

10. For a 100 kV X-ray machine using a tungsten target ($Z = 74$), compute the shortest wave length due to *bremsstrahlung* and also the wave length and energy for characteristic X-rays due to electrons dropping from the 3rd and 2nd shells to the 1st.

REFERENCES

1. Kaplan, Irving, *Nuclear Physics*. 2nd ed. Reading, Mass: Addison-Wesley Publishing Co., Inc., 1963.

2. Halliday, David, *Introductory Nuclear Physics*. New York: John Wiley and Sons, Inc., 1955.

3. Semat, Henry, *Introduction to Atomic and Nuclear Physics*. New York: Holt, Rinehart, and Winston, 1962.

4. Frankel, J. P., *Principles of the Properties of Materials*. New York: McGraw-Hill Book Co., Inc., 1957.

5. Lapp, Ralph E., and H. L. Andrews, *Nuclear Radiation Physics*. Englewood Cliffs, N. J.: Prentice-Hall, Inc., 1963.

6. Liverhant, Solomon E., *Elementary Introduction to Nuclear Reactor Physics*. New York: John Wiley and Sons, Inc., 1960.

7. Cahen, G., and P. Treille, *Nuclear Engineering*, trans. by G. B. Melese. Boston: Allyn and Bacon, Inc., 1961.

8. Pitzer, Kenneth S., *Quantum Chemistry*. Englewood Cliffs, N. J.: Prentice-Hall, Inc., 1953.

9. Kendall, H. W., and W. K. H. Panofsky, "The Structure of the Proton and the Neutron." *Scientific American* **224**, no. 6 (June, 1971), pp. 60–77.

10. Arya, Atam P., *Fundamentals of Nuclear Physics*. Boston: Allyn and Bacon, Inc., 1961.

11. Arya, Atam P., *Fundamentals of Atomic Physics*. Boston: Allyn and Bacon, Inc., 1971.

Chapter 3

The Decay of
Radioactive Nuclei

Radioactivity is due to the decay of unstable nuclei. These nuclei can be:

(1) Heavy elements such as uranium or thorium which have such a slow rate of decay that they have been present since their creation at the beginning of geological time.

(2) The daughter products of the initial heavy elements which are, in turn, radioactive.

(3) Unstable fission products whose N/Z ratio is too high for stability.

(4) Unstable isotopes produced by particle bombardment. Neutron activation is particularly important in this regard. In a reactor the absorption of a neutron produces radiation effects that may be considered a nuisance. However, neutron activation can be used as a powerful analytical tool to identify unknown elements. Here the induced radiation spectrum can be examined to identify the decaying elements.

NATURAL RADIOACTIVITY

The heavy radioactive elements and their unstable daughters emit three types of radiation: alpha particles, beta particles, and gamma rays. The alpha particle is a helium nucleus, having a double positive charge due to its pair of protons which combine with two uncharged neutrons to make the mass approximately 4 u. The beta particle is a negatively charged electron expelled by the nucleus, effectively converting a neutron to a proton. The gamma ray is electromagnetic radiation, as indicated in Chapter 2, which allows an excited nucleus to drop toward the ground state.

Figure 3.1 shows the series of elements formed as ^{232}Th and ^{235}U decay

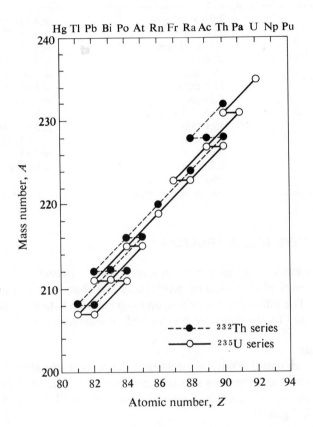

FIG. 3.1 *Natural radioactive decay series for ^{232}Th and ^{235}U.*

through their various daughter products to finally end up as stable ^{208}Pb and ^{207}Pb respectively. Table 3.1 lists the half-lives and types of radiation emitted for each of the reactions in the actinium (^{235}U) decay chain.

The fertile isotope of uranium, ^{238}U, has a half-life of 4.51 billion years. One of its important decay products is radium (^{226}Ra) with a 1620 year half-life. It is present in sufficient quantity in uranium ore to be separated for medical and industrial usage. The stable end product of the ^{238}U decay chain is ^{206}Pb.

TABLE 3.1

THE ACTINIUM DECAY SERIES

Element	Half-Life	Type of Radiation (Energy—MeV)
$_{92}^{235}$U	7.07×10^8 yrs	$\alpha(4.52), \gamma(0.09)$
$_{90}^{231}$Th	25.6 hrs	$\beta, \gamma(0.03)$
$_{91}^{231}$Pa	3.4×10^4 yrs	$\alpha(5.05), \gamma(0.32)$
$_{89}^{227}$Ac	21.6 yrs	$\alpha(5.0), \beta(0.22)$
$_{90}^{227}$Th	18.1 days	$\alpha(6.05), \gamma$
$_{88}^{223}$Ra	11.7 days	$\alpha(5.86), \gamma$
$_{86}^{219}$Rn	3.29 sec	$\alpha(6.82), \gamma$
$_{84}^{215}$Po	1.83×10^{-3} sec	$\alpha(7.36)$
$_{82}^{211}$Pb	36.1 min	$\beta(1.4), \gamma(0.8)$
$_{83}^{211}$Bi	2.16 min	$\alpha(6.62), \beta, \gamma(0.35)$
$_{84}^{211}$Po	0.5 sec	$\alpha(7.43)$
$_{81}^{207}$Tl	4.76 min	$\beta(1.4), \gamma$
$_{82}^{207}$Pb	Stable	

RADIOACTIVE DECAY PROCESSES

Radioactive decay takes place in several ways. In each of these processes the mass of the resultant particles is less than that of the parent nucleus. The difference may show up as gamma radiation or as kinetic energy shared by the daughter nucleus and an emergent particle.

Alpha Decay

When an unstable nucleus ejects an alpha particle, the atomic number is reduced by 2 and the mass number decreases by 4. An example is ^{234}U which decays by the ejection of an alpha accompanied by the emission of a 0.068 MeV gamma.

$$_{92}^{234}\text{U} \longrightarrow {}_{90}^{230}\text{Th} + {}_2^4\alpha + \gamma + KE \tag{3.1}$$

The combined kinetic energy of the resultant nucleus and the emergent particle (in this case the ^{230}Th and the α) is designated as KE. The sum of the kinetic energy and the gamma energy is equal to the difference in mass between the original nucleus and the final particles. This total mass-energy conversion is called Q.

$$Q = KE + \gamma = (m_U - m_{Th} - m_\alpha) \times 931 \tag{3.2}$$

Substituting:

$$Q = (234.0409 - 230.0331 - 4.00260) \times 931 = 4.84 \text{ MeV}$$

This represents the total mass-energy conversion for the process. The kinetic energy shared by the particles is

$$KE = Q - \gamma = 4.84 - 0.068 = 4.77 \text{ MeV}$$

The disintegration of the parent ^{234}U nucleus is shown in Fig. 3.2. The radioactive nucleus is considered to be stationary. The momenta of

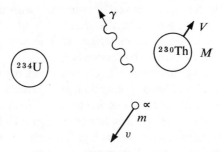

FIG. 3.2   *Alpha decay of ^{234}U nucleus.*

the emergent particle and the recoiling daughter nucleus are therefore equal and opposite.

$$MV + mv = 0 \tag{3.3a}$$

$$V = -(m/M)v \tag{3.3b}$$

Here M and V represent the mass and velocity of the recoiling daughter and m and v represent the mass and velocity of the emergent alpha. The kinetic energy of the two particles is

$$KE = (M/2)V^2 + (m/2)v^2$$

$$= \left(\frac{m+M}{M}\right)\left(\frac{mv^2}{2}\right) = \left(\frac{m+M}{M}\right)KE_\alpha \tag{3.4a}$$

The kinetic energy of the alpha is then

$$KE_\alpha = [M/(m+M)]KE \tag{3.4b}$$

The alpha emitted by the ^{234}U will have a KE as follows:

$$KE_\alpha = (230/234)4.77 = 4.69 \text{ MeV}$$

Alpha radiation is not very penetrating, being effectively stopped by a piece of paper. Thus, external exposure to alpha radiation presents little hazard, but ingestion of an alpha emitter can be very serious. The radioactive material can collect preferentially in various organs of the body and cause great harm.

Beta Emission

Beta particles are electrons that have been expelled by excited nuclei. They can have a charge of either sign. If both energy and momentum are to be conserved, a third type of particle, the neutrino, ν, is involved. The neutrino is associated with positive electron emission and its anti-particle, the antineutrino, $\bar{\nu}$, is emitted with a negative electron. They are similar in all respects, except that the spin vector is in the same direction as the direction of motion for the neutrino, while the spin vector for the antineutrino is opposite to the direction of motion. These uncharged particles have only the very weakest interactions with matter, their rest mass is zero, and they travel with the speed of light. For all practical purposes they pass through all materials with so few interactions that their energy is lost (i.e., cannot be recovered).

Negative electron emission effectively converts a neutron to a proton, thus increasing Z by 1 and leaving A unchanged. This is a common mode of decay for nuclei with an excess of neutrons, as with fission fragments on the high side of the N/Z stability line (refer again to Fig. 2.3). Velocities of the ejected electrons are often high enough to be a considerable fraction of the speed of light. This requires that they be treated in a relativistic fashion. There is a spectrum of beta energy values below some maximum. At the maximum beta energy the beta particle accounts for the total Q value. At lower energies the mass-energy conversion is shared with the antineutrino. The decay of ^{32}P illustrates the negative beta decay process.

$$_{15}^{32}P \longrightarrow {}_{16}^{32}S + {}_{-1}^{0}e + \bar{\nu} \qquad (3.5)$$

The average electron energy is about one-third of the maximum. The intensity of a stream of $_{15}^{32}P$ betas will be attenuated 50 percent by a thickness of 0.1 mm of aluminum.

Positively charged electrons are known as positrons. Except for sign, they are identical with their negatively charged cousins. When a positron is ejected from the nucleus, Z is decreased by 1 and A remains unchanged. A proton has been converted to a neutron. The decay of ^{13}N illustrates this process.

$$_{7}^{13}N \longrightarrow {}_{6}^{13}C + {}_{+1}^{0}e + \nu \qquad (3.6a)$$

In this case the neutrino shares with the positron the loss in mass which has been converted to energy. In the alpha decay and in the beta minus decay discussed previously atomic masses, rather than nuclear masses, could be used for computing the mass change since the electron masses cancelled out. With positron emission this is not so, as is shown by the following example.

$$\begin{aligned} Q &= [(m_N - 7m_e) - (m_C - 6m_e) - m_e] \times 931 \\ &= [(m_N - m_C) - 2m_e] \times 931 \end{aligned} \qquad (3.6b)$$

Note that an orbital electron is released in the conversion from nitrogen to carbon. This or an equivalent electron will later meet and annihilate the positron by producing two gammas with a combined energy equal to the rest mass of the $\pm$ electrons ($2 \times 0.000549 \times 931 = 1.02$ MeV).

Orbital Electron Capture (K-Capture)

Nuclei having an excess of protons but lacking energy for positron emission can move an electron from one of the inner orbits (usually the K-shell) into the nucleus, as shown in Fig. 3.3. Positron emission and K-

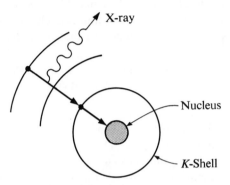

FIG. 3.3 *Orbital electron capture.*

capture are competing processes. However, if the parent's mass is not greater than that of the daughter by more than twice the electron mass, only K-capture is energetically possible (see Eq. (3.6b)). $_4^7$Be is such an isotope which can only decay by orbital electron capture.

$$_4^7\text{Be} + _{-1}^0\text{e} \longrightarrow _3^7\text{Li} + \nu \qquad (3.7)$$

A neutrino must be released by the nucleus to conserve the angular momentum of the nucleus. There may sometimes be accompanying gamma radiation and there will always be characteristic X-rays given off when electrons fill the orbital vacancies.

Proton Decay

Previously, transmutation to a different chemical element was considered possible to occur only by alpha decay, $\pm$ beta decay, and K-capture. However, during 1970 direct proton decay was reported.

Bombardment of ^{40}Ca nuclei by ^{16}O nuclei has resulted in the formation of an unstable ^{53}Co nucleus which decays to ^{52}Fe by the emission of a proton. The same nucleus has been produced by proton bombardment of ^{54}Fe nuclei to yield the same ^{53}Co nuclei and again, proton decay. The half-life of the proton emitting ^{53}Co is very short (245 ms) and the decay process reduces both A and Z by one.

$$_{27}^{53}\text{Co} \longrightarrow _1^1p + _{26}^{52}\text{Fe} \qquad (3.8)$$

As more exotic nuclei are produced it is expected that others will be found that will decay by proton emission.

Neutron Emission

Very energetic nuclei can expel a nuetron ($\sim$8 MeV). Several such isotopes among the fission fragments provide delayed neutrons. This small but important group of neutrons simplifies the control of a reactor, as will be shown in Chapter 10. Iodine 137 is a negative beta emitter which decays to ^{137}Xe which, in turn, immediately expels a neutron. The neutrons appear at a rate determined by the iodine decay.

$$_{53}^{137}\text{I} \xrightarrow[\substack{27\text{sec}}]{\beta^-} {}_{54}^{137}\text{Xe} \xrightarrow[\substack{\text{instantaneous}}]{n} {}_{54}^{136}\text{Xe} \qquad (3.9)$$

Isomeric Transition

Often a daughter isotope is left in an excited state after a radioactive parent nucleus emits a particle. The nucleus will drop to the ground state by the emission of gamma radiation. This commonly occurs immediately on particle emission; however, the nucleus may remain in an excited state for a measurable period of time before dropping to the ground state at its own characteristic rate. A nucleus that remains in such an excited state before decay is known as an *isomer*.

Figure 3.4a shows the decay scheme for ^{107}Cd which includes K-capture, gammas, and positron emission. Each of the three possible modes of Cd decay leaves the ^{107}Ag in an isomeric state from which it decays with a 44.3 second half-life by emitting a 0.0939 MeV gamma.

Internal Conversion

Sometimes nuclear excitation energy is transferred to a K-shell electron rather than having a gamma emitted. This conversion electron is ejected with a discrete energy and without a neutrino. The orbital electrons drop to a lower energy state with the emission of X-rays. These in turn may eject other orbital electrons which are known as *Auger electrons*.

COMPLEX DECAY SCHEMES

Several modes of decay may be available to a single nucleus. A case in point is ^{64}Cu that can decay not only by $\pm\beta$ emission, but also by electron capture that may or may not leave the daughter ^{64}Ni in an excited state, so that a gamma can be produced as well (see Fig. 3.4b). A similar diagram is shown in Fig. 3.4c for ^{213}Bi that emits alphas, betas, and gammas. The decay of ^{107}Cd (shown in Fig. 3.4a) was discussed previously as an example of decay to an isomeric state of the daughter sil-

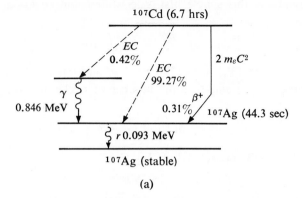

(a)

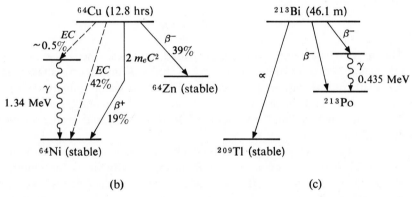

(b)   (c)

FIG. 3.4   *Complex decay schemes:* (a) ^{107}Cd; (b) ^{64}Cu; and (c) ^{213}Bi.

ver isotope.   Many other isotopes have even more complicated decay schemes.

DECAY RATES AND HALF-LIVES

The decay of radioactive isotopes occurs in a random manner.   There is a certain probability that in a given time interval a certain fraction of the nuclei of a particular unstable isotope will decay.   The rate of decay (dN/dt) is equal to minus the probability of decay, λ, times the number of unstable nuclei present, N.

$$dN/dt = -\lambda N \qquad (3.10)$$

The probability of decay is known as the *decay constant*.   Separation of variables allows this simple first-order differential equation to be integrated.

$$\int_{N_o}^{N} \frac{dN}{N} = -\lambda \int_0^t dt \qquad (3.11)$$

Here N_0 represents the original number of unstable nuclei present at the initial time ($t = 0$) and N is the number of nuclei at some subsequent time, t.

$$ln\left(\frac{N}{N_0}\right) = -\lambda t \qquad (3.12)$$

Taking the antilog of each side of Eq. (3.12)

$$N = N_0 e^{-\lambda t} \qquad (3.13)$$

It is well to note here that the activity of a sample, A, is the absolute magnitude of its decay rate.

$$A = \left|\frac{dN}{dt}\right| = \lambda N \qquad (3.14)$$

The activity of a sample is often expressed in curies, where one curie is taken as 3.7×10^{10} disintegrations per second. A microcurie is taken as 3.7×10^4 disintegrations per second. The curie was originally defined as the number of disintegrations per second occurring in one gram of ^{226}Ra. This is slightly less than the value of 3.7×10^{10} disintegrations per second currently in use.

For any sample being monitored only a fraction of the events are recorded. Thus, the count rate, CR, is the activity times the counter efficiency, e. For a given geometry and sample the efficiency is taken as constant.

$$CR = eA = e\lambda N \qquad (3.15)$$

so that $CR \propto A \propto N$. This proportionality of count rate, activity, and the number of unstable nuclei present permits a simple determination of the decay constant from the slope of a log count rate versus time plot for a decaying isotope.

$$\frac{CR_1}{CR_2} = \frac{A_1}{A_2} = \frac{N_1}{N_2} \qquad (3.16)$$

Fig. 3.5 represents the decay of a particular isotope. Equation (3.13) can be integrated between times t_1 and t_2 when N_1 and N_2 unstable nuclei are present.

$$\int_{N_1}^{N_2} \frac{dN}{N} = -\lambda \int_{t_1}^{t_2} dt \qquad (3.17)$$

so that

$$\lambda = \frac{ln N_1 - ln N_2}{t_2 - t_1} = \frac{ln(N_1/N_2)}{t_2 - t_1} \qquad (3.18)$$

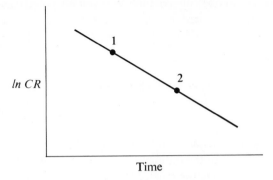

FIG. 3.5 *Typical decay curve for a radioisotope.*

Because of the proportionality between CR and N

$$\lambda = \frac{ln(CR_1/CR_2)}{t_2 - t_1} = \frac{lnCR_1 - lnCR_2}{t_2 - t_1} \quad (3.19)$$

The half-life of a radioisotope, $t_{1/2}$, is defined as the time required to reduce the number of decaying nuclei to one-half their original value.

$$\frac{N_{1/2}}{N_0} = \frac{CR_{1/2}}{CR_0} = \frac{1}{2} = e^{-\lambda t_{1/2}} \quad (3.20)$$

$$2 = e^{\lambda t_{1/2}} \quad (3.21)$$

Taking the log of each side and then solving for the half-life

$$t_{1/2} = \frac{ln2}{\lambda} = \frac{0.693}{\lambda} \quad (3.22)$$

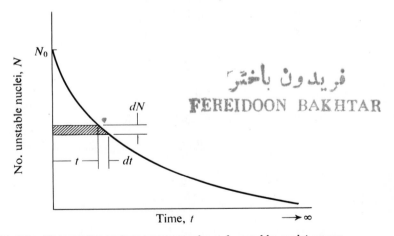

FEREIDOON BAKHTAR

FIG. 3.6 *Decay of a radioisotope: number of unstable nuclei versus time.*

A differential number of radioactive nuclei dN will decay during the time interval between t and $t + dt$. The total lifetime for this small group of nuclei will be

$$T = -t \times dN \tag{3.23a}$$

By differentiating Eq. (3.13) dN may be expressed as a function of time and then

$$T = N_0\lambda t e^{-\lambda t}\, dt \tag{3.23b}$$

Thus, if we integrate this function between $t = 0$ and $t = \infty$, we will have the total lifetime of all of the radioactive nuclei. Dividing by the original number of nuclei will give the mean lifetime for decay, t_m.

$$t_m = \frac{N_0\lambda \displaystyle\int_0^{\infty} t e^{-\lambda t}\, dt}{N_0}$$

$$= t e^{-\lambda t} - \frac{e^{-\lambda t}}{\lambda}$$

$$= \frac{1}{\lambda} \tag{3.23c}$$

The mean lifetime is thus seen to be the reciprocal of the probability of decay.

Example 1. Cesium 132 is an isotope useful in medical research for determining bodily retention of cesium. How long will it take a sample of this isotope to decay to 1 percent of its original activity? What will be the mean life of the ^{132}Cs atoms in a given sample?

$$\text{For } {}^{132}\text{Cs} \qquad t_{1/2} = 9.7 \text{ days}$$

Since $A \propto CR \propto N$

$$\frac{CR}{CR_0} = \frac{N}{N_0} = e^{-\lambda t}$$

$$0.01 = e^{-(0.693/9.7)t}$$

Taking the log of both sides and solving for t,

$$t = \frac{ln\, 100 \times 9.7}{0.693} = 64.1 \text{ days.}$$

The mean life is

$$t_m = \frac{1}{\lambda} = \frac{9.7}{0.693} = 14.0 \text{ days.}$$

It should be noted that bodily rejection of any ingested ^{132}Cs would reduce the time required for attainment of the 1 percent activity level.

COMPOUND DECAY

Often the daughter of a radioactive isotope is not stable and decays to a third nuclide, which also can be unstable. Figure 3.1 illustrated the rather lengthy decay chains for ^{232}Th and ^{235}U.

For the case of an element decaying to an unstable daughter and thence to a third stable isotope, expressions can be written for the number of atoms of each species. If N_{10} represents the original number of parent atoms and N_1 is the number of parent atoms having a decay constant λ_1, at any subsequent time, t,

$$N_1 = N_{10}e^{-\lambda_1 t} \tag{3.24}$$

The rate of change of parent nuclei is

$$\frac{dN_1}{dt} = -N_{10}\lambda_1 e^{-\lambda_1 t} \tag{3.25}$$

The rate of change of the daughter atoms, dN_2/dt, is due to the buildup caused by the decay of the parent less the decay of the daughter with its own decay constant, λ_2.

$$\frac{dN_2}{dt} = -\frac{dN_1}{dt} - \lambda_2 N_2$$

$$= \lambda_1 N_{10}e^{-\lambda_1 t} - \lambda_2 N_2 \tag{3.26}$$

Rearranging,

$$\frac{dN_2}{dt} + \lambda_2 N_2 = \lambda_1 N_{10}e^{-\lambda_1 t} \tag{3.27}$$

which is an equation of the form

$$\frac{dy}{dx} + a_1(x)y = h(x) \tag{3.28}$$

This first-order ordinary differential equation can be solved through the use of an integrating factor, p.

$$p = e^{\int a_1(x)dx} \tag{3.29}$$

The solution for Eq. (3.28) is

$$y = \left(\frac{1}{p}\right) \int ph(x)\, dx + \frac{C}{p} \tag{3.30}$$

where C is a constant of integration.

Since $a_1(x) = \lambda_2$ and $p = e^{\int a_1(x)dx} = e^{\int \lambda_2 dt} = e^{\lambda_2 t}$, then

$$N_2 = \left(\frac{1}{e^{\lambda_2 t}}\right) \int e^{\lambda_2 t}\lambda_1 N_{10}e^{-\lambda_1 t}\, dt + \frac{C}{e^{\lambda_2 t}}$$

$$= \frac{\lambda_1}{\lambda_2 - \lambda_1} N_{10}e^{-\lambda_1 t} + Ce^{-\lambda_2 t} \tag{3.31}$$

The constant of integration can be evaluated with the initial conditions, $t = 0$, $N_2 = 0$

$$C = \frac{-\lambda_1 N_{10}}{\lambda_2 - \lambda_1}$$

Thus, the number of daughter atoms can be expressed as

$$N_2 = \frac{\lambda_1 N_{10}}{\lambda_2 - \lambda_1} (e^{-\lambda_1 t} - e^{-\lambda_2 t}) \qquad (3.32)$$

If the granddaughter element is stable, it will have a number of nuclei present, N_3, equal to

$$N_3 = N_{10} - N_1 - N_2 \qquad (3.33)$$

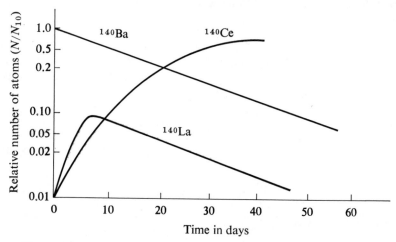

FIG. 3.7   *Decay of radioactive* ^{140}Ba. *After approximately 15 hours the* ^{140}Ba *and* ^{140}La *will be in transient equilibrium.*

Figure 3.7 shows an example of this type of compound decay process for ^{140}Ba which by beta emission decays to ^{140}La which in turn decays by beta emission to stable ^{140}Ce.

$$^{140}\text{Ba} \xrightarrow[12.8d]{\beta^-} {}^{140}\text{La} \xrightarrow[40.2hr]{\beta^-} {}^{140}\text{Ce} \qquad (3.34)$$

Notice here that the decay constant for the ^{140}Ba is smaller (0.0024 hr^{-1}) by a considerable amount than that for the ^{140}La (0.0172 hr^{-1}). After the ^{140}La passes through its maximum it will essentially decay at a rate equal to that of the parent ^{140}Ba. When $\lambda_1 < \lambda_2$ and the daughter and parent decay at essentially the same rate, they are in transient equilibrium. As t becomes large the $e^{-\lambda_2 t}$ term is considerably less than the $e^{-\lambda_1 t}$ term and contributes little to the solution. Thus,

$$N_2 \approx \frac{\lambda_1}{\lambda_2 - \lambda_1} N_{10} e^{-\lambda_1 t} \tag{3.35}$$

The ratio of the numbers of atoms of the two species which are in transient equilibrium is then

$$\frac{N_2}{N_1} = \frac{\lambda_1}{\lambda_2 - \lambda_1}$$

Multiplying both numerator and denominator by the appropriate decay constant gives the activity ratio.

$$\frac{A_2}{A_1} = \frac{N_2 \lambda_2}{N_1 \lambda_1} = \frac{\lambda_2}{\lambda_2 - \lambda_1} \tag{3.36}$$

The activity ratio is fixed and is only slightly larger than unity for the case of transient equilibrium.

Secular equilibrium occurs when the parent has an extremely long half-life. The daughter builds up to an equilibrium amount and decays at what amounts to a constant rate. In this situation $\lambda_1 \ll \lambda_2$ and the rate of formation of daughter atoms balances their rate of decay.

$$\frac{dN_2}{dt} = 0 = \lambda_1 N_1 - \lambda_2 N_2 \tag{3.37}$$

and, thus

$$\lambda_1 N_1 = \lambda_2 N_2 \tag{3.38}$$

In the long decay chain for a naturally radioactive element such as ^{232}Th where all the elements in the chain are in secular equilibrium, each of the descendents has built up to an equilibrium amount, and all decay at the rate set by the original parent. The only exception is the final stable nth element on the end of the chain. Its number of atoms is constantly increasing. In such a chain

$$\lambda_1 N_1 = \lambda_2 N_2 = \lambda_3 N_3 = \lambda_4 N_4 = \cdots = \lambda_{n-1} N_{n-1} \tag{3.39}$$

A third case of particular interest occurs when the parent is short-lived in comparison with its daughter ($\lambda_1 > \lambda_2$). In this instance no equilibrium will be established between the two species. Figure 3.8 shows the decay of 3.05 min ^{218}Po to 26.8 min ^{214}Pb. The daughter builds up to a maximum as the parent is disappearing. After the parent has all but vanished, the daughter decays according to its own half-life.

Example 2. For the ^{218}Po–^{214}Pb system, starting with freshly separated ^{218}Po, how long will it take for equal amounts of the two species to exist? At such time what fraction of the original parent atoms will be Po and Pb? Setting $N_1 = N_2$

$$N_{10} e^{-\lambda_1 t} = \frac{\lambda_1 N_{10}}{\lambda_2 - \lambda_1} (e^{-\lambda_1 t} - e^{-\lambda_2 t})$$

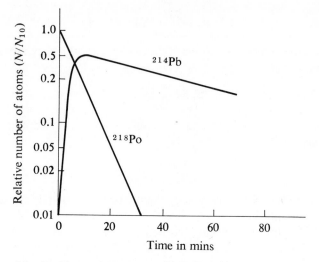

FIG. 3.8   *Buildup and decay of* ^{214}Pb *(26.8 minute half-life) from* ^{218}Po *(3.05 minute half-life).*

By rearranging and taking logs

$$t = \frac{ln\left(\dfrac{2\lambda_1 - \lambda_2}{\lambda_1}\right)}{\lambda_1 - \lambda_2}$$

$$\lambda_1 = \frac{0.693}{3.05} = 0.227 \text{ min}^{-1}$$

$$\lambda_2 = \frac{0.693}{26.8} = 0.0258 \text{ min}^{-1}$$

$$t = \frac{ln\,(2 \times 0.227 - 0.026)/0.227}{0.227 - 0.026} = 3.16 \text{ min.}$$

$$\frac{N_1}{N_{10}} = \frac{N_2}{N_{10}} = e^{-\lambda_1 t} = e^{-0.227 \times 3.16} = 0.484$$

Thus, after 3.16 minutes, Po and Pb each account for 48.4 percent of the original Po atoms.

PROBLEMS

1. ^{213}Po decays by alpha emission. What will be the daughter product? What will be the kinetic energies of the alpha particle and the recoiling nucleus?

2. ^{53}V emits a negative electron and an antineutrino with a combined energy of 2.53 MeV plus a 1.01 MeV gamma. What will be the daughter product? If the average electron energy is one-third of the total shared by the electron

and its antineutrino, find the ratio of the velocity at this average electron energy to the speed of light. What is the atomic mass of the ^{53}V atom?

3. ^{48}V can decay by either electron capture or positron emission. Write an equation describing each process.

4. Carbon dating for archeological materials of organic origin is based on the fact that the organism at its death stops absorbing radioactive carbon 14 as $^{14}CO_2$ from the atmosphere. This radioactive carbon in living materials accounts for about 0.10 percent of the total carbon content. At death the absorption ceases and the ^{14}C decays at its characteristic rate. Wood in an excavated ruin shows a ^{14}C content of 0.082 percent. Estimate the age of the structure.

5. How long will it take the activity of a 5 microcurie ^{60}Co source to decrease to 1.0 microcurie? What weight of ^{60}Co will be required for a 5 μci source?

6. A rock returned from the surface of the moon has a ratio of ^{87}Rb to ^{87}Sr atoms equal to 14.45. Assuming that this was all ^{87}Rb upon the formation of the solar system, estimate the age of the solar system.

7. During the shutdown of the Connecticut Yankee Reactor, a solution of ^{58}Co in the flooded refueling cavity produced a maximum activity of 1.5 $\mu ci/ml$ compared to a normal coolant activity of 1×10^{-3} $\mu ci/ml$. The use of flow-through filters and ion exchangers reduced the activity level by a factor of 14 in about 4 days, permitting refueling to proceed. How long would a similar attenuation take if radioactive decay of the cobalt were the only factor reducing the radiation level? If replacement power costs $50,000 per day, compute the total replacement power cost during the extra time required to wait for attenuation by radioactive decay.

8. How many grams of ^{210}Po will be required to supply a heat source for a thermoelectric generator which will produce 15 watts (th) at the end of a one-year space mission?

9. From the equation for the number of atoms of a radioactive daughter product develop an expression for the time at which this daughter product will be a maximum.

10. A sample of initially pure 4.7 day ^{47}Ca decays to 3.3 day ^{47}Sc which decays to stable ^{47}Ti. How long will it take the ^{47}Sc to reach a maximum? What will be the relative amount of each element at this time?

11. If ^{234}U and ^{226}Ra both occur in the decay chain for ^{238}U, compute the percent of each which is present in natural uranium. How many grams of ^{226}Ra will be present in one metric ton of natural uranium?

12. Starting with a freshly separated sample of ^{140}Ba, plot a curve of the relative amounts of ^{140}Ba, ^{140}La, and ^{140}Ce versus time. Use a Fortran program with a DO loop to calculate these amounts for each day during a 50-day period. Calculate and print out the amounts for the time at which the ^{140}La is a maximum.

13. For a freshly separated nuclide having an unstable daughter and a stable granddaughter, derive an expression for the length of time to have the number of parent and granddaughter nuclei be equal. In the case of ^{140}Ba decay after how many days will there be equal amounts of ^{140}Ba and ^{140}Ce?

REFERENCES

1. Lapp, R. E., and H. L. Andrews, *Nuclear Radiation Physics*. Englewood Cliffs, N. J.: Prentice-Hall, Inc., 1963.

2. Kaplan, I., *Nuclear Physics*. Reading, Mass.: Addison-Wesley Publishing Co., 1955.

3. Halliday, D., *Introductory Nuclear Physics*. New York: John Wiley and Sons, Inc., 1955.

4. Wilson, V. H., W. N. Bishop, and M. Hillman, "Production of Carrier-Free ^{132}Cs and ^{127}Cs," *Nuclear Applications* **1**, no. 6 (December, 1965), pp. 556–59.

5. El Wakil, M. M., *Nuclear Power Engineering*. New York: McGraw-Hill, 1962.

6. Liverhant, S. E., *Elementary Introduction to Nuclear Reactor Physics*. New York: John Wiley and Sons, Inc., 1960.

7. Semat, H., *Introduction to Atomic and Nuclear Physics*, 4th ed. New York: Holt, Rinehart, and Winston, 1962.

8. "Fourth Transformation Mode: Proton Decay," *Nuclear News* 13, no. 12 (December, 1970).

9. Jackson, K. P., et al., "^{53}Co^m: A Proton-Unstable Isomer," *Physics Letters* **33B**, no. 4 (26 October, 1970), pp. 281–283.

10. Cerny, J., et al., "Confirmed Proton Radioactivity of ^{53}Co^m," *Physics Letters* **33B**, no. 4 (26 October, 1970), pp. 284–286.

11. Graves, R. H., "Coolant Activity Experience at Conn. Yankee Reactor," *Nuclear News* **13**, no. 11 (November, 1970), pp. 66–67.

12. Ray, J. W., "Tritium in Power Reactors," *Reactor and Fuel-Processing Technology*, **12,** No. 1 (Winter 1968–69), pp. 19–26.

Chapter 4

Nuclear Reactions

THE COMPOUND NUCLEUS

In a nuclear reaction an incident particle (α, d, p, n, or γ) is absorbed into a target nucleus to form a highly excited compound nucleus. This compound nucleus then ejects a particle and/or gamma radiation to drop to a lower energy state.

If the particle being absorbed to form the compound nucleus is positively charged, it must overcome a potential barrier due to the repulsion of like charged bodies (see Fig. 4.1). As it approaches the nucleus the kinetic energy of a positively charged particle is converted to potential energy until the short-range nuclear forces balance the repulsive force. The particle then enters the nucleus, dropping into the potential well caused by the contribution of its binding energy. Classical mechanics would forbid a particle with less than the energy of the potential barrier from entering the nucleus. However, quantum mechanics predicts that by a process known as tunneling, there is a small probability of some particles having an energy less than that of the potential barrier entering the nucleus. Since neutrons and gammas carry no charge, they may enter the nucleus freely without having to surmount any potential barrier.

The compound nucleus may last only $\sim 10^{-14}$ seconds, but the binding energy of the incoming particle is quickly shared by the nucleons of the compound nucleus. During the lifetime of the compound nucleus the

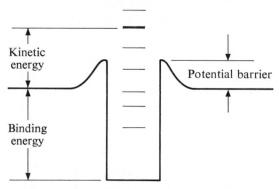

FIG. 4.1 *Energy levels for a compound nucleus. The energy of the compound nucleus is equal to the binding energy contributed by the incident particle plus its kinetic energy.*

nucleons exchange energy among themselves until one of them attains an energy level sufficient for particle ejection. This concept is valid for particle energies below 20 MeV for the lightest nuclei and below 80 MeV for the heaviest ones. For higher particle energies individual nucleons, or groups of nucleons, may be knocked from the nucleus without the formation of a compound nucleus.

A useful example of a nuclear reaction is found in the plutonium-beryllium neutron source. These may be used to provide neutrons for subcritical assemblies or to provide a monitorable neutron flux level on startup of a critical reactor. The plutonium is an alpha emitter. These alphas then have a high probability of being absorbed by the beryllium. The excited compound nucleus formed is $_6^{13}C^*$ which subsequently ejects a neutron to produce stable $_6^{12}C$.

$$_4^9Be + {_2^4}\alpha \longrightarrow {_6^{13}}C^* \longrightarrow {_6^{12}}C + {_0^1}n \tag{4.1}$$

In examining nuclear reactions one must allow for conservation of charge. In Eq. (4.1) there are six positive charges among the incident particles in the compound nucleus and in the emergent particles (in this particular case all six are carried by the $_6^{12}C$). There also must be conservation of nucleons. Again, there are 13 nucleons at each stage of the above reaction.

Momentum and energy must also be conserved in nuclear reactions. As stationary observers, we view reactions in the laboratory frame of reference. The energy of an incident particle is usually given for the laboratory system. It is often convenient to consider reactions in the center of mass (COM) system, where the observer must be imagined to be traveling at the velocity to be attained by the compound nucleus.

Fig. 4.2 shows a reaction occurring in the lab system. Consider first the formation of the compound nucleus. The incident particle of

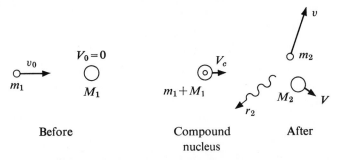

Before   Compound   After
                          nucleus

FIG. 4.2 *Nuclear reaction in the laboratory system showing the formation and decay of a compound nucleus. In this frame of reference
the reaction appears as it would to a stationary observer.*

mass m_1 and velocity v_0 strikes the stationary ($V_0 = 0$) target nucleus of
mass M_1 to form the compound nucleus of mass ($m_1 + M_1$) and velocity
V_c.   A momentum balance gives an expression for the compound nucleus
velocity in terms of the original neutron velocity.

$$m_1 v_0 + M_1(0) = (m_1 + M_1)V_c$$

$$V_c = \left(\frac{m_1}{m_1 + M_1}\right) v_0 \qquad\qquad (4.2)$$

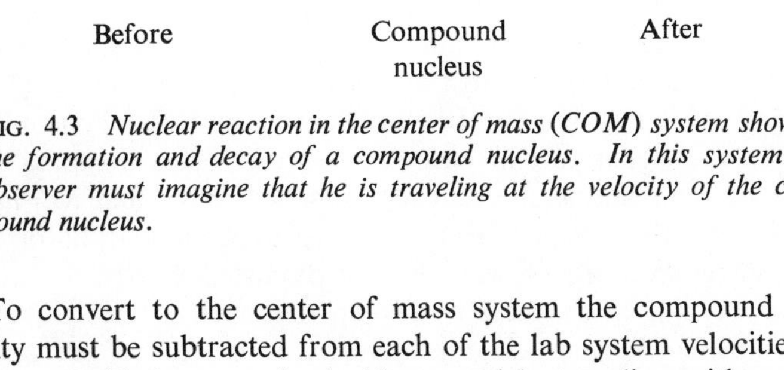

Before   Compound   After
                          nucleus

FIG. 4.3 *Nuclear reaction in the center of mass (COM) system showing
the formation and decay of a compound nucleus. In this system the
observer must imagine that he is traveling at the velocity of the compound nucleus.*

To convert to the center of mass system the compound nucleus
velocity must be subtracted from each of the lab system velocities.   The
observer would then see the incident particle traveling with a reduced
velocity, v_1, approaching the struck nucleus which has a velocity V_1 equal
to $-V_c$.

$$v_1 = v_0 - V_c = v_0 - \left(\frac{m_1}{m_1 + M_1}\right) v_0$$

$$= \left(\frac{M_1}{m_1 + M_1}\right) v_0 \tag{4.3}$$

When they meet, the compound nucleus will appear to hang stationary, possessing no kinetic energy. All of the kinetic energy of the incident particles in the COM system will therefore contribute to the excitation of the compound nucleus.

$$KE_1 = \frac{m_1 v_1^2}{2} + \frac{M_1 V_1^2}{2} \tag{4.4a}$$

Using Eqs. (4.2) and (4.3) KE_1 may be expressed in terms of the original lab system kinetic energy, KE_0, of the incident particle.

$$KE_1 = \frac{m_1 [M_1 v_0/(m_1 + M_1)]^2}{2} + \frac{M_1 [-m_1 v_0/(m_1 + M_1)]^2}{2}$$

$$= \left(\frac{M_1}{m_1 + M_1}\right) \left(\frac{m_1 v_0^2}{2}\right)$$

$$= \left(\frac{M_1}{m_1 + M_1}\right) KE_0 \tag{4.4b}$$

Thus, not all of KE_0 shows up as excitation energy in the compound nucleus. If the lab system kinetic energy of the compound nucleus is subtracted from KE_0, the result will be identical with Eq. (4.4b).

A mass-energy balance may be written for the overall reaction in the COM system.

$$m_1 c^2 + KE_1 + M_1 c^2 = m_2 c^2 + KE_2 + M_2 c^2 + \gamma_2 \tag{4.5a}$$

The difference in the rest masses is often denoted as Q.

$$Q = [(m_1 + M_1) - (m_2 + M_2)] c^2$$
$$= KE_2 + \gamma_2 - KE_1 \tag{4.5b}$$

A decrease in mass indicates an exothermic reaction and an increase in mass says that the reaction is endothermic. For endothermic reactions KE_1 must be at least large enough to offset the negative value of Q. For such endothermic reactions the threshold energy is the lab system kinetic energy of the incident particle (KE_0) necessary to offset the mass deficit, thus making the reaction energetically possible. Note that KE_1 may be considered to include the energy contributed by a gamma photon in the photo-disintegration process which will be discussed shortly.

In considering the breakup of a compound nucleus the COM system is again most convenient. In this system the direction of the emergent particle, θ, is random and the energies of the emergent particle of mass m_2 and velocity v_2 and the recoiling nucleus of mass M_2 and velocity V_2 are independent of direction, θ. When the compound nucleus breaks up, the kinetic energy shared by the emergent particles is

$$KE_2 = Q + KE_1 - \gamma_2 \qquad (4.5c)$$

A momentum balance ignores any momentum of a gamma (with its zero rest mass) and indicates that particle velocities and masses are inversely proportional, with the particles travelling in opposite directions.

$$(m_1 + M_1)0 = m_2 v_2 + M_2 V_2$$

$$V_2 = - \left(\frac{m_2}{M_2}\right) v_2 \qquad (4.6)$$

An expression may then be developed for the COM kinetic energy, KE_2', of the emergent particle, m_2, in terms of the lab system kinetic energy, KE_0, of the incident particle. Combining Eqs. (4.4b), (4.5c), and (4.6)

$$KE_2 = Q + \left(\frac{M_1}{m_1 + M_1}\right) KE_0 - \gamma_2$$

$$= \frac{m_2 v_2^2}{2} + \frac{M_2(m_2 v_2 / M_2)^2}{2} \qquad (4.7a)$$

Rearranging,

$$Q + \left(\frac{M_1}{m_1 + M_1}\right) KE_0 - \gamma_2 = 1 + \frac{m_2}{M_2} \frac{m_2 v_2^2}{2}$$

$$= \left(\frac{m_2 + M_2}{M_2}\right) KE_2'$$

$$KE_2' = \left(\frac{M_2}{m_2 + M_2}\right) \left(Q + \left(\frac{M_1}{m_1 + M_1}\right) KE_0 - \gamma_2\right) \qquad (4.7b)$$

If the compound nucleus velocity is added vectorially to the emergent particle velocity, v_2, and the recoil nucleus velocity, V_2, the lab system velocities may be determined. Both the velocities and the kinetic energies in the lab system are direction dependent. This will be covered more fully for the elastic scattering of neutrons in Chapter 8.

Example 1. A 0.5 MeV neutron is absorbed by a $_3{}^6$Li nucleus and causes an alpha particle to be ejected without any gamma radiation. Compute the COM kinetic energy of the alpha.

$$_3{}^6\text{Li} + _0{}^1\text{n} \longrightarrow _3{}^7\text{Li}^* \longrightarrow _1{}^3\text{H} + _2{}^4\alpha + Q$$

$$Q = [(m_{\text{Li}} + m_{\text{n}}) - (m_{\text{H}} + m_\alpha)]c^2$$
$$= [(6.01513 + 1.008665) - (3.01605 + 4.00260)]931$$
$$= 4.80 \text{ MeV}$$

$$KE_2' = \left(\frac{M_2}{m_2 + M_2}\right) \left(Q + \left(\frac{M_1}{m_1 + M_1}\right) KE_0 - \gamma_2\right)$$

$$= \frac{3}{7}\left(4.80 + \frac{6}{7}0.5 - 0\right)$$

$$= 2.24 \text{ MeV}$$

A compound nucleus may be formed from a variety of events. Its decay is independent of its mode of formation. An example of this is the formation of $_7^{15}N$ by alpha, deuteron, proton, or neutron capture. The decay of this compound nucleus may then occur by ejection of one of a variety of particles and/or by gamma emission, as illustrated by the following.

$$
\left.\begin{array}{c}
_5^{11}B + _2^4He \\
_6^{13}C + _1^2D \\
_6^{14}C + _1^1p \\
_7^{14}N + _0^1n
\end{array}\right\} \longrightarrow {_7^{15}N^*} \longrightarrow
\left\{\begin{array}{l}
_5^{11}B + _2^4He \\
_6^{13}C + _1^2D \\
_6^{14}C + _1^1p \\
_7^{14}N + _0^1n \\
_7^{13}N + 2_0^1n \\
_7^{15}N + \gamma
\end{array}\right.
$$

If decay occurs by ejection of the same type of particle as that which initiated the reaction ($[n, n]$, $[p, p]$, etc.) the process is called scattering. If the emerging particle and recoiling nucleus share all of the available kinetic energy, it is known as elastic scatter. If some of the energy is carried off by gamma radiation, thus reducing the KE to be shared by the emergent particle and the recoiling nucleus, the process is inelastic scatter. If the compound nucleus drops to the ground state solely by gamma emission, the process is called radiative capture.

Fig. 4.4 shows the energy levels of $_7^{15}N$ with some of the various modes of formation and decay. Note that the first excited state exists at 5.28 MeV above the ground level. The binding energy of a neutron is 10.834 MeV. Unless the energy level exceeds the binding energy of one of the particles, decay is only possible by gamma emission. The probabilities (cross sections) of neutron-induced reactions, $^{14}N(n, n)^{14}N$, $^{14}N(n, p)^{14}C$, $^{14}N(n, \alpha)^{11}B$, are shown above this binding energy for the incident neutrons.

Photodisintegration occurs when an incident gamma provides enough excitation energy to make particle ejection possible. The binding energy of the last neutron is normally 5 to 13 MeV, but deuterium and beryllium are exceptions. In the case of beryllium this threshold energy is 1.66 MeV. The value for $_1^2D$ is calculated in the following example. If monoenergetic gammas exceeding the threshold energy are used, neutrons of a single energy will be produced.

Example 2. A ^{24}Na–D_2O combination is used as a monoenergetic source of neutrons produced by the photodisintegration of the deuterium.

$$\gamma_1 + _1^2D \longrightarrow _1^1H + _0^1n$$

$$
\begin{aligned}
Q &= (m_D - m_H - m_n)c^2 \\
&= (2.01410 - 1.007825 - 1.008665)(931) \\
&= -2.225 \text{ MeV}
\end{aligned}
$$

The threshold energy for this reaction is 2.225 MeV. The radioactive

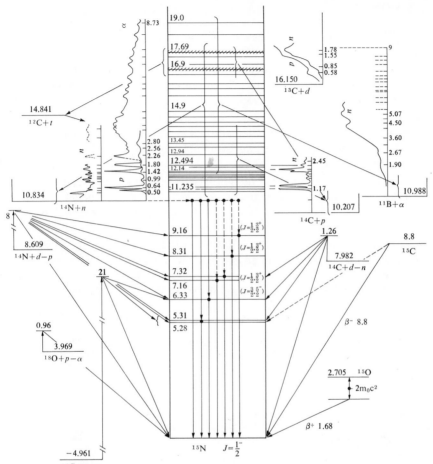

FIG. 4.4 *Energy levels in the* ^{15}N *nucleus.* [*From Ajzenberg, F., and T. Lauritsen, "Energy Levels in Light Nuclei, IV."* Revs. Mod. Phys., **24** (1952), p. 321.]

sodium gives off gammas of 2.75 MeV, 1.37 MeV, etc. Only the 2.75 MeV gamma provides enough energy to exceed the threshold and cause photodisintegration. The energy shared by the neutron and the proton as they fly apart will be

$$KE_2 = Q + \gamma_1 = -2.225 + 2.75 = 0.525 \text{ MeV}$$

Since the neutron and the proton have approximately the same mass, they will share the kinetic energy equally. The kinetic energy of the photoneutrons is

$$KE_n = \frac{1}{2} KE_2 = 0.263 \text{ MeV}$$

FISSION

Fission occurs when a heavy nucleus absorbs a neutron and splits into two fragments with the ejection of several high velocity (fast) neutrons. Among the naturally occurring isotopes only ^{235}U fissions by the absorption of thermal (slow) neutrons. Its more abundant sister isotope, ^{238}U, requires that a neutron have a kinetic energy of 1 MeV or better for fast neutron-induced fission to occur. Likewise, fast neutrons can cause fission of ^{232}Th. Both of these latter isotopes are fertile materials, which may be converted to fissile (thermally fissionable) nuclei, as will be discussed in the next section.

The neutrons emitted per fission vary from 0 to 7 or 8. The average number of neutrons emitted per fission, ν, is energy dependent. It increases linearly with energy. Not all neutron absorptions produce fission. When ν is multiplied by the probability of having fission after the absorption of a neutron, the result is known as the fission factor, η. It is the number of fast neutrons emitted per neutron absorbed. Values of ν and η are shown in Table 4.1 for three different energy levels.

Fig. 4.5 shows a neutron being absorbed by a ^{235}U nucleus to form

TABLE 4.1

FAST NEUTRONS EMITTED PER FISSION (ν) AND PER NEUTRON ABSORBED (η)

Neutron Energy	^{233}U		^{235}U		^{238}U		^{239}Pu	
	ν	η	ν	η	ν	η	ν	η
Thermal (0.025 eV)	2.50	2.30	2.43	2.07	—	—	2.89	2.11
1 MeV	2.62	2.54	2.58	2.38	—	—	3.00	2.92
2 MeV	2.73	2.57	2.70	2.54	2.69	2.46	3.11	2.99

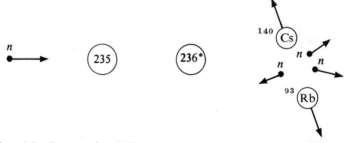

FIG. 4.5 *Fission of a ^{235}U nucleus by neutron absorption. The particular fission fragments shown are ^{140}Cs and ^{93}Rb with three neutrons being ejected.*

^{236}U as a highly excited compound nucleus. It immediately splits into two fission fragments, say ^{140}Cs and ^{93}Rb, plus three neutrons.

$$^{235}\text{U} + {}_0^1\text{n} \longrightarrow {}^{236}\text{U}^* \longrightarrow {}^{140}\text{Cs} + {}^{93}\text{Rb} + 3\,{}_0^1\text{n} \qquad (4.8)$$

Fig. 4.6 shows the variation in mass number for the fission products of ^{235}U. Note of effect of high energy neutrons in changing the relative fission yields. Apparently the probability is best of having one fragment of about 95 u and the other about 139 u, each with a yield of about 6.5 percent. The excess number of neutrons in the fission fragments makes them very unstable beta and gamma emitters. Since there are two fragments per fission when all the yields of fission products are added, the

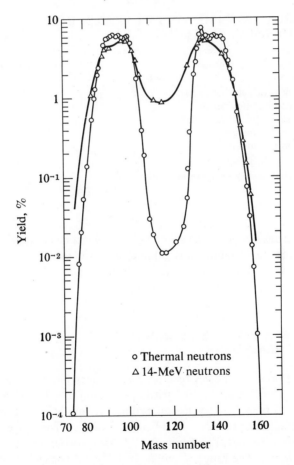

FIG. 4.6 ^{235}U fission yield versus mass number. Curves are shown for fission by thermal neutrons and by 14 MeV fast neutrons. (ANL 5800, p. 11.)

sum will be 200 percent. The yields of the various fission fragments differ slightly for the other fissile nuclei.

The energy distribution of ^{235}U fission neutrons may be expressed by the Watt equation.

$$N(E) = 0.453e^{-E} \sinh \sqrt{2E} \qquad (4.9)$$

where $N(E)$ is the fraction of neutrons of energy E (MeV) per unit energy interval. This relation indicates that for ^{235}U the most probable energy of fission neutrons is 0.72 MeV and the average energy is 2.0 MeV.

The energy release per fission is approximately 200 MeV. Table 4.2

TABLE 4.2

ENERGY DISTRIBUTION FOR FISSION INDUCED
BY THERMAL NEUTRONS IN ^{235}U

Source	Energy (MeV)
Fission product kinetic energy	168
Neutron kinetic energy	5
Fission γ's (instantaneous)	5
Fission γ's (delayed)	6
Fission product β's	7
Total available as heat	191
Neutrino energy (not available as heat)	11
TOTAL	202

indicates the distribution of this energy. The kinetic energy of the fission fragments and the instantaneous gammas are available for heating. The fission product gamma and beta decay energies can only be partially recovered during the lifetime of a nuclear fuel.

TRITIUM AS A TERNARY FISSION PRODUCT IN POWER REACTORS

Tritium occurs in power reactors as a ternary fission product. It is produced at a rate of 8.7×10^{-5} triton per fission in ^{235}U fueled reactors. The energy of these ternary fission product tritons will be less than 14 MeV with the most probable value being 7.5 MeV. The range of tritons in zirconium is estimated at 5 mils for 7.5 MeV tritons and 14.5 mils for 15 MeV tritons. The range is similar in UO_2 and somewhat smaller for stainless steel. Since cladding thicknesses of 16.5 to 33 mils are in use, it would appear that none of the ternary tritons will recoil through the clad.

Also there is little evidence of diffusion of this tritium through the cladding into the reactor coolant. Thus, the fission-induced tritium is delivered to the fuel reprocessing plant in the spent fuel elements. Here it is transferred to the liquid streams in the plant. It can be released after dilution in liquid water, or, after vaporization, be discharged to the atmosphere from a tall stack as a vapor.

CONVERSION OF FERTILE NUCLEI

Since 99.3 percent of natural uranium is the 238 isotope, which cannot be fissioned by thermal neutrons, it would be highly desirable to convert this to fissile material. This can be accomplished by neutron capture, which produces ^{239}U, which decays by β^- emission to ^{239}Np, and subsequently to ^{239}Pu by another β^- decay.

$$_{92}^{238}U + _0^1n \longrightarrow _{92}^{239}U^* \longrightarrow _{93}^{239}Np + _{-1}^0e \qquad \textbf{(4.10a)}$$

$$_{93}^{239}Np \longrightarrow _{94}^{239}Pu + _{-1}^0e \qquad \textbf{(4.10b)}$$

In a similar manner Thorium 232 absorbs a neutron and by subsequent beta decays goes to Protactinium 233 and Uranium 233. Materials which can thus be converted to fissionable nuclei are said to be fertile.

Thermal fission of a ^{235}U nucleus produces an average of 2.43 neutrons. If one of these is used to produce the next fission in a steady state chain reaction, there is a balance of 1.43 neutrons left. These are divided among

(1) Leakage from the core
(2) Capture by nonfuel or nonfertile materials (parasitic capture)
(3) Nonfission capture in the fuel
(4) Capture by the fertile nuclei

If capture by fertile nuclei produces on an average less than one new fissionable nucleus from the available 1.43 neutrons, the reactor is said to be a converter. If it produces more than one new fissionable nucleus, it is a breeder. For a breeder, items 1, 2, and 3 listed above must consume less than 0.43 neutron per fission. In a breeder reactor, more new fissile nuclei are being produced than are consumed by fission. To achieve this end successfully in a power reactor is a challenge to the ingenuity of reactor designers. Breeder reactors hold the promise of extending the supply of fissile material by several orders of magnitude. Because of the high value of η (2.99 at 2 MeV) for ^{239}Pu, this fuel looks to be the best prospect for use in fast breeder reactors. Because of the relatively greater number of nonfission captures in fuel, thermal breeders look less feasible. However, the η of 2.30 for ^{233}U makes it look more promising than the other two isotopes. The Molten Salt Reactor Experiment (MSRE) at Oak Ridge was a step toward the eventual development of a large thermal breeder reactor. It was the first reactor to be completely fueled with ^{233}U.

FUSION

Fusion reactions form $_2^4$He by the combination of lighter nuclei. Unfortunately the probability (cross section) for light hydrogen combining with itself or its heavier isotopes is too small to give hope of containment at reasonable temperatures. However, deuterium has a larger cross section for reaction with itself, as well as with tritium ($_1^3$T) and light helium ($_2^3$He). Fig. 4.7 shows these cross sections for D-D and D-T reactions. Two deuterons may interact by either of two processes. Both have similar probabilities of occurring, hence only one D-D curve is shown.

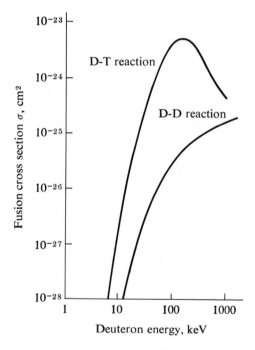

FIG. 4.7 *Fusion cross section versus deuteron energy. The variation in fusion cross section is shown as a function of deuteron energy for both the D-D and D-T reactions.* [*From* Bishop, A. S., Project Sherwood: The U. S. Program in Controlled Fusion. *Reading, Mass.: Addison-Wesley Publishing Co., Inc., 1958.*]

$$_1^2D + _1^2D \longrightarrow _2^3He + _0^1n + 3.27 \text{ MeV} \qquad \textbf{(4.11a)}$$

$$_1^2D + _1^2D \longrightarrow _1^3T + _1^1p + 4.03 \text{ MeV} \qquad \textbf{(4.11b)}$$

The light helium formed in the neutron branch (Eq. 4.11a) of the D-D reaction releases a significant amount of energy when it in turn interacts with a deuteron. However, the probability of this reaction (Eq. 4.12) is too low to be of great interest.

$$_1^2D + _2^3He \longrightarrow _2^4He + _1^1p + 18.3 \text{ MeV} \qquad \textbf{(4.12)}$$

The tritium, on the other hand, can react even faster than plain deuterium and gives off nearly as much energy as the previous reaction.

$$_1^3T + _1^2D \longrightarrow _2^4He + _0^1n + 17.6 \text{ MeV} \qquad \textbf{(4.13)}$$

The energy imparted to the neutron in the D-T reaction is approximately 14 MeV. This energy is sufficient to make the neutron relativistic (see Problem 9 at the end of this chapter).

These 14 MeV neutrons are uncharged and, therefore, cannot be contained by a magnetic field which must envelop the reaction volume to contain the plasma. If the neutrons pass through the wall of the containment vessel, they can enter a surrounding moderator blanket containing ^6Li. On absorption by the ^6Li they can produce an additional source of tritium to be separated and fed back into the fusion chamber.

$$_3^6Li + _0^1n \longrightarrow _3^7Li^* \longrightarrow _1^3T + _2^4He \qquad \textbf{(4.14)}$$

The energy given up by the neutrons slowing down and that produced by the *n-Li* reactions can be used as the heat source for a conventional steam or gas turbine cycle. The transport medium for conveying the thermal energy to a steam generator might be lithium fluoride. Extra neutrons could be produced by either Be or fission in subcritical amounts of U or Th. The Be has an (*n*, 2*n*) reaction. As mentioned earlier, it can also undergo photodisintegration, if sufficiently energetic photons are available.

In order for fusion to occur, tremendous temperatures are required. Two colliding nuclei must have sufficient energy to overcome the electrostatic forces of repulsion due to their like charges. Fig. 4.8 shows the power density attained for both D-D and D-T reactions as a function of kinetic temperature. Since the kinetic energy at the most probable velocity for a group of particles with a Maxwellian energy distribution is the product of the Boltzman constant, k, and the temperature, T, temperature is sometimes expressed in electron volts, with 1 keV being equal to 1.16×10^7 °K. A temperature of 100,000,000°K (8.6 keV) will permit fusion. However, for the D-D reaction the radiation losses from the plasma exceed the energy released and, thus, there is a net power loss. The D-T reaction only requires 4 keV (4.6×10^7 °K) to attain a

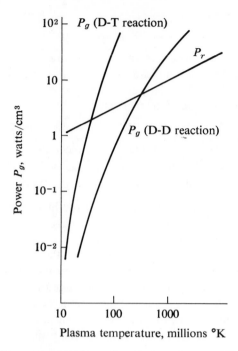

FIG. 4.8 *Power generated vs. plasma temperature. The total power generated (P_g) per cm³ is shown for both the D-D and D-T reactions as a function of temperature. The power radiated (P_r) is also shown. The curves are for plasma densities of about 10^{15} particles per cm³.* [*From Bishop, A. S.,* Project Sherwood: The U. S. Program in Controlled Fusion. *Reading, Mass.: Addison-Wesley Publishing Co., Inc., 1958.*]

balance between energy released and energy lost, as compared to 36 keV (4.1×10^8 °K) for D-D. The major energy loss is due to X-rays induced by *bremsstrahlung*, that is, collisions between electrons and the positive ions. The temperature at which the reaction becomes self-sustaining is called the ignition temperature. At such temperatures the hot plasma must be kept from physical contact with the container walls. This is accomplished by containing the plasma within a magnetic field.

When a particle with a velocity, v, moves across a magnetic field of strength, B, as shown in Fig. 4.9, there is a mutually perpendicular force, F, set up which is equal to the product of the field strength in gauss, the electronic charge, e, and the velocity of the particle.

$$F = Bev \qquad (4.15)$$

It is this force which affects the containment of the plasma. If a heavy current flows in a continuous track containing a high temperature plasma,

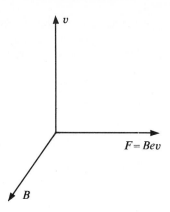

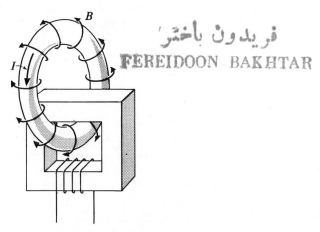

FIG. 4.9 *Vector diagram showing the relationship between particle velocity, v, magnetic field strength, B, and force on the particle, F.*

such as a torus, just the current flow will induce a field around itself. This "pinch effect" squeezes the plasma into the center of the track. A simple fusion reactor might take the form of a torus containing the plasma. The torus acts as the secondary of a transformer. The energy pumped into the torus from the primary windings induces a high current and produces the enormous temperatures necessary for fusion. This current also causes a magnetic field which pinches the plasma.

It is interesting to note that the mean free path, or the average distance a deuteron must travel to undergo fusion, is thousands of miles.

FIG. 4.10 *Simple fusion reactor. The torus acts as the secondary of a transformer and contains the plasma. The current, I, induces the magnetic field of strength, B, which pinches the plasma inward away from the walls.*

The stability of the plasma must be sustained for periods long enough to allow significant numbers of fusion reactions to occur. Control or elimination of the instabilities in plasmas presents a most difficult technological challenge. Successful development of fusion reactors is dependent on its being overcome.

A kinking type of instability is shown in Fig. 4.11. As the plasma

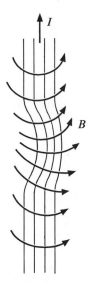

FIG. 4.11 *Kinking type of instability.   As the plasma bends, the magnetic lines are crowded together on the concave side of the kink, pushing the plasma closer to the wall.*

bends, the magnetic lines of force are crowded together on the concave side of the bulge, tending to increase the force on the kink and move it toward the wall. Contact with the wall cools the plasma and quenches the reaction.

Sausage-like instabilities crowd the magnetic lines of force together at the constrictions and tend to interrupt the plasma flow by forcing the bulges apart. A helical coil around the torus creates an axial magnetic field which improves the stability of the plasma.

The Model C stellarator at Princeton used essentially a toroidal track for its plasma. It is shown in Fig. 4.12. Containment has provided stability of the plasma for one millisecond, where only one microsecond would be required for the ions to reach the walls without magnetic confinement. The main field coils and the stabilizing windings are wound at differing angles to provide shear fields which improve confinement. In the divertor the outermost lines of flux are sidetracked

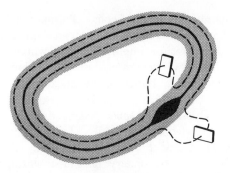

FIG. 4.12 *Model C Stellarator at Princeton. The plasma is confined in an 8-inch diameter stainless steel racetrack that nestles within the primary arms of the large transformer at the left. The plasma forms the secondary of this transformer and when current is applied via the overhead cables, it can be heated to about 500,000°K (50 eV). The racetrack itself is hidden by magnetic coils which can provide field strengths as high as 50 kG to contain the plasma. The outermost lines of flux are diverted into a separate chamber by a set of coils in the center foreground. Here the energetic plasma particles are removed before they are able to strike the racetrack wall and release impurities that would cool the plasma. [From Roderick, H., and A. E. Ruark, "Thermonuclear Power," Int. Sci. and Tech. (September 1965).]*

into a separate chamber by a set of coils. Plasma ions approaching the walls are trapped in the divertor and pumped from the system before they strike the walls to release impurities which would cool the plasma. The fact that the Model C stellarator cost $26 million to build and $4 million annually to operate indicates the magnitude of the controlled fusion effort.

Success of the Russian Tokamak plasma ring led to the Model C Stellarator being converted to the Model ST Tokamak, which has produced results comparable to those of the Russians. In a Tokamak the plasma is stabilized by a secondary plasma-stabilizing magnetic field generated by an electric current flowing in the plasma itself, instead of by helical coils inside the primary coils.

The DCX-1, shown in Fig. 4.13, illustrates an open field magnetic mirror type of fusion device. A straight tube, open at the ends, uses a stronger field at the ends of the tube to make the ions spiral more tightly until they are reflected back, as illustrated in Fig. 4.14. The ions then just spiral back and forth. Unfortunately, some of the particles escape from the ends. It is uncertain whether plasmas can be contained long enough in mirror machines to provide any net power.

To provide a net amount of power once the ignition temperature is attained, plasmas must be contained for a significant period of time. The product of the particle density, n, in particles per cm^3 and the average confinement time, t, in seconds is a measure of the fuel burnup. An nt product of 10^{14} is called the Lawson number. It represents a theoretical target level at which a fusion reactor could produce power. Practically, an even higher nt product would be required to offset various losses.

The closest approach to the Lawson number to date has been obtained with the Russian Tokamak plasma ring. A current flowing along the plasma provides heating. Stability is achieved by providing a longitudinal magnetic field with the field lines parallel to the centerline of the plasma ring. This field is much greater than that produced by the plasma current. It is expected that the Tokamak-10 will come to within 10^{-1} of the Lawson number. During the sixties the values of nt increased by about two orders of magnitude.

The problems of containing plasmas were grossly underestimated early in the fusion program. This overoptimism was replaced by the question of whether a fusion reactor was possible at all. Efforts to date have provided rather steady progress toward achieving the Lawson number without uncovering any overriding negative factors which would preclude construction of a fusion reactor. A new air of quiet optimism is indicated by the fact that various groups currently are concerned with solving fusion-reactor design problems other than plasma containment. Some of these problems will be discussed in Chapter 13.

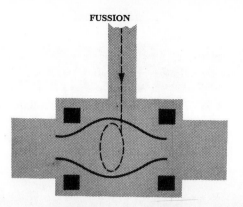

FIG. 4.13   *DCX*-1 *plasma experiment at Oak Ridge.   The plasma is formed by injecting molecular ions from the 600 kV accelerator on top into a magnetic mirror region.   Here the dissociated atomic ions can be trapped for as long as 50 seconds—although so far not at densities high enough for copious fusion reactions to occur.   [From Roderick, H., and A. E. Ruark, "Thermonuclear Power," Int. Sci. and Tech. (September 1965).]*

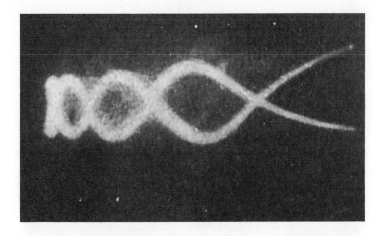

FIG. 4.14   *In a uniform magnetic field the force on a charged particle bends its path into a spiral.   When the field is made nonuniform at, say, the end of an open tube, the lines curve so that the particle is turned back from what is effectively a magnetic mirror.   This photograph shows the tracks of electrons being turned back from such a mirror (at right). The light for the photo comes from the excitation of the background gas.* [*From Roderick, H., and A. E. Ruark, "Thermonuclear Power,"* Int. Sci. and Tech. (*September 1965*).]

TRANSURANIUM ELEMENTS

Elements with an atomic number greater than that for uranium do not exist in nature but can be produced by bombardment of uranium or thorium nuclei with neutrons, deuterons, alphas, or even heavier nuclei. Fig. 4.15 shows how elements between plutonium ($Z = 94$) and rutherfordium ($Z = 104$) can be produced by a combination of intense thermal neutron irradiation and beta decays.

The new element hahnium ($Z = 105$), named in honor of Otto Hahn who received a Nobel prize for discovering nuclear fission, was produced by the bombardment of ^{249}Cf with 84 MeV ^{15}N nuclei to produce hahnium-260 accompanied by the emission of several neutrons.

An even more exciting development has been the possible formation of a superheavy element, eka-mercury ($Z = 112$). This was accomplished by the bombardment of pure tungsten by high energy (24 GeV) protons. Occasionally, a recoiling tungsten nucleus will be energetic enough to cause a fusion with another similar nucleus. The resulting isotope has a long-lived alpha decay (6.73 MeV) different from any known isotope. It also fissions spontaneously with a half-life of approximately 500 years. Such superheavy elements have very interesting

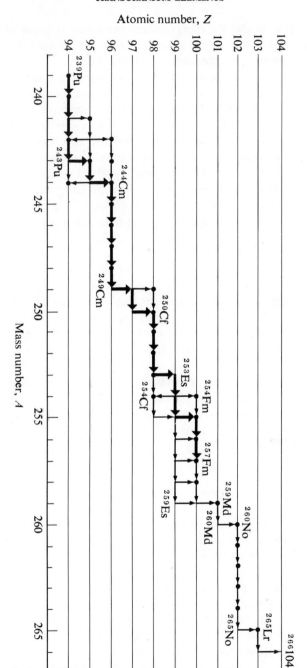

FIG. 4.15 *Nuclear reactions for the formation of transuranium elements by intensive thermal neutron irradiation.* [*From Seaborg, G. T.,* Nuclear Applications and Technology **9**, *no. 6 (December, 1970), p. 843.*]

fission properties in that the energy release per fission is about 50 percent greater than that for U or Pu isotopes. Also the number of neutrons released per fission (v) is estimated to be about 10.5.

Among the transuranium elements ^{239}Pu and ^{241}Pu are established as fissionable fuels, while ^{238}Pu is an important heat source due to alpha decay. ^{242}Cm is not too useful as a heat source because of its 163-day half-life; however, it does decay to ^{238}Pu. ^{244}Cm should ultimately be produced at a lesser cost than ^{238}Pu and be used as a heat source. Because of its spontaneous fission it will require more shielding.

Amerecium-241 emits a 60 keV gamma with 35 percent of the alpha decay events. It has a 433-year half-life and probably has more applications than any of the other actinide isotopes. As a gamma emitter it can be used in thickness gages, to determine sediment concentration in a flowing stream, to measure soil compaction, or as a location sensing device. As an alpha emitter it can be mixed with beryllium as a neutron source for oil-well logging, measuring moisture content of soils, or determining water content in chemical process streams. The ionization of air by its alphas is useful in static eliminators and fire detectors.

Californium-252 is a 2.65-year alpha emitter and also spontaneously fissions with a half-life of 85.5 years. It is useful as an intense source of neutrons and it is particularly effective in cancer therapy. The cells at the center of many cancers are starved for oxygen. These oxygen-starved cells are much more resistant to X-rays than ordinary cancer cells, whereas the effectiveness of the ^{252}Cf is much less effected by the oxygen deficiency. Fig. 4.16 shows a 50-ton shipping cask built at Oak Ridge to transport up to 1 gram of ^{252}Cf, giving some indication of the intensity of its radiation.

HIGH ENERGY REACTIONS

As more energetic projectiles have become available with the advent of more powerful accelerators, a whole family of strange particles have appeared. These result from energy to mass conversions similar to electron pair production at lower energy levels. They may also appear during the decay of other unstable strange particles.

A powerful experimental tool for studying high energy reactions is the bubble chamber. In 1952, Donald A. Glasser reported the operation of the first such unit, a 3 cm $\times$ 1 cm glass bulb filled with diethylether. They have since grown to the 80 $\times$ 27 $\times$ 26 inch chamber at the Brookhaven National Laboratory which is filled with liquid hydrogen at $\sim$27°K (see Fig. 4.17). The pressure on the subcooled liquid is suddenly reduced below the saturation pressure. The passage of a charged particle causes

FIG. 4.16 *Fifty-ton shipping cask built at Oak Ridge National Laboratory for transporting up to 1 gm of* ^{252}Cf. [*From Seaborg, G. T.,* Nuclear Applications and Technology *9, no. 6 (December, 1970), p. 848.*]

ionization along its track in the superheated liquid. This ionization produces a train of bubbles that marks the path of the particle. The track can then be photographed. The chamber is operated in a strong magnetic field so that the path of a charged particle is curved. Particles with opposite charges will have paths with opposite directions of curvature. The curvature of the path is a function of the particle's momentum and the field strength. In the first three years of operation of the 80 inch chamber 3,110,233 pictures were taken. Maintaining and operating the chamber requires the fulltime efforts of 67 engineers, physicists, and technicians. Even larger bubble chambers are being proposed. BNL has designed a unit 14 feet in diameter which will contain 21,000 gallons of liquid.

FIG. 4.17   *BNL 80-inch liquid hydrogen bubble chamber.   View from right side during operation.   [Photograph courtesy of Brookhaven National Laboratory Bubble Chamber Group.]*

At low energy levels gammas can interact in the field of a nucleus to create an electron pair, one being positively charged and one being negatively charged.   A threshold energy of 1.02 MeV is required to produce the rest mass of the two particles.   Any excess energy is shared nearly equally as kinetic energy of the electrons.

$$h\nu = {}_{-1}^{0}e + {}_{+1}^{0}e + 2KE \tag{4.16}$$

Looking ahead at Fig. 4.20, we can see two examples of pair production. The dotted lines in the right half of this figure represent the paths of uncharged particles which leave no track in the actual photograph on the left. The dotted lines marked γ_1 and γ_2 terminate with the sudden appearance of a pair of divergent tracks. The opposite curvature of the tracks indicates the unlike charges of the electrons as they move through the magnetic field in the bubble chamber.

Pair production is but one form of mass-energy conversion. Proton-antiproton and neutron-antineutron pairs have been created as accelerators have been able to produce particles with energies of several billion electron volts (GeV). Particle-antiparticle pairs have the following characteristics:

(1) Masses equal and positive
(2) Charges opposite
(3) Spins equal
(4) Magnetic moments opposite
(5) Equal lifetimes
(6) Creation and annihilation in pairs

To produce an antiproton a proton with an energy of 5.6 GeV is required. The reaction is

$$p + p \longrightarrow 3p + \bar{p} \tag{4.17}$$

where $\bar{p}$ represents the antiproton. Fig. 4.18 is interesting since it shows the disappearance of an antiproton. It may be surmised that it has produced a neutron-antineutron pair (which, being uncharged, causes no visible tracks in the bubble chamber). After travelling 9.5 cm the antineutron is annihilated, producing an annihilation star by interaction with a neutron in a nucleus. The star is formed by the bubble tracks due to several charged particles leaving the nucleus.

In high energy collisions a whole array of unstable particles may be produced. Table 4.3 tabulates some of the properties of the known particles. Those with masses less than 1 atomic mass unit (u) and having a spin of $\frac{1}{2}$ are *leptons*, while those with a mass of less than 1 u with zero spin are *mesons*, and *baryons* are particles of nucleon mass or greater, but less than the mass of a deuteron.

The bombardment of a carbon target with 380 MeV alphas will produce pi mesons (pions). An energy of 139.6 MeV is required to create a pion whose charge can be of either sign. They are unstable and decay with a mean lifetime of only 2.5×10^{-8} seconds.

$$p + p \longrightarrow p + n + \pi^+ \tag{4.18a}$$

$$p + n \longrightarrow p + p + \pi^- \tag{4.18b}$$

$$p + n \longrightarrow n + n + \pi^+ \tag{4.18c}$$

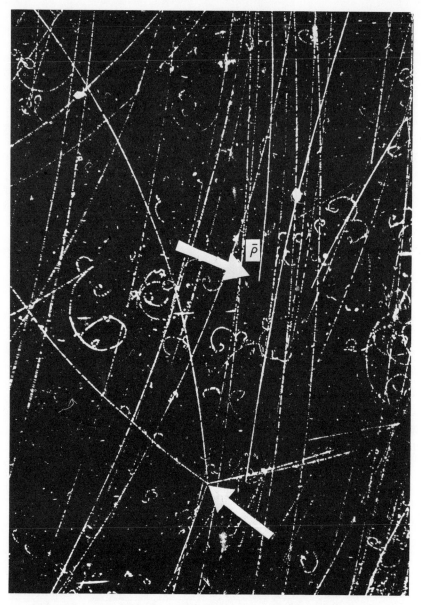

FIG. 4.18 *Photograph showing an antiproton entering a propane bubble chamber. It undergoes a charge exchange with a proton to form a neutron-antineutron pair (upper arrow). The antineutron being uncharged leaves no track. After traveling 9.5 cm it interacts with a nucleus to form an annihilation star. [Photograph courtesy of Professor E. Segré, Lawrence Radiation Lab., University of California, Berkeley, California.]*

TABLE 4.3

PROPERTIES OF ELEMENTARY PARTICLES

Class of Particle	Particle and Antiparticle	Mass in m_e	Mass in MeV	Mean lifetime (seconds)
Photon	γ	0	0	stable
Lepton	ν $\bar{\nu}$	0	0	stable
	e^- e^+	1	0.511	stable
	μ^- μ^+	207	105.7	2.2×10^{-6}
Mesons	π^+ π^-	273.2	139.6	2.55×10^{-8}
	π^0	264.2	135.0	1.8×10^{-16}
	K^+ K^-	966.7	494.0	1.22×10^{-8}
	K° $\bar{K}^\circ$	973.4	497.9	$K_1^0 1 \times 10^{-10}$ $K_2^0 6 \times 10^{-8}$
Baryons	p $\bar{p}$	1836	938.2	stable
	n $\bar{n}$	1838	939.5	1.103×10^3
	Λ $\bar{\Lambda}$	2180	1115.2	2.62×10^{-10}
	Σ^+	2327	1189.4	0.8×10^{-10}
	Σ^0	2331	1191.5	$< 10^{-14}$
	Σ^-	2340	1196	1.74×10^{-10}
	Ξ^0	2577	1311	3.0×10^{-10}
	Ξ^-	2580	1318	1.7×10^{-10}
	Ω^-	3280	1676	0.7×10^{-10}

An uncharged pion (π^0) can be formed by the interaction of a negative pion and a proton.

$$\pi^- + p \longrightarrow n + \pi^0 \tag{4.19}$$

Note that in Table 4.3 the uncharged pion weighs less than its charged sisters by the amount of the neutron-proton mass difference. This pion decays to two gammas in 10^{-16} seconds.

$$\pi^0 \longrightarrow \gamma + \gamma \tag{4.20}$$

The charged pion, however, decays to a lepton, known as a muon, and a neutrino.

$$\pi^+ \longrightarrow \mu^+ + \nu \tag{4.21a}$$

$$\pi^- \longrightarrow \mu^- + \bar{\nu} \tag{4.21b}$$

The muons, in turn, decay with a mean life of 2.2×10^{-6} seconds. They form an electron of the same sign and a neutrino-antineutrino pair.

$$\mu^\pm \longrightarrow e^\pm + \nu + \bar{\nu} \tag{4.22}$$

The strange particle baryons of a mass between one and two nucleons are also called hyperons. They are designated as Λ (lambda), Σ (sigma), and Ξ (xi) particles. Fig. 4.19 is an exceptionally fine one, showing the formation of a positive sigma particle, Σ^+, and a positive kaon, K^+, by the interaction of a positive pion, π^+, and a proton.

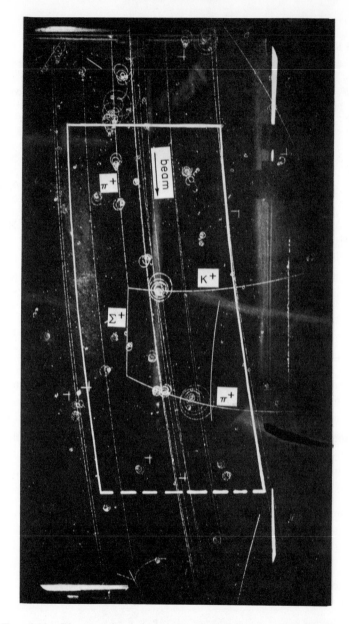

FIG. 4.19 *Photograph of the tracks of particles in a liquid hydrogen bubble chamber showing the production of a positive sigma particle by the interaction of a positive pion and a proton. The initial momentum of the pion is 1.23 BeV/c; the bubble chamber is in a magnetic field of 17,000 gausses.* [*From Baltay, C., et al.,* Revs. Mod. Phys. **33,** (1961) *p. 374.*]

$$\pi^+ + p \longrightarrow \Sigma^+ + K^+ \qquad\qquad (4.23)$$

The positive kaon is a heavy meson with a mass of 966.7 m_e. It leaves the bubble chamber before decaying, but the positive sigma particle decays into a positive pion and an uncharged neutron.

The series of events shown in Fig. 4.20 confirms the existence of the Ω^- particle which had been predicted previously by a gap in the array of

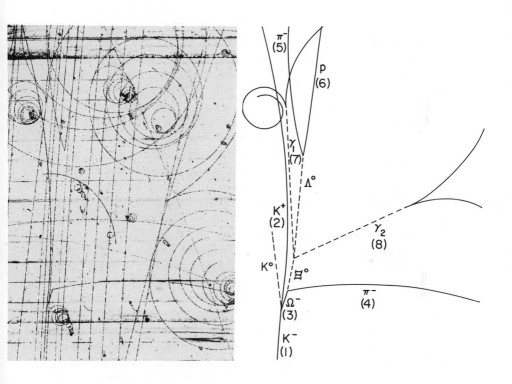

FIG. 4.20 *Photograph and line diagram showing the interaction of a negative kaon with a proton to form an omega minus particle along with a positive kaon and an uncharged kaon. The series of events due to the decay of the Ω^- is also shown. [Photograph courtesy of Brookhaven National Laboratory Bubble Chamber Group.]*

known particles. About 100,000 pictures were taken to find this first example of the event. The bottom of the photograph shows a stream of K^- mesons with a momentum of 5.0 GeV/c entering the bubble chamber. One of these in a collision with a proton produces the Ω^-, as well as a K^+ and a K^0. The omega minus particle then undergoes a sequence of decay events which is detailed below.

$$K^- + p \longrightarrow \Omega^- + K^+ + K^0$$

$$\longmapsto \Xi^0 + \pi^-$$

$$\longmapsto \Lambda^0 + \pi^0$$

$$\longmapsto \gamma_1 + \gamma_2$$

$$\longmapsto e^+ + e^-$$

$$\longmapsto \pi^- + p \longmapsto e^+ + e^-$$

The study of these strange particles has led to their first medical application. At Stanford's Linear Accelerator Center negative pi mesons have been used as a tool in cancer therapy. The π^- mesons have the unique ability to penetrate deeply with little damage to outer tissues. Oxygen atoms capture the negative strange particles causing star explosions which destroy the adjacent malignant cells.

Also at the two-mile long Stanford Linear Accelerator Center, scattering studies using an electron beam with energies up to 21 GeV have shown that neutrons and protons seem to have an internal structure. The observed inelastic scattering cross sections were 40 times higher than those which had been predicted. This indicates that the scatter is taking place on internal structures much smaller than the nucleons themselves. A theoretical model proposed by Dr. R. P. Feynman of Cal Tech seems to explain the inelastic scatter results, at least quantitatively. Dr. Feynman assumes the scatter is taking place on point particles called partons which do not exhibit the known properties of mesons. They seem to be identical to previously proposed entities known as quarks. They have fractional electric charges, either $2/3$ or $-1/3$ for quarks and $-2/3$ or $+1/3$ for antiquarks. Mesons are assembled from a quark and an antiquark. Nucleons and baryons are assembled from three quarks. Whether the parton model will lead to an understanding of nucleon structure and the strong forces which bind the nuclei together is still uncertain. It is felt, however, that electron scattering studies will eventually yield the desired knowledge.

A more complete picture of the work being done on strange particles can be obtained from the references at the end of this chapter.

PROBLEMS

1. ^{37}Cl is struck by a proton and emits a 1 MeV neutron(COM). Write the reaction equation and compute the energy of the incident proton in the lab system.

2. A 2 MeV deuteron stikes a $_3{}^6$Li nucleus. The compound nucleus splits into identical nuclides. Identify the resultant particles and calculate the (COM) kinetic energy of each.

3. A 2 MeV neutron stikes a $_7{}^{14}$N nucleus, causing an alpha particle to be ejected. What element is the recoil nucleus? What will be the kinetic energy of the recoil nucleus?

4. Compute the threshold energy for photoemission of a neutron by a $_4{}^9$Be nucleus. The resultant $_4{}^8$Be nucleus is in turn unstable and splits into two alphas. What will be the velocity of the two emergent alphas if the original gamma had just the threshold energy?

5. Show that in the lab system, when the kinetic energy of the compound nucleus is subtracted from the kinetic energy of the incident particle, the difference is identical to Eq. (4.4b).

6. A light hydrogen atom absorbs a thermal neutron in a radiative capture process. Compute the energy of the gamma emitted. Calculate the recoil velocity and kinetic energy of the deuteron.

7. Thermal fission of a ^{233}U nucleus produces 4 neutrons and 2 fission fragments, one of which is ^{143}La (142.9157 u). What is the other fission fragment? Compute the energy released if the second fragment has a mass of 86.9224 u.

8. If the Watt Eq. (4.9) defines the energy spectrum of the fission neutrons for ^{235}U, show that the most probable fission energy is 0.72 MeV.

9. In a fusion reactor the uncharged neutrons produced in some of the reactions will escape the reaction chamber. Their energy can be transformed to heat by a surrounding moderator. If the moderator contains $_3{}^6$Li, neutron absorption by this isotope will produce an extra source of tritium. Compute the energy available from this reaction per neutron absorbed.

10. Show that the deuterium-tritium fusion reaction produces 17.6 MeV. Determine the kinetic energy of the emergent neutron. Is the neutron relativistic?

11. Show that a lab system energy of 5.6 GeV is required to produce a proton-antiproton pair when a proton strikes another stationary proton.

12. Pions may be produced by high energy photons interacting with nucleons. What threshold energy must a photon have to interact with a proton to produce a positive pion and a neutron?

13. Proton decay of ^{53}Co was mentioned in Chapter 3. To form the ^{53}Co nucleus ^{40}Ca can be bombarded by an energetic ^{16}O nucleus. An alternative method of forming the ^{53}Co is by proton bombardment of ^{54}Fe. What particles are emitted in each case?

REFERENCES

1. Liverhant, S. E., *Elementary Introduction to Nuclear Reactor Physics.* New York: John Wiley and Sons, Inc., 1960.

2. Semat, H., *Introduction to Atomic and Nuclear Physics.* New York: Holt, Rinehart, and Winston, 1962.

3. Kaplan, I., *Nuclear Physics.* Reading, Mass.: Addison-Wesley Publishing Co., Inc., 1955.

4. Lapp, R. E., and H. L. Andrews, *Nuclear Radiation Physics*. Englewood Cliffs, N. J.: Prentice-Hall, Inc., 1963.

5. Roderick, H., and A. E. Ruark, "Thermonuclear Power," *International Science and Technology* 45 (September, 1965), pp. 18–29.

6. Murray, R. L., *Introduction to Nuclear Engineering*. Englewood Cliffs, N. J.: Prentice-Hall, Inc., 1961.

7. Bishop, A. S., *Project Sherwood—The U. S. Program in Controlled Fusion*. Reading, Mass.: Addison-Wesley Publishing Co., Inc., 1958.

8. Glasstone, S., and R. H. Loveberg, *Controlled Thermonuclear Reactions*. Princeton, N. J.: D. Van Nostrand Co., Inc., 1960.

9. Katkoff, S., "Fission Product Yields from U, Th, and Pu," *Nucleonics* 16, no. 4 (April, 1958), p. 78.

10. Jensen, J. E., *The Cryogenic Bubble Chamber—An Accelerator Research Facility*, ASME paper no. 66-WA/NE 22, 1966.

11. Hill, R. D., *Tracking Down Particles*. New York: W. A. Benjamin, Inc., 1964.

12. Barnes, V. E., et al., "Observation of a Hyperon with Strangeness Minus Three," *Phys. Rev. Lett.* 12 (February, 1964), pp. 204–206.

13. Alvarez, L. W., et al., "1660–MeV Y_1^*, Hyperon," *Phys. Rev. Lett.* 10, no. 5 (March, 1963), pp. 184–88.

14. Segré, E., *Nuclei and Particles*. New York: W. A. Benjamin, Inc., 1965.

15. Seaborg, G. T., "The Synthetic Actinides—from Discovery to Manufacture," *Nuclear Appl. & Technology* 9, no. 6 (December, 1970), pp. 830–50.

16. "Final Report of the IAEA Panel on International Co-operation in Controlled Fusion Research and Its Applications," *Nuclear Fusion* 10, no. 4 (December, 1970), pp. 413–21.

17. "Enter Element 105," *Nuclear News* 13, no. 6 (June, 1970), p. 20.

18. "Pi Mesons in Cancer Treatment," *Nuclear News* 13, no. 6 (June, 1970), p. 34.

19. Butler, J. W., et al., "Report of the Argonne Senate Subcommittee on Controlled Thermonuclear Research," *Argonne Reviews* 6, no. 1 (July, 1970), pp. 30–34.

20. "Eka-Mercury, Evidence for Element 112," *Science News* 99, no. 8 (20 February, 1971), pp. 127–28.

21. Kendall, H. W., and W. K. H. Panofsky, "The Structure of the Proton and the Neutron," *Scientific American* 224, no. 6 (June, 1971), pp. 60–77.

Chapter 5

Radiation Detection

Radiation detection results from ionization of the medium through which radiation passes. The charge collected is a measure of the radiation, either in the form of pulses or current. Four general types of radiation which are of interest are discussed in this chapter.

HEAVY CHARGED PARTICLES

The following comments apply to alpha particles and, generally, to fission fragments and protons as well. Of the four interactions which alpha particles have with matter, scattering and nuclear transmutation are rare. Excitation and ionization, therefore, are almost exclusively used as the processes for alpha detection. An alpha particle loses an average of 32–35 eV/ion pair produced. This characteristic is utilized while the alpha particle moves along its straight line path. Ionization can be said to be a property of the particle's passing through matter. The charged particle transfers some of its kinetic energy to the electrons it encounters. The electrons are either raised to an excited state or removed from the atom. The heavy particle (α) loses energy by gradually transferring small amounts of energy to atomic electrons of absorbing material (32–35 eV/ion pair produced). Finally the alpha is stopped and disappears.

Each alpha (or other particle) has a definite range. The range depends on the initial kinetic energy of the alpha and the properties of the absorbing material. Since the mass of electrons is small, they cannot deflect a heavy particle from its path. Occasionally (usually toward the end of its track) an alpha may collide with a nucleus and be deflected through a large angle (see Fig. 5.1). The range for a group of alphas of the same initial energy has a distribution over a small limit, also shown by Fig. 5.1.

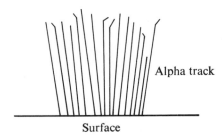

Surface

FIG. 5.1   *Sketch of cloud chamber tracks of alpha particles.*

The Bragg curve, Fig. 5.2, shows that the specific ionization (energy loss) increases along the particle track to a maximum and then rapidly drops to zero. Another relationship, Fig. 5.3, shows that alpha range is energy sensitive.

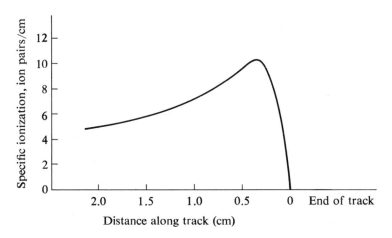

FIG. 5.2   *Bragg curve for single alpha particle track.*   [*From Holloway, M. G., and M. S. Livingston,* Phys. Rev., **54**, *18 (1938).   Reprinted by permission.*]

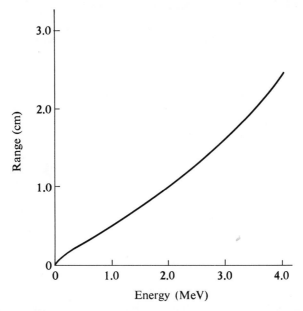

FIG. 5.3 *Mean range for alpha particles in air at 15°C, 760 mm.* [*From Bethe, H. A.,* Rev. Mod. Phys., *22, 213 (1950). Reprinted by permission.*]

Specific ionization is the number of ion pairs produced per centimeter of track. Total ionization is the total number of ion pairs produced. The stopping power of an absorber, dE/dx, is related to the specific ionization, I, by Eq. (5.1).

$$dE/dx = -wI \qquad (5.1)$$

The minus sign occurs because energy, E, decreases as x increases; w is the mean energy expended per ion pair produced. Fortunately, w is nearly independent of the energy of the primary particle. In the case of argon, w is the same for alphas, protons, electrons, and other light particles. Thus, argon is particularly well suited as a gas for use in ion chambers and other counting instruments. Both w and I, as yet, have proven difficult to calculate theoretically; therefore, experimental measurement is relied upon to determine their values. The range of alpha particles can be measured experimentally by measuring the intensity of monoenergetic alphas at different distances from a thin source. The intensity of alphas plotted versus distance from source appears as in Fig. 5.4.

The extrapolated range, R_e, is the range at which the tangent to the

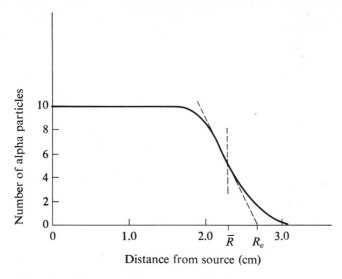

Fɪɢ. 5.4   *Range distribution curve for alpha particles in á gas.*

curve at its inflection point intersects the horizontal axis. The mean range, $\overline{R}$, is the range at which half of the particles have a greater range and half a smaller range. This occurs at the inflection point, and the alphas have a Gaussian distribution about this point. The difference between the mean and extrapolated ranges is the straggling. It occurs because of the random nature of the collisions. If there were no straggling, the curve would drop sharply to zero at the range of the alpha. The mean range and mean energy expended in air of some alpha particles are shown in Table 5.1.

TABLE 5.1

RANGE OF ALPHA PARTICLES

Energy	Range in Air	w	Range in Aluminum	Range in Lead
MeV	cm	eV/ion pair	mg/cm²	mg/cm²
2	1		1.5	3.7
3.5	2		3.1	6.7
5.3	3.7	35.6	5.6	13.7
6.3	5		7.6	18.0
7.8	7.3	35.1	10.8	25.2
9.7	10		14.8	34.5

Data from Aron, W. A., B. D. Hoffman, and F. C. Williams, AECU pamphlet 663, 1949.

Example 1. Determine the number of ion pairs produced and the ionizing current of 100 alphas/sec of 5.3 MeV energy. What is the thickness of aluminum necessary to stop these alpha particles? From Table 5.1

w = 35.6 eV/ion pair for 5.3 MeV alphas.

$$\text{number ion pairs produced} = \frac{(5.3 \times 10^6 \text{ eV}/\alpha)(100 \, \alpha/\text{sec})}{35.6 \text{ eV/ion pair}}$$

$$= 1.489 \times 10^7 \text{ ion pairs/sec}$$

$$I = (1.489 \times 10^7 \text{ electrons/sec})(1.6 \times 10^{-19} \text{ coulomb/electron})$$

$$I = 2.38 \times 10^{-12} \text{ ampere}$$

This is a very small current, but it can be detected by fairly conventional microammeters.

From Table 5.1 the range of 5.3 MeV alpha particles in aluminum is 5.6 mg/cm². If the density of aluminum is taken as 2.7 gm/cm³ the necessary thickness will be

$$x = \frac{5.6 \times 10^{-3} \text{ gm/cm}^2}{2.7 \text{ gm/cm}^3}$$

$$x = 2.1 \times 10^{-3} \text{ cm}$$

Fission fragments have more nuclear collisions and produce less ionization than alpha particles. The fission fragments are initially highly ionized; the ionization is gradually reduced by picking up electrons. The state of ionization decreases therefore, causing less ionization in the material through which it passes. An alpha may also pick up some electrons but will lose them in succeeding collisions. Fission fragments lose most of their energy near the beginning of their track, while alpha energy loss increases along the track (Bragg curve). The total range of an average fission fragment is 6×10^{-4} cm in uranium and 12×10^{-4} cm in aluminum. (For aluminum cladding the thickness is usually 50–100 times this range.) Since few fission fragments can escape, most of the energy loss occurs inside the fuel element; this causes the fuel and cladding to heat up considerably.

LIGHT CHARGED PARTICLES (β)

Light charged particles are not as easy to analyze as heavy charged particles because:

(1) Their path is very irregular.
(2) An electron has a smaller mass, so it suffers many abrupt deflections. It is difficult, therefore, to associate a range with it (see Fig. 5.6).
(3) A mechanical effect is involved since a beta particle and an electron are identical.

(4) The high speed of a beta particle necessitates a relativistic treatment of the collision process.

(5) Beta radiation shows a continuous initial energy distribution. Figure 5.5 is a typical energy spectrum.

While different isotopes emit beta radiation with different spectra, the general shape appears as in Fig. 5.5.

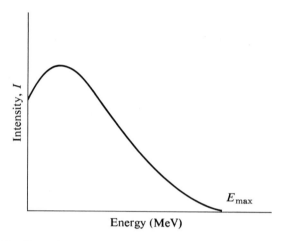

FIG. 5.5 *Typical continuous energy spectrum for a beta emitter.*

The processes by which a beta particle interacts with matter are as follows:

(1) Elastic collision.

(2) Energy conversion. Mass in the form of an electron and a positron is converted to radiation, resulting in two oppositely directed photons.

(3) Inelastic collision (ionization, excitation). This process generally predominates for beta energies of 1 MeV or less. The collision is similar to the ionizing effect of heavy charged particles. The energy loss varies approximately as

$$-\frac{dE}{dx} \propto \frac{NZ}{v^2} \tag{5.2}$$

where Z is the atomic number and N the atomic density of the absorber. The ions produced in the primary ionization often produce further or secondary ionization as they release their excitation energy. The total ionization is the sum of the primary and secondary ionization.

(4) *Bremsstrahlung* (braking radiation). When electrons have an inelastic collision with nuclei they radiate energy in the form of a continuous X-ray emission. The electron path is bent as it nears the nucleus. This path change results in an acceleration of the electron. The radiation emitted is directly proportional to the acceleration squared. With heavier particles

the acceleration as a result of inelastic collision is small and consequently the *bremsstrahlung* is negligible.   *Bremsstrahlung* accounts for the spectrum emitted by X-ray tubes.   The energy loss can be stated as

$$-\frac{dE}{dx} \propto NZ^2E \tag{5.3}$$

where E is the electron energy and N and Z are as before.

By combining the energy loss from *bremsstrahlung* and ionization one can plot the continuous energy loss noted previously (see Fig. 5.6).

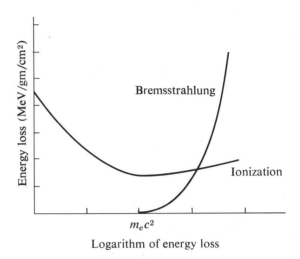

FIG. 5.6   *Energy loss rates for beta particles in a material.*

Since beta particles suffer so many deflections while they lose energy, it is difficult to associate a definite range with a given beta energy.   Figure 5.7 is a plot of number of beta particles versus their range (expressed in gm/cm²).   Note that there is a definite upper limit, but that the curve is not flat up to this range.   The extrapolated range can be used to take the place of an actual range of beta particles.   (*Extrapolated range* is the thickness of material required to reduce the intensity to the background rate.)   Fortunately, this relationship also holds for a continuous beta spectrum if the range is associated with the maximum beta energy (refer to Fig. 5.5).   If the range is extrapolated as in Fig. 5.7, then for the most probable beta energy, $E_p = 1/3\ E_{max}$, the intensity of radiation follows an exponential curve

$$I = I_0\ e^{-\mu x} \tag{5.4}$$

where μ is the linear absorption coefficient and has dimensions of reciprocal centimeters.   A mass absorption coefficient may be defined by

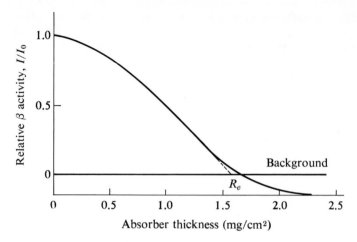

FIG. 5.7 *Absorption curve for a single energy beta particle.*

$$\mu_m = \mu/\rho \qquad (5.5)$$

Equation (5.4) then becomes

$$I = I_0\, e^{-\mu_m d} \qquad (5.6)$$

where d is the absorber thickness in gm/cm².

The result of all this is that one finds that for a given material beta particles have a greater range than alpha particles.

Example 2.   Find the thickness of aluminum absorber necessary to absorb 99 percent of the 5.3 MeV maximum beta particles striking it.   An empirical relationship (see Reference 8)

$$\mu_m = \frac{22}{E_m^{1.33}} * \qquad (5.7)$$

gives mass absorption coefficients for 0.5 MeV $< E_m <$ 6 MeV

$$\mu_m = \frac{22}{(5.3)^{1.33}} = 2.39 \text{ cm}^2/\text{gm}$$

$$I/I_0 = 0.01 = e^{-2.39d}$$

$$-4.59 = -2.39d$$

$$d = 1.92 \text{ gm/cm}^2$$

$$x = \frac{1.92 \text{ gm/cm}^2}{2.7 \text{ gm/cm}^3} = 0.710 \text{ cm}$$

Thus it is seen that a beta particle of 5.3 MeV maximum energy will have a greater range than a corresponding alpha particle.

* [From Goodman, C., ed., *The Science and Engineering of Nuclear Power*, Volume I. Reading, Mass.: Addison-Wesley Publishing Company, Inc., 1947.]

GAMMA (γ) AND X-RAYS

Almost all gamma interaction takes place with electrons.   Normally a gamma ray has only a single interaction with an electron.   The photoelectric effect predominates when low energy gammas interact with tightly bound atomic electrons.   It is believed that the interaction is with K-shell electrons about 80 percent of the time.   In the process the atomic electron becomes detached from its atom and acquires kinetic energy equal to the gamma energy less the binding energy for the electron; the gamma ray is used up in the process.   When the outer shell electrons fill the gap they emit X-rays.   The photoelectric effect is predominant for energies of about 0.1 MeV or less.

The Compton effect is an inelastic scattering between a photon and an individual electron.   Practically speaking, the Compton effect becomes important for gamma energies of about 0.1 MeV and up.   Since the gamma radiation is absorbed by the interacting medium, a linear absorption coefficient can be defined for gamma radiation.   Fig. 5.8 shows

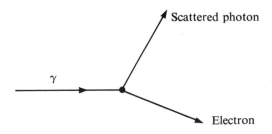

FIG. 5.8   *Compton collision between a gamma ray and an electron.*

that the Compton coefficient consists of two parts one portion caused by scattering of the photon and the remainder due to true absorption.   The photon energy is reduced by scattering and eventually the photoelectric process will take place.   There is essentially no gamma scattering in the photoelectric effect so there need be no division of the absorption coefficient.   However, Compton scattering occurs between a gamma ray and an electron, so the linear absorption coefficient for Compton scattering must be dependent upon the number of electrons present (Z of absorber).

Pair production results in complete absorption of the gamma ray and production of a positron-electron pair.   This energy-to-mass conversion takes place normally in the vicinity of a nucleus.   Since the rest energy of the positron-negatron pair is $2m_0c^2$ the incident photon must have at least this energy (1.022 MeV).   Any excess energy will be shared between the positron and electron.

Combining the linear absorption coefficients for a given material results in a graph similar to Fig. 5.9. It should be noted that the curves will be different for different materials. As in the case of beta radiations, we can define linear and mass absorption coefficients.

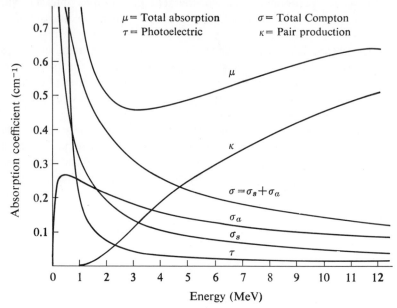

FIG. 5.9 *Absorption coefficients of gamma rays in lead.*

A mean range, $\overline{R}$, for gamma penetration in matter can be defined as the average distance a photon travels before it is absorbed.

$$\overline{R} = \frac{\int_{I_0}^{0} x\,dI}{\int_{I_0}^{0} dI} = \frac{\int_{0}^{\infty} xe^{-\mu x}\,\mu\,dx}{\int_{0}^{\infty} e^{-\mu x}\,\mu\,dx} = \frac{1}{\mu} \tag{5.8}$$

Example 3. Calculate the half-thickness, mean range, and mass absorption coefficients for ^{60}Co gamma rays in lead. An experiment has shown that 4.5 cm thickness of lead reduced the uncollided radiation intensity by 95 percent.

$$I = I_0 e^{-\mu x}$$

$$0.05 = e^{-\mu(4.5)}$$

$$\mu = 0.666 \text{ cm}^{-1}$$

$$\mu_m = \mu/\rho = \frac{0.666}{11.32} = 0.0588 \text{ cm}^2/\text{gm}$$

The *half-thickness* is the thickness of lead which will reduce the intensity by one-half.

$$I/I_0 = 0.5 = e^{-\mu x_{1/2}}$$

$$x_{1/2} = \frac{0.693}{\mu} = \frac{0.693}{0.666}$$

$$x_{1/2} = 1.041 \text{ cm}$$

$$\bar{R} = \frac{1}{\mu} = \frac{1}{0.666} = 1.5 \text{ cm}$$

NEUTRONS

The detection of neutrons is based on neutron interactions with matter. Since a neutron carries no charge, nuclear forces rather than coulomb forces act between it and a nucleus. The six neutron interactions are as follows:

(1) Elastic collision occurs when the neutron shares its kinetic energy with a nucleus without exciting the nucleus. This is the primary mode of energy loss for neutrons as they are slowed to thermal by the light nuclei of a moderator.

(2) Inelastic collision usually occurs with fast neutrons. Here the target becomes excited, emits a gamma, and shares the remainder of the available kinetic energy with the scattered neutron.

(3) Radiative capture (n, γ) takes place when a neutron is absorbed to produce an excited compound nucleus which attains stability by emission of a gamma. These reactions are more probable with thermal and epithermal neutrons.

(4) Ejection of a charged particle occurs normally with fast neutrons. This process is frequently used for detection of neutrons (both fast and thermal). An (n, p) reaction is used for fast neutrons, and an (n, α) reaction is used for thermal detectors such as $B^{10} + n^1 \longrightarrow {}^7Li^* + \alpha$.

(5) Fission reactions occur with both fast and thermal neutrons. Certain fission reactions are energy sensitive. These are also used in detectors.

(6) Shower occurs for very high neutron energies (greater than 100 MeV). The neutron energy appears as a shower of photons and light particles. The total shower energy produced by the neutrons equals the sum of all energies of photons, light particles, etc., produced.

It should be noted that all six interactions can occur, but the probability of a given interaction occurring depends on the neutron energy. A more complete treatment of neutron interactions is to be found in Chapter 8.

ELECTROSTATIC CHARGE ACCUMULATING INSTRUMENT (DOSIMETER)

One of the simplest means of detecting (and measuring) ionizing radiation is with an electroscope (illustrated schematically in Fig. 5.10). The support and quartz fiber are positively charged to about 150 volts dc. This is done by depressing the charging spring into contact with the support and simultaneously applying the dc voltage between the wall (ground) and the charging spring.

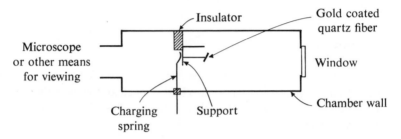

FIG. 5.10   *Sketch of a typical electrostatic dosimeter.*

The support and quartz fiber are repelled and assume an equilibrium position.   The electrostatic force balances the spring force of the quartz fiber.   When an ionizing particle (γ) ionizes the gas, the negative ion which is formed discharges the quartz fiber and the deflection diminishes. When the deflection is observed with a microscope it can be calibrated in units of radiation dose.

SIMPLEST IONIZATION TYPE DETECTOR

Incoming radiation ionizes gas in the gas-filled tube.   The ions produced are collected at the electrodes.   A negative ion collected on the

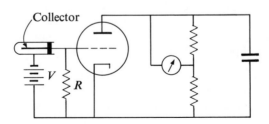

FIG. 5.11   *Simple ionization type detector.*

anode drives the vacuum tube grid negative and causes the meter to deflect. If the voltage, V, on the tube is gradually increased, a characteristic curve (Fig. 5.12) can be plotted.

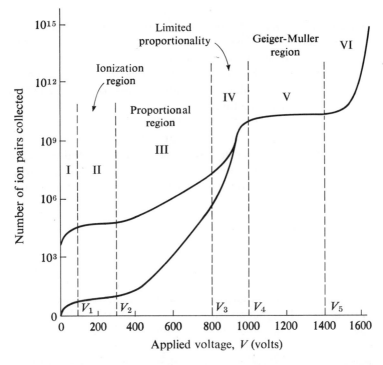

FIG. 5.12   *Curves illustrating ionization, proportional, and Geiger-Müller region.*

Below V_1 some ions recombine. As V increases, the drift velocity of ions increases and recombination decreases. At saturation voltage, V_1, the recombination is at a minimum. Region II is called the ionization region and extends over a few hundred volts. In this region all ion pairs are collected. The voltage range is normally about 100–300 volts. Region III is the proportional region. Here the primary ions acquire enough energy (from V) to cause secondary ionization (gas amplification) and increase the charge collected. The secondary ionization may cause further ionization. In this region there is a linear relationship between number of ion pairs collected and voltage V. In region IV no linear relationship exists between ions collected and primary ions. An avalanche of ions starts and increases as V increases. In region V there is a complete discharge in the vicinity of the central wire. This region is called the Geiger-Müller region. The complete discharge is independent of the initial ionizing radiation and an avalanche of electrons develops all over the central wire and in the gas. V_4 is called the *threshold voltage.* Here the number of ion pairs levels off and remains relatively independent of the applied voltage V. This leveling-off is called the *Geiger plateau.* The plateau extends over a region of 200–300 volts; the threshold is normally about 1000 volts. The operating voltage of the tube is normally about 1200 volts. It should be recalled that the ionization in this region is independent of the nature and energy of the original radiation. An increase in V above V_5 produces a continuous discharge in the tube and will very quickly destroy the tube.

The different methods of detecting ionizing radiation (ion chamber, G-M counter, etc.) depend on the varying behavior of ions produced by radiation in their passage through the tube. Thus, one type of detector may have advantages over another in certain applications (i.e., proportional counter as neutron counter, Geiger tube for small specific ionization).

ION CHAMBERS

An ion chamber can be used as either a pulse or a rate type detector. In pulse operation the output of the chamber is indicated as a series of signals (usually voltage) separated in time. In rate operation no attempt is made to resolve individual actions. Instead, the output is the time average of many interactions. Measuring the output current of the ion chamber is an example of a mean level system. When the total dose measured is averaged over the time interval of measurement, the electrostatic dosimeter of the last section becomes an example of a mean-level type ionization detector.

In a pulse-type ionization chamber the magnitude and duration of the voltage pulse produced by the tube becomes important. If the detector is to count only the number of particles, the voltage pulses must be short enough to be distinguished from one another; they only need to be large enough to be picked up by the amplifier. However, if energy is to be measured, the pulse amplitude is important. When current flows in the external circuit of Fig. 5.11 the ions begin to drift to the collectors. When all charge is collected the current ends. Curve a of Fig. 5.13 shows the voltage output pulse of the ionization tube for a long time constant. The electrons are normally collected within 10^{-6} seconds and the positive ions within 10^{-3} seconds. There is no multiplication. This type of ionization chamber is, therefore, limited to low counting rates (usually less than 100 counts/sec). To remove this restriction of low

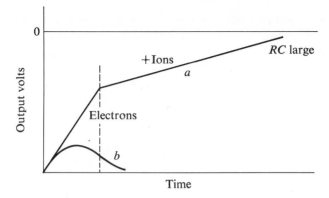

FIG. 5.13   *Output voltage pulse from a typical ionization chamber.*

counting rates, the time constant of the chamber is usually made less than the maximum collection time.   A typical value is 0.2 times the maximum electron collection time.   This gives a uniform pulse height but a much more reduced amplitude.   Curve *b* shown in Fig. 5.13 illustrates the shorter time constant.

The gas filling is usually air, at or near atmospheric pressure.   Almost any gas can be used if it has a small electron affinity.   The insulators (between + and − electrodes) are commonly made of aluminum oxide, quartz, polystyrene, or teflon.   Organic materials are generally not used for high dose rate applications because of their susceptibility to radiation damage.   Teflon is least susceptible to water absorption which may reduce surface leakage resistance.   Stress currents appear across an insulator after it receives electrical or mechanical stress.   Aluminum oxide and quartz have very low stress currents and are used for low current measurements.   Guard rings are used in one type of ionization chamber (parallel plate).   The guard ring defines the active volume of the chamber and reduces the leakage current through the insulators. The guard rings and electrodes are usually made from tungsten or platinum.

PROPORTIONAL COUNTERS

Proportional counters can be used either as pulse type or rate type detectors, but pulse type operation is the most frequent.   Proportional counters are useful in beta radiation measurements because ionization chambers do not have high enough sensitivity.   They also offer an advantage because the voltage pulse retains a proportional relationship with energy but produces a larger pulse than an ionization chamber.   In the proportional region shown in Fig. 5.12 ionization is produced in the region surrounding the anode. The resulting pulse (Fig. 5.14) is independent of the exact region where primary ionization is produced. The discharge stops as soon as all the electrons are swept to the collector. The + ions form a localized sheath on the collector and the tube can receive a second pulse as long as the + ions collect at a different place.

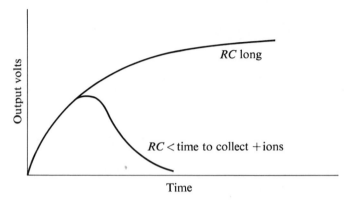

FIG. 5.14   *Output voltage pulse from a proportional counter.*

If the multiplication is too large, the + ion sheath enlarges and the sensitive time of the tube decreases. If the amplitude of the pulses must be measured, the time between pulses must be great enough for the effect of collecting the + ions on the cathode to be negligible. In most cases this can be less than 100 μ sec.

Multiplications resulting from secondary ionization of 10^4 are normal and 10^6 is a possibility. The multiplication must be independent of the position of the primary ionization. This is made possible by making the electrode of fine platinum wire 0.001 or 0.002 inch in diameter. Consequently, the secondary ionization is produced close to the wire. The gas filling is normally a mixture of 90 percent argon and 10 percent methane at atmospheric pressure. The methane absorbs photons, reducing photoemission of electrons and limiting multiplication. The photons are produced with the secondary electrons.

A proportional counter is a fast counter and pulse rates as high as 10^6 per second can be counted with it. A proportional counter also can be used to discriminate energies. The multiplication is linearly dependent on operating voltage. If the counts at lower operating voltages are compared with those at higher voltages, the contribution of highly ionizing particles is compared with those of low ionization. An electronic differential pulse height analyzer is used for this type of discrimination.

These analyzers measure the slope of the energy distribution curves. The discriminator allows pulses of height between set limits, say H and $H + \Delta H$, to be passed to a counter. The height, H, and $H + \Delta H$ can be varied as desired. As the difference ΔH is decreased the result approaches a true differential pulse-height distribution. The instruments which perform these differential energy-distribution measurements are commonly known as spectrometers.

GEIGER-MÜLLER COUNTERS

The Geiger-Müller counter has been the most widely used detector. It has been popular primarily because: (a) it is highly sensitive to even the smallest radiations; (b) it can be used with many different types of radiation; (c) it has a very high voltage pulse output; and (d) its cost is reasonable. The Geiger-Müller is frequently used as a pulse-type detector.

The applied voltage, V (refer to Fig. 5.12), is so high that the primary ionization produces an avalanche of ions. A multiplication as high as 10^8 is common. The avalanche is independent of the nature and energy of the original radiation; in addition, electrons may be ejected from the tube walls by gamma interaction. The immediate region around the anode becomes insensitive to more radiation very quickly. This occurs because the free electrons are collected rapidly, leaving a sheath of + ions all along the anode. The output voltage pulse from the tube resembles that of the proportional counter, shown in Fig. 5.14. As in the proportional counter, the time constant of the tube is made much less than the time to collect the + ions. The tube remains insensitive to more radiation until the + ions move away from the anode. The + ions finally collect on the cathode and quenching must be supplied to prevent an undesirable afterpulse. The afterpulse would take the form either of an electron emitted from the cathode or a photon radiated from the cathode. Either of these could start another avalanche. Quenching may be provided by: (a) lowering the tube voltage for a few μ seconds (external quenching); (b) introducing an organic gas into the tube; (c) introducing a halogen gas. External quenching is very seldom used. The + ions transfer their energy to quench gas molecules ar_d when the quench gas molecules reach the cathode they dissociate rather than produce an electron. Alcohol-quenched tubes have a lifetime of about 10^{10} events, while halogen ions recombine, thereby extending the lifetime of the tube almost indefinitely. The gas is generally about 90 percent argon at a total pressure of 10 cm Hg.

The ionization depends on the physical characteristics and construction of the tube. Normally the tube output pulse is high (on the order of volts). The tube is usually cylindrical with a 0.003 or 0.004 inch diameter center electrode made of tungsten. The cathode is usually the wall of the tube and is made of glass coated with a stainless steel or nickel conductor.

When electrons collect on the anode (collector), the positive ions originating near the anode reduce the electric field intensity too low to support discharges and there is no output. The dead time, t_d, is the time for a subsequent small pulse to appear. The recovery time, t_r, is the time for a full amplitude pulse to appear. The effective dead time, D, depends on the electronics of the system and the tube characteristics. It is generally less than $t_d + t_r$ (Fig. 5.15). Dead time is normally introduced

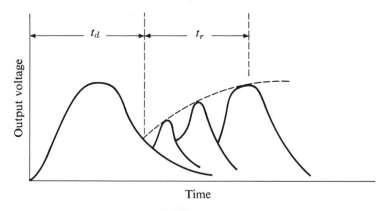

FIG. 5.15 *Dead time in a G-M tube.* [*From Stever, H. G.,* Phys. Rev. **61,** *38 (1942). Reprinted by permission.*]

electronically after each count. This enables each operator to accurately determine the true count. The dead time also limits the maximum number of counts. The true counting rate is determined as follows:

$$n = \text{observed counts per second}$$
$$N = \text{true counts per second}$$
$$D = \text{effective dead time, seconds per count}$$

then

$$nD = \text{total time not counted}$$
$$1 - nD = \text{total time counted}$$
$$n = N(1 - nD)$$
$$N = \frac{n}{1 - nD} \qquad (5.9)$$

Thus $1/(1 - nD)$ is the factor by which the observed count rate may be multiplied to give the true count rate.

Example 4. What is the counting error for a G–M counter with a dead time of 200 μ sec and an observed counting rate of 1500 cpm?

The counting error may be expressed by the factor

$$\frac{1}{1-nD} = \frac{1}{1-(1500/60)(200 \times 10^{-6})}$$

$$= \frac{1}{1-5 \times 10^{-3}} = 1.00503$$

The true count would then be

$$N = \frac{n}{1-nD}$$

$$N = 1500(1.00503) = 1508 \text{ cpm}$$

SCINTILLATION COUNTERS

Scintillators can be used for any radiation but are most widely used for gamma counting. The scintillators discriminate energy levels and therefore can be used to detect unknown gamma emitters.

Radiation entering the crystal (Fig. 5.16) causes luminescence in the

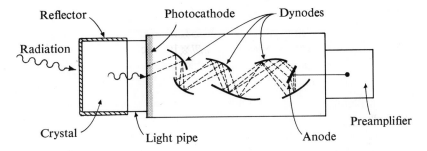

FIG. 5.16 *Schematic diagram of scintillation crystal and photomultiplier.*

scintillation crystal. This light is reflected through the light pipe to the photomultiplier. The scintillation crystal absorbs gamma energy by one of the three means of gamma interaction. Each interaction lifts an electron to an excited state. The electron is brought to rest in the scintillator and in doing so emits light [for NaI(Tl) one photon per 50 eV of energy]. The intensity of the emitted light is directly proportional to the energy lost by the incident particle. The focusing of emitted photons onto the photocathode is very critical. MgO or Al_2O_3 (aluminum foil) is used to reflect photons into the light pipe and to prevent light transmission to the outside. The reflector normally covers all but one side of the scintillator. Impurities are added to inorganic crystals to "soften" them (i.e., make them more transparent to photons).

Scintillators are made in many shapes, including disks, right circular cylinders, cylinders with holes, etc. The light pipe is commonly made from glass, lucite, or plexiglass. Its purpose is to provide a large critical angle of incidence so that radiation will not be trapped within the crystal. It also serves to separate the crystal from the photomultiplier (if desired), to spread the light over a large cathode area, and to shape the surface to a flat photocathode if necessary. On striking the photocathode the photons emit electrons. The electrons are collected and focused from one dynode to another. Each dynode is at a higher potential than the previous one and emits several electrons for each electron incident on its surface. Thus, by using several dynodes ($\sim$10) amplifications of 10^7 to 10^{11} can be obtained. The photocathode is usually a thin coating of antimony-cesium on the inside of the photomultiplier while the dynodes are either antimony-cesium or silver-magnesium.

A good scintillator emits light in less than 10^{-8} seconds. Since all the light flashes occur so nearly simultaneously they are integrated into a single pulse. The time for the emission of 63.2 percent of the photons is called the time constant (τ).

For

NaI (Tl)	$\tau = 0.25 \times 10^{-6}$ sec
Anthracene	$\tau = 0.27 \times 10^{-7}$ sec
ZnS	$\tau = 10^{-5}$ sec
Plastics	$\tau = 5 \times 10^{-9}$ sec

Scintillators have several advantages over other methods of counting gammas. Among them are: (a) a pulse height proportional to energy; (b) an efficiency for gammas which may be as high as 50 percent since there are more atoms in a solid than a gas; (c) a short dead time (10^{-9} sec); and (d) the probability of absorbing a scattered gamma which increases with crystal size, thereby enhancing the photopeak. Table 5.2 lists some scintillators with their applications.

One of the most useful applications of a scintillation crystal is the scintillation spectrometer. A typical gamma spectrometer is illustrated in Fig. 5.17. In this setup the scintillator-photomultiplier output combination is fed into a single channel pulse height analyzer. The lower discriminator will only pass pulses from the linear amplifier which are greater than its setting (45 V). The upper discriminator will only pass pulses greater than its setting (55 V). The anticoincidence circuit will only pass pulses which do not arrive in coincidence from the two discriminators. Therefore, only pulses falling within a preset value (window) will

TABLE 5.2

APPLICATIONS OF SCINTILLATORS

Scintillator	Most Common Use
Anthracene	β, neutron
Trans-stilbene	β
ZnS(Ag)	Alpha particles
NaI(Tl)	γ-ray
LiI(Sn)	neutrons
p-terphenyl	$\beta(^{14}C, {}^{3}H)$
Diphenylorazole	β, neutrons
Tetraphenyl butadiene	β
Terphenyl in polystyrene	
Xenon	neutrons

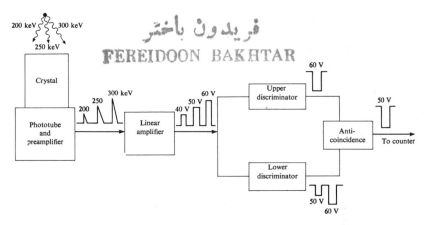

FEREIDOON BAKHTAR

فریدون باختر

FIG. 5.17   Schematic arrangement of a scintillation spectrometer.

be passed on to the counter (45–55 V in this case).   This insures that only pulses between the two discriminator settings will be passed to the counter. The discriminator settings and/or the window width may be varied over any desired range.   Fig. 5.18 illustrates a pulse-height curve for ^{137}Cs gammas taken with a single channel pulse height analyzer and a NaI(Tl) crystal.   Notice that the photopeak appears very sharp while the scatter peak is spread over a wider range.   At this energy level the gammas interact by both the photoelectric process and Compton scatter.   All of the photoelectric interactions contribute to the photopeak, as well as those Compton events where both the scattered electron and the attenuated gamma dump their energy in the scintillator during its resolving time.   If the attenuated gamma interacts elsewhere, then only the scat-

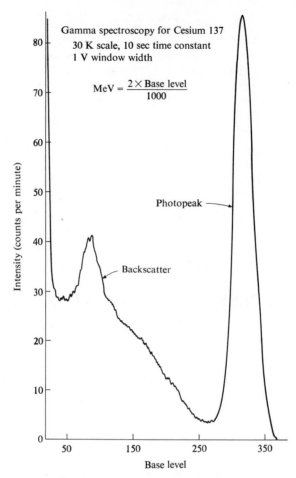

Gamma spectroscopy for Cesium 137

30 K scale, 10 sec time constant

1 V window width

$$MeV = \frac{2 \times Base\ level}{1000}$$

Photopeak

Backscatter

FIG. 5.18   *Pulse height distribution for* ^{137}Cs.   [*Courtesy Northeastern University Nuclear Engineering Laboratory.*]

tered electron converts its energy to light.   These events cause a significant number of counts to occur at energies below that of the photopeak.

NEUTRON DETECTORS

The products of neutron interactions are measured because neutrons themselves cannot be detected.   The most useful neutron interactions are as follows: (a) transmutations (n, α), (n, p), (n, γ), $(n,$ fission$)$; (b) elastic collision (n, p); (c) foil activation.

Transmutations are generally energy sensitive. For example, the reaction $^{10}B + n^1 \longrightarrow {}^7Li + \alpha$ is very sensitive to thermal neutrons (0.025 eV) but relatively insensitive to neutrons above 100 keV.

Gas chambers, scintillators, and thermopiles are used for neutron detection. Gas chambers are lined with B_4C or filled with BF_3 gas. A chamber may be lined with ^{235}U (for thermal neutrons) or ^{238}U (for fast neutrons). In a ^{10}B chamber the ^{10}B must be extremely pure to prevent capture of neutrons and thereby reduce the ionization present.

A BF_3 filled counter is normally cylindrical in shape with a 0.002 inch diameter center anode and a cathode about 0.8 inch in diameter and is 4 to 6 inches long. The BF_3 filling is at about 10 cm Hg pressure. The detector must not disturb the neutron flux. As long as the product $\Sigma_a d$ is very small the absorption will be negligible. Σ_a is the macroscopic absorption cross section for neutrons and d is the distance a neutron can travel through the BF_3.

One type of boron lined counter is sketched in Fig. 5.19. The po-

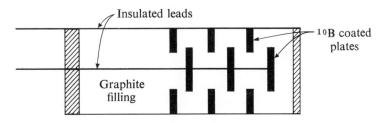

Insulated leads

^{10}B coated plates

Graphite filling

FIG. 5.19 *Schematic diagram of a parallel circular plate neutron chamber (uncompensated ion chamber).*

larity of alternate plates is the same; therefore, the chamber is in effect one large parallel plate chamber. It is sensitive to both gamma and neutrons, but by making the surface large in comparison to volume, the sensitivity to gamma can be kept at a minimum. The alpha and ^7Li produced by the reaction in turn produce ionization which is measured in a current type ionization chamber. The boron is applied in thin layers to make it transparent to neutrons from outside and to produce reactions such that the particles can escape into the chamber. ^{10}B chambers are usually used for neutron fluxes in the order of 10^4–10^{10} neutrons/cm² sec.

When a pulse-type proportional chamber is used to measure the neutron flux, the gamma radiation accompanying the neutrons can be discriminated by the circuit electronics. One type of compensated ion chamber which isolates the neutron induced ionization from the gamma induced ionization is sketched in Fig. 5.20. With this compensated ion chamber an accurate measure of the neutron flux (and power level) in a

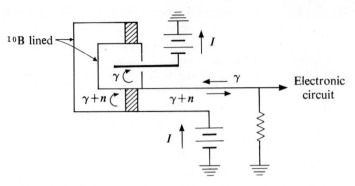

FIG. 5.20   *Schematic diagram of a compensated ion chamber.*

reactor can be made.   The net current flow is proportional to current due to $\gamma + n$ minus current due to γ, or the neutron current alone.   The internal pressure, volume, and voltage are adjusted so that the γ just balances the γ contribution in the $\gamma + n$.

FISSION CHAMBERS

Fission chambers are used during reactor startup because of the large energy released during fission relative to the flux of γ-rays present. Neutrons are absorbed and the fission fragments produce ionization either through kinetic energy or radioactivity.   The resulting ionization is measured either in a pulse-type ion chamber or a proportional counter. One type of fission chamber has enriched ^{235}U electroplated on the inside surface; the chamber is filled with high pressure oxygen-free argon.   The fission fragments lose their energy in the gas.   If fast neutrons are desired, ^{10}B or Cd is used to screen out the thermal neutrons and the fast neutrons react with the ^{238}U.   Other materials such as ^{232}Th which are fissionable only by fast neutrons are also used as the lining in fast neutron fission chambers.

FAST NEUTRON DETECTORS

The elastic scattering (n, p) is the method most used for detecting fast neutrons.   One type of chamber is lined with polyethylene and filled with hydrogenous gas such as methane.   Thermal neutrons will not impart an appreciable amount of energy to the protons.   On the other hand, fast neutrons will impart energy to the hydrogen nuclei through elastic scattering. The recoil protons will then induce ionization or excitation by inelastic collision. The chamber can be either a pulse or rate type detector, but is usually a pulse type proportional counter. If the pulse heights are made proportional to the proton recoil energies, the fast neutron energies can be determined.

Neutron-induced foil activation as a means of detection is discussed in Chapter 8. The general use of neutron detectors in reactor instrumentation is shown in Fig. 5.21.

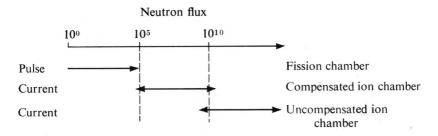

Fig. 5.21   *Examples of neutron detectors used in reactor instrumentation.*

SOLID-STATE DETECTORS

There are two principal types of solid-state radiation detectors: bulk and barrier layer. They both offer some extremely attractive advantages over other methods of detection.

They have, for example, high energy resolution, linear output with particle energy regardless of the nature of the particle, almost 100 percent detection efficiency, very fast pulse rise time, and no apparent dead time. In addition, the detectors are quite stable, low in cost, and very small in size.

Unfortunately, all the manufacturing problems have not yet been overcome; the detectors have a small output (millivolts), and they are sensitive to high temperatures. Their life is also quite limited under strong radiation.

The theory and operation of semiconductor type detectors depend on an understanding of quantum mechanics, a specialized and complex field. The action of radiation in semiconductors, therefore, will only be described qualitatively. A schematic diagram of the electron energy bands of semiconductors (Fig. 5.22) will aid in the description of particle interaction in a semiconductor. The uppermost filled band is separated from a higher empty band by a small forbidden zone. At sufficiently high

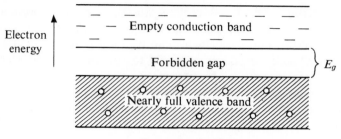

Lower bands filled

FIG. 5.22   *Schematic representation of semiconductor energy bands.*

temperatures (100 − 300°K) some electrons cross the forbidden zone. These electrons are now able to conduct, and the empty band is then called the conduction band.   The minimum energy needed for an electron to cross the forbidden gap and enter the conduction band ranges from about 0.1 to 3.0 eV.

When an electron leaves the filled valence band it leaves a "hole." This hole corresponds to a positive charge carrier.   The electrons in the conduction band and these holes in the valence band become carriers of charge and will respond to an electric field placed across them.   The concentration of electrons (n) and holes (p) is given by

$$n = p = 10^{19}\, e^{-E_v/2KT} \qquad (5.10)$$

where E_g = minimum energy for an electron to enter the conduction band.   Table 5.3 lists some properties of semiconductors used in particle detection.

TABLE 5.3

PROPERTIES OF SOME SEMICONDUCTORS USED
IN RADIATION DETECTION

Semiconductor	*Energy E_g* eV	*Electron Carrier Lifetime* sec	*Density* gm/cm³
Silicon	1.08	10^{-3}	2.33
Germanium (77°K)	0.75	10^{-3}	5.32
Germanium (300°K)	0.66	10^{-3}	5.32
Gallium arsenide	1.39	10^{-8}	5.3

Example 5.   What is the concentration of charge carriers in silicon at room temperature?   Compare this with the concentration in a metal conductor.

$$n = p = 10^{19} e^{-E_g/2KT}$$
$$= 10^{19} e^{-1.08/2(293.6)(8.65\times10^{-5})}$$

$$n = 2 \times 10^{10}/cm^3$$

The carrier concentration of a metal is about $10^{22}/cm^3$. Thus the carrier concentration of a semiconductor is much less and is temperature dependent.

If impurities (dope) are introduced into the crystal, it is possible for an electron to reach the conduction band without originating in the valence band. In this situation one of the valence electrons remains bonded to its parent nucleus. It can, therefore, move into the conduction band with less than the necessary E_g. If this occurs there will be no hole left by the electron, the impurity is called a *donor*, and the crystal is called an *n-type semiconductor*. If the opposite effect occurs with the introduction of an impurity it is called an *acceptor*, and the crystal is a *p-type semiconductor*.

When radiation enters a bulk detector it creates hole-electron pairs. These hole-electron pairs, acting with the electric field applied to the detector (Fig. 5.23) produce an output pulse which can be counted. The

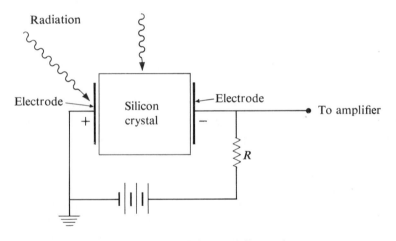

FIG. 5.23 *Bulk-type solid state radiation detector.*

number of carriers released is proportional to the incident energy of the particle, making solid-state detectors useful for spectrometry. The energy necessary to create a hole-electron pair is about one-tenth that necessary to create an ion pair in gas. Thus the particles can be stopped in a small volume (~ 1 cm^3). The problem is that there is no multiplication in the semiconductor which necessitates a very sensitive counting circuit. On the other hand, the statistical variation is not multiplied, either. The bulk detector requires a high electric field to collect the carriers in a short time. This means that the resistivity must be high to prevent leakage current. One way to increase the resistivity is to "dope" silicon with gold, but this increases carrier collection time. Another method has been to dope the silicon with boron. A typical carrier collection time is 10^{-7} seconds.

The barrier layer detectors are of two types: diffused-junction and surface-barrier. The two are very similar; they differ mainly in the method of obtaining a surface junction of p- and n-type semiconductors. In the junction type, practically the whole crystal is p-type but there is an extremely small portion of n-type material on the surface (see Fig. 5.24). The n-type material is usually about one micron or less. The

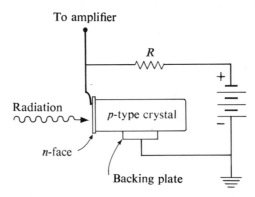

FIG. 5.24 *Diffused junction barrier-type solid state radiation detector.*

radiation enters the crystal through the n-face. The carriers on the two sides of the junction can cross the potential existing across the junction if they are given energy. The incoming radiation does this (3.6 eV/pair for silicon and 3.0 eV/pair for germanium). When the holes and electrons cross the junction they produce an output pulse which can be counted. The pulse is small and is proportional to the energy of the incident particle but is independent of the nature of the particle. The barrier layer detectors are extremely small (<1 cm³) and the collection time is about 10^{-9} seconds. Silicon detectors of the p-type are used as diffused junction types while n-type silicon and n-type germanium have been used for surface barrier-type detectors.

Barrier layer type detectors can be used as neutron detectors. One such detector employs the reaction ^{6}Li (n, α) ^{3}H. Lithium fluoride is coated onto the surfaces of two silicon surface barrier type detectors. The two detectors are placed so that the lithium fluoride is sandwiched between the sensitive surfaces of the detectors. The detectors are placed about 0.5 mm apart. The products of the neutron reaction are recorded on a pulse height analyzer. If a fissionable material is substituted for the lithium fluoride a fission product spectrum can be obtained.

STATISTICS

The emission of radioactive particles is a random process. In addition, there is always a small amount of background radiation present from cosmic sources and natural radiation from nearby sources. Radiation from nuclear reactors or X-ray machines may also affect the background radiation. The effect of background radiation is reduced by taking a separate measurement of the background count and subtracting it from the measured count. It is also helpful to place shielding around the counting equipment to minimize the effect of radiation from outside the apparatus.

The number of counts recorded on a counting apparatus will be different each time a measurement is made. It is desired to approach as nearly as possible a true average counting rate. To do this, the deviation to be expected due to the random fluctuations must be known.

Since each radioactive decay is an independent event the average disintegration rate can only be determined exactly by counting for an infinite time. The deviation from this true average will, however, obey the laws of random processes. In the decay process the binomial distribution law

$$p(n) = \frac{N_o!}{m! \, n!} \, p^n \, q^m \tag{5.11}$$

may be applied. In this expression $p(n)$ is the probability that n events out of a total of N_o will occur and q the probability that n events will not occur: $m = (N_o - n)$. The average value n then becomes pN_o. Several deviations from the average are used to indicate the precision of the resulting n events. These are (a) standard deviation, (b) probable error, and (c) average error. The most frequently used is the standard deviation, σ.

$$\sigma = \left[\sum_0^{N_o} (n - \bar{n}) \right]^{1/2} \tag{5.12}$$

For the case of radioactive decay the binomial distribution can be put in a more convenient form. The probability that an atom will not decay in time t is $e^{-\lambda t}$, and the probability that it will decay is $1 - e^{-\lambda t}$. Also, for radioactive decay $\lambda t \ll 1$, $N_o \gg 1$, and $n \ll N_o$. Making these substitutions into Eq. (5.11) gives us the Poisson distribution.

$$p(n) = \frac{(\bar{n})^{1/2} e^{-n}}{n!} \tag{5.13}$$

The standard deviation becomes

$$\sigma = (pN_o)^{1/2} = (\bar{n})^{1/2} \tag{5.14}$$

The Poisson distribution is applicable for λt as large as 0.01 and N_o as small as 100.

The standard deviation from the mean then equals $n^{1/2}$. For the population as a whole 68.26 percent of measurements have a smaller deviation than the standard, and 95.44 percent of measurements have smaller deviation than two times the standard. If several count rates are made the average count rate will also have a standard deviation from the mean. The standard deviation when several count rates are made is $(\bar{n}/\text{number counting intervals})^{1/2}$. If one count is made

$$R(\text{count rate with standard deviation}) = \frac{n \pm \sqrt{n}}{t} \tag{5.15}$$

If several counts are made

$$R = \frac{\bar{n} \pm \sqrt{\bar{n}/\text{no. intervals}}}{t} \tag{5.16}$$

where t is the time interval of counting and n is the number of counts. It can be seen that longer counting periods increase the probability of getting a true average.

Example 6. A radioactive sample was counted for 9 minutes. The average counting rate was 3476 counts per minute. The background was counted for 5 minutes and was 562 counts. What is the counting rate with its standard deviation?

The standard deviation of the resulting count squared is the sum of the standard deviations squared of the sample counting and the background counting.

$$\sigma^2 = \sigma_s^2 + \sigma_b^2$$
$$\sigma_s = \sqrt{3476}$$
$$\sigma_b = \sqrt{112}$$
$$\sigma^2 = 3476 + 112$$
$$\sigma = 59.8$$

The counting rate due to the source alone, therefore, is

$$R = (n_s - n_b) \pm \sigma$$
$$R = (3476) - 112) \pm 60$$
$$R = 3364 \pm 60 \text{ counts per minute}$$

The preceding material can be used to aid in the design of counting experiments for minimum error. There are three situations of interest to be considered when specifying a given standard deviation:

(1) Minimum total counting time.   In this case the differential $d(t_s + t_b) = 0$, and

$$t_s = \frac{R_s + \sqrt{R_s R_b}}{\sigma^2} \tag{5.17}$$

(2) Equal counts.   In this case $n_s = n_b$ and

$$n_s = \frac{R_s^2 + R_b^2}{\sigma^2} \tag{5.18}$$

(3) Equal counting times.   In this case $t_s = t_b$ and

$$t_s = \frac{R_s + R_b}{\sigma^2} \tag{5.19}$$

PROBLEMS

1. Determine the thickness of lead and aluminum necessary to absorb 4.0 MeV alpha particles.
2. Compare the ionization loss of beta particles of maximum energy 1.7 MeV in aluminum and lead.
3. Using Fig. 5.9, calculate the half-value thickness for 1.25 MeV gamma radiation from a source.   What is the mass absorption coefficient for lead at this gamma energy?   What is the mean range of gammas?
4. Calculate the maximum thickness of aluminum window in a G–M tube to permit counting of 2.7 MeV beta particles.
5. The capacitance of an electroscope is 15 $\mu\mu$ f, and it is charged to 150 volts. If it is subjected to a count rate of 29.5 cps of 1.60 MeV gammas for one hour, how much will the dosimeter deflect?   Assume deflection proportional to charge.
6. How many ions would be required to neutralize all the quench gas in a 100 cm³ G–M tube if it did not recombine?   The quench gas is 0.1 percent Cl by volume of argon at atmospheric pressure.
7. A G-M counter has an operating voltage of 1200 volts.   The Geiger plateau has a slope of 2.5 percent.   What is the maximum permissible voltage fluctuation if the count rate fluctuation is not to be more than 0.1 percent?
8. Determine the counting error for a counter dead time of 150 μ sec at an observed counting rate of 100 counts per sec.
9. Plot a curve of observed counting rate versus percent error for errors from 0 to 10 percent at a dead time of 180 μ sec.
10. The background counting rate is 25 ± 4 counts per minute.   The sample counting rate is 126 ± 10 counts per minute.   Determine the net counting rate with its standard deviation.
11. It is desired to make a measurement of counting rate with the largest possible statistical accuracy.   The requirements limit the total counting time to 15 minutes.   A test count gave a background of 37 counts/minute and a sample including background of 1012 counts/minute.   What should be the counting schedule for minimum error?

REFERENCES

1. Birks, J. B., *Scintillation Counters*. New York: McGraw-Hill Book Co., Inc., 1953.

2. Goldstein, H., *Fundamental Aspects of Reactor Shielding*. Reading, Mass.: Addison-Wesley Publishing Co., Inc., 1959.

3. Halliday, D., *Introductory Nuclear Physics*. New York: John Wiley and Sons, Inc., 1955.

4. Evans, R., *The Atomic Nucleus*. New York: McGraw-Hill Book Co., Inc., 1955.

5. Lapp, R. E., and H. L. Andrews, *Nuclear Radiation Physics*. Englewood Cliffs, N. J.: Prentice-Hall, Inc., 1965.

6. Price, W. J., *Nuclear Radiation Detection*. 2d edition. New York: McGraw-Hill Book Co., Inc., 1964.

7. Taylor, J. M., *Semiconductor Particle Detectors*. London: Butterworth and Co., Ltd., 1963.

8. Goodman, C., ed., *The Science and Engineering of Nuclear Power*, Vol. I. Reading, Mass.: Addison-Wesley Publishing Co., Inc., 1947.

9. Hurst, G. S., and J. E. Turner, *Elementary Radiation Physics*. New York: John Wiley & Sons, Inc., 1969.

Chapter 6

Health Physics and Biological Radiation Protection

Radiation is either a form of energy or a particle carrying energy with it. As we have seen, this radiation can have certain interactions with matter; both the matter and the radiation will be altered. If the matter undergoing the reaction happens to be a living organism, the effects of the interaction can damage the living tissue to the point of severe illness or death. The exact effects and mechanism of radiation damage to biological tissue are not known. "Health Physics" is concerned not only with the effects of radiation on living tissue but also with the detection of radiation that may be injurious to persons. Health physicists evaluate permissible exposure levels of radiation for persons, and devise procedures and methods to protect individuals from excess exposure to radiation.

It was partly by accident that people became aware of the damaging nature of radiation on living tissue. Early workers suffered "burns" on their skin after exposure to X-rays. This naturally led to the study of the biological effects of radiation. Unfortunately, there were some deaths and severe injuries as a result of overexposure to radiation before the serious nature of radiation damage was known. The classic example of this is the case of workers who painted watch dials. They died as a result of accidentally ingesting some of the radium that the paint contained.

It was not until the 1920s (over 25 years after X-rays were discovered) that safety measures for handling radioactive materials were proposed.

In the 1930s maximum permissible levels for exposure were set. The general acceptance of the maximum permissible exposure levels has kept down the incidence of radiation injuries.

UNITS AND MEASUREMENTS

An amount of radiation is usually referred to as a *dose*. It is important to make a distinction between an exposure and a delivered dose. For personnel protection, it is the exposure which is of interest, while for biological (or structural) damage the absorbed dose would be of concern. The first unit of radiation, the roentgen, was adopted in 1928 and modified in 1937. It is still the most prevalent unit in use. The *roentgen* is "that quantity of X or γ radiation such that the associated corpuscular emission per 0.001293 gm of air produces, in air, ions carrying one esu of quantity of electricity of either sign." This means that one roentgen, when ionizing one cubic centimeter of air at STP will produce ions such that the total charge on all the ions will be one esu. Notice that only the primary ionization need be produced in the 1.0 cm³, but secondary ionization can be produced in any air. The secondary ionization contributes to the one esu of charge. Note also that one roentgen expresses a charge density and applies only to X or γ rays in air and, therefore, is considered a unit of exposure. Exposure expressed in roentgens does not depend on time, so an exposure rate can be expressed in terms of roentgen per unit time.

Example 1. What energy is imparted to air when it completely absorbs one roentgen of radiation?

The charge on an electron is 4.8×10^{-10} esu, and it requires 34 eV to produce one ion pair. The latter unit of 34 eV/ion pair was adopted by the International Commission on Radiological Units in 1956.

$$1 R = \frac{1 \text{ esu}}{0.001293 \text{ gm air}} \times \frac{1 \text{ ion pair}}{4.8 \times 10^{-10} \text{ esu}} \times \frac{34 \text{ eV}}{\text{ion pair}} = 54.8 \times 10^{12} \frac{\text{eV}}{\text{gm}}$$

$$1 R = \frac{54.8 \times 10^{12} \text{ eV}}{\text{gm air}} \times \frac{1.6 \times 10^{-12} \text{ erg}}{\text{eV}} = 87.7 \frac{\text{ergs}}{\text{gm air}}$$

Even though 1 R is a reasonably large quantity of radiation it is trivial from a physical energy standpoint. For example, it takes about 85.5 ergs to move a new sharpened No. 2 lead pencil one sixteenth of an inch. As we will see later, the amount of energy delivered in a lethal dose of radiation is also trivial.

It seems desirable to have a more general unit of radiation which is independent of both the type of radiation and the irradiated material. This unit would then express an absorbed or delivered dose. The unit has been named rad and can be defined as being equal to the absorption of 100 ergs/gram at the point of interest.   The rad, therefore, applies to any material and any radiation.   Obviously 1 R will deliver a dosage to a material dependent on its absorption coefficient.   The absorption coefficient is the probability of absorption and is expressed as cm^2/cm^3 or cm^2/gm.

Unfortunately, the picture is complicated further by the fact that not all radiations have the same effect on body tissue even though they may dissipate the same energy in the tissue.   This biological effectiveness depends upon the specific ionization of the ionizing particle.   To account for this problem, quality factor QF is defined as

$$QF = \frac{\text{physical absorbed dose of 250 kV X-rays to produce a given effect}}{\text{physical absorbed dose of comparison radiation to produce the same effect}} \qquad (6.1)$$

Table 6.1 gives recommended values of QF.   *Quality factor* is the same

TABLE 6.1

QF FOR VARIOUS RADIATIONS

Radiation	QF
X and γ rays	1
Electrons	1
Thermal n's	2–5
Fast n's (10 MeV)	5–10
Alpha	20
Protons (10 MeV)	10

as *relative biological effectiveness*, RBE, but is a more appropriate term. In reality, the ratio in Eq. (6.1) depends on biological effect, dose, dose rate, physiological conditions, and other conditions so that quality factor implies an application to all tissue under a variety of conditions.   Conceivably, different RBE's might be used under differing definitions and methods used for diagnosis.   Quality Factor, however, is conservative and is the value used in establishing permissible limits.

Probably the most significant characteristic of passage of radiation through matter relating to biological damage is the *linear energy transfer*. LET expresses a rate of energy loss per micron of particle track.

$$LET = wS = \frac{dE}{dL} \qquad (6.2)$$

where S = specific ionization, number of ion pairs produced per centimeter of tissue, and w = energy (eV) necessary to produce one ion pair. Neither S nor w is well known, but dE/dL can be predicted from theoretical considerations. The QF would then depend on the values of LET for the particular type of damage and particular radiation. For most biological changes QF increases as LET or S increases, from small values for secondary electrons to largest values for protons or alpha particles.

We can now define a unit of biological dose, the *roentgen equivalent man, rem*. The *rem* can be defined as the dose in tissue that results in biological damage equivalent to that produced per rad of X-ray (about 250 kV) having a LET to water of 3.5 keV/micron.

$$rem = QF \times \text{dose in rads} \qquad (6.3)$$

The advantage in using units of rems is that dosages of different radiations (when expressed in rems) are additive. Thus, maximum permissible exposures for persons can be expressed in rems without regard to the type of radiation present. It must be remembered, though, that the values of QF are not exact. Furthermore, the rem should not be used for acute exposure (accidents) because the QF's may be different from those for chronic exposure.

Unfortunately, radiation exposure causes no bodily sensation (except possibly at high intensities). This means that instruments must be used to survey the areas where radiation hazards may exist. A good survey meter should respond in a manner proportional to tissue ionization produced.

All areas around a reactor are monitored frequently to determine the radioactivity present on surfaces and in the air. There is usually an instrument that continuously monitors the radiation present in the air. In addition, all wastes discharged from a plant are monitored to insure that they do not cause an environmental hazard. Personnel are provided with dosimeters to measure the radiation to which they are exposed. The dosimeter can be read as often as desired in an area where radiation levels are high. Workers may be taken off a project before they receive more than a permissible exposure. Anyone exposed to an above normal dose can be identified and measures must be taken to prevent further injury.

In the U. S. the National Committee on Radiation Protection recommends maximum levels of radiation exposure for individuals. It is the responsibility of the health physics organizations to enforce these recommendations and to conduct radiation monitoring. It is well to remember that, despite the efforts of health physicists, an individual is ultimately responsible for his own safety.

Radiation monitoring instruments must be calibrated regularly and kept in perfect operating condition. Ionization chamber instruments are widely used for quantitative surveys since they respond to a wide range of energies. This means, of course, that their response can be designed to be proportional to tissue ionization. Geiger-Müller counters are also used for survey measurements; since they respond to the number of ionizing events rather than energy, however, they should not be used for quantitative measurements. A geiger counter is a radiation detector rather than an instrument for radiation measurement. Preferably a geiger counter used for radiation monitoring should read in counts rather than in milliroentgens per minute. The milliroentgen per minute reading would apply only to the radiation for which the instrument was calibrated. Figures 6.1 and 6.2 show available radiation monitoring instruments.

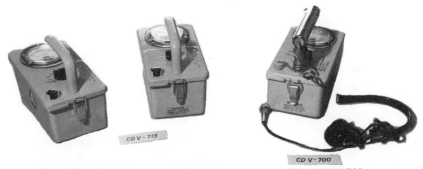

FIG. 6.1 *Radiation monitoring instruments. The CDV-715 is a gamma survey meter, the CDV-700 a Geiger counter.*

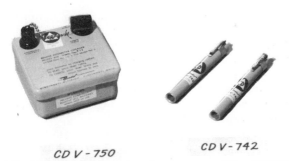

FIG. 6.2 *Radiation monitoring instruments. The CDV-750 is a dosimeter reader-charger and the CDV-742 is a dosimeter.*

To calculate a dose rate the flux of radiation (photons/cm² sec) must be multiplied by the rate at which energy is delivered to the absorbing material (MeV/cm³). The product can be converted to rads/gm-hr. It is general procedure to use the absorption coefficient, μ, as the total coefficient minus the Compton scattering coefficient. Fig. 6.3 shows the

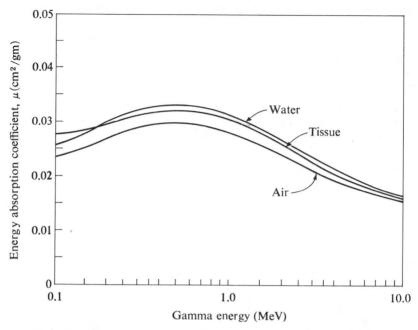

FIG. 6.3   *Energy absorption coefficients for gamma absorption in air, water, and tissue.* [*Data from ORNL-421, Absorption of gamma rays.*]

variation of μ with gamma energy for air, water, and tissue.   The density of tissue is taken as 1.0 gm/cm³.

Example 2.   Calculate the dose rate in tissue at a distance of 10 cm from a one millicurie source of ⁶⁰Co.   ⁶⁰Co emits γ-rays of energies 1.17 MeV and 1.332 MeV.   Since μ is a function of energy the dose rate will be different for each of the two gammas; therefore, each must be calculated separately and added to give the total dose rate.   The absorption of radiation by air in the 10 cm interval will be neglected.   The flux can be calculated from a point source using the inverse square law.

$$\phi = \frac{\text{source strength}}{4\pi R^2}$$

$$\phi = \frac{3.7 \times 10^7}{4(100)} = 2.94 \times 10^4 \text{ photons/cm}^2 \text{ sec}$$

From Fig. 6.3

$$1.17 \text{ MeV} \qquad \mu = 0.029 \text{ cm}^2/\text{gm}$$

$$1.332 \text{ MeV} \qquad \mu = 0.0275 \text{ cm}^2/\text{gm}$$

$$\text{Dose rate} = \phi\mu E$$

$$D_{1.17} = 0.029(2.94 \times 10^4)(1.17)(1.0) \quad = \quad 997 \text{ MeV/cm}^3 \text{ sec}$$

$$D_{1.332} = 0.0275(2.94 \times 10^4)(1.332)(1.0) = 1080 \text{ MeV/cm}^3 \text{ sec}$$

Total dose rate $= 2077 \text{ MeV/cm}^3 \text{ sec}$

This is equivalent to

$$D = \frac{(2077 \text{ MeV/cm}^3 \text{ sec})(1.6 \times 10^{-6} \text{ erg/MeV})}{(100 \text{ erg/gm rad})(1.0 \text{ gm/cm}^3)}$$

$$D = 3.32 \times 10^{-5} \text{ rad/sec} = 1.99 \text{ mrem/min}$$

EXPOSURE AND BIOLOGICAL DAMAGE

Radiation exposure can occur in two ways: (1) external exposure to the body or clothing directly from a source: (2) internal exposure from sources inhaled, injested, or absorbed into the body.

Irradiation of a cell (by internal or external exposure) can cause damage to the cell nucleus or to any of the other cell components. It is generally believed that cells can repair damage unless the interaction is with the cell nucleus. In this case, the cell may be destroyed or the chromosomes in a reproductive cell may be altered, resulting in a mutation in the daughter cell. These mutations are retained by the daughter cells and the organism which ultimately grows from these cells will be different (better or worse) from one which suffered no radiation absorption. In man, it may take a long time (generations) for these mutations to become evident. Thus, many of the long term effects of radiation are still unknown.

The potential results of these genetic effects cause great concern to health physicists. Many feel that mutations will be disadvantageous to man because he is so highly developed. This means that offspring will be more or less defective and these defects may be passed on to succeeding generations. It seems possible that a general *large* increase in level of radiation may increase the number of members of society who are unable to contribute their proper share to the general welfare.

More specifically, all radiation effects stem from ionization of the cells. The ionization can be produced in any of the interaction processes described in Chapter 5. It should be noted, however, that the LET of a particle plays an important part in the cell damage. The radiation produces ionization and excitation in the cells which interfere with their normal functioning. This is evidenced by: (a) the breaking apart of cells; (b) the displacement of cells or the swelling of cell nuclei beyond their normal position; (c) the increasing permeability of cell membranes; and (d) the forming of radioactive isotopes which themselves decay.

Almost all the effects of radiation result from secondary ionization by the electron and free radical of the original cell. Large amounts of radiation destroy many cells and a large quantity of tissue is damaged.

The effects on the body of exposure to radiation are heavily dependent upon the nature of the exposure. *Acute exposure* is a large dose of radiation received over a short period of time. For example, radiation absorbed due to an accident would be acute. *Chronic exposure* means relatively low dosages received over a long period of time, such as that experienced in normal everyday handling of radioactivity. In general, chronic exposure is less serious than acute exposure because the body can make continuing repairs to the damage.

The most striking and most significant characteristic of biological radiation exposure is the *latent period*. This is observed as a delay in appearance of symptoms. It is comparable to sunburn in which the redness and soreness usually become more marked several hours after one has come out of the sun. Radiation exposure produces an effect similar to sunburn but is much more serious since the radiation can penetrate to tissue beneath the skin. The latent period applies as well to other effects of radiation exposure. In some cases the latent period may even be longer than the individual's lifetime.

If a large dose is absorbed, most of the apparent changes will be observed within a few weeks and apparent recovery will take place within a few months. These relatively short-term effects show themselves as reddening of the skin (erythema), nausea, vomiting, decrease in both white and red blood cell count, loss of appetite, diarrhea, and formation of ulcers. The time lag in the appearance of these symptoms depends upon the absorbed dose. As little as 100 rems received as an acute dose will cause vomiting and fatigue in most persons, but some persons will show no effects for larger doses. Thus it is nearly impossible to assign strict levels that cause specific biological damage.

In an emergency or an accident an individual might suffer a large acute dose of radiation. We can estimate the probable effects of an acute whole-body dose. These whole-body effects are shown in Table 6.2.

If exposure occurs daily for a long period, no symptoms will be immediately observed (possibly for years). The damage, however, worsens as long as exposure continues. If the exposure is stopped, the damage may be repaired or long-term effects may occur years later. It is difficult to tell when recovery is completed because of these long-term effects. With a moderate dose there will be only a few such effects, but the delay may be as long as 25 years. In the interval between recovery from short-term effects and appearance of long-term effects, the victim may be completely free of symptoms. As the dose is increased, the interval between short- and long-term effects becomes shorter.

TABLE 6.2

EFFECTS OF ACUTE WHOLE-BODY RADIATION DOSES

Dose (rems)	0 to 100	100 to 200	200 to 600	600 to 1000	1000 to 5000
Vomiting	None	5% to 50%	100% at 300 rems	100%	100%
Latent period	None	3 hours	2 hours	1 hour	30 minutes
Character-istic sign		Leuko-penia	Leuko-penia Purpura Hemorrhage	Diarrhea Fever	Convulsions Tremor Lethargy
Therapy	Reassur-ance	Reassur-ance	Blood transfusion Antibiotics	Possible bone marrow transplant	Sedatives
Conva-lescent period	None	Several weeks	1 to 12 months	Long	
Incidence of death	None	None	0 to 80%	80 to 100%	90 to 100%
Time of death			2 months	2 months	2 weeks
Cause of death			Hemorrhage Infection	Hemorrhage Infection	Circulatory collapse

Data from Reference 1.

There may also be some synergism; that is, irradiation from a mixture of two types of radiation and/or exposure of two or more body organs may produce damage greater than the sum of individual components when received separately.

Some organisms are more sensitive to radiation than others. The most sensitive cells are those which are constantly reproducing or growing. Examples are the blood-forming organs, intestines, reproductive organs, lenses of the eye, the skin, and the thyroid. The most insensitive cells are those which are not growing or reproducing themselves such as adult brain cells and muscles. Recovery can take place in cells and tissue which can grow new ones; no recovery is possible in cells which do not repair or reproduce themselves.

This table is based on doses received by large numbers of individuals and on extrapolations from animal studies. For up to 200 rems the information is based on reliable information, but beyond 200 rems the data from exposed humans decrease rapidly. Above 600 rems the information is based almost entirely on observations made on animals ex-

posed to radiation.   For a comprehensive discussion of radiation effects
see Reference 1.

EXTERNAL EFFECTS, INTERNAL EFFECTS, AND TREATMENT

The following outline lists the noted biological effects. of radiation.
The single most significant effect is the LD 50–30.   This is the acute
dose that would prove fatal to some 50 percent of the population within
30 days of exposure.

(1) LD 50–30 acute dose in rads.

Examples:	man	450	guinea pig	250
	monkey	500	dog	300–430
	rat	590	sheep	520
	rabbit	790–875	donkey	580–780
	chicken	1000	turtle	1500

(2) Erythema.   A reddening of the skin similar to sunburn, but different because of the more penetrating effect of radiation.

(3) Growth rate and stunting of growth.

(4) Growth abnormalities.   Various localized abnormal growths, such as
tumors, may be produced.

(5) Blood count.   The most reliable indication of degree of exposure.   First
indication is a decrease in the white blood count followed somewhat later
by a loss in red blood count.   Blood count by itself, however, is not used
as a measure of overexposure to radiation.

(6) Mitotic index.   A quantitative and rapidly responding measure of radiation exposure.   Mitotic index is a ratio of the number of cells in a particular phase of their development to the total number of cells of the same
kind.   The mitotic index changes normally and continually, but exposure
to radiation will cause an abnormal change.

(7) Life span.   So far this is only a statistical measure of the effects of radiation.   It is fairly certain, however, that chronic exposure will reduce the
normal lifespan slightly.

Examples:	general population	65.6 years
	some exposure	63.3 years
	radiologists	60.7 years

(8) Cataracts.   The eye is not particularly sensitive to gamma rays but is
quite sensitive to fast neutrons.   It is estimated that about 3×10^9 neutrons will cause an eye cataract.

(9) Cancer and leukemia.   The latent period for the incidence of cancer and
leukemia is very long (about 25 years).   For this reason the usual practice
is to limit exposure to levels that show no permanent deleterious changes
which might lead to cancer.

(10) Genetic effects.   The complete genetic effects on man cannot yet be given,
because it will take about ten generations for them to be produced.
However, it has been shown that radiation-induced mutations are about

the same as those occurring in nature.   Therefore, it is desirable to limit the exposure to as few persons as possible and, among those persons, to limit exposure through the reproductive years.

Overexposure of the gonads to radiation in both men and women may produce temporary or permanent sterility.   This reduction in fertility or sterility may be passed on to descendents.   The sensitivity of the gonads, however, is not as high as that of the blood-forming organs so that the level of permissible exposure for the blood-forming organs is also satisfactory for the gonads.

Hands almost inevitably will receive a higher dose rate than other parts of the body.   It is improbable, therefore, that the maximum permissible dose rate of the rest of the body will be exceeded if the hands do not receive it.   It is difficult to measure the exposure of hands, so the usual practice is to measure the dose rate to the whole body by a film badge and/or pocket dosimeter similar to that of Fig. 5.10.

The effects of exposure from internal sources are no different except that the source presents more concentrated exposure near vital organs. This is particularly important in the case of alpha and beta particles. Once the radioactive source has been introduced into the body through (a) wounds, (b) the gastro-intestinal tract, or (c) the lungs, there is no way to control the damage.   The duration of internal exposure depends on the half-life of the source and body elimination.   Some materials are rapidly eliminated in body wastes.   Others, such as plutonium, strontium, and radium, concentrate in the bone.   Uranium concentrates in the kidneys, but tritium distributes itself throughout the body.   In this regard the critical organ refers to the most vital organ to which the isotope goes. In evaluating internal hazards two concepts are useful: effective half-life and maximum permissible body content.

$$\frac{1}{t_{1/2\text{eff}}} = \frac{1}{t_{1/2\text{biol}}} + \frac{1}{t_{1/2\text{rad}}} \tag{6.4}$$

where $t_{1/2\text{eff}}$ = effective half-life
$\quad\quad\ t_{1/2\text{biol}}$ = biological half-life or the length of time to eliminate one-half the isotope biologically
$\quad\quad\ t_{1/2\text{rad}}$ = radioactive half-life

The effective half-life cannot be predicted exactly for all persons because of normal variation in biological half-life.   The effective half-life for ^{90}Sr, for example, is 3000–5000 days.   The maximum permissible body content is the amount of radioactive isotope that gives the maximum permissible internal dose rate to a critical organ.   The rate of intake into the body, which eventually results in a specified body content, is inversely proportional to the effective half-life in the critical organ.

Treatment of radiation sickness can only minimize the effects of exposure to radiation. The usual treatment is bed rest for long periods of time. Antibiotics are given to increase body resistance and blood transfusions are given to counteract the blood damage. In some recent serious cases bone marrow has been transplanted, but transplants have not met with complete success because the body tends to reject any foreign tissue.

EXPOSURE PROTECTION GUIDES

Evidence suggests that there is no threshold below which no injury from radiation occurs. Thus, everyone working in an area of radiation works in a hazardous environment. All the effects discussed in the preceding section have been carefully taken into account in arriving at guides for maximum exposure of persons working in the field.

Radiation Guides for permissible exposures of persons working in areas subject to radiation have been recommended by the National Committee on Radiation Protection and Measurement (NCRP). This organization is affiliated with the International Committee on Radiation Protection (ICRP). In addition, the U. S. Federal Radiation Council is active in establishing radiation exposure guides. The Guides, of course, are subject to continuing study and revision.

The Radiation Protection Guides for individuals exposed to radiation in their occupations are as follows:

(1) Total accumulated dose over a period of years $\leqslant 5(n - 18)$ rems, where n = the individual's age. Notice that persons under 18 years are not permitted to work where they will be exposed to radiation.
(2) The dose cannot exceed an average of 5 rems per year or 12 rems in any given year.
(3) The maximum exposure also should not exceed 3 rems over any period of 13 weeks.
(4) If a person is continuously exposed to radiation during his working hours, the maximum recommended dose rate would be 2.5 mrems/hr or 100 mrem/wk.

The above figures apply to the gonads and blood-forming organs. Specific parts of the body can be exposed to larger values, but the Guides are usually considered for the whole body. In an emergency the Guides provide for a maximum exposure of 12 rems, if the accumulation limit has not been reached. This exposure might occur, for example, when an area is decontaminated after an accident.

The human body has probably adapted itself to small continuous doses of radiation because it has always been exposed to natural background radiation. This background radiation is cosmic rays and radioactive material in the soil, air, water, and ^{14}C and ^{40}K in the body. Now small additional amounts of radiation from atomic weapons tests and operating reactors have been added. For the population as a whole the Guides limit exposure to 0.5 rems per year to the gonads or whole body and 1.5 rems for other parts of the body. By the time he is 30, an individual should not have accumulated more than 1.5 rems to the whole body or the gonads.

For internal hazards, Radioactivity Concentration Guides (RCG) have been postulated for maximum average concentrations of isotopes in air and water. These indicate amounts of radiation which will not result in excessive accumulation in the body. Unfortunately, RCG values are not known for most isotopes. Table 6.3 shows some RCG values.

TABLE 6.3

RADIOACTIVITY CONCENTRATION GUIDES

Element	Maximum Body Concentration	RCG in Water	RCG in Air	Critical Organ
	μc	$\mu c/cm^3$	$\mu c/cm^3$	
^{226}Ra	0.1	4×10^{-7}	3×10^{-11}	Bone
^{90}Sr	1.0	4×10^{-6}	3×10^{-10}	Bone
^{239}Pu	0.04	10^{-4}	2×10^{-12}	Bone
^{131}I	0.3	6×10^{-5}	9×10^{-9}	Thyroid
U^*	5×10^{-3}	5×10^{-4}	7×10^{-11}	Kidney

*Chemical toxicity overshadows the hazard due to radioactivity.
(Data from NBS 52 and USAEC Rules and Regulations, Part 20.)

SHIELDING

Chapter 1 indicated that shielding must be provided around a reactor to protect both personnel and material. Shielding which is adequate for neutrons and gamma rays will also stop alpha and beta particles. Previous sections of this chapter have indicated that neutrons are potentially more dangerous than gamma rays in causing biological damage. Even so, the contribution of neutrons to total dose is much less than that of gamma rays. The problem, then, is basically one of providing protection from (1) primary gamma radiation, (2) radiation due to n–γ reactions in the shield, and (3) fast neutrons.

The weight of shielding to be used is almost independent of the shielding material itself. It is usually advantageous to use dense material, particularly concrete, lead, and water. Water can be used where heating (due to absorption of gamma energy) is important and for storage purposes. Because of its low cost and structural characteristics, concrete is the most commonly used shielding material.

In its simplest form shielding involves interposing distance and materials between the source and recipient of radiation. Design considerations and the calculation of the resultant dose complicate the problem.

To gain some insight into shielding calculations we shall consider an oversimplified situation which involves a point source of radiation. Fig. 6.4 shows a point source radiating isotropically through a vacuum.

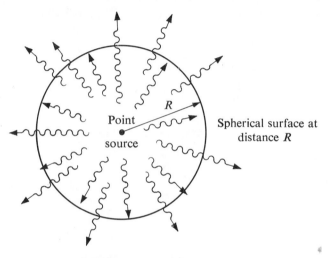

FIG. 6.4 *Point source of radiation in a vacuum.*

According to the inverse square law, the intensity of radiation on the surface of a sphere of radius R will be

$$I = \frac{S}{4\pi R^2} \qquad (6.5)$$

where S is the source strength (number of particles or rays per unit time). If we place enough distance between ourselves and the source, the intensity of radiation will be reduced to safe levels. However, if we place material between ourselves and the source, we can take advantage of attenuation provided by the material. For the case of a collimated beam of gamma particles, Eq. (5.4) predicts the intensity at a point in the material

$$I = I_0 e^{-\mu R} \qquad (6.6)$$

where μ is the total linear absorption coefficient. Equation (6.6) applies strictly to a collimated beam and only when scattered radiation is removed from the beam.   In a thick shield such as that in Fig. 6.5, Eq. (6.6) would give a low result because some of the radiation is backscattered into the path.   This is the result of Compton scatter in the shield; the gammas decrease in energy.   To correct for this backscattering an experimental buildup factor, $B(\mu R)$, is employed.   Equation (6.6) becomes

$$I = B(\mu R)I_0 e^{-\mu R} \qquad\qquad (6.7)$$

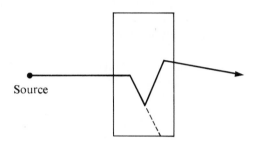

FIG. 6.5   *Backscattering of radiation in a shield.*

The buildup factor, a function of linear absorption coefficient and shield thickness, is commonly given in the form

$$B(\mu R) = 1 + a\mu R \qquad\qquad (6.8)$$

where a is a value depending on gamma energy and material.   For example, the buildup factor for ^{60}Co gammas in air is

$$B = 1 + 0.55 R \text{ (see Reference 12)} \qquad\qquad (6.9)$$

Combining Eqs. (6.5) and (6.7) gives the intensity from an isotropic point source of radiation

$$I = \frac{SB(\mu R)e^{-\mu R}}{4\pi R^2} \qquad\qquad (6.10)$$

Example 3.   What is the intensity of gamma rays from a 10 curie source of ^{22}Na surrounded by 5 cm of lead?   The buildup factor is 2.1

$$I = \frac{SB(\mu R)e^{-\mu R}}{4\pi R^2}$$

From Appendix D the ^{22}Na gamma energy is 1.28 MeV.   The total linear absorption coefficient (Fig. 5.9) is 0.66 cm^{-1}.

$$I = \frac{10(3.7 \times 10^{10})(2.1)e^{-(0.66)(5)}}{4\pi(5)^2}$$

$$I = 9.03 \times 10^7 \text{ photons/cm}^2\text{-sec}$$

This can be converted to a dose rate in the manner of Example 2.

Equation 6.9 is applicable only to a point source of radiation. With the introduction of a buildup factor, it is seen that intensity in a shield is not an exponential function. However, it would be convenient if we could devise an expression that retains the exponential character. This can be done by representing intensity as:

$$I = I_o e^{-\lambda/a} \qquad (6.11)$$

where λ is defined as the relaxation length. In other words, it is the length in which the intensity decreases by a factor of $1/e$. Equation (6.11), therefore, includes a contribution for scattering in the material. Relaxation length is frequently used in rough shielding calculations. If the radiation variation is not exponential, this means that the relaxation length varies from point to point in the material. For thick shields variation is very nearly exponential. Table 6.4 gives relaxation lengths

TABLE 6.4

RELAXATION LENGTHS

Material	Density	Fast Neutrons	8 MeV Gamma
	g/cm³	cm	cm
Water	1.00	10	40
Concrete	2.30	12	18
Lead	11.30	9	2
Beryllium	1.85	9	30
Graphite	1.65	9	25

for some common shielding materials. Notice that the relaxation length for both neutrons and gammas is about the same in concrete.

Almost all sources of radiation are larger than point sources. Fortunately, gamma rays do not interact with each other, so total radiation can be considered as the sum of radiations from point sources. For example, consider a circular plane uniform isotropic source, Fig. 6.6. If the source is considered to be made up of a number of point sources having a total strength S, the dose (intensity) at point P is

$$D = \int_0^R \frac{S e^{-\mu a}}{4\pi a^2} 2\pi r \, dr \qquad (6.12)$$

In terms of the distance from P to the plane, Eq. (6.12) becomes

$$D = 2\pi S \int_z^{(z^2+a^2)^{1/2}} G(a) a \, da \qquad (6.13)$$

$G(a)$ is called the point attenuation kernel. It is the radiation intensity observed at distance a from a unit isotropic point source. In our case

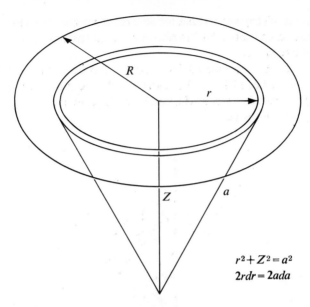

$$r^2 + Z^2 = a^2$$
$$2r\,dr = 2a\,da$$

FIG. 6.6   *Circular plane uniform isotropic source.*

$$G(a) = \frac{B(\mu a)e^{-\mu a}}{2\pi a^2} \tag{6.14}$$

Integration of (6.13) for a plane surface leads to an exponential integral of the first kind. By employing this concept of a point kernel the intensity for other geometries can be evaluated.

A volume source can be related to a surface source as follows. Let S_v represent a uniform source strength within the volume element dV of Fig. 6.7. The source strength due to the volume element is $S_v\,dV$. The width of the element is $r \sin \psi\, d\theta$, its height dr and its length is $r\,d\psi$. The radiation at the surface due to the volume dV is

$$dS = S_v\,G(a)a^2 \sin \psi\, d\theta\, d\psi\, da \tag{6.15}$$

and the total intensity at the surface due to the entire volume is

$$S = S_v \int_0^{2\pi} \int_0^{\pi/2} \int_0^D G(a)a^2 \sin \psi\, d\theta\, d\psi\, da \tag{6.16}$$

Introducing the relaxation length into the point kernel and letting the buildup factor equal 1

$$G(a) = \frac{e^{-a/\lambda}}{4\pi a^2} \tag{6.17}$$

Evaluating Eqs. (6.16) and (6.17) gives

$$S = 1/2\, S_v\lambda \tag{6.18}$$

and since Eq. (6.16) was written for sources from one direction only, Eq. (6.18) must be multiplied by 2 to obtain the total surface source equivalent of the volume source.

If S_v can be represented by a simple function, Eq. (6.18) can be combined with Eq. (6.13) and integrated. In the more general case, an average S_v is used and assumed constant throughout the core. This leads to a conservative result.

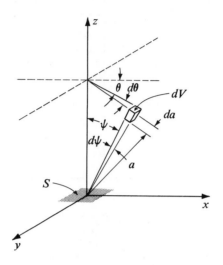

FIG. 6.7   *Volume distributed source.*

The shielding materials used in reactor systems are dictated not only by neutrons, primary, and secondary gammas but also by the purpose of the reactor. For example, in a submarine reactor the weight of the shielding is of extreme importance, but in a power reactor it is mostly an economic consideration. Radiation level outside the reactor is of prime importance, of course.

Frequently, shielding is designed by a comparison method. An existing reactor is used as the basis for predicting the shielding characteristics of the reactor being designed.

When the physical layout of the reactor system has been determined, the maximum radiation exposure at various points is computed. Of course, some knowledge of the reactor power and core materials is necessary to determine the distribution of radiation. If this information is known, a comparison can be made. A mock-up of the design can then be tested in a facility such as the Bulk Shielding Facility at Oak Ridge, Tennessee.

If no similar system is available, analytic calculations are made. Because of the complexity of radiation interactions the calculations cannot be exact, and normally recourse must be made to experimental models. Finally, as the reactor design is finalized the shielding determination becomes more and more refined.

PROBLEMS

1. Is there a difference between the contributions of dose rate and total dose to the biological damage done by radiation? Explain.

2. How long will it take to receive a weekly dose of 2 MeV gammas to the hands and forearms from a 1 μc source? Assume a weekly dose to be that recommended by the Radiation Guides.

3. Calculate the total energy dissipated if a 160-pound man received an LD 50–30.

4. Calculate the dose rate in tissue given by a 10 millicurie source of ^{137}Cs gammas. Neglect any absorption of gammas in the air between tissue and source. The source distance is 100 cm.

5. How long will it take a worker to receive his weekly dose of neutrons (according to radiation protection guides) if he is exposed to a flux of 10^8 thermal neutrons/cm^2-sec and a flux of 10^4 fast neutrons/cm^2-sec?

6. If a worker was exposed to 50 mR of ^{60}Co gammas and 20 mrad of fast neutrons, what would be his total exposure?

7. The radiation protection guides are intended to prevent what injuries during the lifetime of the individual?

8. A man exposed to radiation receives a dose of 40 mrad of fast neutrons. What is his whole body dose? Did he exceed the recommended weekly dose on any part of his body?

9. What should be done in the case of the man exposed to radiation in the preceding problem?

10. If a test tube containing 400 mg of ^{90}Sr was dropped and broken in a room 40 feet square and 10 feet high, would there be a dangerous concentration of ^{90}Sr in the air in the room?

11. What distance must an experimenter remain from a 3 curie ^{226}Ra source if he is not to receive more than the recommended maximum weekly dosage?

12. Find the thickness of lead necessary to reduce the dose rate from a 100 curie ^{60}Co source to safe levels for continuous exposure. Note: use a buildup factor of 5.8 for both the ^{60}Co gammas.

REFERENCES

1. Glasstone, S., ed., *The Effects of Nuclear Weapons.* USAEC, 1964.
2. *Nuclear Safety*, USAEC quarterly publication.

3. *Proceedings of the Second United Nations International Conference on the Peaceful Uses of Atomic Energy*, Vol. XXI, 1958.

4. Glasstone, S., and A. Sesonske, *Nuclear Reactor Engineering*.   New York: D. Van Nostrand Co., Inc., 1963.

5. Etherington, E., *Nuclear Engineering Handbook*.   New York: McGraw-Hill Book Co., Inc., 1958.

6. Blatz, H., ed., *Radiation Hygiene Handbook*.   New York: McGraw-Hill Book Co., Inc., 1959.

7. *Radiation Protection: Recommendations of the International Commission on Radiological Protection*.   New York: Pergamon Press, Inc., 1959.

8. "Maximum Permissible Body Burdens and Maximum Permissible Concentrations of Radionuclides in Air and Water for Occupational Exposure," N. B. S. *Handbook* 69 (1959).

9. E. L. Saenger, ed., *Medical Aspects of Radiation Accidents*.   USAEC, 1963.

10. *Radiological Health Handbook*.   U. S. Department of Health, Education, and Welfare, 1962.

11. *Occupational Radiation Protection*.   U. S. Department of Health, Education, and Welfare, 1965.   Ch. 5.

12. Batter, J. F., "Cobalt and Iridium Buildup Factors Near the Ground/Air Interface," *Trans. Amer. Nucl. Soc.* **6,** no. 1 (1963).

13. Spencer, L. V., "Structure Shielding Against Fallout Radiation from Nuclear Weapons," *N. B. S. Monograph 42* (1962).

14. Eisenhauer, C., "An Engineering Method for Calculating Protection Afforded by Structures Against Fallout Radiation," *NBS Monograph 76*, 1964.

15. "Shelter Design and Analysis-Volume 1 Fallout Protection," U. S. Office of Civil Defense, 1967.

16. "Radiation Effects on Man," *Nucleonics* **21,** no. 3 (March 1963).

17. "New ICRU Recommendations on Radiation Quantities and Units," *Nucleonics* **21,** no. 7 (July 1963).

Chapter 7

Radioisotope
Application

CATEGORIES OF RADIOISOTOPES

Almost every industry and service organization in the world has a potential use for radiation. This chapter aims to acquaint the reader with some examples of current uses of radioisotopes. Because of the magnitude of present and future uses of radioisotopes, the discussion is limited; however, the reader can gain some knowledge and, hopefully, will be stimulated to explore other uses in detail.

It is convenient to classify the usage of radioisotopes in four categories:

(1) Irradiation of a target material to make a change in its physical properties. The change may enhance the usefulness of the material or destroy it. Examples are production of wood-plastic materials and destruction of cancerous tissue.

(2) Injection of a small amount of radioisotope with normal material in order to trace it through some process. Examples are wear studies and tracing water flow to locate water supplies.

(3) Fixed sources of radiation used as gages. Examples are thickness gages and radiographic inspection.

(4) Fixed sources of radiation used for power generation, heat, or illumination.

The use of radioisotopes, although it does not now represent a large capital outlay by the nuclear industry, is increasing rapidly. In addition to the users of radioisotopes the industry encompasses producers of primary isotopes, processors who prepare radioactive chemicals and specialized sources for medical applications, fabricators who prepare large sources such as those used in radiography and medical therapy, and equipment manufacturers who make the radiography equipment, power generators, process irradiators, etc.   The number of companies involved in these activities is small.   Fig. 7.1 shows sales and exports of radioactive sources.

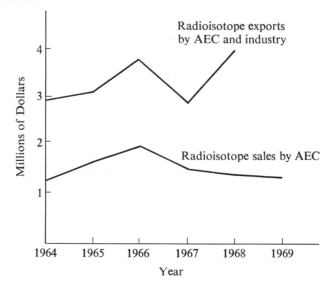

FIG. 7.1   *Value of radioisotope sales.   [Source: U. S. Bureau of the Census: Statistical Abstract of the U. S. (1969).]*

INDUSTRIAL APPLICATIONS

Industrial companies use radioisotope gages to measure thickness, density, and level of materials.   These measurements are frequently combined with other mechanical measurements, such as speed, to determine other properties of the material.

Radioisotope gages have a big advantage over other gages in that they can continuously monitor without contacting the material to be measured.   Also, since the radioisotopes are used in conjunction with an electronic detector, it is relatively easy to amplify the output signal and use it to control a process.

The radioisotope sources are sealed and emit beta or gamma radiation. ^{192}Ir, ^{90}Sr, and ^{60}Co are popular sources.   The gages are set up either as transmission or backscatter types. In the transmission gage the source and detector are on opposite sides of the material to be gaged. The attenuation depends on the thickness and density of material between source and detector. The detector is commonly an ionization chamber. A backscatter gage has the source and detector on the same side of the material to be gaged. Shielding prevents any direct radiation from entering the detector. Only the reflected radiation is detected. The degree of reflection, or backscatter, depends on the thickness of the material. Thickness measurement by backscatter requires access to only one side of the sample. When a β particle is incident on a surface it will undergo scattering with nuclei of the material. It is probable that at some time the β may be scattered back out from the surface. Fig. 7.2 shows the intensity of backscattered radiation in relation to material thickness. The intensity of this radiation is a function of β energy and the scattering characteristics of the material being measured.

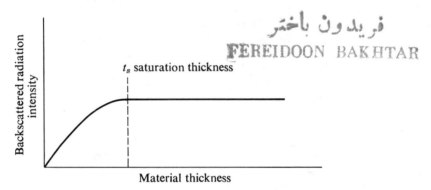

FIG. 7.2 *Intensity of backscattered radiation with thickness of material.*

At the saturation thickness, t_s, the intensity reaches a limiting value. Thus, it is only necessary to have a large enough difference in backscattered intensity from two materials to measure. An example of this measurement is shown in Fig. 7.3.

Coating thicknesses in the range 5–100 μ inches can be measured in this manner as long as the geometry of the detection system is fixed, the film thickness is less than the saturation thickness of the plating material, and the plated material has a thickness greater than its saturation thickness.

A successful use of thickness gages has been in the manufacture of sandpaper and emery cloth. Gages are placed before and after successive coating operations. The difference in detector responses represents the difference in weight; the response automatically adjusts the coating appli-

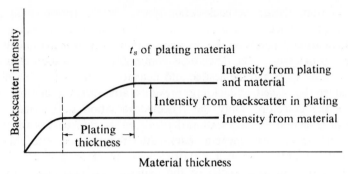

FIG. 7.3   *Film thickness measurement by backscattering.*

cators.   This technique results in an extremely uniform product and may save up to $12,000 per year for a large manufacturer.

Example 1.   Fig. 7.4 shows a schematic arrangement for measuring the thickness of a material using a transmission gage.   Suppose that such a gage is to be used for monitoring the thickness of rolled steel plate.   The source is ^{192}Ir which has a half-life of 74.5 days and emits several gammas, 0.316 MeV being the most abundant.   What should be the reduction in intensity if the steel thickness is to be 0.100 inch?   The reduction in gamma ray intensity can be represented as an exponential function.

$$I = I_0 e^{-\mu_m \rho x} \qquad (7.1)$$

The mass attenuation coefficient for 0.316 MeV gammas in steel is 0.107 cm²/gm.

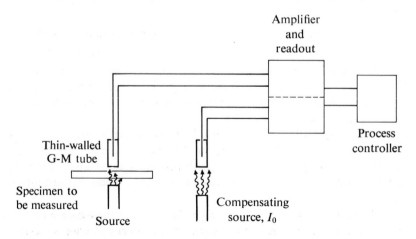

FIG. 7.4   *Schematic of a thickness measuring and controlling gage.*

$$I = I_0 e^{-(0.107)(7.80)(0.100)(2.54)}$$
$$I = I_0 e^{-0.212} = 0.808\ I_0$$

The reduction in intensity is therefore 19.2 percent of the intensity with no specimen present for 0.316 MeV gamma rays.

Probably the best-known use of radioisotope gages is in the control of cigarette density. It has been estimated that 80–90 percent of cigarette production is controlled by radioisotope gaging (see Reference 1). In a typical application a 20 microcurie source of ^{90}Sr is used in the density gage. The gage measures the density of cigarette rod before it is cut and assembled into packages. The output of the detector controls the rate of tobacco feed, maintaining a constant weight of tobacco from pack to pack. This technique enables an automatic production of about 2000 cigarettes per minute.

Some of the newer industrial uses of radioisotopes include using ^{32}S to study the constituents of stack gas, ^{60}Co treatment to break down detergents, in pesticides, and to treat bacteria in sewage treatment plants, activation analysis of trace elements in air and in polluted waterways to pinpoint polluters, and measurement of contaminants in uranium mines.

Radiography using radioactive isotopes amounts to about 60–70 percent of the total radiography done in the U. S. Most of the radiography is done using ^{60}Co with a specific activity of about 160 curies/gm. In some applications ^{192}Ir with a specific activity of about 300 curies/gm is used. The tendency is to make specific activity larger, since this results in a higher sensitivity. The sensitivity is akin to the shadow a light source makes. In other words, the smaller the source size the more sensitive the radiography.

The most valuable use of radioisotopes is in portable radiography work where it would be impossible to transport X-ray machines. For example, radioisotopes are used extensively for weld inspection in pipelines, bridges, boilers, and other custom-built structures. Radioisotopes are frequently used in routine maintenance inspections. Airlines use a ^{60}Co inspection for the core of jet engines. With routine radiographic inspection flaws can be detected inexpensively. Boiler tubes have been inspected with ^{60}Co sources. Even with insulation and furnace walls corroded boiler tubes could be identified. Ordinarily, some tubes would not be seen in a visual inspection.

Research programs employ many radioactive tracer studies. In a tracer study a radioisotope is attached to a larger quantity of nonradioactive material. The radioisotope does not lose its identity during chemical or physical reactions. Thus, its path can be followed at all times.

Radioisotopes are added to material being traced in several ways. A small amount of liquid or gaseous isotope may be mixed with a larger amount of nonradioactive compound. In some cases, chemicals are made from radioactive starting materials. With solid parts, a sealed source can be physically attached to the object to be traced. In other situations, the whole piece may be irradiated by neutrons in a reactor.

One of the most profitable uses of tracers has been in wear studies. In a typical study, a pinion gear is irradiated in a reactor. It is then run with a nonradioactive gear and the rate of wear is measured by the activity of the lubricating oil. An additional benefit can be gained from a test such as this, by autoradiographing the initially nonradioactive gears. The radiograph will show any areas that have picked up radioactive ^{59}Fe from the pinion. The gears can then be redesigned easily to prevent this wear. In internal combustion engine wear tests the cylinder is frequently plated with ^{51}Cr (.32 MeV gamma) and the piston rings are irradiated to produce ^{59}Fe (1.11 and 1.13 MeV gammas). Using a pulse height analyzer it is possible to separate the ring and cylinder wear. Alternatively, the rings could be labeled with different isotopes to compare the wear rates of those rings. To make studies of piston ring rotation a small amount of another isotope (such as ^{60}Co) could be embedded in the ring. Wear tests can also be made by impregnating the surface with ^{14}C or ^{32}P. The surface can be scanned to determine the time variations in radioactivity. This method is most valuable in cases where wear particles are difficult to collect. In any wear tests, precaution must be taken to obtain accurate measurements such as, for example, by screening the engine from the detector. The significant difference between the wear tests using more conventional physical measurements and the radioactive tracers methods lies in the fact that the radioisotope experiments can be made in days while conventional tests take about six months.

A unique tracer study was made in studying the rate of tool wear in a production machining operation. Instead of activating the tool, as is done in laboratory experiments, the chips were collected and irradiated to activate tungsten from the cutting tool.

The Atomic Energy Commission has sponsored development of a tracer technique that should find wide applicability in studies of solid surfaces. In this method the material is either bombarded with positive radioactive krypton ions or radioactive krypton ions are diffused into the substance at high pressures and temperatures. The krypton is a mixture of approximately 5 percent ^{85}Kr (half-life 10.7 years) and 95 percent stable krypton isotopes. Some of the ^{85}Kr gas is substituted in the lattice structure and some is located interstitially. Almost any solid material can be made radioactive by "kryptonation." An important side effect of kryptonation allows determination of the surface temperature distribution. Kryptonates lose krypton at high temperatures in a reproducible and controlled way. That is, when the temperature of a kryptonate is raised to a certain point a fixed percentage of ^{85}Kr is lost. If the temperature is held at this point, or lowered, no further loss of krypton occurs. Surface temperature distributions of jet engine blades have been made using this technique. Kryptonates have also been proposed for use in corrosion studies, phase change studies, and stress-strain studies.

The chemical and electronic industries are making use of radiation for processing. The most successful radiation processing has been with polyethylene film and electrical insulation. The radiation used for these products is mainly electron beams from accelerators. The irradiated polyethylene film or insulation has a tensile strength up to six times as great as the conventional product and it possesses a "thermal memory." In the case of polyethylene, a sheet or tube is irradiated, heated, and stretched to double its original size then cooled under tension. When the polyethylene is used (for packaging, say) it is again heated. The second application of heat causes it to shrink to its normal size.

Wood-plastic combinations promise an interesting use of radiation processing. In this process, the wood fibers are impregnated with a plastic compound. The impregnated wood is then exposed to a high dose rate ^{60}Co source (up to 10^6 rads total dose) which polymerizes the plastic compound within the wood. Most of the impregnation has been done with styrene, methyl methacrylate, polymethyl methacrylate, or vinyl acetate.

The resulting wood-plastic combination has the natural appearance of wood, but it is much more durable. The combination has increased strength, dimensional stability, and hardness. It can be fabricated by normal methods used for other woods; the only finishing required is sanding to the desired surface characteristics. The major difficulty in making the process economically feasible has been lack of quantity markets for the product, difficulty in producing uniform impregnation, and fabrication difficulties. Recently published research indicates that flooring and veneer modification are the two most likely applications for this material.

Studies in the USA and Germany indicate that production of detergents in the presence of γ radiation enhances their biodegradable characteristics. The original detergents are composed of alkyl benzene sulfonates. By reacting oxygen and sulfur dioxide with hydrocarbons in the presence of γ radiation an alkane sulfonate compound is produced. The alkyl benzene sulfonates are only about 25 percent decomposed in sewage plants. Tests of the alkane sulfonate compounds showed them 100 percent degraded after two days while the alkyl benzene sulfonate was degraded only 10 percent in two days. The physical properties and detergent action were nearly the same.

POWER GENERATORS

In 1956, the U. S. Atomic Energy Commission began developing direct conversion devices to convert the energy of decaying isotopes into electricity. The impetus for this program was the potential use of the generators in space and in isolated locations such as Antarctica, and in their use as navigational buoys. The first isotopic power generator was produced in 1959. It employed a thermoelectric generator, produced 2.5 watts of power, and used ^{210}Po as fuel. The whole generator weighed only four pounds. Contrast this with a conventional nickel-cadmium battery (weighing about 700 pounds) producing equivalent energy. The first commercial isotopic power generator became available in 1966. It was produced through the joint efforts of the Martin Company and the Atomic Energy Commission. The unit is a thermoelectric device powered by ^{90}Sr. Initial prices for the unit ranged from $53,587 to $63,230 for a unit guaranteed to produce 25 watts of electricity for five years. Fig. 7.5 is a picture of a Martin Marietta Corporation isotopic power generator.

Two types of direct conversions have been proposed for isotopic power generators: thermoelectric and thermoionic. Fig. 7.6 is a simplified sketch of a thermoelectric radioisotope generator. The outer shell serves as the heat radiator as well as the container for the generator itself. Theoretically, the radiation shield could be placed on either side of the thermoelectric converters. Placing it inside the converters reduces the hot junction temperature and the generator efficiency. Placing it outside the converters, as in the figure, increases the volume of shield material and the cost. Uranium is a common shield; consequently, the mass and cost of the shield may be the major portion of the whole generator. In fact, the shield may go as high as 90 percent of the generator mass.

The Apollo missions have included some of the more spectacular applications of radioisotope generators. The first use was in the Apollo-11 mission where a ^{238}Pu fueled heater in the seismometer keeps the equipment warm. The Apollo-12 mission left a SNAP-27 generator as the sole source of power on the moon. The SNAP-27 generator produces 63 watts of electricity. It is fueled by ^{238}Pu. The ^{238}Pu capsule was encased in graphite and carried on the side of the LEM. This permitted a simpler design and the graphite protected the ^{238}Pu in the event the mission was aborted and the LEM re-entered the earth's atmosphere.

In 1969, the first Nimbus weather satellite using a radioisotope generator was launched. The power supply was PuO_2 fuel. The heat from

FIG. 7.5 *Cutaway view of the SNAP-7B 60-watt isotopic generator showing 7 of the 14 tubular fuel capsules at its center which contain strontium titanate pellets providing the source of power. Around the capsules are 120 pairs of lead telluride thermocouples which convert heat from the decaying radioisotope into electricity.* (*Courtesy Martin Marietta Corporation.*)

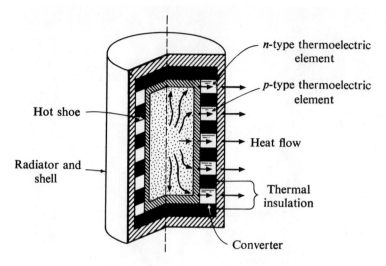

FIG. 7.6   *Thermoelectric isotopic power generator.*

the decaying ^{238}Pu is converted into electrical power in a bank of PbTe thermocouples. The thermocouples are wired in series and parallel to provide the optimum current-voltage relationship. The heat rejected is radiated into space by four fins. The Nimbus satellite has two 25-watt generators each about 9 inches high × 20 inches in diameter.

THERMOELECTRIC CONVERTERS

Ordinary metal wire thermocouples were used originally, but their low efficiencies (<1%) made them impractical. All thermoelectric isotopic power generators now use doped semiconductors as the conversion device. Unfortunately, there are many problems with semiconductor thermoelectric elements, not the least of which is efficiency. Several doped materials have been used for the *n*- and *p*-type semiconductors. Either *n*- or *p*-type semiconductors can be used alone for conversion, but a couple makes a much better converter.

The efficiency of a thermoelectric generator can be expressed as

$$\eta_t = \frac{I^2 R_L}{\alpha_{pn} I T_H + K \Delta T - \frac{1}{2} I^2 R} \qquad (7.2)$$

The current I is determined by the thermoelectric potential, $\alpha_{pn} \Delta T$, divided by the sum of the couple resistance, R, and the load resistance, R_L.

$$I = \frac{\alpha_{pn} \Delta T}{R + R_L} \qquad (7.3)$$

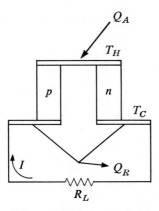

FIG. 7.7 *Schematic of a thermoelectric generator.*

The useful output is the energy dumped in the load, I^2R_L. The input energy is made up of the Peltier effect, which is the product of the Seebeck coefficient, α_{pn}, the current, and the hot junction temperature, plus the thermal heat leak from the hot side to the side through the semiconductor elements, minus one-half the joule internal heating effect which is returned to the hot junction.

$$Q_1 = \alpha_{pn}IT_H + K\Delta T - \frac{1}{2}I^2R \qquad (7.4)$$

If the p and n legs have their area ratio as follows

$$\frac{A_p}{A_n} = \left(\frac{\rho_p k_n}{\rho_n k_p}\right)^{1/2} \qquad \begin{array}{l} \rho = \text{electrical resistivity} \\ k = \text{thermal conductivity} \end{array} \qquad (7.5)$$

the KR product will be a minimum and the figure of merit becomes

$$Z = \frac{\alpha_{pn}}{[(\rho_n k_n)^{1/2} + (\rho_p k_p)^{1/2}]^2} \qquad (7.6)$$

It can be seen that for a high figure of merit the Seebeck coefficient should be as large as possible, while the thermal conductivity and electrical resistivity should be as low as possible. Using this optimized geometry, and using the value of R to give the maximum efficiency, an expression depending only on the temperatures and the figure of merit will result

$$\eta_{opt} = \frac{\Delta T}{\dfrac{\sqrt{1 + ZT_m} + 1}{\sqrt{1 + ZT_m} - 1}T_m + \dfrac{\Delta T}{2}} \qquad (7.7)$$

where $T_m = (T_H + T_C)/2$. The ratio of the load resistance to the internal couple resistance is

$$\frac{R_L}{R} = \sqrt{1 + ZT_m} \tag{7.8}$$

When the load resistance equals the internal couple resistance the maximum output results, but the efficiency is somewhat lower. Fig. 7.8 shows the figure of merit for various combinations. The higher the Z value the better will be the thermoelectric material. Even with good design and placement of insulation only about 5–10 percent of the heat

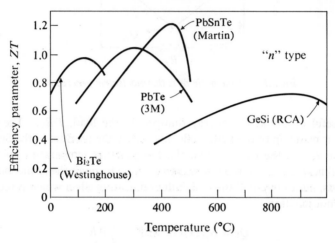

FIG. 7.8a *Figure of merit as a function of temperature for* n-*type materials.* [*From Schulman, F.,* Nucleonics, **21,** 9 (1953), *p. 56. Reprinted by permission.*]

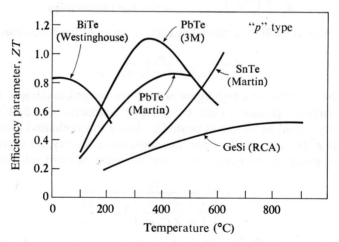

FIG. 7.8b *Figure of merit as a function of temperature for* p-*type materials.* [*Ibid. Reprinted by permission.*]

produced by the decaying elements can be converted into electricity. If the thermal conductivity of the converters is too high and too much heat is conducted to the cold junction not enough will be converted to electricity. On the other hand, if the electrical resistance is too high too much of the power converted appears as I^2R loss. Thus the importance of the figure of merit, Z.

Example 2. A thermoelectric generator is to be designed to operate between a high side temperature of 327°C and a sink temperature of 27°C. The n-type couples are to be made of 75 percent Bi_2Te_3 — 25 percent Bi_2Se_3, while the p-type material is to be 25 percent Bi_2Te_3 — 75 percent Bi_2Se_3 with 1.75 percent excess Se. The properties of these semiconductor materials at the average couple temperature are given as follows:

$$\text{Seebeck coefficient, } \alpha_{pn} = 430 \ \mu V/C$$
$$\text{Electric resistivity, } \rho_p = 0.00175 \text{ ohm cm}$$
$$\rho_n = 0.00135 \text{ ohm cm}$$
$$\text{Thermal conductivity, } k_p = 0.012 \text{ W cm}^{-1} \text{ C}^{-1}$$
$$k_n = 0.014 \text{ W cm}^{-1} \text{ C}^{-1}$$

The elements are to be 0.25 cm in length and the diameter of the n-type elements is to be 0.3 cm. The diameter of the p-type units should produce the minimum value of the RK product. The load is to match the generator so as to produce the optimum value of thermal efficiency. There are to be 20 couples in series electrically and in parallel thermally. Find the heat which would have to be supplied by an isotopic heat source, the watts of power provided to the load, and the thermal efficiency.

The diameter of the positive leg should be determined first.

$$\frac{A_p}{A_n} = \left(\frac{\rho_p k_n}{\rho_n k_p}\right)^{1/2} = \left(\frac{0.00175 \times 0.014}{0.00135 \times 0.012}\right)^{1/2} = 1.23$$
$$d_p^2 = 1.23 \ d_n^2 = 1.23 \times 0.3^2 = 0.1108$$
$$d_p = 0.333 \text{ cm}$$

The electrical resistance and the thermal conductance for the individual couples must be calculated.

$$R = \frac{\rho_p l_p}{A_p} + \frac{\rho_n l_n}{A_n} = \frac{0.00175 \times 0.25}{(\pi/4)(0.333)^2} + \frac{0.00135 \times 0.25}{(\pi/4)(0.30)^2}$$

$$= 0.00505 + 0.00479 = 0.00815 \text{ ohms/couple}$$

$$K = \frac{A_p k_p}{l_p} + \frac{A_n k_n}{l_n} = \frac{(\pi/4)(0.333)^2(0.012)}{0.25}$$

$$+ \frac{(\pi/4)(0.30)^2(0.104)}{0.25} = 0.0042 + 0.00395$$

$$= 0.00815 \text{ WC}^{-1}$$

The optimized figure of merit is

$$Z = \frac{\alpha_{pn}^2}{(\sqrt{\rho_p k_p} + \sqrt{\rho_n k_n})^2}$$

$$= \frac{(430 \times 10^{-6})^2}{(\sqrt{0.00175 \times 0.012} + \sqrt{0.00135 \times 0.014})^2}$$

$$= 0.00232$$

The load ratio which will result in the best efficiency is

$$\frac{R_L}{R} = \sqrt{1 + ZT_m} = \sqrt{1 + 0.00232 \times 450}$$

$$= 1.43$$

The load resistance is then

$$R_L = 1.43 \times 0.00982 = 0.0143 \text{ ohms/couple}$$

The current developed by the unit will be

$$I = \frac{\alpha_{pn} \Delta T}{R + R_L} = \frac{430 \times 10^{-6} \times 300}{0.00982 + 0.01403} = 5.41 \text{ amps}$$

The heat input required from an isotopic heat source is

$$Q_1 = \alpha_{pn} T_1 I + K \Delta T - \frac{1}{2} I^2 R$$

$$= (430 \times 10^{-6} \times 600 \times 5.41) + (0.00815 \times 300)$$

$$- \left(\frac{1}{2} \times 5.41^2 \times 0.00982 \right)$$

$$= 1.395 + 2.44 - 0.1435$$
$$= 3.69 \text{ W/couple}$$
$$73.8 \text{ W for the assembly of 20 couples}$$

The power generated by the thermoelectric unit is

$$W = I^2 R_L = (5.41)^2 \times 0.01403 = 0.411 \text{ W/couple}$$
$$8.22 \text{ W for the total unit}$$

The thermal efficiency is then

$$\eta_t = \frac{W}{Q_1} = \frac{8.22}{73.8} = 11.13\%$$

This could also have been calculated using Eq. 7.7.

$$\eta_t = \frac{\Delta T}{\dfrac{\sqrt{1 + ZT_m} + 1}{\sqrt{1 + ZT_m} - 1} \times T_m + \dfrac{1}{2} \Delta T}$$

$$= \frac{300}{(2.43/0.43)(450) + 300/2} = 11.13\%$$

There are other mechanical difficulties in the development of thermoelectric converters. For example, it is extremely difficult to bond the thermoelectric converters to the hot junction. The delicately doped semiconductors must be protected from any chemical reactions with their surroundings. Finally, the thermoelectric materials are very fragile.

THERMIONIC CONVERTERS

Thermionic converters offer the advantage of higher efficiency than thermoelectric converters, but require higher temperatures. Fig. 7.9 is a schematic sketch of an isotopic power generator utilizing thermionic conversion.

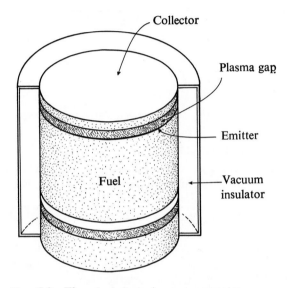

FIG. 7.9 *Thermionic isotopic power generator.*

Heat from the fuel boils out electrons from the emitter which are captured by the collector. The flow of electrons provide current flow through an external load. Ideally the efficiency can be made to approach Carnot cycle efficiency by adjusting the collector and emitter energy levels.

In practice the Carnot efficiency will not be reached because of inherent losses. Figure 7.10 shows these losses. The efficiency of this device can be expressed as:

$$\eta = \frac{J_n(V_1 - V_2 - \Delta V)}{J_1(V_1 + ZkT_1) - J_2(V_1 + ZkT_2) + \Sigma Q} \tag{7.9}$$

J_n represents the net current flow and ΔV accounts for electrical leakages. The Q terms in the denominator represent an increase in input energy to allow for thermal conduction and radiation in the gaseous plasma gap

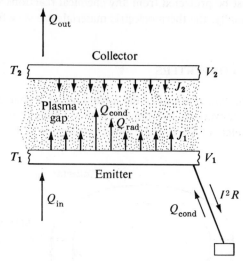

FIG. 7.10   *Schematic of a thermionic converter.*

and losses in the electrical leads connected to the electrodes.   The kinetic energy of the plasma gas electrons also contributes to a decrease in the efficiency.   Practical thermionic devices have attained efficiency of just over one-third their Carnot efficiencies.

High power and current densities require very high emitter temperatures to produce a satisfactory flow of electrons.   To work, the emitter and collector must have different work functions.   The electron that binds other electrons to the metal surface is measured by its work function.   Thus, the greater the work function the more electrons emitted. To provide useful current densities the work function of the emitter must be lowered.   In thermionic converters this is done by enclosing the emitter surface with cesium gas.   The presence of a partially ionized gas between electrodes produces electron scattering which reduces the passage of electrons across the space.   Some of the energy of the emitted electrons must be used to produce ions in the space.   These ions make up a large fraction of the current flow.   The collector while collecting electrons also collects contaminants present.   These contaminants may come from emitter and collector materials and possibly fuel clad.   Even small amounts of contaminants reduce collector absorption.   The effectiveness of the collector is affected by the plasma and it is necessary to optimize the conditions of the emitter and collector.   The high temperature emitter surface can be tungsten.   The plasma gap is about 0.02 cm wide. A difficulty in producing an isotope fueled thermionic power generator will be in insulating the high temperature emitter.   As much as one-half of the heat produced may escape the converter. Lower temperatures will, of course, reduce the output and efficiency. If the temperature becomes too high the electron kinetic energy will be converted to waste heat in the collector, raising its temperature.

ISOTOPE FUELS

The selection of a fuel for a radioisotope generator is of critical importance. Of special concern is safety. The fuel must not subject anyone to unnecessary exposure to radiation and it must be safe from possible nuclear reaction. Extensive tests have been made of all fuel capsule configurations to ensure that they are completely safe under all possible operating or accident conditions. Other equally important considerations are reliability, weight (for space applications), power density, and cost.

There are over 1300 possible radioisotopes from which to choose. However, a suitable isotope must have a long half-life, low gamma emission, power density of at least 0.1 watt/gram; it must be cheap to produce, easy to shield, and it must have desirable physical properties. These restrictions narrow the selection to nine practical isotope fuels. Four of these are beta emitting fission products which can be recovered in fuel reprocessing. Four are alpha emitters which must be produced in reactors and, consequently, are more expensive. The ninth, ^{60}Co, is available in plentiful supply but is a gamma emitter. Table 7.1 lists the nuclear and physical properties of available isotopic power sources.

So far the most successful fuel has been ^{90}Sr, but the only fuel used so far in space applications has been ^{238}Pu. Plutonium has been used because it is easily shielded, and there is no danger of nuclear reaction.

^{90}Sr is cheap and plentiful. There are millions of curies available in the AEC's waste facility in the state of Washington. It has a half-life of 27.7 years and has a fairly high power density; its disadvantage is its affinity for bone and consequent damage to blood production. Strontium titanate was chosen as the fuel form because $SrTiO_3$ is insoluble in water, resistant to shock, and has a high melting point. Furthermore, ^{90}Sr is a beta emitter and does not require extremely heavy shielding. Fig. 7.11 traces schematically the flow of ^{90}Sr from fission products to final fabrication into small cylindrical pellets. ^{90}Sr has found its most publicized use in the SNAP–7 series of power generators. The SNAP–7 series is used for navigational and weather station purposes. Presently ^{90}Sr produces more electric power than any other isotope.

Example 3. Calculate the theoretical initial power density of $SrTiO_3$. The composition of the Sr is 55 percent ^{90}Sr, 43.9 percent ^{88}Sr, 1.1 percent ^{86}Sr.

TABLE 7.1

PROPERTIES OF AVAILABLE RADIOISOTOPIC POWER SOURCES

	^{144}Ce	^{90}Sr	^{137}Cs	^{147}Pm	^{60}Co	^{242}Cm	^{244}Cm	^{210}Po	^{238}Pu
Compound	Ce_2O_3	$SrTiO_3$		Pm_2O_3		Cm_2O_3	Cm_2O_3	$GdPo$	PuO_2
Half-life	284.5d	27.7y	30y	2.67y	5.26y	162.5d	18.1y	138d	86y
Activity (curie/gm)	440**	33	16	742	360 max	3044	72.6	140	0.4
Specific Power (watt/gm)	2.84	0.223	0.0774	0.41	5.32	44.1	2.53	31.2	
Thermal Energy (curie/watt)	126	148	207	2440	65.1		29.2	590	
Melting Point (°C)	2680	1910		2350	1480	1950	1950		
Strength		fair	brittle	good	excellent				good
Stability	good in air	good	decreases above 1000°C	good	excellent in inert gas	fair	fair		good
Shielding*	3.5	1.0	3.6	little	5.7	neutron	neutron		neutron
Capsule compatability	reacts above 1400°C	excellent	excellent	excellent	excellent	neutron	neutron		

*Number of centimeters of uranium necessary to attenuate radiation to 10 rads/hr at 100 cm distance with 100 watts power.
** After one-year decay.

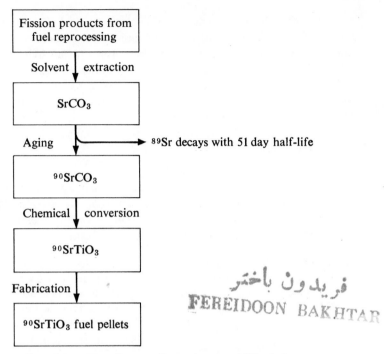

$$A_0 = \frac{0.693(6.023 \times 10^{23})}{27.7(8760)} = 1.72 \times 10^{18} \frac{\text{dis}}{\text{hr-atom } ^{90}\text{Sr}}$$

power density $= 1.72 \times 10^{18}$ dis/hr-atom ^{90}Sr [0.55 atom ^{90}Sr/
atom SrTiO$_3$][1 atom SrTiO$_3$/185 gm SrTiO$_3$]
[0.54 MeV/dis][4.44 $\times 10^{-17}$ watt-hr/MeV]

power density $= 0.1223$ watt/gm SrTiO$_3$ or 0.457 watt/gm ^{90}Sr

¹⁴CARBON DATING

Cosmic ray bombardment of the earth produces a constant supply of neutrons in the earth's atmosphere. The neutrons react with atmospheric nitrogen to produce ^{14}C, ^{3}H, and probably a small amount of ^{4}He with ^{11}Be. The ^{14}C and ^{3}H are radioactive, ^{14}C having a half-life of 5568 years. It is assumed that the radioactive carbon reacts with oxygen to form CO$_2$ and that the CO$_2$ mixes with atmospheric CO$_2$. It is possible, therefore, to say that absorption of cosmic ray neutrons is equivalent to production of radioactive carbon dioxide mixed with atmospheric carbon dioxide. Since plants and animals eventually live off carbon dioxide, they too will be radioactive.

Extensive theorizing and experimentation reveal that there is equilibrium between the rate of decay of radioactive carbon atoms and the rate of assimilation of radioactive carbon atoms for all living organisms. When the living organism dies, the assimilation stops and the radioactive ^{14}C in the tissue decays. The equilibrium value has been determined to be 15.3 disintegrations per minute per gram of carbon (see Reference 2). This value provides a method for determining the age since death of organic materials. The equation for the specific activity of ^{14}C in an organic material is

$$\text{Sp act} = 15.3 \, e^{-0.693t/5568} \tag{7.10}$$

where t is the number of years since death. When age is to be measured, the specimen must be very carefully sampled. It must contain only carbon atoms originally present at the time of death; chemical changes cannot have caused replacement of the carbon atoms.

Example 4. A charred log recovered from ruins being excavated in the central United States was found to have an activity of 0.510×10^{-3} microcuries. The sample weighed 525 grams after separation and processing. What is the approximate age of the civilization existing at the time the tree was cut? The specific activity of the tree log in dis/min-gm is

$$\text{Sp act } ^{14}C = \frac{0.510 \times 10^{-9} c (3.7 \times 10^{10} \, dps)(60s)}{525 gm \qquad c \qquad m}$$

$$2.16 \text{ dpm/gm}$$

$$\text{Sp act} = 15.3 \, e^{-0.693t/5568}$$
$$2.16 = 15.3 \, e^{-0.693t/5568}$$
$$t = 16,000 \text{ years}$$

Normally the ^{14}C dating method is used only to corroborate other archeological dating methods. It is difficult to separate ^{14}C specimens; since specimens are susceptible to many changes over the thousands of years following their death, ^{14}C dating in itself is not reliable.

FOOD PROCESSING

Radiation can be used to aid in the preservation of foods. Small doses can be used in pasteurization and large doses can be used to sterilize foods. Sterilization requires 2 to 4.5 million rads, while a dose of 200,000 to 500,000 rads is used to pasteurize. Both gamma radiation and electrons produced by accelerators are used.

In addition to retarding spoilage, small doses of radiation can tenderize vegetables and will inhibit maturing of vegetables and fruits, thereby increasing shelf life.

The major problem in radiation-processed foods has been a slight alteration of taste and color. As in all preservation or sterilization of foods, there will be some slight alterations. The problems of undesirable tastes can be partially eliminated by controlling the irradiation conditions. For example, irradiating meats at $-78°F$ virtually eliminates undesirable tastes.

The AEC and the FDA continue to make lengthy and exhaustive tests of radiation-processed foods to ensure wholesomeness and quality. No radiation-processed food may be offered for public consumption without the FDA's specific approval of both the food and its packaging. Packaging of preserved food is a considerable problem because the food must be packaged before it is processed. The radiation (particularly the doses used in sterilization) may be harmful to the packaging; there could possibly be some interaction between the food and packaging. The ordinary metal cans used in heat processing have been found most satisfactory for radiation-sterilized foods. Radiation pasteurizing does not present as great a packaging problem as does radiation sterilizing.

One of the earliest and most successful programs utilizing radiation processing has been in the fish industry. This program has been a cooperative venture between the AEC and private industry. It has been shown that irradiation can easily double the refrigerated shelf life of fish and shellfish. Increasing shelf life in this fashion will permit much wider distribution of fish and fish products. It is hoped that this wider distribution will make the process more attractive economically. The first instrument designed specifically for fish irradiation was the Marine Products Development Irradiator at Gloucester, Mass. The alternative to this is the more recently developed Experimental Marine Irradiator, Fig. 7.12. These irradiators are small and are capable of irradiating (100,000 rads) 150 pounds of fish per hour immediately after the catch. The irradiated fish are given a second dose on land after processing and packaging.

AGRICULTURE

Only about one percent of the energy that plants receive from the sun is used to manufacture food. The remaining 99 percent is wasted. Agriculturists are using radioisotopes to study photosynthesis. In one study CO_2 and H_2O were labeled with ^{15}O. The labeled compounds were supplied separately to plants. The result was that no ^{15}O was liberated when the plants were fed labeled CO_2, but ^{15}O was liberated when labeled H_2O was supplied. Thus, through a relatively simple test using radioisotopes, an important discovery concerning photosynthesis was made.

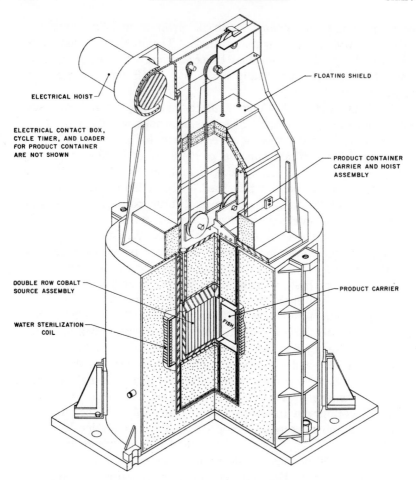

FIG. 7.12 *Experimental marine irradiator (EMI).* [*Courtesy of Nuclear Materials and Equipment Corporation.*]

Labeled fertilizers are also used successfully in agriculture. The labeled fertilizers proved conclusively that plants absorb fertilizer through leaves, bark, and roots. In fact, about 95 percent of fertilizer applied to leaves is absorbed while only about 10 percent applied to soil is absorbed.

Almost all food used by animals as well as by plants can be tagged with radioactive compounds to trace its utilization. For example, calcium and phosphorus have been labeled to show exactly how bone is formed and destroyed. Vitamin B_{12} has been tagged with ^{60}Co and fed to sheep and chickens. The results help show the effect of B_{12} and why it makes the chicken and sheep grow faster.

Radiation is also used to produce mutations in plants. Much of this work was done at Brookhaven National Laboratory. Plants are set out in circular rows in a one-acre plot. The source can be lowered into the ground to limit exposure and to permit personnel to harvest and examine the plants, vegetables, fruit, and shrubs. If a mutation is produced, cuttings or seeds are taken from it and planted in a normal environment for tests of hardiness and fruitfulness. Through this "gamma field" and other irradiating fields many spectacular developments have been made in a very short time.

Irradiation has been successfully used for insect control. Radiation-sterilized male insects are released into a controlled wild population. Mating by the sterilized males results in a decline in size of successive generations. Advantages of this procedure include avoidance of insecticides and increasing efficiency as population of the pest is reduced. In order to be successful, however, an economic method of raising large numbers of insects must be available, the insects must be easily dispersed, and the females must mate only once.

The screw-worm fly was irradicated from southeastern United States in about 18 months after the initial release of sterile screw-worm flies. At the height of the project about 50 million flies per week were raised, and a total of 2.5 billion sterile flies were released. The initial cost was about $10,000,000.

MEDICINE

In the medical profession the use of radioisotopes is focused into three categories: diagnosis, therapy, and research.

Physicians have used radium in therapy for many years, but it has always been very expensive. When radioisotopes became readily available ^{60}Co replaced radium as the chief source for therapeutical applications. It is estimated that the activity of $100 of ^{60}Co is equivalent to $20,000 of radium. ^{60}Co, however, is limited to external applications. In many instances it is desirable to have the isotope inside the body. Phosphorus 32 (a beta emitter) has been used to treat polycythema vera, a disease of the blood. A patient is fed ^{32}P which concentrates in bone marrow. The radioactive ^{32}P slows the production of red blood cells in the marrow, arresting the polycythema vera. ^{32}P is also being used to control rejection of transplanted organs. It helps destroy some of the blood factors that cause rejection.

As a treatment for cancer ^{198}Au has been physically implanted in the diseased cells. The gamma radiation destroys the cells and the gold eventually decays to negligible activity. An important side benefit is the fact that the radioactive gold inside the body can be used as a radiography source to accurately locate its position.

As important or more important than therapy uses are tracers. For example, a small quantity of NaCl containing ^{24}Na ($t_{1/2} = 15$ hr) is injected into the blood. By following the radioactive buildup with a geiger counter the circulation can be gaged. If there is a restriction to blood flow the activity may even drop sharply at the restriction, pinpointing its exact location. ^{99}Tc and ^{67}Ga have been used to detect certain kinds of brain tumors. The radioactive elements have a preference for certain kinds of tumors and are absorbed into them. By tracing this absorption externally the location and type of tumor can frequently be diagnosed.

^{252}Cf is being investigated as a treatment for cancer. ^{252}Cf is a high intensity neutron source. Therefore, it may be implanted to give a highly localized radiation dose to diseased tissue while healthy tissue is exposed to lesser radiation.

Of course, in medical research and diagnosis the isotope must be carefully chosen. Both its decay energy and its effective half-life must be minimal in order to prevent any harmful effects to the patient. Even so, the use of radioisotopes is limited only by the enthusiasm and ingenuity of the experimenter.

PROBLEMS

1. What phenomena must be taken into account for the interpretation of measurements made with tracers?

2. A transmission gage is to be used to control the thickness of coating on a certain paper. The source of radiation is ^{90}Sr. The paper is composed of material with density 1.0 gm/cm^3 and backscattering coefficient 0.224 cm^2/gm. The coating material has density of 1.38 gm/cm^3 and back-scattering coefficient of 0.235 cm^2/gm. What should be the reduction in intensity if the paper is 0.092 inch thick and the coating 0.019 inch thick?

3. In controlling the weight of sugar in a refining process a transmission gage is used. The gage is set to control the limits of flow between 0.70 and 0.75 of initial intensity. For a ^{137}Cs source what is the mass flow rate of sugar if the six-inch conveyor travels at a speed of 2.25 cm/sec? The sugar density is 0.308 gm/cm^3.

4. Carbon believed to be from a cremation was found in the northeastern United States. After separation and processing, 12 grams of carbon remained. The carbon had an activity of 94.3 counts per minute above background. What is the age of the cremation?

5. In the southwestern United States several corncobs were found in a cave. After processing, 5.54 grams of carbon with an activity of 66 counts per minute remained. The background was 1.7 cpm. How many years ago was the corn eaten?

6. Repeat Example 2, but make the load resistance equal to the resistance of the generator. Assume it is to work between the same temperature limits. Determine the required heat input, power output, and thermal efficiency of the unit.

7. The generator in the preceding problem is to be fueled with ^{210}Po. The source at the start of the mission is adequate to provide the necessary amount of heat. After 138 days what will be the heat supply temperature (T_1), the power output, and the generator efficiency? Assume that the sink temperature is maintained at 27°C.

8. What is the minimum ^{147}Pm that must be produced to have an initial power of 100 watts?

9. Theoretically, how many curies of ^{242}Cm would be required initially to fuel the generator of Problem 7? Assume all conditions the same except the fuel.

10. An engine piston weighing 1 kg was made radioactive by neutron activation. The resulting initial activity was 8.5 millicuries. After a few hours of running the lubricating oil was indicating a true count rate of 13,000 cts/min corrected for background. Estimate the piston wear that has taken place.

REFERENCES

1. Stone, E. W., et al., *Isotopes in Industry.* USAEC Report 3337–16.

2. Libby, W. F., *Radiocarbon Dating,* 2d ed. Chicago: University of Chicago Press, 1955.

3. *Isotopes and Radiation Technology.* USAEC Quarterly.

4. *Proceedings of the Third United Nations International Conference on the Peaceful Uses of Atomic Energy,* vol. XV (1964).

5. Angrist, S. *Direct Energy Conversion.* Boston: Allyn and Bacon, Inc., 1965.

6. Urbain, W. M., "Food Irradiation." *Nuclear News* **9,** 7 (September, 1966).

7. Wagner, H. M., "Radiopharmaceuticals—Their Use in Nuclear Medicine," *Nucleonics* **24,** 7 (July, 1966).

8. *Strontium-90 Fueled Thermoelectric Generator Power Source for Five Watt U. S. Coast Guard Light Buoy.* U. S. Dept. of Commerce Report MND–P–2720, 1962.

9. Bormat, M., et al., "SNAP–III Electricity from Radionuclides and Thermo-electric Conversion," *Nucleonics* **17,** 166 (May, 1959).

10. "Radionuclide Power for Space," Parts 1, 2, and 3. *Nucleonics* **21,** 3 (March, 1963), 4 (April, 1963), 9 (September, 1963).

11. *Shipboard ^{60}Co Radiopasteurizer.* BNL Report 808, USAEC, 1963.

12. Desrosier, N. W., *The Technology of Food Preservation.* Westport, Conn.: AVI Publishing Company, 1959.

13. Goldsmid, H. J., *Applications of Thermoelectricity.* Methuen Co. Ltd., 1960.

14. Chleck, D., R. Maehl, and O. Cucchiare, *Development of ^{85}Kr as a Universal Tracer.* USAEC Report NYO–2757 (February, 1966).

15. Coombe, R. A., *An Introduction to Radioactivity for Engineers.* New York: Macmillan Co., 1968.

16. Lewis, J., and Henley, E. J., ed., *Advances in Nuclear Science and Technology*, vol. 5. New York: Academic Press, 1969.

Chapter 8

Neutron Interactions

Fission neutrons are born with an average energy of 2 MeV. These fast neutrons interact with the core materials in absorption and scattering reactions. Collisions that result in scatter are useful in slowing neutrons to thermal energies. Thermal neutrons can be absorbed by fissionable nuclei to produce more fissions or can be absorbed in fertile material for conversion to fissionable fuel. Unfortunately, parasitic absorption by structural material, moderator, or coolant removes some neutrons without their having fulfilled any useful purpose.

CROSS SECTIONS

The cross section (σ) for a reaction is the probability that a particle (neutron) will interact with a nucleus. Loosely, this can be considered as the target area through which the particle must pass if an interaction is to occur. A square centimeter is tremendous in comparison to the effective area of a nucleus; hence, it is convenient to express cross sections in barns, where

$$1 \text{ barn} = 10^{-24} \text{ cm}^2$$

Nuclear folklore suggests that a physicist referred to a particularly large cross section as being "big as a barn door." The name has persisted.

NEUTRON INTERACTIONS

Scattering reactions are important because they allow the moderation or slowing down process to occur. When neutrons reach thermal energy levels they have much higher cross sections for fission. The mechanics of neutron energy loss during slowing down will be discussed later in this chapter.

Elastic scatter occurs when both the kinetic energy and momentum of the incoming and emergent particles are conserved. The neutrons may bounce off the struck nucleus, as when one billiard ball strikes another (potential scatter). They may also be absorbed into the nucleus and subsequently be expelled. This resonant scatter accounts for the resonance peaks in the elastic scattering cross section when it is plotted versus energy.

Inelastic scatter occurs when the nucleus is raised to an excited state and emits a gamma ray in addition to a neutron. Since light elements commonly have excited energy levels one MeV or more apart, the slowing down process is usually considered as taking place by elastic scatter only. With heavy nuclei the energy levels are only about 0.1 MeV apart and inelastic scatter is more prominent. Generally, only fast neutrons engage in inelastic scatter where, because of the energy of the gamma, the emergent particles have less kinetic energy and momentum than the incident particles.

Absorption processes may be of three types:

(1) Radiative capture (n, γ). The nucleus absorbs a neutron and the new isotope drops to ground state by the emission of a gamma. This type of reaction accounts for the relatively high absorption cross section of light hydrogen.

$$_1^1H + _0^1n \longrightarrow _1^2H^* \longrightarrow _1^2H + \gamma$$

For a reaction such as this we can use a shorthand notation having the incident and emergent particles within a bracket preceded by the target nucleus and followed by the recoil nucleus.

$$_1^1H \, (n, \gamma) \, _1^2H$$

Not all neutrons absorbed by fissionable nuclei produce fission. ^{235}U, for example, has a radiative capture cross section of 112 b at 0.025 eV.

(2) Capture with particle emission. The capture of a neutron may result in the compound nucleus decaying by the ejection of a charged particle. Examples of this are:

$$_4^7Be \, (n, p) \, _3^7Li$$
$$_7^{14}N \, (n, p) \, _6^{14}C$$
$$_5^{10}B \, (n, \alpha) \, _3^7Li$$

The last of the above reactions is important in neutron detection where a BF_3 counter measures thermal neutron flux. Uncharged neutrons produce little ionization in a counting chamber, but the alphas produced in boron trifluoride gas are highly ionizing. Each alpha emission indicates a neutron interaction within the counting chamber.

(3) Fission. The capture of a neutron by ^{233}U, ^{235}U, ^{239}Pu, or ^{241}Pu may result in splitting the heavy nucleus. As the fission fragments fly apart an average of between 2 and 3 neutrons are emitted. One of these must cause a subsequent fission if a steady state chain reaction is to take place. A detailed discussion of the fission process can be found in Chapter 4.

ATTENUATION OF A NEUTRON BEAM

Consider a collimated beam of neutrons impinging perpendicularly on a surface of area A, as shown in Fig. 8.1.

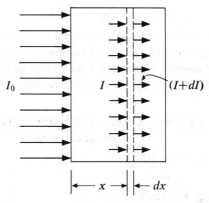

FIG. 8.1 *Collimated beam of neutrons impinging on material with cross-sectional area of A, cm². Note that, since neutrons are being removed, dI will be negative.*

A = surface area, cm²
x = distance from front face, cm
I_0 = initial beam intensity, n/cm² sec
I = intensity at distance x from front face, n/cm² sec
σ = microscopic cross section, cm²/nucleus
N = density of target atoms, nuclei/cm³
$NA\,dx$ = number of target atoms in the differential thickness, dx.
$\sigma NA\,dx$ = total effective area presented by nuclei to the neutrons, cm².

The ratio of the total effective area in the differential slab to the full area gives the probability of interaction in the distance dx.

$\sigma NA\,dx/A$ = probability of interaction (fraction of beam that undergoes an interaction), cm² effective area/cm² total area

The decrease in intensity, dI, as the neutrons pass through the differential slab, is the intensity at that point times the probability of interaction.

$$dI = -I\sigma N\,dx \qquad (8.1)$$

Separating variables,

$$\frac{dI}{I} = -\sigma N\,dx$$

Then, integrating for a thickness x

$$\int_{I_0}^{I} \frac{dI}{I} = -\sigma N \int_0^x dx$$

$$\ln\left(\frac{I}{I_0}\right) = -\sigma Nx$$

$$I = I_0 e^{-\sigma Nx} = I_0 e^{-\Sigma x} \qquad (8.2)$$

Where $\Sigma = \sigma N$ = macroscopic cross section, cm^2/cm^3. This represents the effective target area per unit volume of material.

The number density of the target atoms can be found by the product of the density multiplied by Avagadro's number divided by the mass number.

$$N = \frac{\rho \text{ gm/cm}^3 \times 6.023 \times 10^{23} \text{ atoms/gram atom}}{A \text{ gm/gram atom}}$$

$$N = \frac{6.023 \times 10^{23}\,\rho}{A} \qquad (8.3)$$

Differentiating Eq. (8.2),

$$\frac{dI}{dx} = -I_0 \Sigma e^{-\Sigma x} \qquad (8.4)$$

Thus, the rate of absorption decreases exponentially.

MEAN FREE PATH

The average distance travelled by a neutron before interaction is known as the mean free path, λ. From Eq. (8.4) it may be seen that the decrease in intensity while travelling a distance dx is due to the number of neutrons interacting and, hence, removed from the beam.

$$dI = -I_0 \Sigma e^{-\Sigma x}\,dx$$

These neutrons have travelled a distance x without interaction. The total distance travelled by all the neutrons as they interact in an infinite thickness of material is

$$- \int_{x=0}^{x=\infty} x \, dI = +I_0 \Sigma \int_0^\infty x e^{-\Sigma x} \, dx$$

This represents the summation for the infinite slab of the distance travelled by neutrons absorbed in each differential thickness. The mean free path is then this total interaction distance divided by the original beam intensity.

$$\lambda = \frac{+I_0 \Sigma \int_0^\infty x e^{-\Sigma x} \, dx}{I_0} = \Sigma \int_0^\infty x e^{-\Sigma x} \, dx = \frac{1}{\Sigma} \qquad (8.5)$$

Thus, the reciprocal of the macroscopic cross section (cm^2/cm^3) is the mean free path (cm). This same result is useful for considering neutron flux where the neutrons are not collimated but are travelling in random directions.

Since cross sections are probabilities of interaction, individual probabilities can be summed to give a total probability. The total cross section is the sum of the absorption and scatter cross sections

$$\sigma_T = \sigma_a + \sigma_s \qquad (8.6)$$

In turn, for a fissionable nucleus the absorption cross section is the sum of the fission and radiative capture cross sections.

$$\sigma_a = \sigma_f + \sigma_c \qquad (8.7a)$$

Similarly, the scattering cross section is made up of an elastic plus an inelastic value.

$$\sigma_s = \sigma_{se} + \sigma_{si} \qquad (8.7b)$$

Macroscopic cross sections can also be added:

$$\Sigma_T = \Sigma_f + \Sigma_c + \Sigma_s = \frac{1}{\lambda_f} + \frac{1}{\lambda_c} + \frac{1}{\lambda_s} = \frac{1}{\lambda_T} \qquad (8.8a)$$

Thus, the total mean free path is

$$\lambda_T = \frac{\lambda_f \lambda_s \lambda_c}{\lambda_c \lambda_s + \lambda_f \lambda_s + \lambda_f \lambda_c} \qquad (8.8b)$$

The relaxation length for a material is the thickness of material necessary to attenuate the neutron beam by a factor of e. Setting $x = \lambda$

$$I_\lambda = I_0 e^{-\Sigma \lambda} = I_0 e^{-1} = \frac{I_0}{e} \qquad (8.9)$$

Therefore, the mean free path is also the relaxation length.

Example 1. For a 95 percent Al — 5 percent Si (by weight) alloy determine the absorption, scatter, and total macroscopic cross sections for 2200 m/sec neutrons. What are the corresponding mean free paths? The density of the alloy is 2.66 gm/cm³.

$$N_{Al} = \frac{0.95 \times 2.66 \times 6.023 \times 10^{23}}{26.98} = 5.59 \times 10^{22} \text{ Al nuclei/cm}^3$$

$$N_{\text{Si}} = \frac{0.05 \times 2.66 \times 6.024 \times 10^{23}}{28.06} = 2.85 \times 10^{21} \text{ Si nuclei/cm}^3$$

$$\begin{aligned}
\Sigma_a &= N_{\text{Al}}\sigma_{a\text{Al}} + N_{\text{Si}}\sigma_{a\text{Si}} \\
&= 5.59 \times 10^{22} \times 0.23 \times 10^{-24} + 2.85 \times 10^{21} \times 0.16 \times 10^{-24} \\
&= 0.01283 + 0.000456 = 0.01329 \text{ cm}^2/\text{cm}^3
\end{aligned}$$

$$\begin{aligned}
\Sigma_s &= N_{\text{Al}}\sigma_{s\text{Al}} + N_{\text{Si}}\sigma_{s\text{Si}} \\
&= 5.59 \times 10^{22} \times 1.4 \times 10^{-24} + 2.85 \times 10^{21} \times 1.7 \times 10^{-24} \\
&= 0.0782 + 0.00485 = 0.0831 \text{ cm}^2/\text{cm}^3
\end{aligned}$$

$$\Sigma_t = \Sigma_a + \Sigma_s = 0.01329 + 0.0831 = 0.0964 \text{ cm}^2/\text{cm}^3$$

$$\lambda_a = \frac{1}{\Sigma_a} = \frac{1}{0.01329} = 75.3 \text{ cm}$$

$$\lambda_s = \frac{1}{\Sigma_s} = \frac{1}{0.0831} = 12.02 \text{ cm}$$

$$\lambda_t = \frac{1}{\Sigma_t} = \frac{1}{0.0964} = 10.37 \text{ cm}$$

Thus, it is seen that a 2200 m/sec neutron must travel an average of 75.3 cm to interact by absorption, 12.02 cm to interact by scatter, but only 10.37 cm to have an interaction by either scatter or absorption.

NEUTRON CROSS SECTIONS

High scattering cross sections are imperative for effective slowing of fast neutrons to thermal energy levels. (Values change only slowly with energy.) Both thermal and epithermal cross sections are listed in Appendix A, as well as 2200 meter/sec absorption cross sections. It can be seen that sometimes the epithermal cross section is larger than the thermal scattering cross section and sometimes it is the smaller of the two. For example, the thermal value of the scattering cross section for deuterium is 7 b, while the epithermal value is 3.4 b. In the case of copper, the values are 7.2 b thermal and 7.7 b epithermal. For most of the lighter elements scattering cross sections run 2 to 6 b, while the heaviest ones run up to 12 b. Light hydrogen is an exception. At low energies a single atom has a scattering cross section of 38 barns. In the epithermal region the value drops to 20 b. When in the bound state as light water composite values of 80 b thermal and 44 b epithermal can be used for each molecule. Figure 8.2 shows the total cross section for $_1^1\text{H}$ and $_6^{12}\text{C}$ as a function of energy. Since absorption cross sections are small for these isotopes, the total cross section is approximately equal to the scattering cross section.

Neutron absorption cross sections are highly energy dependent. In the thermal region they are usually inversely proportional to neutron velocity. When values in the thermal region are plotted versus energy on

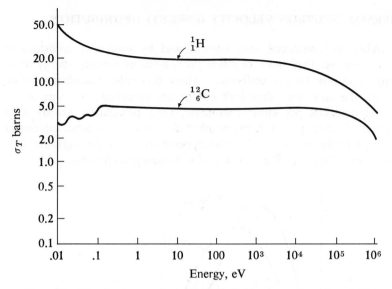

FIG. 8.2 *Total cross sections for light hydrogen and carbon. Since* $\sigma_a \ll \sigma_s$, $\sigma_s = \sigma_T$ *for these two isotopes.*

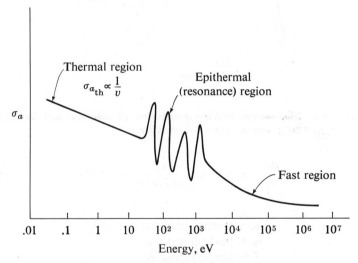

FIG. 8.3 *Typical curve of neutron absorption cross section versus energy.*

a log-log plot, the curve will have a slope of $-\frac{1}{2}$, as illustrated in Fig. 8.3. As energies increase, resonance peaks are apt to be prominent in the epithermal region. Many of these resonances are due to radiative capture. As energies continue to increase into the fast region, cross sections drop to low values of the order of 1 barn.

THERMAL NEUTRON VELOCITY (ENERGY) DISTRIBUTION

When fast neutrons have been slowed by successive collisions to thermal energy, they have as much probability of gaining energy as of losing it on any further collisions. These thermalized neutrons diffuse through the core until they leak out or are absorbed. If there are n_0 thermal neutrons per cubic centimeter, their population density as a function of velocity, $n(v)$, is the number of neutrons per cubic centimeter per unit velocity interval. The velocity (or energy) distribution is assumed to be Maxwellian (see Fig. 8.4) and it is expressed as follows:

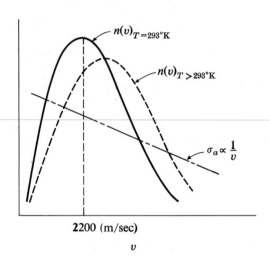

FIG. 8.4 *Maxwellian velocity distribution of neutrons and thermal absorption cross section (for a 1/v absorber).*

$$\frac{dn}{dv} = n(v) = n_0 \frac{4\pi v^2}{(2\pi kT/m)^{3/2}} e^{-mv^2/2kT} \tag{8.10}$$

where

$$n_0 = \text{thermal neutrons per cm}^3$$
$$m = \text{neutron rest mass}$$
$$T = \text{temperature, °K}$$
$$k = \text{Boltzmann constant}$$

Let

$$B = \frac{4\pi}{(2\pi kT/m)^{3/2}}$$

Then,

$$n(v) = n_0 B v^2 e^{-mv^2/2kT} \tag{8.11}$$

The most probable neutron velocity, v_p, is found by setting the derivative of $n(v)$ with respect to velocity equal to zero.

$$\frac{dn(v)}{dv} = 2n_0Bve^{-mv^2/2kT} + n_0Bv^2\left(\frac{-mv}{kT}\right)e^{-mv^2/2kT} = 0$$

$$v_p = \left(\frac{2kT}{m}\right)^{1/2} \tag{8.12}$$

The kinetic energy of neutrons at the most probable velocity is

$$KE_p = \frac{mv_p^2}{2} = \frac{m}{2}\frac{2kT}{m} = kT \tag{8.13}$$

This is not the average kinetic energy which has a value of $\frac{3}{2}kT$. Note that the kinetic energy is independent of the particle mass. For neutrons at 20°C

$$v_p = \left(\frac{2 \times 1.38 \times 10^{-16} \times 293}{1.66 \times 10^{-24}}\right)^{1/2} = 2.2 \times 10^5\frac{cm}{sec}$$

$$= (2200 \text{ m/sec})$$

At the most probable velocity the kinetic energy is

$$KE_p = 1.38 \times 10^{-16} \text{ erg/°K} \times 293°K \times \left(\frac{1}{1.6 \times 10^{-12}}\right) \text{ eV/erg}$$

$$= 0.025 \text{ eV}$$

It is at these conditions that neutron absorption cross sections are tabulated in Appendix A.

To find the average neutron velocity

$$\bar{v} = \frac{\int_0^\infty n(v)v\,dv}{\int_0^\infty n(v)\,dv} = \frac{\int_0^\infty \dfrac{4\pi n_0v^3e^{-mv^2/2kT}\,dv}{(2\pi kT/m)^{3/2}}}{n_0} \tag{8.14}$$

Let $y = v^2$; then, $dy = 2v\,dv$ and $v\,dv = dy/2$. Also, let $b = -m/2kT$.

$$\bar{v} = \frac{4\pi}{(2\pi kT/m)^{3/2}}\int_0^\infty ye^{by}\frac{dy}{2}$$

$$= \frac{2\pi}{(2\pi kT/m)^{3/2}} \cdot \left[\frac{e^{by}}{b^2}(by-1)\right]_0^\infty$$

$$= \sqrt{\frac{8kT}{\pi m}} \tag{8.15}$$

Therefore, the ratio of the average velocity to the most probable velocity is

$$\frac{\bar{v}}{v_p} = \frac{\sqrt{8kT/\pi m}}{\sqrt{2kT/m}} = \frac{2}{\sqrt{\pi}} = 1.128 \tag{8.16}$$

CORRECTED ABSORPTION CROSS SECTIONS

In the thermal region most materials have an absorption cross section that varies inversely with neutron velocity. Therefore, the absorption cross section will vary inversely as the square root of both the kinetic energy and the absolute temperature.

$$\sigma_a \propto \frac{1}{v} \propto \frac{1}{KE^{1/2}} \propto \frac{1}{T^{1/2}} \qquad (8.17)$$

$$\sigma_a' = \sigma_{a_{293}} \sqrt{\frac{293}{T}} \qquad (8.18)$$

Since the average neutron velocity is larger than the most probable neutron velocity by the factor of $2/\sqrt{\pi}$, the absorption cross sections at these velocities are in the inverse of this ratio. The cross section at the average neutron velocity at a temperature T is

$$\bar{\sigma}_a' = \sigma_{a_{293}} \left(\frac{\sqrt{\pi}}{2} \right) \sqrt{\frac{293}{T}} \qquad (8.19)$$

NEUTRON FLUX

At a given point in a reactor, neutrons will be travelling in all directions. The flux is defined as

$$\phi = \int n(v)v \, dv \qquad (8.20)$$

Dividing both sides of Eq. (8.20) by n_0, the total number of neutrons per cubic centimeter,

$$\frac{\phi}{n_0} = \frac{\int n(v)v \, dv}{\int n(v) \, dv} = \bar{v} \qquad (8.21)$$

This represents the average neutron speed.

Although flux is velocity (or energy) dependent, it is often convenient to treat thermal neutrons as a monoenergetic group travelling at the average neutron speed.

$$\phi_{th} = n_0 \bar{v} \qquad (8.22)$$

Thus, ϕ_{th} is equivalent to a flux of neutrons at a single speed and the velocity distribution can be ignored. Thus the flux can be considered as the sum of the distances travelled per second by the neutrons in one cubic centimeter of volume.

Dividing the distance travelled per second, ϕ, by the mean free path for interaction, λ, results in the interaction rate, R.

$$R = \frac{\phi}{\lambda} = \phi\Sigma = \phi N\sigma \qquad \text{interactions/sec cm}^3 \qquad (8.23)$$

NEUTRON ACTIVATION

When a material is placed in a neutron flux it will absorb neutrons in proportion to its cross section. The next heavier isotope will be formed, which may or may not be stable. This results in radioactivity of structural materials in a reactor core, permits the production of sources of radioactivity, and is useful where foils can be inserted at various points in a reactor core to infer the flux level from the resultant activity.

If a newly formed isotope is unstable, it will begin to decay at the same time it is being formed. If N is the number of nuclei of the new isotope, and N_0 is the number of original target nuclei, a differential equation may be written. The rate of change of new nuclei is equal to their rate of formation less their rate of decay. V is the volume of the irradiated sample.

$$\frac{dN}{dt} = \phi N_0\sigma_a - \lambda N = \phi V\Sigma_a - \lambda N \qquad (8.24)$$

Rearranging,

$$\frac{dN}{dt} + \lambda N = \phi V\Sigma_a$$

This is a first-order differential equation of the form

$$\frac{dy}{dx} + a(x)y = h(x)$$

An integrating factor $p = e^{\int a(x)dx}$ gives a solution of the form

$$y = \left(\frac{1}{p}\right) \int ph(x)\, dx - \frac{C}{p}$$

where C is a constant of integration. In this particular case $a(x) = \lambda$ (constant) and $h(x) = \phi\Sigma_a$ (constant).

$$p = e^{\int \lambda dt} = e^{\lambda t}$$

$$N = \frac{1}{e^{\lambda t}} \int e^{\lambda t}\, \phi V\Sigma_a\, dt - \frac{C}{e^{\lambda t}}$$

$$= \frac{\phi V\Sigma_a}{\lambda} - \frac{C}{e^{\lambda t}}$$

$$C = \frac{e^{\lambda t}\phi V\Sigma_a}{\lambda} - e^{\lambda t} N$$

Starting with an unirradiated sample when $t = 0$ and $N = 0$, the constant of integration can be evaluated:

$$C = \frac{e^0 \phi V \Sigma_a}{\lambda} - e^0 N = \frac{\phi V \Sigma_a}{\lambda}$$

$$N = \frac{\phi V \Sigma_a}{\lambda} (1 - e^{-\lambda t}) \tag{8.25}$$

Fig. 8.5 shows the buildup of radioactive nuclei during irradiation

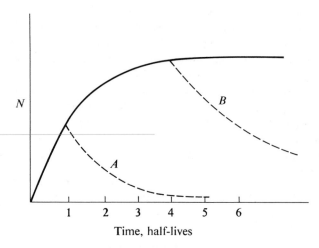

Time, half-lives

FIG. 8.5 *Buildup of radioactive nuclei during neutron irradiation. Curves A and B represent decay upon removal after 1 and 4 half-lives of irradiation.*

in a neutron flux. When the irradiated sample is removed from the core, it will decay with its characteristic half-life.

Example 2. A cobalt wire one foot long and one-sixteenth inch in diameter is left in a subcritical reactor core for two years. The flux is 10^6 n/cm² sec. What will be the activity (μc) of the wire on removal? What will be its activity after another two years out of the reactor core? The wire temperature during the irradiation is 100°C.

When ^{59}Co is irradiated by neutrons, the resultant ^{60}Co has two isomeric states, one with a 10.5 minute half-life and the other with a 5.24 year half-life. The cross section for producing the short-lived isomer is 18 barns and the cross section for the long-lived isomer is 37.0 barns. Note that in Appendix A the cross section for direct formation of ^{60}Co with the 5.24 year half-life is 19 barns. Since the 10.5 minute ^{60}Co promptly decays from its higher energy level to the 5.24 year level, the effective cross section is 37 barns.

The decay constants for the two isomers are

$$\lambda_1 = \frac{0.693 \times 60}{10.5} = 3.97 \text{ hr}^{-1}$$

$$\lambda_2 = \frac{0.693}{5.24 \times 365 \times 24} = 1.505 \times 10^{-5} \text{ hr}^{-1}$$

The volume of the cobalt wire is

$$V = 0.785 \times \left(\frac{1}{16}\right)^2 \times 12 \times 2.54^3 = 0.604 \text{ cm}^3$$

The number of target nuclei is

$$N_0 = \frac{V\rho N_{Av}}{A} = \frac{0.604 \times 8.71 \times 6.023 \times 10^{23}}{58.94}$$

$$= 0.541 \times 10^{23} \, {}^{*59}\text{Co nuclei}$$

The corrected cross sections are

$$\overline{\sigma_{a_1}} = 18 \times \frac{\sqrt{\pi}}{2} \sqrt{\frac{293}{373}} = 14.16 \, b$$

$$\overline{\sigma_{a_2}} = 37.0 \times \frac{\sqrt{\pi}}{2} \sqrt{\frac{293}{373}} = 29.1 \, b$$

Because the two-year irradiation period will saturate the short half-lived isomer, the second term in Eq. (8.25) will drop out in the expression for N_1.

$$N_1 = \frac{\overline{\sigma_{a_1}} N_0 \phi}{\lambda_1} = \frac{14.16 \times 10^{-24} \times 0.541 \times 10^{23} \times 10^6 \times 3600}{3.97}$$

$$= 6.94 \times 10^8 \, {}^{60}\text{Co nuclei with a 10.5 minute half-life}$$

For the 5.24 year ^{60}Co

$$N_2 = \frac{\overline{\sigma_{a_2}} N_0 \phi}{\lambda_2} (1 - e^{-\lambda_2 t})$$

$$= \frac{29.1 \times 10^{-24} \times 0.541 \times 10^{23} \times 10^6 \times 3600}{1.505 \times 10^{-5}} (1 - e^{-0.693 \times 2/5.24})$$

$$= 8.7 \times 10^{13} \, {}^{60}\text{Co nuclei with a 5.24 year half-life}$$

The activity on removal will be

$$A_0 = N_1\lambda_1 + N_2\lambda_2 = \frac{6.94 \times 10^8 \times 3.97}{3600 \times 3.7 \times 10^4} + \frac{8.7 \times 10^{13} \times 1.505 \times 10^{-5}}{3600 \times 3.7 \times 10^4}$$

$$= 20.7 + 9.84 = 30.5 \, \mu c$$

After an additional two years out of the core the short-lived activity will have disappeared and only that activity due to the longer half-life will remain.

$$A = A_0 e^{-\lambda_2 t} = 9.84 e^{-0.693 \times 2/5.24} = 7.54 \, \mu c$$

On irradiation for a short period, less than 0.1 half-life, say, the number of radioactive nuclei is so small that their decay may be ignored and

$$\frac{dN}{dt} = \phi V \sum_a \tag{8.26}$$

Integrating,

$$N = \phi V \sum_a \int_0^t dt = \phi V \sum_a t \tag{8.27}$$

NEUTRON ACTIVATION ANALYSIS

Activation analysis is a powerful tool for determining the elements present in an unknown sample. This particularly valuable technique can identify trace amounts of elements as small as a few parts per million, or, in some cases, parts per billion. Upon neutron irradiation of the unknown material, radioactive isotopes are formed. Examination of the energy spectrum of the radiation being emitted will identify the elements present. A multichannel analyzer with as many as several hundred channels can display on an oscilloscope the gamma spectrum being given off. The elements are identified by the energies at which photopeaks occur. Knowledge of such factors as the height of the photopeak, irradiation time, post irradiation time, and counter efficiency will allow the determination of the amount of each element present. It should be noted that neutron activation analysis is insensitive to the chemical form or state of the element being bombarded.

The uses of activation analysis are myriad. It has been used to determine trace level impurities in semiconductors such as germanium and silicon. It also can determine the dopant levels in finished semiconductor devices. It is useful in determining trace amounts of oxygen in steel, titanium, sodium, and beryllium. It can detect deleterious traces of catalyst residues in plastics. In agriculture it is useful for determining residual amounts of bromine on crops and in foodstuffs. Fig. 8.6 indicates how an oil slick can be identified by comparing the spectrogram of a known sample with the spectrograms of various unknown samples.

The results of activation analysis are being used successfully as evidence in court. In criminal investigations it can trace a sample of paint, grease, tire rubber, etc. to its manufacturer by the amounts of trace elements present. Gunpowder residues on the skin of a suspect can be identified in a reliable manner.

One particularly attractive use of activation analysis is in the introduction of minor amounts of several easily activated trace elements as coding to guard against counterfeiting of the protected product. This method of identification is being considered for products as diverse as drugs, foodstuffs, cement, alkali metals, and legal tender.

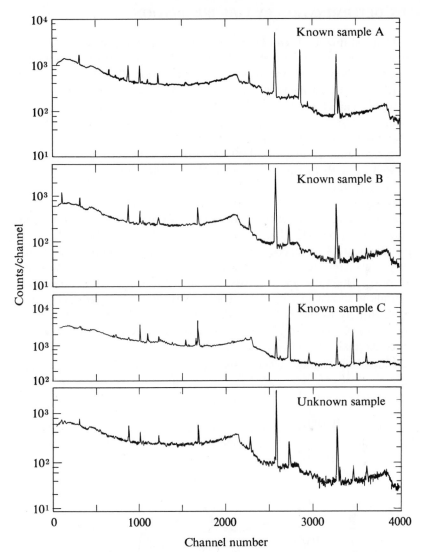

FIG. 8.6 *Oil slick identification. Trace elements can be identified from the peaks in each spectrum. The trace element fingerprint of the unknown sample closely matches that of Sample B.* [*From John, J., Lukens, H. R., and Schlesinger, H. L.,* Industrial Research **13**, 9 (*September, 1971*), *p. 50.*]

FLUX DETERMINATION BY FOIL IRRADIATION

Neutron flux levels can be inferred by inserting foils or wires of such metals as gold or copper into a neutron field. The gold, for example, has a fairly large neutron absorption cross section (98.8 barns at 2200 meters/sec). Upon neutron capture the ^{198}Au atoms formed will decay with their characteristic 2.7-day half-life. The initial count rate will be proportional to the flux at the point of irradiation, as shown by Eq. (8.25).

Indium foil is often used to determine flux levels. Because of a strong resonance absorption of 29,400 barns at 1.44 eV, the ^{115}In will be activated by both thermal neutrons and those neutrons absorbed in the resonance region.

A second foil can be covered with cadmium and irradiated in a similar position. A large resonance exists in cadmium at the upper end of the thermal region. The cross section then falls rapidly to about 10 barns at the 1.44 eV energy level. The cadmium covers are, therefore, nearly transparent to the epithermal neutrons and opaque to the thermal neutrons. The variation in cross section with energy for the two foil materials is shown in Fig. 8.7. The activity of the covered foil is due almost entirely to the epithermal neutrons. The difference between the bare and the Cd-covered foil readings indicates the activity due to absorption of thermal neutrons.

Fig. 8.8 shows data taken with a bare indium foil and a Cd-covered

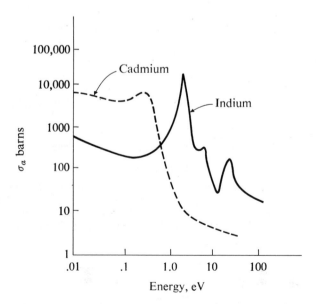

FIG. 8.7   *Cadmium and indium neutron absorption cross sections.*

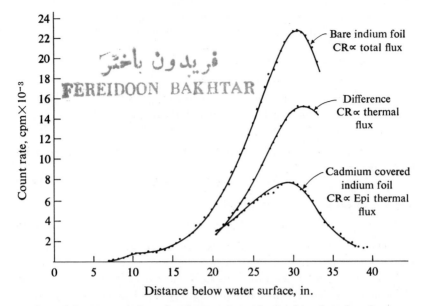

FIG. 8.8 *Vertical flux distribution from data taken 4 inches from source tube in a Nuclear Chicago Student Training Reactor, Model 9000. The foil-traversing technique uses bare and Cd-covered indium foils, a Nuclear Chicago D-47 Gas Flow Counter, and a Nuclear Chicago Actigraph (foil speed 1½ inch per minute, window width ½ inch).*

indium foil in a vertical direction, 4 inches from the central source tube of a light-water moderated, natural uranium fueled, subcritical assembly. The ratio of the count induced by the thermal neutrons is roughly twice that for the epithermal count rate. This ratio gives an indication as to the degree of thermalization of the flux.

POLONIUM PRODUCTION

The activation of a particular nuclide in itself may not be as useful as its daughter or granddaughter element. For example, ^{210}Po, an alpha emitter, is a popular isotopic heat source (see Prob. 3.6). It is the unstable daughter of the ^{210}Bi formed by activation of naturally available ^{209}Bi. In the conversion of ^{232}Th and ^{238}U to fissionable ^{233}U and ^{239}Pu the fissile isotopes are the granddaughters of the ^{233}Th and ^{239}U formed upon neutron activation.

The production of ^{210}Po will be used as an example of neutron activation for the production of an isotope other than the one originally activated in the target material.

$$_{83}^{209}\text{Bi} + {}_0^1n \rightarrow {}_{83}^{210}\text{Bi} \xrightarrow[5d]{\beta^-} {}_{84}^{210}\text{Po} \xrightarrow[138d]{\alpha} {}_{82}^{206}\text{Pb}$$

In the following derivations

N_1 = No. target nuclei (^{209}Bi)

N_2 = No. nuclei of activated isotope (^{210}Bi)

N_3 = No. nuclei of radioactive daughter (^{210}Po)

N_4 = No. nuclei of granddaughter (^{206}Pb)

The rate of change of activated ^{210}Bi nuclei is developed from Eq. (8.24) as

$$dN_2/dt = \phi N_1 \sigma_{a_1} - \lambda_2 N_2 \tag{8.28}$$

and Eq. (8.25) gives the number of ^{210}Bi nuclei as

$$N_2 = (\phi V \Sigma_{a_1}/\lambda_2)(1 - e^{-\lambda_2 t}) \tag{8.29}$$

The rate of change of ^{210}Po nuclei will be equal to its rate of formation due to ^{210}Bi activity less its own decay rate. Note that any removal of ^{210}Bi and ^{210}Po by neutron capture is ignored as having a probability $\phi \sigma_a$ much less than its probability of decay λ. This effect may not be ignored for ^{233}U and ^{239}Pu.

$$dN_3/dt = N_2 \lambda_2 - N_3 \lambda_3 \tag{8.30a}$$

Substituting Eq. (8.29)

$$dN_3/dt = \phi V \Sigma_{a_1}(1 - e^{-\lambda_2 t}) - N_3 \lambda_3 \tag{8.30b}$$

Rearranging

$$dN_3/dt + N_3 \lambda_3 = \phi V \Sigma_{a_1}(1 - e^{-\lambda_2 t}) \tag{8.30c}$$

This is again a first-order differential equation, which may be solved through the use of an integrating factor.

$$p = e^{\int \lambda_3 \, dt} = e^{\lambda_3 t} \tag{8.31}$$

The solution then becomes

$$N_3 = \frac{1}{e^{\lambda_3 t}} \int e^{\lambda_3 t} \phi V \Sigma_{a_1}(1 - e^{-\lambda_2 t}) - C/e^{\lambda_3 t}$$

$$N_3 = (\phi V \Sigma_{a_1}/e^{\lambda_3 t}) \int (e^{\lambda_3 t} - e^{(\lambda_3 - \lambda_2 t)}) \, dt - Ce^{-\lambda_3 t}$$

$$N_3 = \phi V \Sigma_{a_1} \left[\frac{1}{\lambda_3} - \frac{e^{-\lambda_2 t}}{(\lambda_3 - \lambda_2)} \right] - Ce^{-\lambda_3 t} \tag{8.32}$$

If unirradiated bismuth is placed in the neutron flux, the initial conditions are that when $t = 0$, then $N_3 = 0$. This allows the constant of integration to be evaluated.

$$0 = \phi V \Sigma_{a_1} \left[\frac{1}{\lambda_3} - \frac{1}{\lambda_3 - \lambda_2} \right] - C$$

$$C = \phi V \Sigma_{a_1} \lambda_2 / \lambda_3 (\lambda_2 - \lambda_3) \tag{8.33}$$

Substituting Eq. (8.33) back into Eq. (8.32)

$$N_3 = \frac{\phi V \sum a_i(\lambda_2(1 - e^{-\lambda_3 t}) - \lambda_3(1 - e^{-\lambda_2 t}))}{\lambda_3(\lambda_2 - \lambda_3)} \tag{8.34}$$

Fig. 8.9 shows the grams of polonium present per kg of bismuth

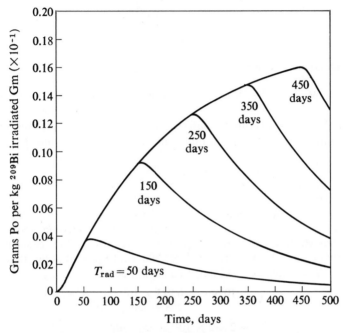

FIG. 8.9 *Polonium production by irradiation of ^{209}Bi for various times (T_{rad}) followed by removal from the reactor. During irradiation the thermal flux is 10^{14} n/cm^2 sec at a temperature of 200°C.*

irradiated as a function of time. The smooth upper curve shows the buildup of polonium during irradiation as decreed by Eq. (8.34). After various irradiation times the irradiated material is removed from the neutron flux and decay will occur. After the shorter irradiation periods (t_{rad}) the decay of activated ^{210}Bi will offset the ^{210}Po decay for a period of time and the polonium content will rise to a maximum before starting to fall. After longer irradiation, say 350 days, the decay rate of the polonium on removal is larger than its formation from the decay of activated bismuth. Thus, the amount of polonium will start to fall immediately on removal from the thermal neutron flux.

After removal from the flux the dual decay is described by Eq. (3.31), but the initial conditions differ from those of a freshly separated sample due to the fact that polonium is already present.

$$N_3 = \frac{\lambda_2}{\lambda_3 - \lambda_2} N_2' e^{-\lambda_2(t - t_{rad})} + C e^{-\lambda_3(t - t_{rad})} \qquad (8.35)$$

When $(t - t_{rad}) = 0$, $N_2' = $ No. ^{210}Bi atoms at time of removal, and $N_3' = $ No. ^{210}Po atoms at the time of removal.

$$N_3' = \frac{\lambda_2 N_2'}{\lambda_3 - \lambda_2} + C$$

$$C = N_3' - \frac{\lambda_2 N_2'}{\lambda_3 - \lambda_2} \qquad (8.36)$$

Thus, after removal

$$N_3 = \frac{\lambda_2}{\lambda_3 - \lambda_2} N_2' (e^{-\lambda_3(t - t_{rad})} - e^{-\lambda_2(t - t_{rad})}) + N_3' e^{-\lambda_3(t - t_{rad})} \qquad (8.37a)$$

If Eq. (8.37a) is differentiated and set equal to zero, the time at which a maximum amount of polonium is present can be determined.

$$(t - t_{rad})_{max} = \frac{ln \cdot \left[\dfrac{(\lambda_2 - \lambda_3)\lambda_3 N_3'}{\lambda_2^2 N_2'} + \dfrac{\lambda_3}{\lambda_2} \right]}{(\lambda_3 - \lambda_2)} \qquad (8.37b)$$

Example 3. If one kilogram of bismuth is irradiated for 100 days in a thermal flux of 10^{14} n/cm^2 sec at a temperature of 200°C, determine the weight of ^{210}Po which will be present on removal. How long after removal will the ^{210}Po peak? How many grams of ^{210}Po will be present at this time?

The number of ^{210}Bi target nuclei will be

$$N_1 = \frac{10^3 \text{ gm} \times 6.023 \times 10^{23} \text{ (atoms/gm at)}}{208.98 \text{ gm/gm at}}$$

$$= 2.882 \times 10^{24} \text{ atoms } ^{209}\text{Bi}$$

The macroscopic cross section for these atoms will be

$$V\Sigma_{a1} = N_1 \frac{\sqrt{\pi}}{2} \sqrt{\frac{293}{T}} \sigma_a^{209}$$

$$= 2.882 \times 10^{24} \times \frac{\sqrt{\pi}}{2} \times \sqrt{\frac{293}{473}} \times .015 \times 10^{-24}$$

$$= 0.03004 \text{ cm}^2$$

The decay constants for the 5-day ^{210}Bi and 138-day ^{210}Po are

$$\lambda_2 = 0.693/5.0 \times 24 \times 3600 = \frac{1.6041 \times 10^{-6} \text{ sec}^{-1}}{(0.1386 \ d^{-1})}$$

$$\lambda_3 = 0.693/138 \times 24 \times 3600 = \frac{0.581 \times 10^{-7} \text{ sec}^{-1}}{(0.00502 \ d^{-1})}$$

At the end of the 100-day irradiation of the original natural bismuth the number of polonium atoms present will be

$$N_3 = N_3' = (\phi V \sum a_1 / (\lambda_2 - \lambda_3)) \left[\frac{\lambda_2}{\lambda_3} (1 - e^{-\lambda_3 t}) - (1 - e^{-\lambda_2 t}) \right]$$

$$= \frac{10^{14} \, (\text{n/cm}^2 \text{ sec}) \times (.03004 \text{ cm}^2) \times 1 \text{ atom Po/n}}{(16.041 - 0.581) \times 10^{-7} \text{ sec}^{-1}}$$

$$\times ((16.041 \times 10^{-7}/0.581) \times 10^{-7})(1 - e^{-.502}) - (1 - e^{-13.86})$$

$$= 1.9194 \times 10^{19} \text{ atoms } {}^{210}\text{Po}$$

The corresponding mass of polonium produced in the 1 kg of bismuth will be

$$m_3 = \frac{1.9194 \times 10^{19} \text{ atoms Po} \times 210 \text{ gm } {}^{210}\text{Po/gm atom}}{6.023 \times 10^{23} \dfrac{\text{atoms } {}^{210}\text{Po}}{\text{gm atom}}}$$

$$= 0.0067 \text{ gm Po}$$

Before determining the time at which the maximum amount of polonium will be present, the number of ^{210}Bi atoms present at the end of irradiation must be determined. For the ^{210}Bi the 100-day irradiation period is 20 half-lives and, thus, saturation exists.

$$N_2 = N_2' = \phi V \sum a_1 / \lambda_2 = \frac{10^{14} \times 0.03004}{16.041 \times 10^{-7}}$$

$$= 1.8704 \times 10^{18} \text{ atoms}$$

The time after removal at which the maximum amount of Po will be present will be

$$(t - t_{rad})_{max} = \frac{\ln \left[\dfrac{(\lambda_2 - \lambda_3)\lambda_3 N_3'}{\lambda_2^2 N_2} + \dfrac{\lambda_3}{\lambda_2} \right]}{(\lambda_3 - \lambda_2)}$$

$$= \frac{\ln \left[\dfrac{(16.041 - 0.581) \times 0.581 \times 1.9194}{16.041^2 \times 0.18704} + \dfrac{0.581}{16.041} \right]}{(0.00502 - 0.1386)}$$

$$= 6.955 \text{ days}$$

When the irradiated material is held for approximately a week after irradiation the maximum number of polonium atoms will be present.

$$N_{3max} = \frac{\lambda_2 N_2'}{\lambda_2 - \lambda_3} \left(e^{-\lambda_3(t - t_{rad})max} - e^{-\lambda_2(t - t_{rad})max} \right) + N_3' e^{-\lambda_3(t - t_{rad})max}$$

$$N_{3max} = \frac{16.041 \times 10^{-7} \times 1.8074 \times 10^{18}}{(16.041 - 0.581)10^{-7}} \left(e^{-.00502 \times 6.955} - e^{-.1386 \times 6.955} \right)$$

$$+ 1.9194 \times e^{-.00502 \times 6.955}$$

$$= 2.044 \times 10^{19} \, {}^{210}\text{Po atoms}$$

$$m_{3max} = \frac{2.044 \times 10^{19} \times 210}{6.023 \times 10^{23}} = 0.007127 \text{ gm Po}$$

By waiting 6.955 days after removal before chemical processing there would be an increase of 6.8 percent in the polonium recovery. Again, it should be noted that an increase of this sort will occur only at the shorter irradiation periods where the decay rate of the bismuth exceeds that of the polonium.

TRITIUM ACTIVATION IN BORATED WATER

In pressurized water reactors the addition of boric acid acts as a chemical shim. That is, the boron acts as a poison which, as it is burned out, offsets the reduction in reactivity due to fuel burnup. Both thermal and fast neutron reactions are involved in the activation of significant amounts of tritium. The following reactions predominate:

(1) $^{10}B(n, 2\alpha)T$ which has a threshold of 1 MeV with a cross section increasing from 15 mb at 1 MeV and increasing to 75 mb at 5 MeV and remaining constant from 5 to 10 MeV. A cross section of 50 mb may be used for the fast flux ($E > 1$ MeV).

(2) $^{10}B(n, \alpha)^7Li(n, n\alpha)T$, a duplex reaction where the first reaction is a thermal neutron reaction and the second has a 3 MeV threshold whose cross section increases linearly from 0 at 3 MeV to 400 mb at 6 MeV and remains constant from 6 MeV to 10 MeV. The cross section for the $^7Li(n, n\alpha)T$ reaction can also be taken as approximately 50 mb for the fast flux ($E > 1$ MeV).

Fig. 8.10 shows the tritium production rate from boron shim in the coolant of a typical 1000 Mw(e) PWR. The accumulated tritium activity must be considered as contributing to the hazard of any leakage from the primary loop and one of the contributors to the seriousness of a loss of coolant accident.

The rate from the first reaction falls off as the chemical shim is reduced from an initial level of 1500 ppm to 400 ppm after 350 days of reactor full-power operation. In the duplex reaction the rate builds up as the ^7Li concentration builds up due to ^7Li activation by thermal neutrons.

SLOWING DOWN OF NEUTRONS

Neutrons slow from an average energy of 2 MeV at birth, as the result of fission, to 0.025 eV for 2200 meter per second thermal neutrons. This energy reduction is accomplished essentially by elastic scattering in which both kinetic energy and momentum are conserved. More energy is lost in scattering with light nuclei; therefore, materials of this sort (light water, heavy water, beryllia, graphite, etc.) make effective moderators.

For elastic scattering one must take measurements in the laboratory system where the observer is stationary, as opposed to the center of mass

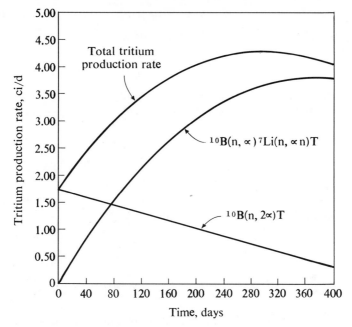

FIG. 8.10 *Estimated tritium production rate from boron shim in a 1000 Mw(e) PWR vs. time.*

system where the observer travels at the velocity of the compound nucleus. The rest mass of the neutron is 1 u and the struck nucleus has a rest mass of A u. Fig. 8.11 shows the scattering process in the lab system.

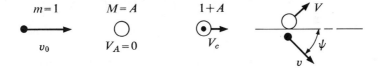

FIG. 8.11 *Lab system scatter.*

v_0 = original neutron velocity in lab system, cm/sec
$V_A = 0$ = velocity of struck nucleus in lab system
V_c = velocity of compound nucleus in lab system, cm/sec
V = velocity of scattered nucleus in lab system, cm/sec
v = velocity of scattered neutron in lab system, cm/sec
ψ = scattering angle in lab system of emergent neutron with respect to original direction of motion.

Since the struck nucleus has little or no velocity, the momentum of the compound nucleus is equal to the momentum of the incident neutron.

$$1 \times v_0 = (1 + A)V_c \tag{8.38}$$

Thus, the velocity of the compound nucleus is

$$V_c = \frac{v_0}{(1 + A)} \tag{8.39}$$

To examine the breakup of the compound nucleus it is convenient to transfer to the center of mass (COM) system. (See Fig. 8.12.) To do

$$v_{-1} = v_0 - V_c \qquad v_{-1} = V_c \qquad 0$$

FIG. 8.12   *Scatter in center of mass system.*

this, the observer must imagine that he is travelling at the speed and in the direction that the compound nucleus will have after the collision. This amounts to subtracting V_c from both the velocity of the incident neutron and the target nucleus. Note that in this system the compound nucleus will appear to hang stationary after the collision.

The velocity of the incoming neutron in COM system is

$$v_1 = v_0 - V_c = v_0 - \frac{v_0}{(1 + A)} = \frac{Av_0}{(1 + A)} \tag{8.40}$$

In the COM system the kinetic energy before the collision must equal the kinetic energy of the particles as they fly apart. The binding energy to form and break up the compound nucleus cancels and, therefore, only KE must be considered. The KE available for the compound nucleus is the sum of the KEs of the incoming neutron with a velocity $(v_0 - V_c)$ and the nucleus with a velocity $(-V_c)$.

$$KE_{COM} = \frac{1}{2}(v_0 - V_c)^2 + \frac{1}{2}A(-V_c)^2$$

Substituting from Eqs. (8.40) and (8.39)

$$KE_{COM} = \frac{1}{2}\left(\frac{A}{(1 + A)}\right)^2 v_0^2 + \frac{1}{2}A\left(\frac{v_0}{(1 + A)}\right)^2$$

$$= \frac{A}{(1 + A)} KE_0 \tag{8.41}$$

where KE_0 is the original KE of the neutron in the lab system.   The same result may be obtained in the lab system by subtracting the KE of the compound nucleus from that of the incident neutron.

Note that the KE_{COM} will be 235/236 that of the incident neutron, KE_0, when a ^{235}U nucleus is struck, while it is only $\frac{1}{2}KE_0$ when a light hydrogen nucleus is hit.   Thus, the difference between the lab and the center of mass systems is more pronounced for lighter elements.

Referring to Fig. 8.12, KE_{COM} is shared by the scattered particles which fly apart in opposite directions in the COM system.

V_2 = the velocity of the scattered nucleus in the COM system, cm/sec
v_2 = the velocity of the scattered neutron in the COM system, cm/sec
θ = the neutron scattering angle in the COM system

In the COM system the KE imparted to the compound nucleus is equal to that of the emergent particles.

$$\frac{A/(1+A)v_0^2}{2} = \frac{AV_2^2}{2} + \frac{v_2^2}{2} \tag{8.42}$$

The momentum of the compound nucleus is zero in the COM system and, thus, the momenta of the particles as they fly apart are equal and opposite.

$$1 \times v_2 + AV_2 = 0$$
$$v_2 = -AV_2 \tag{8.43}$$

When Eqs. (8.42) and (8.43) are combined

$$\frac{AV_2^2}{2} + \frac{A^2V_2^2}{2} = \frac{(A/(1+A))v_0^2}{2} = \frac{AV_2^2}{2A^2} + \frac{v_2^2}{2}$$

$$V_2 = \frac{v_0}{(1+A)} \tag{8.44}$$

$$v_2 = \frac{Av_0}{(1+A)} \tag{8.45}$$

It is useful to convert back to the lab system to compare the KE of the scattered neutron in this system with its original value, KE_0.   As shown in Fig. 8.13, this is accomplished by adding the velocity of the compound nucleus, V_c, to the COM velocity of the scattered neutron, v_2. By using the Pythagorean theorem

$$v^2 = (v_2 \sin \theta)^2 + (v_2 \cos \theta + V_c)^2 \tag{8.46}$$

Substituting from Eqs. (8.45) and (8.39)

$$v^2 = \left[\frac{A}{1+A} v_0 \sin \theta\right]^2 + \left[\frac{A}{1+A} v_0 \cos \theta + \frac{v_0}{1+A}\right]^2$$

which reduces to

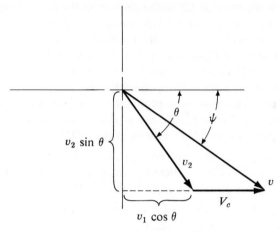

FIG. 8.13   *Conversion from* COM *to Lab system.*

$$v^2 = \frac{(A^2 + 2A \cos \theta + 1)v_0^2}{(1 + A)^2} \tag{8.47}$$

The ratio of the new neutron kinetic energy, KE, to its original value, KE_0, is

$$\frac{KE}{KE_0} = \frac{v^2/2}{v_0^2/2} = \frac{A^2 + 2A \cos \theta + 1}{(1 + A)^2} \tag{8.48}$$

Note that this energy ratio is maximum when $\theta = 0$.

$$\left(\frac{KE}{KE_0}\right)_{max} = \frac{A^2 + 2A + 1}{(1 + A)^2} = 1 \tag{8.49}$$

This indicates that with forward scatter the neutron energy is unchanged. The minimum value of the energy ratio occurs when $\theta = \pi$.

$$\alpha = \left(\frac{KE}{KE_0}\right)_{min} = \frac{A^2 - 2A + 1}{(1 + A)^2} = \frac{(A - 1)^2}{(A + 1)^2} \tag{8.50}$$

For hydrogen ($A = 1$) the value of α is

$$\alpha_H = \left(\frac{1 - 1}{1 + 1}\right)^2 = 0$$

This indicates that backscatter of a neutron by a hydrogen atom can cause the neutron to lose all its energy in a single collision.   For Be ($A = 9$)

$$\alpha_{Be} = \frac{(9 - 1)^2}{(9 + 1)^2} = 0.64$$

This relatively light moderator material can cause a neutron to lose a maximum of 36 percent of its energy in a single collision.   For ^{235}U ($A = 235$)

$$\alpha_{235} = \frac{(235 - 1)^2}{(235 + 1)^2} = 0.984$$

This heavy fuel atom can reduce a neutron's energy by a maximum of 1.6 percent on a single collision.

These few examples have illustrated the advantage of using light nuclei as moderating materials.

SCATTER IN THE *COM* SYSTEM

In the *COM* system the breakup of the compound nucleus is independent of its mode of formation. Neutrons scatter in a random or isotropic manner in *all* directions.

A number of neutrons, n, are considered to scatter in an isotropic manner about a point. The sphere shown in Fig. 8.14 is considered to

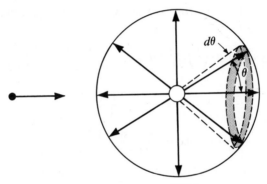

FIG. 8.14 *Isotropic scatter in* COM *system.*

have a unit radius.* The probability of scatter into the angle between θ and $\theta + d\theta$ is the ratio of the area of the elemental ring subtended by the differential angular element to the total area of the unit sphere, or it is the ratio of the solid angle subtended by the elemental ring to the total solid angle. It may be expressed as

$$\frac{2\pi \sin \theta \, d\theta}{4\pi} = \frac{\sin \theta \, d\theta}{2} \qquad (8.51a)$$

When the probability of scatter into the differential angle is multiplied by the total number of neutrons scattering, one has the differential number of neutrons scattering into the angle between θ and $\theta + d\theta$.

$$dn = \frac{1}{2} n \sin \theta \, d\theta \qquad (8.51b)$$

---

* Solid angle is defined as the area subtended by a particular surface on a unit sphere which has a total solid angle of 4π steradians.

LOGARITHMIC ENERGY DECREMENT

The energy loss of a neutron on collision is dependent on the scattering angle, as shown in Eq. (8.48). If one defines the logarithmic energy decrement, ξ, as the average change in the logarithm of neutron energy per collision, the result will turn out to be independent of energy level.

$$\xi = \overline{\ln E_0 - \ln E} = \overline{-\ln (E/E_0)} \tag{8.52}$$

The product of the number of neutrons scattering into the angle between θ and $\theta + d\theta$ is multiplied by the log decrement at the angle θ.

$$-\ln\left(\frac{E}{E_0}\right) dn = \frac{n}{2} \sin \theta \, d\theta \cdot \left[-\ln \frac{A^2 + 2A \cos \theta + 1}{(1 + A)^2}\right] \tag{8.53}$$

Eq. (8.53) is then integrated between 0 and π to give the sum of the log decrements of all n neutrons. Therefore, the average value can be found by dividing by n.

$$\xi = -\ln (\overline{E/E_0}) = \left(\frac{1}{n}\right) \int_0^\pi -\ln\left(\frac{A^2 + 2A \cos \theta + 1}{(1 + A)^2}\right)\left(\frac{n}{2}\right) \sin \theta \, d\theta \tag{8.54}$$

Let

$$x = \frac{A^2 + 2A \cos \theta + 1}{(1 + A)^2}$$

$$dx = \frac{-2A \sin \theta \, d\theta}{(1 + A)^2}$$

The limits for the integration must be changed to the proper values of x. When

$$\theta = 0, \quad x = 1$$
$$\theta = \pi, \quad x = \alpha$$

Therefore,

$$\xi = \int_1^\alpha \frac{\ln x}{2} \cdot \frac{(A + 1)^2}{2A} \, dx = \frac{(A + 1)^2}{4A} \int_1^x \ln x \, dx$$

Note that

$$\frac{(A + 1)^2}{4A} = \frac{(A + 1)^2}{(A + 1)^2 - (A - 1)^2} = \frac{1}{1 - [(A - 1)^2/(A + 1)^2]} = \frac{1}{1 - \alpha}$$

So that

$$\xi = \frac{1}{1 - \alpha} \int_1^\alpha \ln x \, dx = \frac{1}{1 - \alpha} [x \ln x - x]_1^\alpha$$

$$1 + \frac{\alpha}{1 - \alpha} \ln \alpha \tag{8.55}$$

or combining with Eq. (8.50)

$$\xi = 1 + \frac{(A-1)^2}{2A} \ln\left(\frac{A-1}{A+1}\right) \tag{8.56}$$

Thus the average loss in the log of the energy per collision is a function of the mass of the struck nucleus and is independent of energy level. Equation (8.56) can be approximated rather closely by

$$\xi = \frac{2}{A + 2/3} \tag{8.57}$$

For $A = 2$ Eq. (8.57) is in error by only 3.3 percent. The accuracy improves with larger values of A, as shown by Fig. 8.15.

Let $E_0, E_1, E_2, \ldots, E_n$ represent average neutron energies after each of n collisions during the slowing down process from some original energy, E_0, to reach some lower energy, E_n.

$$\ln \frac{E_0}{E_n} = \ln \left(\frac{E_0}{E_1} \cdot \frac{E_1}{E_2} \cdot \frac{E_2}{E_3}, \ldots, \frac{E_{n-1}}{E_n}\right)$$

$$= \ln \left(\frac{E_0}{E_1}\right)^n = n \ln \frac{E_0}{E_1}$$

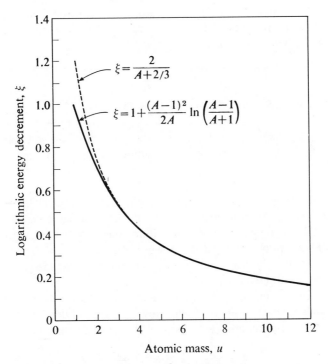

FIG. 8.15 *Comparison of exact and approximate values for logarithmic energy decrement.*

If E_n represents the average thermal neutron energy, the number of collisions to thermalize is

$$n = \frac{\ln (E_0/E_n)}{\xi} \qquad (8.58)$$

Example 3. Compute the number of collisions in beryllium required to reduce 2.0 MeV neutrons to 0.025 eV

$$\xi = \frac{2}{A + 2/3} = \frac{2}{9 + 2/3} = 0.207$$

$$n = \frac{\ln (E_0/E_n)}{\xi} = \frac{\ln (2.0 \times 10^6/0.025)}{0.207} = 86 \text{ collisions}$$

Note that for fast neutrons energy loss will occur on subsequent collisions until thermal energies are reached. Further collisions are as apt to have a gain in energy as a loss in energy. The larger ξ, the smaller the number of collisions to thermalize and, hence, the more effective is the material as a moderator. However, the log energy decrement (or the number of collisions to thermalize) does not completely describe the excellence of a material as a moderator. As neutrons interact with moderator nuclei there must be a high probability for scatter and a low probability of being absorbed.

MACROSCOPIC SLOWING DOWN POWER

Macroscopic slowing down power is the product of the log decrement times the macroscopic scattering cross section for epithermal neutrons.

$$\text{MSDP} = \xi\Sigma_s \qquad (8.59)$$

This indicates how rapidly slowing down will occur in material. It represents the slowing down power of all the nuclei in a cubic centimeter of material. For a light gas, such as helium, there would be a good log decrement but a poor slowing down power because of the small probability of scatter. Not only is σ_s small, but the atom density of the gas is much too low to be attractive.

For a compound or a mixture the log decrement can be found as the sum of the macroscopic slowing down powers divided by the total macroscopic scattering cross section of all the constituents.

$$\xi = \frac{\xi_1\Sigma_{s1} + \xi_2\Sigma_{s2} + \xi_3\Sigma_{s3}}{\Sigma_{s1} + \Sigma_{s2} + \Sigma_{s3}} \qquad (8.60)$$

MODERATING RATIO

The macroscopic slowing down power still does not tell the complete story about the effectiveness of a moderator. An element such as boron has a high log decrement and a good slowing down power, but it is a poor moderator because of its high probability of absorbing neutrons. This can be accounted for by dividing the macroscopic slowing down power by the macroscopic absorption cross section. This is called the *moderating ratio*.

$$MR = \frac{\xi \Sigma_s}{\Sigma_a} \qquad (8.61)$$

For a single element this reduces to

$$MR_1 = \frac{\xi \sigma_s}{\sigma_a} \qquad (8.62)$$

and for a two component mixture or a compound of two elements it is

$$MR_2 = \frac{\xi_1 \Sigma_{s1} + \xi_2 \Sigma_{s2}}{\Sigma_{a1} + \Sigma_{a2}} \qquad (8.63)$$

A good moderator, then, has a high moderating ratio and a large macroscopic slowing down power.

Table 8.1 indicates the relative merits of several materials as mod-

TABLE 8.1

COMPARISON OF THE MODERATING CHARACTERISTICS OF MATERIALS

Material	ξ	No. Collisions to Thermalize	MSDP	Moderating Ratio
H_2O	0.927	19	1.425	62
D_2O	0.510	35	0.177	4830
He	0.427	42	*8.87×10^{-6}	51
Be	0.207	86	0.724	126
B	0.171	105	0.092	0.00086
C	0.158	114	0.083	216

* 1 atm and 20°C.

erators. Light water has a high log decrement and a good macroscopic slowing down power, but because of a 0.332 b cross section for absorption it has the lowest moderating ratio of any of the commonly used moderators. Its availability and low cost justify its use, even though the use of enriched fuel is required to achieve criticality in a reactor core.

The vastly superior moderating ratio of heavy water is offset by its extremely high cost.   Beryllium and carbon (graphite) have similar moderating ratios.   The difficulty of fabrication of beryllium, its cost, and its toxicity are not conducive to its common use.   Graphite has been commonly used as a moderator because of its availability in quantities, its low cost, and ease of fabrication.

Helium is ruled out on the basis of its low density which results in an extremely poor MSDP.   Boron is also a poor moderator, but in this case it is because of the high cross section for absorption.   It does find use, however, as a neutron absorber in control rods.

AVERAGE VALUE OF THE COSINE
OF THE SCATTERING ANGLE

Figure 8.16 shows that when the velocity of the compound nucleus is added to the velocity of scattered monoenergetic neutrons in the *COM*

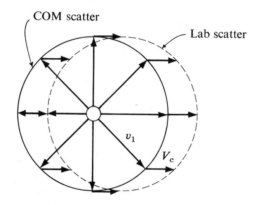

Fig. 8.16 *Isotropic scatter in* COM *system and an isotropic scatter in the Lab system.*

system, the scatter in the lab system is anisotropic.   There is preferential forward scatter.

The average value of the cosine of the scattering angle in the *COM* system is found by multiplying the number of neutrons scattering into the angle between θ and $\theta + d\theta$ by $\cos \theta$.   When this product is integrated from 0 to π and divided by the number of scattered neutrons, the average value of $\cos \theta$ results.

$$\overline{\cos \theta} = \frac{1}{n} \int_0^\pi \cos \theta \frac{n}{2} \sin \theta \, d\theta = \frac{1}{4} \int_0^\pi \sin 2\theta \, d\theta$$

$$= \frac{1}{8} \cos 2\theta \bigg]_0^\pi = 0 \qquad (8.64)$$

For this value of the cosine theta is 90°, which indicates that just as many neutrons scatter forward as scatter backward. The scatter is isotropic.

This will not be so in the lab system. Fig. 8.13 shows how the cosine of the scattering angle in the lab system can be expressed in terms of the *COM* scattering angle, θ.

$$\cos \psi = \frac{v_1 \cos \theta + V_c}{\sqrt{(v_1 \cos \theta + V_c)^2 + (v_1 \sin \theta)^2}}$$

$$= \frac{\dfrac{Av_0}{A+1} \cos \theta + \dfrac{v_0}{A+1}}{\sqrt{\left(\dfrac{Av_0}{A+1}\cos \theta + \dfrac{v_0}{A+1}\right)^2 + \left(\dfrac{Av_0 \sin \theta}{A+1}\right)^2}}$$

$$= \frac{A \cos \theta + 1}{\sqrt{A^2 + 2A \cos \theta + 1}} \qquad (8.65)$$

The average value of the scattering angle in the lab system can now be determined

$$\overline{\cos \psi} = \frac{1}{n} \int_0^\pi \cos \psi \, \frac{n}{2} \sin \theta \, d\theta$$

$$= \int_0^\pi \frac{A \cos \theta + 1}{\sqrt{A^2 + 2A \cos \theta + 1}} \frac{\sin \theta}{2} \, d\theta = \frac{2}{3A} \qquad (8.66)$$

For graphite

$$\overline{\cos \psi} = \frac{2}{3 \times 12} = 0.056 \qquad (\psi = 87.2°)$$

which indicates nearly isotropic scatter in the lab system.

For hydrogen

$$\overline{\cos \psi} = \frac{2}{3} \qquad (\psi = 41.8°)$$

which indicates quite strong forward scatter.

TRANSPORT MEAN FREE PATH

The *transport mean free path* is a scattering mean free path that has been corrected for the somewhat greater distance travelled in the lab system due to the preferential forward scatter. It can be determined by dividing the scattering mean free path by 1, minus the average value of cos ψ. Its reciprocal is the macroscopic transport cross section.

$$\lambda_{tr} = \frac{\lambda_s}{1 - \overline{\cos \psi}} = \frac{1}{\Sigma_s(1 - \overline{\cos \psi})} = \frac{1}{\Sigma_{tr}} \qquad (8.67)$$

Example 5. Compute the transport mean free path for thermal neutrons in beryllia.

$$\rho_{Be0} = 2.70 \text{ gr/cm}^3$$

$$N_{Be} = N_0 = \frac{\rho \times 6.023 \times 10^{23}}{A}$$

$$= \frac{2.7 \times 6.023 \times 10^{23}}{25.01} = 6.51 \times 10^{22} \text{ atoms/cm}^2$$

$$\overline{\cos \psi}_{Be} = \frac{2}{9 \times 3} = 0.0741$$

$$\overline{\cos \psi}_0 = \frac{2}{16 \times 3} = 0.0417$$

$$\lambda_{tr} = \frac{1}{N_{Be}\sigma_{sBe}(1 - \overline{\cos \psi}_{Be}) + N_0\sigma_{s0}(1 - \overline{\cos \psi}_0)}$$

$$= \frac{1}{6.51 \times 10^{22} \times 7 \times 10^{-24}(1 - 0.0741)}$$

$$\frac{1}{+ 6.51 \times 10^{22} \times 4.2 \times 10^{-24}(1 - 0.0417)}$$

$$= \frac{1}{0.422 + 0.262} = 1.46 \text{ cm}$$

PROBLEMS

1. A collimated beam of 2200 m/sec neutrons has an intensity of 100,000 neutrons/cm² sec. What would be its intensity after passing through a sheet of 0.10 inch thick boral? Boral has a density of 2.56 gr/cm³ and its composition is 50 percent Al, 40 percent B, and 10 percent C by weight.

   What would be the beam intensity after passing through a sheet of pure aluminum of the same thickness?

2. If $n(E) = dn/dE$, show that by starting with Eq. (8.10)

$$n(E) = \frac{2\pi n_0 E^{1/2}}{(\pi kT)^{3/2}} e^{-E/kT}$$

   and that the most probable kinetic energy is $kT/2$.

3. If the temperature in a reactor core is 500°C, what will be the most probable thermal neutron velocity? What will be the average thermal neutron velocity? What will be the most probable kinetic energy?

4. At 500°C, 3 percent enriched UO₂ has a density of 10.5 gr/cm³. Compute the following:
   (a) the macroscopic fission cross section,
   (b) the absorption mean free path,

(c) the mean free path for the interaction of thermal neutrons by either scatter or absorption.

5. Three gold foils are irradiated in a thermal flux of 10^{10} neutrons/cm² sec. The foil is 1 inch in diameter and 0.010 inch thick. The temperature during irradiation is 100°F.

(a) How many curies will each foil emit upon removal after irradiation for periods of 2 hours, 2 days, and 2 months respectively?

(b) What will be the activity of the foil which was irradiated for 2 days at the end of the 24-hour period following removal?

6. An iron Charpy specimen $\frac{3}{8}$ inch by $\frac{3}{8}$ inch by $2\frac{1}{4}$ inch is irradiated in a thermal flux of 10^{12} neutrons/cm² sec for 30 days at 100°C. The resultant activity is due to the 0.31 percent ^{58}Fe atom which is present. The ^{59}Fe which is produced has a 45-day half-life. Determine:

(a) the number of curies emitted by the specimen upon removal, and

(b) the activity 60 days after removal.

7. A copper foil weighing 0.10 gram is irradiated in a thermal neutron flux of 10^{14} n/cm² sec for a period of 5.1 minutes. The average neutron velocity is 2200 m/sec. Compute the activity 25.5 minutes after removal.

8. One kg of thorium is irradiated for 1 year in a thermal flux of 10^{14} n/cm² sec at a temperature of 650°C. Note the short half-life of ^{233}Th (22.1 min.) allows us to ignore the ^{233}Th and assume that neutron absorption by ^{232}Th leads directly to ^{233}Pa. Also for the ^{233}U its long half-life (1.62×10^5 yrs.) means that its probability of decay is much smaller than its probability of removal by neutron absorption. Hence, $\phi\sigma_a^U$ replaces λ_U.

How many grams of ^{233}Pa and ^{233}U will be present at the end of the irradiation period? By what percent will the uranium yield increase if the Pa is allowed to decay before separation?

9. A 1000 MWe pressurized water reactor (PWR) is to have a boron shim which decreases from 1500 ppm to 400 ppm over a 350 day period. Tritium is produced due to the ^{10}B(n, 2 α)T and ^{10}B(n, α)^{7}Li(n, αn)T reactions. The fast flux ($E > 1$ MeV) is 6×10^{13} n/cm² sec and the cross section for the fast reactions can be taken as 50 mb for the ^{10}B(n, 2α)T and 75 mb for the ^{7}Li(n, αn)T reactions. The ^{10}B(n, α)^{7}Li reaction occurs due to thermal neutron absorption in a thermal flux of 4×10^{13} n/cm² sec. The water is at an average temperature of 550°F and a pressure of 2000 psia. It has a volume of 650 ft³. Leakage fraction $= 0.0012$d⁻¹.

Estimate the rate of tritium production (ci/day) when the reactor has been on line for 200 days at the given power (flux) level.

10. For a Be moderator at 800°F determine:

(a) the number of collisions to thermalize,

(b) macroscopic slowing down power,

(c) moderating ratio, and

(d) transport mean free path.

11. 2 MeV neutrons are being thermalized in beryllia at 1000°F. Compute the following:

(a) the log decrement,

(b) the macroscopic slowing down power,

(c) the number of collisions to thermalize,

(d) the moderating ratio, and

(e) for elastic scattering with a Be atom, the value of α and also E/E_0 when $\theta = 90°$.

12. Show that $\overline{\cos \psi} = \displaystyle\int_0^{\pi} \cos \psi \sin \theta \, d\theta/2 = 2/3A$.

REFERENCES

1. Glasstone, S., and M. C. Edlund, *The Elements of Nuclear Reactor Theory.* Princeton, N. J.: D. Van Nostrand Co., 1952.

2. Glasstone, S., and A. Sesonske, *Nuclear Reactor Engineering.* Princeton, N. J.: D. Van Nostrand Co., 1963.

3. Murray, R. L., *Introduction to Nuclear Engineering.* Englewood Cliffs, N. J.: Prentice-Hall, Inc., 1961.

4. El-Wakil, M. M., *Nuclear Power Engineering.* New York: McGraw-Hill Book Co., Inc., 1962.

5. Lamarsh, J. R., *Introduction to Nuclear Reactor Theory.* Reading, Mass.: Addison-Wesley Publishing Co., Inc., 1966.

6. King, C. D. G., *Nuclear Power Systems.* New York: Macmillan Co., 1964.

7. Guinn, V. P., "Activation Analysis," *Industrial Research* (October, 1964) pp. 30–36.

8. *Reactor Physics Constants*, 2d ed., ANL 5800, July, 1962.

9. John, J., Lukens, H. R., Schlesinger, H. L., "Trace Analysis—the Nuclear Way," *Industrial Research* **13**, no. 9 (September, 1971), pp. 49–51.

10. Ray, J. W., "Tritium in Power Reactors," *Reactor and Fuel-Reprocessing Technology*, **12**, no. 1 (winter 1968–1969), pp. 19–26.

11. Briggs, R. B., "Tritium in Molten Salt Reactors," *Reactor Technology*, **14**, no. 4 (winter 1971–1972) pp. 335–342.

Chapter 9

The Steady State
Reactor Core

In a thermal reactor core fast neutrons are born of fission. They slow to thermal energies by collisions with moderator nuclei. Some are then absorbed by fissionable nuclei with the subsequent fissions producing a new generation of neutrons. The ratio of neutrons in the new generation to the number in the previous generation is called the *multiplication factor*. In a core of finite size there is a probability of neutron leakage and a probability that absorption will occur before leakage. The sum of these probabilities is unity; the neutrons either leak out or they don't leak out.

INFINITE MULTIPLICATION FACTOR

In a core of infinite extent there can be no leakage. For such a core the infinite multiplication factor, k_∞, is the ratio of the number of neutrons, n', in the current generation to the number in the previous generation, n.

$$k_\infty = \frac{n'}{n} \qquad (9.1)$$

In an actual core it is necessary to study the diffusion of neutrons from the center toward the physical boundaries where they may leak out and be lost for subsequent fissions. The effective multiplication factor is the product of the nonleakage probability, P_{NL}, and the infinite multiplication factor.

$$k_{eff} = k_\infty P_{NL} \tag{9.2}$$

The nonleakage probabilities can be determined only after the diffusion of neutrons and the critical size of the core are examined later in this chapter.

For a reactor to be critical the effective multiplication factor must be unity. Thus, there is a constant number of neutrons in each generation and the fission energy is released at a constant rate. When k_{eff} is greater than unity the reactor is said to be supercritical and the power level will rise exponentially. Great care must be exercised that the rate of increase be kept within reasonable limits. When k_{eff} is less than 1, the reactor is subcritical and there will be a decrease in neutron population and power.

For a real core to be critical ($k_{eff} = 1$), k_∞ must be larger than 1 to allow for

(1) leakage of neutrons;
(2) buildup of fission fragments, some of which have very significant absorption cross sections;
(3) consumption of fissionable nuclei. This may be partially offset by conversion of ^{232}Th to ^{233}U or ^{238}U to ^{239}Pu, etc. (In a true breeder reactor there will be a net gain in fissionable nuclei. This is a goal toward which the nuclear industry is striving); and
(4) changes in temperature and pressure in the core.

FOUR-FACTOR EQUATION

The infinite multiplication factor can be evaluated as the product of

(1) the fast fission factor, ε,
(2) the resonance escape probability, p;
(3) the thermal utilization factor, f; and
(4) the thermal fission factor, η.

$$k_\infty = \varepsilon p f \eta \tag{9.3}$$

Taking an infinite core with n fast neutrons which have been produced by thermal neutrons absorbed in fissionable fuel, let us examine the life history of these neutrons.

First, their number can be increased slightly, due to fast fission. Not only can the high energy neutrons cause fission in the fissionable isotopes, but the fertile nuclei, ^{232}Th and ^{238}U, have a small cross section for fission above a threshold energy of about 1 MeV. In a homogeneous core, there is little probability of much fast fission as there are apt to be several collisions with the more numerous moderator nuclei before a neutron will collide with a fuel nucleus. In a heterogeneous core where the fuel is in sizeable chunks (rods, pins, plates, pellets, etc.), the fast neutrons must travel through fuel for some distance before contacting the moderator. Here there may be enough fast collisions to increase the neutron population by several percent. The fast fission factor, ε, is defined as the ratio of the total number of fast neutrons to the number of fast neutrons induced by thermal fission. The total number of fast neutrons is then

$$n\varepsilon = \text{total fast neutrons}$$

These fast neutrons scatter and slow down. Absorption cross sections are small in the fast region and absorption can be ignored until neutrons reach epithermal energies where large resonances exist for both ^{238}U and ^{232}Th. These fertile isotopes, if present, will prevent many neutrons from ever reaching the thermal region. The *resonance escape probability* is the ratio of the number of neutrons thermalized to the total fast neutrons. It expresses the probability that a neutron will escape resonant capture and will reach thermal. The number of thermal neutrons available for fission is now

$$n\varepsilon p = \text{number of thermal neutrons.}$$

A method of evaluating the resonance escape probability will be considered after the discussion of the four-factor equation is completed.

Not all thermal neutrons are absorbed in fuel. The *thermal utilization factor* is the ratio of the number of neutrons absorbed in the fuel to the total number of absorptions in fuel, moderator, cladding, etc.

$$f = \frac{\Sigma_{abs}^{fuel}\phi_{fuel}}{\Sigma_{abs}^{fuel}\phi_{fuel} + \Sigma_{abs}^{mod}\phi_{mod} + \Sigma_{abs}^{clad}\phi_{clad}} \tag{9.4}$$

In a heterogeneous core there can be considerable difference in the flux in the fuel, the flux with the moderator, and the flux in the cladding. If the difference is small or nonexistent, as in a homogeneous core, the fluxes cancel and

$$f = \frac{\Sigma_{abs}^{t}}{\Sigma_{abs}^{t} + \Sigma_{abs}^{m} + \Sigma_{abs}^{cl}} = \frac{\sigma_{a}^{t}}{\sigma_{a}^{t} + \dfrac{N_{m}\sigma_{a}^{m}}{N_{f}} + \dfrac{N_{cl}\sigma_{a}^{cl}}{N_{f}}} \tag{9.5}$$

Thus, the number of thermal neutrons absorbed in the fuel becomes

$$n\varepsilon pf = \text{thermal neutrons absorbed in fuel}$$

The *thermal fission factor* is the number of fast neutrons produced per thermal neutron absorbed in the fuel. This is found by multiplying the ratio of fission absorptions in the fuel to total absorptions in the fuel by ν, the number of fast neutrons emitted per fission.

$$\eta = \frac{\Sigma_{\text{fis}}^{\text{f}}}{\Sigma_{\text{abs}}^{\text{f}}} \nu \tag{9.6}$$

The total number of fast neutrons in the next generation is then

$$n' = n\varepsilon pf\eta = nk_\infty \tag{9.7a}$$

so that

$$k_\infty = \frac{n'}{n} = \varepsilon pf\eta \tag{9.7b}$$

Checking the units on k_∞

$$k_\infty = \quad \varepsilon \quad \times \quad p \quad \times \quad f \quad \times \quad \eta \tag{9.7c}$$

$$\frac{\text{fast } n}{\text{fast } n \text{ from}} \qquad \frac{\text{thermal } n}{\text{fast } n} \quad \frac{\text{thermal } n \text{ abs.}}{\text{in fuel}} \quad \frac{\text{fast } n \text{ from}}{\text{thermal fission}}$$

thermal fission $\qquad\qquad\qquad$ thermal n $\qquad \dfrac{\text{thermal fission}}{\text{thermal } n \text{ absorbed}}$

$$\text{in fuel}$$

Fig. 9.1 shows the life cycle for neutrons in a finite critical core. Leakage and absorption just balance the production of neutrons by both

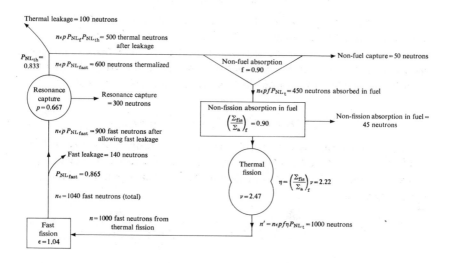

FIG. 9.1 *Life cycle for neutrons in the core of a critical reactor ($k_{eff} = 1$) where both fast and thermal leakage occur.*

fast and thermal fission with the result that each successive generation has the same number of neutrons.

CALCULATION OF RESONANCE ESCAPE PROBABILITY

In considering the resonance escape probability observe Fig. 9.2 which shows the absorption cross section for ^{238}U. Radiative capture cross sections reach about 7×10^3b at 6.7 eV, 5.4×10^3b at 21 eV, and 4.3×10^3b at 37 eV. Also fertile ^{232}Th shows two close peaks of 500

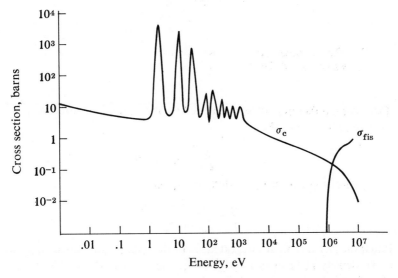

FIG. 9.2   *Absorption (capture and fission) cross sections for* ^{238}U.

and 700b between 20 and 25 eV and two lesser peaks between 50 and 75 eV. Therefore, for both of these resonance absorbers the absorption cross sections are strongly energy dependent. One must consider the neutron slowing down density, $q(E)$, which is the number of neutrons per cm^3-sec slowing down past a given energy level, E.

In Fig. 9.3 it can be seen that the slowing down density at the lower end of the energy interval, $q(E)$, is less than the value at the upper end, $q(E + \Delta E)$, by the number of neutrons which have been absorbed (leakage being neglected).

The probability of absorption is

$$P_{abs} = \frac{\sum_a}{\sum_a + \sum_s} \tag{9.8}$$

The number of scattering collisions per neutron in the energy interval ΔE is

$$n = \frac{\Delta \ln E}{\xi} = \frac{\Delta E}{\xi E} \tag{9.9}$$

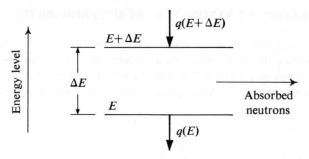

FIG. 9.3 *Neutron slowing down density with absorption as energy drops from $E + \Delta E$ to E.*

Thus, the number of neutrons removed by absorption in scattering through the energy interval, ΔE, is

$$\Delta q = \frac{\Sigma_a}{\Sigma_a + \Sigma_s} \frac{\Delta E}{\xi E} q \tag{9.10}$$

Expressing Eq. (9.10) in differential form

$$\frac{dq}{q} = \frac{\Sigma_a}{\Sigma_a + \Sigma_s} \frac{dE}{\xi E} \tag{9.11}$$

Equation (9.11) is then integrated from the average fast neutron slowing down density at birth (q_o) and average energy at birth (E_o) to the values after thermalization, q_{th} and E_{th}.

$$\int_{q_o}^{q_{th}} \frac{dq}{q} = \int_{E_o}^{E_{th}} \frac{\Sigma_a}{\Sigma_a + \Sigma_s} \frac{dE}{\xi E} \tag{9.12}$$

$$\ln\left(\frac{q_{th}}{q_o}\right) = \int_{E_o}^{E_{th}} \frac{\Sigma_a}{\Sigma_a + \Sigma_s} \frac{dE}{\xi E} = -\int_{E_{th}}^{E_o} \frac{\Sigma_a}{\Sigma_a + \Sigma_s} \frac{dE}{\xi E} \tag{9.13}$$

Taking antilogs of both sides and realizing that the ratio of thermal slowing down density to the initial fast slowing down density is essentially the definition of resonance escape probability

$$p = q_{th}/q_o = e^{-\int_{E_{th}}^{E_o} \frac{\Sigma_a}{\Sigma_a + \Sigma_s} \frac{dE}{\xi E}} \tag{9.14}$$

Through the epithermal region the scattering cross sections are essentially constant and are primarily contributed by the moderator. On the other hand, absorption cross sections vary wildly in the epithermal region, the principal resonances being contributed by the fertile resonance absorber atoms (^{232}Th or ^{238}U) which may be present. For the present discussion assume that only ^{238}U is present and σ_a^{238} and N_{238} represent the absorption cross section and atom density for this resonance absorber.

$$p = e^{-\int_{E_{th}}^{E_o} \frac{N_{238}\sigma_a{}^{238}}{N_{238}\sigma_a{}^{238}+\Sigma_s} \frac{dE}{\xi E}} = e^{-\frac{N_{238}}{\xi\Sigma_s} \int_{E_{th}}^{E_o} \frac{\sigma_a{}^{238}\Sigma_s}{N_{238}\sigma_a{}^{238}+\Sigma_s} \frac{dE}{E}}$$

$$= e^{-\frac{N_{238}}{\xi\Sigma_s} \int_{E_{th}}^{E_o} (\sigma_a{}^{238})_{eff} \frac{dE}{E}} \qquad (9.15)$$

where $(\sigma_a{}^{238})_{eff}$, the effective resonance absorber cross section, is defined as

$$(\sigma_a{}^{238})_{eff} = \frac{\sigma_a{}^{238}\Sigma_s}{N_{238}\sigma_a{}^{238} + \Sigma_s} = \frac{\sigma_a{}^{238}}{\dfrac{N_{238}\sigma_a{}^{238}}{\Sigma_s} + 1} \qquad (9.16)$$

The effective resonance integral is given as

$$I_{eff} = \int_{E_{th}}^{E_o} (\sigma_a{}^{238})_{eff} \frac{dE}{E} \qquad (9.17)$$

making

$$p = e^{-\left(\frac{N_{238}}{\xi\Sigma_s} I_{eff}\right)} \qquad (9.18)$$

When the effective resonance integral for a homogeneous reactor is laboriously evaluated by mechanical integration through the resonance region it can be represented for either ^{232}Th or ^{238}U by the equation

$$I_{eff} = 3.9 \left(\frac{\Sigma_s}{N_{238}}\right)^{0.415} \qquad (9.19)$$

Note that Σ_s/N_{238} must be expressed in barns and the effective resonance integral has the units of barns. Observe that I_{eff} is a function only of the scattering cross section per resonance absorber atom (Σ_s/N_{238}).

Equation (9.19) is satisfactory for ratios of Σ_s/N_{238} less than 1000 barns. The effective resonance integral for ^{238}U runs from 9.25 b for pure metal to an upper limit of 240 b for an infinitely dilute mixture of ^{238}U in moderator. For thorium the values run between 11.1 b for pure metal and 69.8 b for the infinitely dilute mixture.

Example 1. Compute the infinite multiplication factor for a homogeneous mixture of 200 moles of graphite per mole of 5 percent enriched uranium. From the mole ratio and the given enrichment

$$\frac{N_{238}}{N_{235}} = \frac{0.95}{0.05} = 19$$

$$\frac{N_c}{N_{235}} = \frac{200 \text{ moles C/mole U}}{0.05 \text{ mole } ^{235}\text{U/mole U}} = 4000 \frac{\text{moles C}}{\text{mole } ^{235}\text{U}}$$

For a homogeneous mixture $\varepsilon = 1$

$$I_{eff} = 3.9 \left(\frac{\Sigma_s}{N_{238}}\right)^{0.415} = 3.9 \left[\frac{\dfrac{N_u}{N_{235}}\sigma_s^u + \dfrac{N_c}{N_{235}}\sigma_s^c}{N_{238}/N^{235}}\right]^{0.415}$$

$$= 3.9 \left[\frac{20 \times 8.3 + 4000 \times 4.66}{19} \right]^{0.415}$$

$$= 3.9 (978)^{0.415} = 68 \text{ b}$$

$$\xi_c = \frac{2}{A + \frac{2}{3}} = \frac{2}{12.67} = 0.158 \qquad \xi_u = \frac{2}{238.6} = 0.0084$$

$$\xi_{avg} = \frac{N_u \sigma_s^u \xi_u + N_c \sigma_s^c \xi_c}{N_u \sigma_s^u + N_c \sigma_s^c}$$

$$= \frac{20 \times 8.3 \times 0.0084 + 4000 \times 4.66 \times 0.158}{20 \times 8.3 + 4000 \times 4.66} \approx 0.158$$

$$p = e^{-\frac{N_{238}}{\xi \Sigma_s} I_{eff}} = e^{-\frac{1}{0.158(978)} \times 68}$$

$$= e^{-0.442} = 0.641$$

$$f = \frac{\sigma_a^{235} + (N_{238}/N_{235})\sigma_a^{238}}{\sigma_a^{235} + \frac{N_{238}}{N_{235}} \sigma_a^{238} + \frac{N_c}{N_{235}} \sigma_a^c}$$

$$= \frac{694 + 19(2.71)}{694 + 19(2.71) + 4000(0.0034)} = 0.985$$

$$\eta = \frac{\sum_f^{235}}{\sum_a^u} \nu = \frac{\sigma_f^{235}\nu}{\sigma_a^{235} + \frac{N_{238}}{N_{235}} \sigma_a^{238}}$$

$$= \frac{582 \times 2.43}{694 + 19(2.71)} = 1.898$$

$$k_\infty = \varepsilon p f \eta = 1.0 \times 0.641 \times 0.985 \times 1.898 = 1.198$$

Note that in calculating f and η the fuel was considered as being the fissionable ^{235}U and the fertile ^{238}U. One could use only the fissionable isotope as the fuel without affecting k_∞; however, the values of f and η would be different. Care must be taken that a similar basis is used for evaluating Σ_a^f in these two items.

HETEROGENEOUS CORES

In Example 1 the value of k_∞, is 1.198; allowing for a modest neutron leakage the mixture of graphite and 5 percent enriched uranium should experience little difficulty in achieving criticality. However, in Problem 3 the same calculation with natural uranium as a fuel will result in $k_\infty = 0.778$. The homogeneous mixture with 200 moles of graphite per mole of natural uranium cannot achieve criticality even in an infinite core.

Why then could CP-1, the original reactor constructed by Enrico Fermi and his associates at the University of Chicago, go critical? Its fuel was natural uranium and its moderator was graphite.

The answer is that it was a heterogeneous assembly of graphite blocks and lumps of natural uranium. In a heterogeneous reactor where the neutrons must travel through a significant amount of fuel before entering the moderator there may be a gain in the total fast neutron population of several percent, as indicated by the fast fission factor, ε. An even more important improvement occurs in the resonance escape probability, p. Fast neutrons are born in the fuel but are mainly slowed down in the moderator. After thermalization by the moderator they must diffuse back into the fuel elements. Any epithermal neutrons diffusing into the fuel are quickly absorbed by the large ^{238}U resonances in the outer layer of fuel. This effect is called self-shielding and it permits the interior of the fuel to see few, if any, epithermal neutrons. The result is a marked improvement in the resonance escape probability since only a small fraction of the fuel volume is involved in resonance capture.

The thermal utilization factor is not as good in a heterogeneous core as it is in a homogeneous one. If Eq. (9.4) is rearranged

$$f = \frac{\Sigma_a^{\text{fuel}}}{\Sigma_a^{\text{fuel}} + \dfrac{\phi_m}{\phi_f} \Sigma_a^{\text{mod}} + \dfrac{\phi_{cl}}{\phi_f} \Sigma_a^{\text{clad}}} \tag{9.20}$$

it can be seen that if the flux in the moderator and clad are larger than the average value in the fuel the thermal utilization factor will suffer a reduction. The ratios ϕ_m/ϕ_f and ϕ_{cl}/ϕ_f are known as the thermal disadvantage factors for the moderator and clad respectively. Fig. 9.4 shows the variation of fast and thermal flux in a heterogeneous core. Fast neutrons are born in the fuel and leak into the moderator where they are lost to the thermal group by slowing down collisions. The reverse is true of the thermal flux where the slow neutrons are born in the moderator as their fast ancestors lose energy. The fuel elements act as a strong sink or absorber of the thermal neutrons. Thus, the thermal flux dips in the fuel and peaks in the moderator.

As power levels have increased in reactors, it has become necessary to use smaller diameter rods or pins or thinner plate type elements to prevent excessive temperatures in the fuel. The smaller each individual element, the closer a heterogeneous core approaches the homogeneous core. The result is that the small dips in flux can be averaged out and the core can be treated as though it were homogeneous without serious error in many instances.

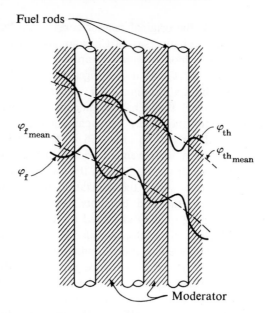

FIG. 9.4   *Variation in ϕ_{th} and ϕ_f in a heterogeneous reactor lattice.*

NEUTRON CURRENT DENSITY

As neutrons diffuse through matter, if the scattering is isotropic, "simple" diffusion theory will describe their travels.   For a heavier moderator such as graphite, the deviation from isotropic scatter is not serious, as shown in Chapter 8, where for graphite $\overline{\cos \psi} = 0.056$.   Later in this chapter a correction will be introduced to allow for the anisotropy of the scatter which is especially necessary with lighter moderators.   Further, the "simple" diffusion theory assumes that a monoenergetic group of neutrons be considered where the velocity is the average value for the group.   Since scattering cross sections do not vary strongly with neutron energy, an average cross section for scatter can be used.

Neutron current density is the number of neutrons per second crossing a unit area normal to the direction of neutron flow.

Fig. 9.5 shows a differential volume, dV, from which neutrons will scatter through the area dS downward, contributing a differential current flow in the z direction, dJ_{z-}.   The net current flow in the z direction is found by subtracting the downward current flow in the z direction, J_{z-}, from the upward flow from the lower hemisphere, J_{z+}.   Thus,

$$J_z = J_{z+} - J_{z-} \tag{9.21}$$

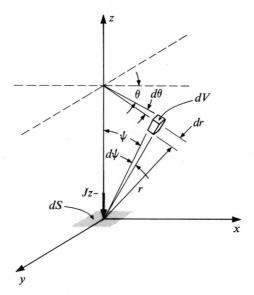

Fig. 9.5 *Neutron scatter in differential volume, dV, contributes a differential current density, dJ$_{z-}$, to the flow of neutrons through the area, dS.*

The elemental volume in terms of spherical coordinates is

$$dV = rd\psi \cdot r \sin \psi \, d\theta \cdot dr = r^2 \sin \psi \, d\theta \, d\psi \, dr \qquad (9.22)$$

The neutron flux is position dependent and at any position of the differential volume, dV, the number of scatterings within the elemental volume will be $\Sigma_s \phi dV$. The effective surface area as seen from dV is $\cos \psi \cdot dS$. The fraction of neutrons scattered through the effective area, dS, is $\cos \psi \, dS/4\pi r^2$, assuming there are no interactions as the neutrons travel from dV to dS. Interactions between these two locations result in an attenuation by a factor of $e^{-\Sigma r}$. If the medium is assumed to be only weakly absorbing, then $\Sigma \approx \Sigma_s$ and the neutron flow through dS in the z-direction becomes

$$dJ_{z-} \cdot dS = \Sigma_s \phi dV \cdot \frac{\cos \psi \cdot dS}{4\pi r^2} e^{-\Sigma_s r} \qquad (9.23)$$

Rearranging, substituting Eq. (9.22) for dV, and integrating over the entire upper hemisphere gives

$$J_{z-} = \frac{\Sigma_s}{4\pi} \int_0^{2\pi} \int_0^{\pi/2} \int_0^\infty \phi \, e^{-\Sigma_s r} [\cos \psi \sin \psi \, d\theta \, d\psi \, dr] \qquad (9.24)$$

The flux is a function of position

$$\phi = f(x, y, z) = f'(r, \theta, \psi) \qquad (9.25)$$

ϕ may be expanded in a Maclaurin series in terms of the flux at the origin

$$\phi\,(x, y, z) = \phi_0 + x\left(\frac{\partial \phi}{\partial x}\right)_0 + y\left(\frac{\partial \phi}{\partial y}\right)_0 + z\left(\frac{\partial \phi}{\partial z}\right)_0$$

$$+ \frac{x^2}{2}\left(\frac{\partial^2 \phi}{\partial x^2}\right)_0 + \frac{y^2}{2}\left(\frac{\partial^2 \phi}{\partial y^2}\right)_0 + \frac{z^2}{2}\left(\frac{\partial^2 \phi}{\partial z^2}\right)_0 + \cdots \quad (9.26)$$

Fortunately, any terms resulting from the second-order partial derivatives cancel and the results would be exactly the same if only the first-order terms were considered in Eq. (9.26). Since the flux gradient in the x or y directions makes no contribution to the neutron flow in the z direction Eq. (9.24) becomes

$$J_{z-} = \frac{\Sigma_s}{4\pi}\phi_0 \int_0^{2\pi} \int_0^{\pi/2} \int_0^{\infty} e^{-\Sigma_s r} \cos \psi \sin \psi\, d\theta\, d\psi\, dr$$

$$+ \frac{\Sigma_s}{4\pi}\left(\frac{\partial \phi}{\partial z}\right)_0 \int_0^{2\pi} \int_0^{\pi/2} \int_0^{\infty} \underbrace{r \cos \psi}\, e^{-\Sigma_s r} \cos \psi \sin \psi\, d\theta\, d\psi\, dr \quad (9.27)$$
$$\qquad\qquad\qquad\qquad\qquad\qquad\quad z$$

Integrating

$$J_{z-} = \frac{\Sigma_s \phi_0}{4\pi}\left[\frac{-e^{-\Sigma_s r}}{\Sigma_s}\right]_0^{\infty} (1/2) \sin^2 \psi \Big]_0^{\pi/2} \theta \Big]_0^{2\pi}$$

$$+ \frac{\Sigma_s}{4\pi}\left(\frac{\partial \phi}{\partial z}\right)_0 \left[\frac{e^{-\Sigma_s r}}{\Sigma_s^2}(-\Sigma_s r - 1)\right]_0^{\infty} - \frac{\cos^3 \psi}{3}\Big]_0^{\pi/2} \theta \Big]_0^{2\pi} \quad (9.28)$$

substituting limits

$$J_{z-} = \frac{\Sigma_s \phi_0}{4\pi}\left(\frac{1}{\Sigma_s}\right)\left(\frac{1}{2}\right)(2\pi) + \frac{\Sigma_s}{4\pi}\left(\frac{\partial \phi}{\partial z}\right)_0 \left(\frac{1}{\Sigma_s^2}\right)\left(\frac{1}{3}\right)(2\pi)$$

$$J_{z-} = \frac{\phi_0}{4} + \frac{1}{6\Sigma_s}\left(\frac{\partial \phi}{\partial z}\right)_0 \quad (9.29)$$

The upward current flow through ds from the lower hemisphere is found by a similar integration with the limits ψ going from π to $\pi/2$. This results in

$$J_{z+} = \frac{\phi_0}{4} - \frac{1}{6\Sigma_s}\left(\frac{\partial \phi}{\partial z}\right)_0 \quad (9.30)$$

Taking the difference in (9.30) and (9.29) results in the net current flow in the z direction

$$J_z = -\left(\frac{1}{3\Sigma_s}\right)\left(\frac{\partial \phi}{\partial z}\right)_0 \quad (9.31)$$

In a similar manner the component of current in the x and y directions can be obtained. When the three are added

$$J = -\left(\frac{1}{3\Sigma_s}\right)\left[\frac{\partial \phi}{\partial x} + \frac{\partial \phi}{\partial y} + \frac{\partial \phi}{\partial z}\right] = -D\,(\text{grad }\phi) \quad (9.32)$$

This is known as *Fick's law of diffusion.* It indicates that the neutron current will flow in a direction opposite to a positive gradient of the flux. It will be in proportion to the diffusion constant, D, and current will be minimum when flux is maximum.

The diffusion constant is corrected for anisotropic scatter by using the transport mean free path or the macroscopic transport cross section in place of the scattering values.

$$D = \frac{1}{3\sum_{tr}} = \frac{1}{3\sum_s(1 - \overline{\cos \psi})} = \frac{\lambda_{tr}}{3} \qquad (9.33)$$

DEVELOPMENT OF DIFFUSION EQUATION

As neutrons diffuse through a reactor core they may (1) be absorbed by fuel, moderator, coolant, cladding, structure, etc.; (2) leak out at the core boundaries; or (3) act as a source for new fission neutrons. If one considers the neutrons in a differential volume, dV, an expression can be

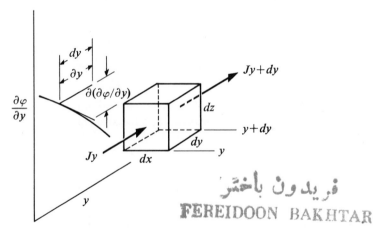

FIG. 9.6   *Neutron leakage in the y-direction from a differential volume.*

developed for the net neutron leakage from this elemental volume.   First consider only neutrons leaking into the front face in the y-direction.

$$L_y = J_y \, dx \, dz = -D \left(\frac{\partial \phi}{\partial y}\right) dx \, dz \qquad (9.34)$$

From the rear face the leakage is

$$L_{y+dy} = J_{(y+dy)} \, dx \, dz = -D \left(\frac{\partial \phi}{\partial y} + \frac{\partial(\partial \phi/\partial y)}{\partial y} \, dy\right) dx \, dz \qquad (9.35)$$

The net leakage in the y direction is the difference between (9.35) and (9.34).

$$L_{y_{net}} = L_{y+dy} - L_y = -D\left[\frac{\partial\phi}{\partial y} + \frac{\partial^2\phi}{\partial y^2} dy\right] dx\, dz$$

$$+ D\frac{d\phi}{\partial y} dx\, dz = -D\frac{\partial^2\phi}{\partial y^2} dx\, dy\, dz \quad (9.36)$$

Similarly,

$$L_{x_{net}} = -D\frac{\partial^2\phi}{\partial x^2} dx\, dy\, dz \tag{9.37}$$

$$L_{z_{net}} = -D\frac{\partial^2\phi}{\partial z^2} dx\, dy\, dz \tag{9.38}$$

The total leakage for a unit volume (neutrons/cm³ sec) is

$$L_t = -D\left[\frac{\partial^2\phi}{\partial x^2} + \frac{\partial^2\phi}{\partial y^2} + \frac{\partial^2\phi}{\partial z^2}\right] = -D\nabla^2\phi \tag{9.39}$$

The expression for the neutrons absorbed in a unit volume per second is

$$\text{no. abs} = \phi\Sigma_a \tag{9.40}$$

If fuel is present in the volume being considered, there will be a source of neutrons due to fission. For thermal neutrons k_∞ new thermal neutrons will appear for each neutron absorbed and thus the source strength is

$$S_{th} = k_\infty\phi\Sigma_a \tag{9.41}$$

The rate of change of neutron population density is equal to the rate of production, less the leakage, less the absorption of neutrons

$$\frac{\partial n}{\partial t} = k_\infty\Sigma_a\phi - (-D\nabla^2\phi) - \Sigma_a\phi \tag{9.42}$$

For a steady state core

$$\frac{\partial n}{\partial t} = 0 \tag{9.43}$$

and, therefore, under these conditions

$$0 = D\nabla^2\phi + (k_\infty - 1)\Sigma_a\phi \tag{9.44}$$

Dividing by Σ_a

$$0 = \frac{D}{\Sigma_a}\nabla^2\phi + (k_\infty - 1)\phi \tag{9.45}$$

The ratio D/Σ_a is called the *square of the thermal diffusion length*, L^2. Therefore

$$L = \sqrt{D/\Sigma_a} = \sqrt{\lambda_{tr}\lambda_a/3} \tag{9.46}$$

The diffusion length can be thought of as more or less a "representative average" distance for interaction as a neutron diffuses.

Substituting the diffusion length into the steady state diffusion equation and rearranging

$$0 = \nabla^2\phi + \left(\frac{k_\infty - 1}{L^2}\right)\phi \qquad (9.47a)$$

$$0 = \nabla^2\phi + B^2\phi \qquad (9.47b)$$

B is called the buckling of a reactor since this second-order partial differential equation is analogous to the one which describes the buckling of a column. In one-group theory only the leakage of thermal neutrons from the core will be considered. Later two-group theory will be developed where the leakage of fast neutrons must also be taken into account.

$$B^2 = \frac{k_\infty - 1}{L^2} \qquad (9.48a)$$

This is sometimes called the material buckling for a core lattice. Its magnitude bears an inverse relation to the size that a core must have to be critical. That is, the overall neutron production must just balance the absorption and leakage during steady state operation. After the next example the diffusion equation will be solved for several simple geometries to illustrate this point.

When (9.48a) is rearranged

$$1 = k_\infty\left[\frac{1}{B^2L^2 + 1}\right] \qquad (9.48b)$$

and (9.48b) is compared with (9.2), it is seen that for the steady state critical reactor ($k_{eff} = 1$) the bracket $[1/(B^2L^2 + 1)]$ represents the non-leakage probability for the thermal group of neutrons.

$$P_{NL_{th}} = \frac{1}{B^2L^2 + 1} \qquad (9.48c)$$

Example 2. Determine the material buckling for the mixture of 200 moles of graphite per mole of 5 percent enriched uranium.* The core temperature is 20°C. For a critical core of these materials what will be the thermal nonleakage probability?

$$\rho_g = 1.6 \text{ gr}^c/\text{cm}^3 \qquad \rho_u = 18.9 \text{ gr}^v/\text{cm}^3$$

$$\text{Vol U} = \frac{238 \text{ gr/mole}}{18.9 \text{ gr/cm}^3} = 12.6 \text{ cm}^3/\text{mole U}$$

---

* Enrichment is the atom percent of ^{235}U in uranium when it is increased above the abundance as found in nature. Thus, 5 percent enriched uranium will have 5 percent of its atoms ^{235}U and 95 percent of them ^{238}U.

$$\text{Vol Graphite} = \frac{200 \text{ moles C/mole U} \times 12 \text{ gr C/mole C}}{1.60 \text{ gr C/cm}^3}$$

$$= 1500 \text{ cm}^3/\text{mole U}$$

$$\text{Total Vol} = 1500 + 12.6 = 1512.6 \text{ cm}^3 \text{ mixture/mole U}$$

$$N_u = \frac{6.024 \times 10^{23} \text{ atoms U/gm mole U}}{1512.6 \text{ cm}^3/\text{gm mole U}}$$

$$= 3.98 \times 10^{20} \text{ atoms U/cm}^3 \text{ mixture}$$

$$N_{235} = 0.05 \times 3.98 \times 10^{20} = 0.199 \times 10^{20} \text{ atoms } ^{235}\text{U/cm}^3 \text{ mixture}$$

$$N_{238} = 0.95 \times 3.98 \times 10^{20} = 3.78 \times 10^{20} \text{ atoms } ^{238}\text{U/cm}^3 \text{ mixture}$$

$$N_c = 200 \text{ atom C/atom U} \times 3.98 \times 10^{20} \text{ atom U/cm}^3$$

$$= 7.96 \times 10^{22} \text{ atoms C/cm}^3 \text{ mixture}$$

$$\left(\sum_{tr}\right)_{th} = N_c \sigma^c_{s_{th}}(1 - \overline{\cos \psi_c}) + N_u \sigma^U_{s_{th}}(1 - \overline{\cos \psi_u})$$

$$= 7.96 \times 10^{22} \times 4.8 \times 10^{-24} \left[1 - \frac{2}{3(12)}\right]$$

$$+ 3.98 \times 10^{20} \times 8.3 \times 10^{-24} \left[1 - \frac{2}{3(238)}\right]$$

$$= 0.361 + 0.0033 = 0.364 \text{ cm}^2/\text{cm}^3 \text{ mixture}$$

$$\sum_a = [N_{235}\sigma^{235}_a + N_{238}\sigma^{238}_a + N_c\sigma^c_a]\frac{\sqrt{\pi}}{2}$$

$$\sum_a = [0.199 \times 10^{20} \times 694 \times 10^{-24} + 3.78 \times 10^{20} \times 2.73 \times 10^{-24}$$

$$+ 7.96 \times 10^{22} \times 0.0034 \times 10^{-24}]\frac{\sqrt{\pi}}{2}$$

$$= 0.0151 \times \frac{\sqrt{\pi}}{2} = 0.0134 \text{ cm}^2/\text{cm}^3 \text{ mixture}$$

Note that the only correction to $\sum_a$ is for the average velocity being larger than the most probable $\left(\frac{\sqrt{\pi}}{2}\right)$ since the core temperature is 20°C.

$$L^2 = \frac{1}{3 \sum_a \sum_{tr}} = \frac{1}{3(0.364)(0.0134)} = 68.2 \text{ cm}^2$$

$$B^2 = \frac{k_\infty - 1}{L^2} = \frac{1.198 - 1}{68.2} = 0.00290 \text{ cm}^{-2}$$

$$B = 0.0538 \text{ cm}^{-1}$$

$$P_{NL_{th}} = \frac{1}{B^2L^2 + 1} = \frac{1}{(0.00290)(68.2) + 1} = 0.835$$

INFINITE SLAB REACTOR

The diffusion equation, (9.47), will first be solved for an infinite slab reactor in order to determine the slab thickness for criticality. Fig. 9.7 shows the slab with the origin taken at its center. Since the slab is

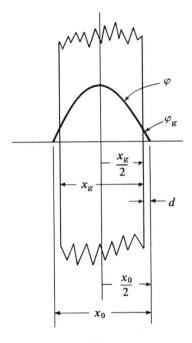

FIG. 9.7 *Infinite slab reactor.*

considered infinite there is no leakage of neutrons in the y or z direction. Leakage occurs only in the x direction through the slab faces. There will therefore be a flux gradient (and hence neutron flow) only in the x direction. The flux must fall as one approaches either face from the center in order to have a current flow toward the outside. The flux, however, is still finite at the slab faces ($x = \pm x_g/2$) and does not fall to zero until the extrapolated half-thickness is reached ($x = \pm x_0/2$).

$$\frac{x_0}{2} = \frac{x_g}{2} + d \qquad (9.49)$$

d is the extrapolation distance by which the geometrical boundary of the core must be extended for the flux to drop to zero.

At the boundary of a bare core neutrons stream out into space and few, if any, are scattered back (the atmosphere is for all intents like a vacuum to the escaping neutrons). Thus the return current J_{x-} may be set equal to zero.

$$J_{x-} = 0 = \frac{\phi}{4} + \frac{D}{2}\frac{d\phi}{dx} \tag{9.50}$$

From this it follows that

$$\frac{d\phi}{dx} = -\frac{\phi}{2D} \tag{9.51}$$

If the extrapolation of the flux is assumed to be a straight line, the slope is also

$$\frac{d\phi}{dx} = \frac{-\phi_g}{x_0/2 - x_g/2} = -\frac{\phi_g}{d} \tag{9.52}$$

Equating (9.51) and (9.52)

$$d = 2D = \frac{2\lambda_{tr}}{3} \tag{9.53}$$

The use of more sophisticated transport theory gives

$$d = 0.71\lambda_{tr} \tag{9.54}$$

Since the extrapolation distance is usually small in comparison to the critical dimensions of a core, the difference is not serious. It must be remembered that the extrapolation distance does not represent an actual finite distance in the reactor, but only a simplified mathematical treatment of the boundary conditions.

The flux in the infinite slab varies only in the x direction; the diffusion equation reduces to an ordinary second-order linear differential equation.

$$0 = \nabla^2\phi + B^2\phi = \frac{d^2\phi}{dx^2} + B^2\phi \tag{9.55}$$

Using operator notation

$$D^2 + B^2 = 0$$

$$D = \pm Bi$$

The imaginary roots for the operator give a sine and cosine solution of the form

$$\phi = A_1 \cos Bx + A_2 \sin Bx \tag{9.56}$$

The boundary conditions demand that

(1) The flux drops to zero at the extrapolated boundaries; it is finite at the geometrical boundaries.
    When

$$x = \pm\frac{x_0}{2}, \qquad \phi = 0$$

(2) The flux be symmetrical and finite about the origin.

When

$$x = 0, \qquad \frac{d\phi}{dx} = 0$$

Taking the second requirement first, determine the expression for the flux gradient.

$$\frac{d\phi}{dx} = -A_1 B \sin Bx + A_2 B \cos Bx \qquad (9.57)$$

At the origin the slope of the flux is zero, $\sin Bx = 0$, and $\cos Bx = 1$.

$$\therefore 0 = 0 + A_2 B$$

Therefore, since B is real and positive

$$A_2 = 0 \text{ and the flux is}$$

$$\phi = A_1 \cos Bx \qquad (9.58)$$

Applying the first condition, that at the extrapolated boundary the flux must be zero

$$0 = A_1 \cos B \frac{x_0}{2}$$

This can occur when $Bx_0/2$ is equal to odd multiples of $\pi/2$.

$$\frac{Bx_0}{2} = \frac{\pi}{2}, \frac{3\pi}{2}, \frac{5\pi}{2}, \ldots \qquad (9.59)$$

From this, various values of x_0, called *eigenvalues*, will satisfy the differential equation. Fortunately, only the first value or fundamental eigenvalue is needed to describe the flux in a minimum size critical reactor.

$$x_0 = \frac{\pi}{B}, \frac{3\pi}{B}, \frac{5\pi}{B} \ldots \qquad (9.60)$$

fundamental eigenvalue └→harmonic eigenvalues

$$\phi = A_1 \cos \frac{\pi x}{x_0} + \left[A_{12} \cos \frac{3\pi x}{x_0} + A_{13} \cos \frac{5\pi x}{x_0} + \cdots \right]$$

drop for critical reactor   (9.61)

Retaining only the fundamental value, the flux for a steady state critical infinite slab reactor can be written as

$$\phi = A \cos \frac{\pi x}{x_0} \qquad (9.62)$$

The value π/x_0 is known as the geometric buckling for this reactor configuration. It will be different for other core geometries, but in each case must equal the value of the material buckling for the critical core.

Note that A is an arbitrary constant, which in this case is equal to the maximum flux at the center of the core.   To raise the flux in an operating reactor, the control rods are removed sufficiently to allow the reactor to be slightly supercritical and for the flux to increase in a controlled manner.   At the desired flux level the control rods are inserted just enough to stabilize the flux and return the value of k_{eff} to 1.   In theory, then, a reactor can be critical at any flux level.

Example 3.   For the homogeneous graphite-uranium mixture considered in Examples 1 and 2, what will be the thickness of a critical infinite slab?

$$x_0 = \frac{\pi}{B} = \frac{\pi}{0.0538} = 58.4 \text{ cm}$$

$$d = 0.71 \, \lambda_{tr} = \frac{0.71}{\sum_{tr}} = \frac{0.71}{0.364} = 1.93 \text{ cm.}$$

$$x_g = x_0 - 2d = 58.4 - 2(1.93) = 54.5 \text{ cm.}$$

FLUX DISTRIBUTION IN A RECTANGULAR PARALLELEPIPED

To extend the solution for the infinite slab to a real core where the flux varies in each of the principal directions, consider the rectangular parallelepiped, as shown in Fig. 9.8, with the origin at the center of the core.   The diffusion equation is written as

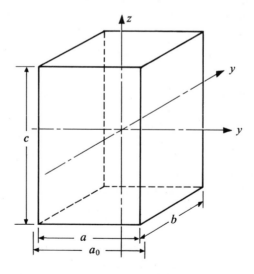

FIG. 9.8   *Rectangular parallelepiped core.*

$$\frac{\partial^2 \phi}{\partial x^2} + \frac{\partial^2 \phi}{\partial y^2} + \frac{\partial^2 \phi}{\partial z^2} + B^2 \phi = 0 \tag{9.63}$$

The equation can be solved by the separation of variables. Assume a solution which is the product of three functions, X, Y, and Z, each of which is a function of only a single variable, or

$$\phi = X(x) \cdot Y(y) \cdot Z(z) = XYZ \tag{9.64}$$

This is to say that the flux variation in the x direction is independent of that in the y and z directions. The flux variation in the y or z direction is similarly independent of variation in the other two directions. Differentiating Eq. (9.64) twice with respect to each variable yields

$$\frac{\partial \phi}{\partial x} = YZ \frac{\partial X}{\partial x}; \qquad \frac{\partial^2 \phi}{\partial x^2} = YZ \frac{\partial^2 X}{\partial x^2} \tag{9.65a,b}$$

$$\frac{\partial \phi}{\partial y} = XZ \frac{\partial Y}{\partial y}; \qquad \frac{\partial^2 \phi}{\partial y^2} = XZ \frac{\partial^2 Y}{\partial y^2} \tag{9.66a,b}$$

$$\frac{\partial \phi}{\partial z} = XY \frac{\partial Z}{\partial z}; \qquad \frac{\partial^2 \phi}{\partial z^2} = XY \frac{\partial^2 Z}{\partial z^2} \tag{9.67a,b}$$

Substituting these second-order partial derivatives into Eq. (9.63)

$$YZ \frac{\partial^2 X}{\partial x^2} + XZ \frac{\partial^2 Y}{\partial y^2} + XY \frac{\partial^2 Z}{\partial z^2} + B^2 XYZ = 0 \tag{9.68}$$

Dividing by XYZ

$$\frac{1}{X} \frac{\partial^2 X}{\partial x^2} + \frac{1}{Y} \frac{\partial^2 Y}{\partial y^2} + \frac{1}{Z} \frac{\partial^2 Z}{\partial z^2} + B^2 = 0 \tag{9.69}$$

Each of the first three terms in (9.69) is a function of a single variable. Therefore, each of the three must be equal to a constant.

$$\frac{1}{X} \frac{\partial^2 X}{\partial x^2} = -\alpha^2 \tag{9.70a}$$

$$\frac{1}{Y} \frac{\partial^2 Y}{\partial y^2} = -\beta^2 \tag{9.70b}$$

$$\frac{1}{Z} \frac{\partial^2 Z}{\partial z^2} = -\gamma^2 \tag{9.70c}$$

From this the square of the buckling becomes

$$B^2 = \alpha^2 + \beta^2 + \gamma^2 \tag{9.71}$$

Taking (9.70a), and using a total second derivative since it is a function of x only, the form is similar to (9.55).

$$\frac{d^2 X}{dx^2} + \alpha^2 X = 0 \tag{9.72a}$$

The solution of this equation is

$$X = A_1' \cos \alpha x + A_2' \sin \alpha x \qquad (9.72b)$$

When this is multiplied by YZ for particular values of y and z an expression for the flux variation in the x direction results.

The boundary conditions are

(1) when $x = \dfrac{a_0}{2}$, $X = 0$

(2) when $x = 0$, $\dfrac{\partial X}{\partial x} = 0$

Applying these conditions, in a manner similar to that for the infinite slab,

$$\alpha = \frac{\pi}{a_0} \qquad (9.73a)$$

similarly

$$\beta = \frac{\pi}{b_0} \qquad (9.73b)$$

and

$$\gamma = \frac{\pi}{c_0} \qquad (9.73c)$$

The three functions of a single variable that are multiplied to give the flux are

$$X = A' \cos \frac{\pi}{a_0} x \qquad (9.74a)$$

$$Y = A'' \cos \frac{\pi}{b_0} y \qquad (9.74b)$$

$$Z = A''' \cos \frac{\pi}{c_0} z \qquad (9.74c)$$

The flux can be written

$$\phi = A \cos \frac{\pi x}{a_0} \cos \frac{\pi y}{b_0} \cos \frac{\pi z}{c_0} \qquad (9.75)$$

If the core is a cube, the buckling then becomes

$$B^2 = 3 \frac{\pi^2}{a_0^2} \qquad (9.76)$$

or

$$a_0 = \sqrt{3} \frac{\pi}{B} \qquad (9.77)$$

The extrapolated length of the side of a cubic core is greater than the extrapolated thickness of an infinite slab of the same materials by a factor of $\sqrt{3}$.

SPHERICAL REACTOR CORE

The spherical core is attractive because its low surface area to volume ratio cuts neutron leakage to a minimum. This results in the minimum amount of fuel to achieve criticality.

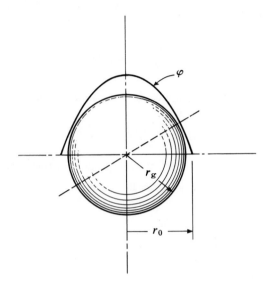

FIG. 9.9 *Spherical reactor core and flux variation along a diameter.*

Since the flux varies only in the radial direction the diffusion equation can be written in spherical coordinates as

$$\nabla^2\phi = \frac{d^2\phi}{dr^2} + \frac{2}{r}\frac{d\phi}{dr} \tag{9.78}$$

Substituting (9.78) into the diffusion equation yields

$$\frac{d^2\phi}{dr^2} + \frac{2}{r}\frac{d\phi}{dr} + B^2\phi = 0 \tag{9.79}$$

Let

$$u = \phi r \tag{9.80a}$$

Taking the derivative of u with respect to r gives

$$\frac{du}{dr} = \phi + r\frac{d\phi}{dr} \tag{9.80b}$$

and the second derivative is

$$\frac{d^2u}{dr^2} = r\frac{d^2\phi}{dr^2} + 2\frac{d\phi}{dr} \tag{9.80c}$$

Thus

$$\frac{1}{r}\frac{d^2u}{dr^2} = \frac{d^2\phi}{dr^2} + \frac{2}{r}\frac{d\phi}{dr} \tag{9.80d}$$

Substituting (9.80a) and (9.80d) into (9.79) gives

$$\frac{1}{r}\frac{d^2u}{dr^2} + B^2\frac{u}{r} = 0 \tag{9.81}$$

which reduces to

$$\frac{d^2u}{dr^2} + B^2u = 0 \tag{9.82}$$

Therefore

$$u = C_1 \cos Br + C_2 \sin Br = \phi r \tag{9.83}$$

and

$$\phi = \frac{C_1 \cos Br}{r} + \frac{C_2 \sin Br}{r} \tag{9.84}$$

If it is required that the flux remain finite at the origin

$$C_1 = 0 \qquad \text{since}$$

$$\lim_{r\to 0} \frac{\cos Br}{r} = \frac{1}{0} = \infty$$

The second boundary condition requires that the flux drop to 0 at the extrapolated radius.

When

$$r = r_0, \qquad \phi = 0$$

$$0 = C_2 \sin Br_0$$

This can occur only when

$$Br_0 = 0, \qquad \pi, \qquad 2\pi, 3\pi, \text{ etc.}$$
$$\downarrow \qquad \downarrow \qquad \downarrow$$
$$\text{trivial} \quad \text{fundamental} \quad \text{harmonic eigenvalues} \tag{9.85}$$
$$\text{eigenvalue}$$

The first value gives a trivial solution and the fundamental eigenvalue is

$$Br_0 = \pi \tag{9.86a}$$

Thus

$$r_0 = \frac{\pi}{B} \tag{9.86b}$$

and

$$r_0 = \frac{\pi}{B} - 0.71\lambda_{tr} \tag{9.87}$$

The flux in the spherical core is

$$\phi = \frac{C_2 \sin \pi r/r_0}{r} \tag{9.88}$$

POWER DEVELOPED BY A SPHERICAL CORE

The flux level at any point in a core will determine the number of interactions by fission. The differential power developed, dP, in a unit volume of core is

$$dP = G\sum_{\text{fis}}\phi\, dV \tag{9.89}$$

where G is energy released per fission.

For the spherical geometry

$$dV = 4\pi r^2\, dr \tag{9.90}$$

Substituting (9.90) into (9.89) and integrating from the origin to the geometrical radius will give the power developed by the core.

$$P = 4\pi G\sum_{\text{fis}} \int_0^{r_g} r^2\, \frac{C_2 \sin Br}{r}\, dr$$

$$= 4\pi G\sum_{\text{fis}} C_2 \int_0^{r_g} r \sin Br\, dr$$

$$= 4\pi G\sum_{\text{fis}} C_2 \left[\frac{1}{B^2} \sin Br_g - \frac{r_g}{B} \cos Br_g \right] \tag{9.91}$$

It may be convenient to replace C_2 by an expression in terms of the maximum flux, ϕ_{max}.

$$\lim_{r\to 0} \phi = \frac{C_2 \sin Br}{r} = \frac{0}{0}$$

Since this is indeterminate, differentiate both numerator and denominator (L'Hôpital's rule) and check this limit.

$$\lim_{r\to 0} \phi = \lim_{r\to 0} \frac{C_2 B \cos Br}{1} = C_2 B = \phi_{\text{max}}. \tag{9.92a}$$

$$C_2 = \frac{\phi_{\text{max}}}{B} \tag{9.92b}$$

Substituting (9.92b) into (9.91) the power developed by the core becomes

$$P = \frac{4\pi G\sum_{\text{fis}}\phi_{\text{max}}}{B^2} \left[\frac{1}{B} \sin Br_g - r_g \cos Br_g \right] \tag{9.93}$$

Example 4. For the homogeneous graphite-uranium mixture used previously in Examples 1, 2, and 3 what will be the critical radius of a bare critical sphere? What must be the maximum flux if the core is to produce 1 kW thermal? Compare the flux at the center of the core to that at the geometrical radius.

$$r_g = \frac{\pi}{B} - 0.71\, \lambda_{tr} = \frac{\pi}{0.0538} - 1.93 = 56.5 \text{ cm}.$$

$$\sum_{\text{fis}} = N_{235}\sigma_{\text{fis}}^{235} \frac{\sqrt{\pi}}{2}$$

$$= 0.199 \times 10^{20} \times 582 \times 10^{-24} \times \frac{\sqrt{\pi}}{2}$$

$$= 0.0103 \ \text{cm}^2/\text{cm}^3_{\text{mix}}$$

$$\phi_{\text{max}} = \frac{B^2 P}{4\pi G \sum_{\text{fis}} [(1/B) \sin Br_g - r_g \cos Br_g]}$$

$$= \frac{0.0538^2 \times 1}{4\pi \times 8.9 \times 10^{-18} \times 0.0103 \times 3600[(1/0.0538) \sin (0.0538 \times 56.5) - 56.5 \cos (0.0538 \times 56.5)]}$$

$$= 1.200 \times 10^{10} \ \frac{n}{\text{cm}^2 \ \text{sec}}$$

$$\frac{\phi_{\text{max}}}{\phi_{r_g}} = \frac{\phi_{\text{max}}}{(\phi_{\text{max}}/Br_g) \sin Br_g} = \frac{Br_g}{\sin Br_g}$$

$$= \frac{0.0538 \times 56.5}{\sin (0.0538(56.5))} = 29.9$$

CYLINDRICAL CORE

To determine the buckling of a cylindrical core the diffusion equation must have the Laplacian operator expressed in cylindrical coordinates. It becomes

$$\frac{\partial^2 \phi}{\partial r^2} + \frac{1}{r} \frac{\partial \phi}{\partial r} + \frac{\partial^2 \phi}{\partial z^2} + B^2 \phi = 0 \tag{9.94}$$

Using the method of separation of variables, as was done for the rectangular parallelepiped, the flux becomes

$$\phi = A J_0 \left(\frac{2.405r}{r_0} \right) \cos \frac{\pi z}{z_0} \tag{9.95}$$

where r_0 is the extrapolated core radius, z_0 is the extrapolated core height, and $J_0 \left(\frac{2.405r}{r_0} \right)$ is a Bessel function of the first kind of zero order.

The buckling for the cylinder is

$$B^2 = \left(\frac{2.405}{r_0} \right)^2 + \left(\frac{\pi}{z_0} \right)^2 \tag{9.96}$$

REFLECTED REACTOR CORE

A reactor core is frequently surrounded by a reflecting material to reduce the ratio of peak flux to the flux at the edge of the core fuel and to reduce the amount of fissionable material required to achieve criticality. Essentially, good moderator materials are effective reflectors. Neutrons leaking into material having a large macroscopic scattering (or transport) cross section will have some scattering collisions return neutrons to the fuel lattice, thus producing additional fissions. Since there are few absorptions in the reflector the thermal flux may actually increase slightly beyond the outermost fuel, as shown in Fig. 9.10.

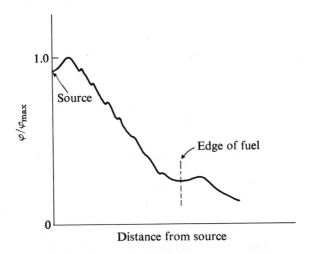

FIG. 9.10 *Horizontal flux traverse in water moderated, natural uranium fueled subcritical assembly.*

The one-group theory to be developed here will not show this rise in flux as one moves into the reflector; however, it will show the higher relative flux at the core lattice boundary and the savings in fuel.

SPHERICAL CORE WITH FINITE REFLECTOR

Two diffusion equations are required to describe the flux in this two-region system. In the core itself there is a source term due to fission.

$$k_\infty \Sigma_a^c \phi_c - (-D_c \nabla^2 \phi_c) - \Sigma_a^c \phi_c = 0 \qquad (9.97)$$

When the constants are combined into the material buckling for the core, this becomes

$$\nabla^2 \phi_c + B_c^2 \phi_c = 0 \qquad (9.98)$$

Equation (9.98) describes the core flux, ϕ_c, from the origin to the core radius, r_c.

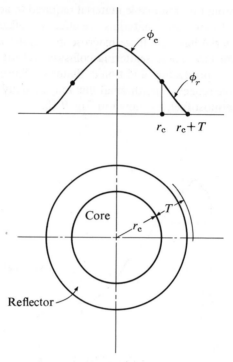

FIG. 9.11   *Spherical core with finite reflector and flux variation along a diameter.*

In the reflector there is no source term and the diffusion equation becomes

$$-(-D_r\nabla^2\phi_r) - \sum_a^r\phi_r = 0 \qquad (9.99)$$

Rearranging, and letting $D_r/\sum_a^r = L_r^2$, the square of the thermal diffusion length for the reflector material,

$$\nabla^2\phi_r - \frac{1}{L_r^2}\phi_r = 0 \qquad (9.100)$$

This equation describes the reflector flux, ϕ_r, from the core boundary at $r = r_c$ to the extrapolated boundary of the reflector at $r = r_c + T$. The following boundary conditions will determine the four constants which will result from the solutions of the two diffusion equations (9.98) and (9.100):

(1) the flux, ϕ_c, at the center of the core must remain finite;
(2) the flux, ϕ_r, at the extrapolated reflector boundary $(r_c + T)$ must be zero;
(3) at the core-reflector interface $(r = r_c)$ the core flux must equal the reflector flux; and

(4) at the core-reflector interface ($r = r_c$) the neutron current must be continuous. Therefore, the current leaving the core must equal that entering the reflector ($J_c = J_r$).

Equation (9.98) can be solved in a manner identical to that used for the bare core. The core flux is

$$\phi_c = \frac{C_1 \cos B_c r}{r} + \frac{C_2 \sin B_c r}{r} \tag{9.101}$$

The first boundary condition dictates that $C_1 = 0$ since

$$\lim_{r \to 0} \frac{C_1 \cos B_c r}{r} = \frac{C_1}{0} = \infty$$

Thus, the core flux is described as

$$\phi_c = \frac{C_2 \sin B_c r}{r} \tag{9.102}$$

Returning to the reflector equation and expressing it in terms of spherical coordinates where the flux varies only in a radial direction will give

$$\frac{d^2\phi r}{dr^2} + \frac{2}{r}\frac{d\phi}{dr} - \frac{1}{L_r^2}\phi_r = 0 \tag{9.103}$$

Letting

$$u = \phi_r r \tag{9.104a}$$

$$\frac{du}{dr} = r\frac{d\phi_r}{dr} + \phi_r \tag{9.104b}$$

$$\frac{d^2u}{dr^2} = r\frac{d^2\phi_r}{dr^2} + 2\frac{d\phi_r}{dr} \tag{9.104c}$$

Dividing (9.104c) by r

$$\frac{1}{r}\frac{d^2u}{dr^2} = \frac{d^2\phi_r}{dr^2} + \frac{2}{r}\frac{d\phi}{dr} \tag{9.105}$$

Hence

$$\frac{d^2u}{dr^2} - \frac{1}{L_r^2}u = 0 \tag{9.106}$$

Using operator notation

$$D^2 - \frac{1}{L_r^2} = 0$$

$$D = \pm\frac{1}{L_r}$$

giving as a solution

$$u = C_3 e^{r/L_r} + C_4 e^{-r/L_r} = \phi_r r \tag{9.107}$$

The reflector flux is then

$$\phi_r = \frac{C_3 e^{r/L_r}}{r} + \frac{C_4 e^{-r/L_r}}{r} \tag{9.108}$$

The second boundary condition is next examined. When

$$r = r_c + T, \qquad \phi_r = 0$$

$$0 = \frac{C_3 e^{(r_c+T)/L_r}}{r_c + T} + \frac{C_4 e^{-(r_c+T)/L_r}}{r_c + T}$$

Therefore

$$C_4 = -C_3 e^{2(r_c+T)/L_r}$$

The reflector flux can now be written

$$\phi_r = \frac{C_3 e^{r/L_r}}{r} - \frac{C_3 e^{2(r_c+T)/L_r}}{r} \cdot e^{-r/L_r} \tag{9.109}$$

$$= \frac{C_3}{r} e^{(r_c+T)/L_r} [e^{(r-r_c-T)/L_r} - e^{-(r-r_c-T)/L_r}]$$

$$= \frac{C_3 e^{(r_c+T)/L_r}}{r} \cdot 2 \sinh \left(\frac{r - r_c - T}{L_r} \right) \tag{9.110}$$

Let $C_3' = 2C_3$ and then

$$\phi_r = \frac{C_3' e^{(r_c+T)/L_r}}{r} \sinh \left(\frac{r - r_c - T}{L_r} \right) \tag{9.111}$$

Equating fluxes at the interface

$$\frac{C_2 \sin B_c r_c}{r_c} = \frac{C_3' e^{(r_c+T)/L_r}}{r_c} \sinh \left(-\frac{T}{L_r} \right)$$

$$C_2 = -\frac{C_3' e^{(r_c+T)/L_r}}{\sin B_c r_c} \sinh \frac{T}{L_r} \tag{9.112}$$

Turning to the final boundary condition, the neutron currents at the interfaces must be evaluated.

$$J_c \bigg|_{r = r_c} = -D_c \frac{d\phi_c}{dr} = \frac{-D_c C_2 (r_c B_c \cos B_c r_c - \sin B_c r_c)}{r_c^2} \tag{9.113}$$

$$J_r \bigg|_{r = r_c} = -D_r \frac{d\phi_r}{dr} = \frac{-D_r C_3' e^{(r_c+T)/L_r}[(r_c/L_r) \cosh(-T/L_r) - \sinh(-T/L_r)]}{r_c^2} \tag{9.114}$$

setting (9.113) and (9.114) equal and substituting (9.112)

$$\frac{D_c \sinh T/L_r}{\sin B_c r_c} (r_c B_c \cos B_c r_c - \sin B_c r_c) =$$

$$-D_r \left(\frac{r_c}{L_r} \cosh \left(\frac{T}{L_r} \right) + \sinh \left(\frac{T}{L_r} \right) \right) \tag{9.115}$$

Rearranging,

$$\frac{D_c}{D_r}[1 - r_c B_c \cot B_c r_c] = \frac{r_c}{L_r} \coth\left(\frac{T}{L_r}\right) + 1 \qquad (9.116)$$

Notice that this rather cumbersome expression for the core radius, r_c, involves core and reflector properties (D_c, B_c, D_r, and L_r) plus the reflector thickness, T. In its present form (9.116) may be solved for r_c only by trial and error if the other parameters are known. However, if the core and reflector diffusion constants are approximately equal ($D_c \approx D_r$)

$$\cot B_c r_c = -\frac{1}{B_c L_r} \coth (T/L_r) \qquad (9.117)$$

Cotangents in the second quadrant are negative and will have the same magnitude but opposite sign from the cotangent of the supplement of the angle.

$$\cot (\pi - B_c r_c) = -\cot (B_c r_c) \qquad (9.118)$$

Therefore,

$$\cot (\pi - B_c r_c) = \frac{1}{B_c L_r} \coth (T/L_r) \qquad (9.119)$$

Now, solving for r_c explicitly

$$r_c = \frac{\pi - \cot^{-1}[(1/B_c L_r) \coth (T/L_r)]}{B_c} \qquad (9.120)$$

When the ratio of T/L_r increases, the $\coth (T/L_r)$ decreases toward 1 as a limit. When the reflector thickness is 2.65 times the thermal diffusion length for the reflector material

$$\coth 2.65 = 1.01$$

and the coth is only 1 percent greater than if the reflector were infinitely thick. For practical purposes if $T/L_r \geq 2.65$, the reflector can be considered infinitely thick and the expression for the core radius becomes

$$r_c = \frac{\pi - \cot^{-1}(1/B_c L_r)}{B_c} \qquad (9.121)$$

Reflector savings, δ, is the difference between the radius of an unreflected core and the radius of a core with reflector.

$$\delta = \frac{\pi}{B_c} - d - \frac{\pi - \cot^{-1}[(1/B_c L_r) \coth (T/L_r)]}{B_c}$$

$$= \frac{\cot^{-1}[1/B_c L_r \coth (T/L_r)]}{B_c} - d \qquad (9.122)$$

Example 5. For the homogeneous graphite uranium mixture used previously, determine the critical radius of a spherical core reflected with an infinite thickness of graphite. What will be the reflector savings, the ratio of the peak flux to the flux at the core-reflector interface, and the maximum flux when the reflected core develops 1 kW (th)?

$$N_c = \frac{1.6 \times 6.03 \times 10^{23}}{12} = 8.03 \times 10^{22} \frac{\text{graphite nuclei}}{\text{cm}^3}$$

$$\Sigma_a^r = 8.03 \times 10^{22} \times 0.0034 \times 10^{-24} \times \frac{\sqrt{\pi}}{2} = 2.42 \times 10^{-4}\,\text{cm}^{-1}$$

$$D_r = \frac{\lambda_{tr}}{3} = \frac{1}{3\,\Sigma_{tr}} = \frac{1}{3 \times 8.03 \times 10^{22} \times 4.8 \times 10^{-24}[1 - (2/3 \times 12)]}$$

$$= 0.915\;\text{cm}$$

$$L_r^2 = \frac{D_r}{\Sigma_a} = \frac{0.915}{2.42 \times 10^{-4}} = 3780\;\text{cm}^2$$

$$L_r = 61.5\;\text{cm}$$

$$\cot(\pi - B_c r_c) = \frac{1}{B_c L_r} = \frac{1}{0.0538 \times 61.5} = 0.302$$

$$\pi - B_c r_c = 1.277$$

$$r_c = \frac{\pi - 1.277}{0.0538} = 34.7\;\text{cm}$$

$$\delta = \frac{\pi}{B_c} - d - r_c = \frac{\pi}{0.0538} - 1.93 - 34.7$$

$$\delta = 21.9\;\text{cm}$$

$$\frac{\phi_{max}}{\phi_{r_c}} = \frac{B_c r_c}{\sin B_c r_c} = \frac{0.0538(34.7)}{\sin(0.0538 \times 34.7)} = 1.95$$

$$\phi_{max} = \frac{B_c^2 P}{4\pi G \,\Sigma_{fis}\,[(1/B_c)\sin B_c r_c - r_c \cos B_c r_c]}$$

$$= \frac{(0.0538)^2 \times 1}{4 \times \pi \times 8.9 \times 10^{-18} \times 0.0103 \times 3600[(1/0.0538)\sin(0.0538}$$

$$\overline{\times 34.7) - 34.7\cos(0.0538 \times 34.7)]}$$

$$= 2.51 \times 10^{11}\;\text{n/cm}^2\;\text{sec.}$$

Comparing the results of examples 4 and 5, it can be seen that the reflected core has a volume which is only 23.2 percent that of the bare core. This means that only 23.2 percent as much fissionable ^{235}U will be required for criticality. Although the peak flux for a given power is an order of magnitude greater, the ratio of ϕ_{max}/ϕ_{r_c} is only 1.95 as compared to a ratio of 29.0 in the bare core. The flux is considerably flattened by the addition of a reflector, thus making the consumption of fissionable nuclei much more uniform across the core.

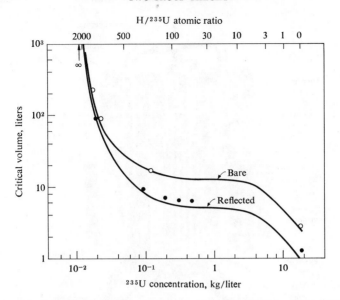

FIG. 9.12 *Transport theory calculation of the critical volume of bare and water reflected (reflector thickness = 20 cm) spheres as a function of* ^{235}U *concentration (or* $H/^{235}U$ *atomic ratio) of homogeneous* ^{235}U-H_2O *systems. The open and filled circles represent experimental results.* [*Soodak, H.,* Reactor Handbook, *Vol. III, Physics, New York: Interscience Publishers, 1962.*]

Fig. 9.12 shows the advantage of using a reflector for a spherical core for a $^{235}U - H_2O$ system. When the $H/^{235}U$ atomic ratio is 100, the bare core requires a critical volume of about 14 liters as compared to 7 liters (experimental) for the reflected core. The saving of 50 percent in the fuel inventory for the core is very worthwhile.

The importance of the reflector in achieving a critical configuration was emphasized with the successful orbiting of the SNAP-10A space nuclear auxiliary power system. After the vehicle was launched into a successful orbit criticality was achieved by rotation of the Be reflectors into place around the core. The system then began to produce its rated 600 watts (e) output with the heat supplied by the core to the thermoelectric generator. Fig. 9.13 shows the SNAP-10A reactor.

TWO-GROUP THEORY

Between birth and thermalization a fast neutron makes on the average n collisions, traveling a distance $(\lambda_{tr})_f$ in the lab system between

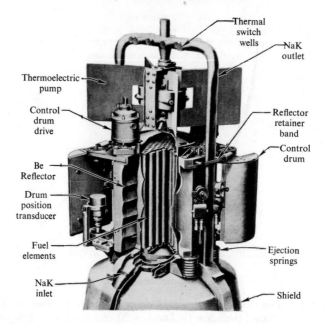

FIG. 9.13   *Cutaway view of the SNAP-10A Reactor.* [*Courtesy Atomics International, a division of North American Aviation, Inc.*]

each collision. $(\lambda_{tr})_f$ is the corrected scattering or transport mean free path based on the epithermal scattering cross sections. The slowing down mean free path, λ_{sl} is the total distance traveled during slowing down. Its reciprocal is the macroscopic slowing down cross section, which may be thought of as the probability of slowing down.

$$\lambda_{sl} = n\lambda_{tr} = \frac{1}{\sum_{sl}} \qquad (9.123)$$

In two-group theory the neutrons are considered as either fast or thermal. The thermal neutrons diffuse, having leakage and absorption. The absorption further causes fission. The fast neutrons are lost by slowing down. Their source is thermal fission, while the source of the thermal neutrons is provided by the fast neutrons slowing down. To describe this situation the diffusion equation must be written for each group. The fast group will be considered first.

$$-(-D_f)\nabla^2\phi_f - \sum_{sl}\phi_f + f\eta\sum_{ath}\phi_{th} = 0$$

| fast neutron leakage | slowing down (removal by thermalization) | source of fast n's from thermal fission |

$$(9.124)$$

Note that the leakage involves a fast diffusion constant, D_f, and the Laplacian operator for the fast flux, $\nabla^2 \phi_f$. The second term represents the number of slowing down interactions in a unit volume. This can be thought of as slowing down, more or less, in one collision. Leakage and slowing down must be balanced by fast neutron production. The number of fast neutrons produced in a unit volume is the number of thermal neutrons absorbed times the product of the thermal utilization factor and the thermal fission factor. Dividing Equation (9.124) by D_f gives

$$\nabla^2 \phi_f - \frac{\sum_{sl}}{D_f} \phi_f + \frac{f\eta\sum_{ath}\phi_{th}}{D_f} = 0 \tag{9.125}$$

The ratio of $D_f/\sum_{sl}$ in the fast neutron diffusion equation is analogous to L^2 in the one-group diffusion equation, (9.47a). It can be designated as L_s^2, the square of the slowing down length.

$$L_s^2 = \frac{D_f}{\sum_{sl}} = \frac{n_f\lambda_{tr}^2}{3} \tag{9.126}$$

Equations (8.48) and (8.57) can be combined with (9.126) to give

$$L_s^2 = \frac{\ln(E_0/E_{th})}{3\xi(\sum_s)^2(1 - \overline{\cos\psi})^2} \tag{9.127}$$

$$L_s = \sqrt{\frac{\lambda_{sl}\lambda_{tr}}{3}} \tag{9.128}$$

Thus, the slowing down length is seen to be more or less an average of the mean free path for slowing down and the mean free path for scatter. The fast diffusion equation has now become

$$\nabla^2 \phi_f - \frac{\phi_f}{L_s^2} + \frac{f\eta\sum_{ath}\phi_{th}}{D_f} = 0 \tag{9.129}$$

In a similar manner a thermal diffusion equation can be written as

$$-(-D_{th})\nabla^2\phi_{th} - \sum_{ath}\phi_{th} + \varepsilon p\sum_{sl}\phi_f = 0$$

$\uparrow$ Leakage of thermal neutrons $\qquad$ $\uparrow$ Absorption of thermal neutrons $\qquad$ $\uparrow$ Source thermal neutrons from the slowing down of fast neutrons

$$\tag{9.130}$$

This equation is similar to (9.43) for one-group theory, except that the source of thermal neutrons is from the slowing down of fast neutrons. The number of slowing down interactions can be increased slightly by the fast fission factor, ε, and is reduced by the resonance escape probability, p.

Rewriting,

$$\nabla^2\phi_{\text{th}} - \frac{\phi_{\text{th}}}{L^2} + \frac{\varepsilon p\sum_{sl}\phi_f}{D_{\text{th}}} = 0 \qquad (9.131)$$

Experiment has shown that fast and thermal fluxes in a large bare core will have the same shape, differing primarily in magnitude (see Fig.

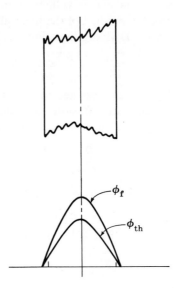

Fig. 9.14   *Fast and thermal neutron flux distributions in a bare slab reactor.*

9.14).   It is assumed that in both instances, for steady state operation, the same buckling can be used in the diffusion equation.

$$\nabla^2\phi_{\text{th}} + B^2\phi_{\text{th}} = 0 \qquad (9.132)$$

$$\nabla^2\phi_f + B^2\phi_f = 0 \qquad (9.133)$$

Comparing 9.132 with (9.131), and (9.133) with (9.129), it is seen that

$$B^2\phi_{\text{th}} = -\frac{\phi_{\text{th}}}{L^2} + \frac{\varepsilon p\sum_{sl}\phi_f}{D_{\text{th}}} \qquad (9.134)$$

and

$$B^2\phi_f = -\frac{\phi_f}{L_s^2} + \frac{f\eta\sum_a\phi_{\text{th}}}{D_f} \qquad (9.135)$$

Solving (9.135) for ϕ_f

$$\phi_f = \frac{f\eta\sum_a\phi_{\text{th}}L_s^2}{D_f[B^2L_s^2 + 1]} \qquad (9.136)$$

Substituting (9.136) into (9.134),

$$[B^2L^2 + 1]\phi_{th} = \frac{\varepsilon p \sum_{sl} L_s^2 f \eta \sum_{a \phi_{th}} L_s^2}{D_{th} D_f [B^2 L_s^2 + 1]} \tag{9.137a}$$

Simplifying,

$$[B^2L^2 + 1][B^2L_s^2 + 1] = k_\infty \tag{9.137b}$$

Rearranging,

$$1 = k_\infty \left[\frac{1}{B^2L^2 + 1} \right]\left[\frac{1}{B^2L_s^2 + 1} \right] \tag{9.137c}$$

At the critical condition the effective multiplication factor is unity. For two-group theory the non-leakage probability is the product of the thermal non-leakage probability and the non-leakage probability for fast neutrons. Since (9.48c) defined the thermal non-leakage probability, the fast non-leakage probability is

$$P_{NL_f} = \frac{1}{B^2L_s^2 + 1} \tag{9.138}$$

The total non-leakage probability is

$$P_{NL} = \frac{1}{B^4L_s^2L^2 + B^2L_s^2 + B^2L^2 + 1} \tag{9.139}$$

For large cores with small values of buckling the $B^4L_s^2L^2$ term can be omitted and

$$P_{NL} = \frac{1}{B^2(L_s^2 + L^2) + 1} \tag{9.140}$$

The sum of the squares of the diffusion length and the slowing down length is known as the square of the migration length, M^2.

$$M^2 = L_s^2 + L^2 \tag{9.141}$$

when M^2 replaces L^2 in (9.48a), this is often called *modified one-group theory*. Buckling is handled as with one-group theory and the results are those for *two-group theory* when the $B^4L_s^2L^2$ term can be ignored.

$$B^2 = \frac{k_\infty - 1}{M^2} \tag{9.142}$$

Example 6.   Compare the diameter of the critical sphere in Example 4 with that for the same material using both modified one-group theory and full two-group theory.

First the slowing down length must be determined.

$$E_{av} = \frac{3}{2} kT = 1.5 \times 0.025 = 0.0375 \text{ eV}$$

This is the average neutron energy for the thermal group.
The number of collisions to thermalize is

$$n = \frac{\ln E_0/E_{th}}{\xi} = \frac{\ln [(2 \times 10^6)/0.0375]}{0.158} = 113$$

$$(\textstyle\sum_{tr})_f = N_c \sigma^c_{s_f}(1 - \overline{\cos \psi_c}) + N_u \sigma^u_{s_f}(1 - \overline{\cos \psi_u})$$

$$= 7.96 \times 10^{22} \times 4.66 \times 10^{-24} \left(1 - \frac{2}{3 \times 12}\right)$$

$$+ 3.98 \times 10^{20} \times 8.3 \times 10^{-24} \left(1 - \frac{2}{3(238)}\right)$$

$$= 0.351 + 0.0033 = 0.354 \text{ cm}^2/\text{cm}^3$$

$$L^2_s = \frac{n_f}{3 \sum_{tr}^2} = \frac{113}{3 \times (0.354)^2} = 302 \text{ cm}^2$$

$$M^2 = L^2_s + L^2 = 302 + 68.2 = 370 \text{ cm}^2$$

$$B^2 = \frac{k_\infty - 1}{M^2} = \frac{1.198 - 1}{370} = 0.000536$$

$$B = 0.0232$$

$$r_g = \frac{\pi}{B} - d = \frac{\pi}{0.0232} - 1.93 = 135.2 - 1.93$$

$$= 133.3 \text{ (modified one-group theory)}$$

$$B^4 L^2_s L^2 + B^2(L^2_s + L^2) + (1 - k_\infty) = 0$$

$$B^4 + \left(\frac{L^2_s + L^2}{L^2_s L^2}\right) B^2 - \left(\frac{k_\infty - 1}{L^2_s L^2}\right) = 0$$

$$B^4 + \frac{370}{(302)(68.2)} B^2 - \frac{0.198}{(302)(68.2)} = 0$$

$$B^4 + 0.017963 \, B^2 - 0.00000961 = 0$$

$$B^2 = \frac{-0.017963 \pm \sqrt{0.017963^2 + 4(0.00000961)}}{2}$$

$$= \frac{-0.01796 + 0.01900}{2} = 0.00052$$

$$B = 0.0228$$

$$r_g = \frac{\pi}{0.0228} - 1.93 = 137.6 - 1.93 = 135.7 \text{ cm (two-group theory)}$$

Fermi age theory assumes that neutrons lose energy in a smooth manner, rather than in discrete steps. For a heavier moderator like graphite, where 113 collisions are required for thermalization, this model is quite adequate. It is less satisfactory for a light water moderator where, on the average, only 19 collisions are required.

Consideration of the variation in the slowing down density during thermalization shows that the fast non-leakage probability is

$$P_{NL_f} = e^{-B^2 \tau} \qquad (9.143)$$

where $\tau = L_s^2 =$ Fermi age. The Fermi age and the square of the slowing down length are identical. When the fast non-leakage probability is expanded in a series

$$P_{NL_f} = \frac{1}{1 + L_s^2 B^2 + L_s^4 B^4 + \cdots} \qquad (9.144)$$

For larger cores where B^2 is small, the terms beyond the second one in the denominator contribute very little. Then the results of Fermi age theory and the two-group theory used here are comparable.

COMPARISON OF ONE-GROUP, MODIFIED ONE–GROUP, AND TWO-GROUP THEORY FOR A MOLTEN SALT CORE

The molten salt reactor concept is being studied because of its possible development as a thermal breeder (see Chapter 13). A typical salt with mole fractions of 0.72 LiF$_2$, 0.16 BeF$_2$, 0.115 ThF$_4$, and 0.005 ^{233}UF$_4$ will have an infinite multiplication factor of only 0.1435. The value is low because of insufficient moderation. As graphite is added to a core assembly the value of k_∞ will increase until it surpasses 1 at 82 percent graphite and 18 percent salt content. As the graphite content is further increased k_∞ increases until there is about 96 percent graphite and 4 percent salt. Then it falls rapidly to 0 for pure graphite. The reasons for this can be inferred from Fig. 9.15. As the salt fraction increases, the thermal utilization factor, f, increases because a larger fraction of the neutron captures take place in the fissile ^{233}U. At the same time the resonance escape probability, p, decreases as the probability of resonance capture by the fertile ^{232}Th nuclei increases with the larger salt fraction. The other two factors in the four factor equation remain unchanged, and thus, a peak occurs for k_∞.

The buckling shown in Fig. 9.15 is for modified one-group theory. It indicates that a volume fraction of approximately 6 percent salt will result in the minimum core size. The fact that a 13 percent salt fraction has been proposed for a molten salt breeder core is indication that minimum core size is not always a primary consideration.

Fig. 9.16 shows the effect of varying the mole fraction of ^{233}UF$_4$ on the critical size and power developed by a cylindrical core (diam. = ht.) using one-group, modified one-group, and two-group theory. Note that the one-group theory, which ignores the leakage of fast neutrons, results in smaller critical sizes and much less power for a given peak flux. The closeness of the curves for the modified one-group and two-group theories indicates that the two models are in close agreement for this type

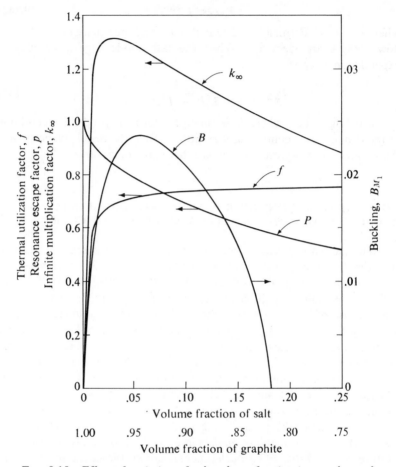

FIG. 9.15 *Effect of variation of salt volume fraction in a molten salt core with graphite as the moderator. Salt composition (mole fractions): 0.72 $^7LiF_2$, 0.16 BeF_2, 0.115 ThF_4, and 0.005 $^{233}UF_4$. Average core temperature 650°C.*

of reactor. It also emphasizes the importance of considering the fast leakage. With smaller mole fractions of $^{233}UF_4$ in the salt $(k_\infty - 1)$ is smaller, reducing the buckling, and increasing the core size. For large power reactors this is desirable, as the specific core power (kW/liter) may be limited by heat transfer and materials considerations.

Fig. 9.17 illustrates the effect of three different mole fractions of $^{233}UF_4$ on k_∞ and B (modified one-group) as the salt fraction is increased. For a given salt fraction larger amounts of fissile material will increase k_∞ and reduce B, resulting in smaller critical sizes.

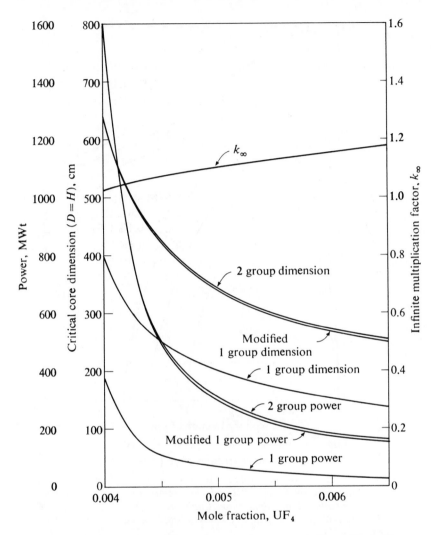

FIG. 9.16 k_∞, critical size, and power for a bare, cylindrical $(D = H)$, molten salt core vs. mole fraction of $^{233}UF_4$ in salt. Salt composition (mole fractions): 0.72 $^7LiF_2$, 0.16 BeF_2, (0.12-UF_4) ThF_4, and (0.004 to 0.006) $^{233}UF_4$. Average core temperature 650°C and peak thermal flux 10^{14} n/cm² sec.

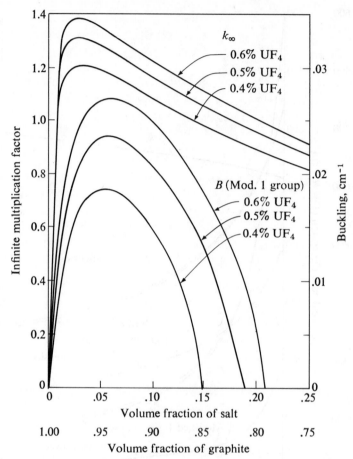

Fig. 9.17 *Effect of salt volume fraction in a graphite moderated molten salt core on k_∞ and B (modified one-group) for three different* $^{233}UF_4$ *contents. Salt composition (mole fractions): 0.72 $^7LiF_2$, 0.16 BeF_2, (0.12-UF_4) ThF_4, and $^{233}UF_4$ as labeled on curves. Core temperature 650°C.*

FAST REACTORS

In a fast reactor system the average neutron energy lies between 0.1 and 0.5 MeV. There is no moderator material to cause scattering collisions and produce a large degradation of energy. Steam, gas, and liquid metals are being considered as coolants; liquid sodium is the most popular current choice. A principal requirement of fast reactor coolants is that they should not appreciably moderate neutrons. Thus, light nuclei should be kept to a minimum in a fast core.

At high neutron energies the ratio of fission cross section to capture cross section is significantly greater, so that more neutrons are available for absorption by fertile nuclei. ^{239}Pu is most attractive for a fast reactor system since η, the number of fast neutrons emitted per neutron absorbed by the fissile nucleus, is 2.92 at 1 MeV and 2.4 for the neutron spectrum in an oxide-fueled fast reactor, as compared to 2.11 at thermal energies. Thus, the oxide-fueled breeder will have 0.4 neutrons per fission to divide between breeding, leakage, and parasitic capture in nonfuel material.

The fission mean free path and the diffusion length for a fast spectrum of neutrons are larger than in a thermal system producing a tendency for the fast reactor to leak more neutrons. This requires that the enrichment of the fuel be increased by a factor of about 5. To get the same output per kg of fissile material in the more highly enriched fuel, the power density of the core must increase similarly. The excellence of the heat transfer characteristics of sodium is some help. Also, the fuel rod diameters are smaller than in water cooled reactors, the diameters being about 3/16 inch rather than the order of $\frac{1}{2}$ inch for thermal systems.

The small fuel rod size coupled with the longer diffusion length tends to allow the core to be treated as homogeneous with even less error than is involved in a thermal reactor.

ONE-GROUP THEORY FOR FAST CORES

One-group theory can be applied fairly effectively to the determination of the critical size of a fast reactor, provided that properly averaged values for the neutron spectrum are used. For example, a metallic fuel produces a harder (higher average energy) spectrum than does an oxide-fueled reactor, while carbide-fueled reactors are intermediate between the other two types. The presence of oxygen or carbon in the fuel provides some moderation due to elastic collisions with the light nuclei, resulting in a softer neutron spectrum. Metallic fuels with their harder spectrum would give a higher breeding ratio but would be unable to stand the temperatures resulting from the high power density. Carbide fuels are being developed, but at the present time it appears that at least the first generation of fast breeders will be designed for oxide fuel. Appendix E lists values of cross sections and η appropriate for an oxide-fueled fast neutron spectrum.

For a fast core the expression for the infinite multiplication factor reduces to

$$k_\infty = f\eta \tag{9.145}$$

Since few neutrons reach thermal energies the resonance escape probability, p, is no longer a problem of significance and the fast fission factor, ε, is inappropriate due to the lack of a significant number of thermal fissions.   If one expands eq. 9.145

$$k_\infty = \frac{\sum_a^{\text{fuel}} \eta}{\sum_a^{\text{fuel}} + \sum_a^{\text{clad}} + \sum_a^{\text{Na}}} \qquad (9.146)$$

If more than one fissionable species is present the $\sum_a^{\text{fuel}}\eta$ terms are added to account for the contribution of each to the next generation of neutrons (See Example 7).   Note that the fertile isotopes ^{232}Th, ^{238}U, ^{240}Pu, and ^{242}Pu can provide significant numbers of neutrons in a fast spectrum.

Example 7.   An oxide-fueled fast reactor is to have a core containing 3.5 v/o ^{239}PuO$_2$, 26.5 v/o ^{238}UO$_2$, 25 v/o stainless steel clad and structure, and 45 v/o sodium as coolant.
   a. Compute the infinite multiplication factor for the core.

Material	$\sum_a$	$\times$ Vol. Frac. =	net $\sum_a$
^{239}PuO$_2$	0.060	0.035	0.0021
^{238}UO$_2$	0.008	0.265	0.00212
Na	4×10^{-5}	0.45	0.000018
SS	0.0015	0.25	0.000375
		1.00	0.004613

$$k_\infty = \frac{\sum_a^{\text{fuel}} \eta}{\sum_a^{\text{fuel}} + \sum_a^{\text{SS}} + \sum_a^{\text{Na}}}$$

$$k_\infty = \frac{0.0021 \times 2.4 + 0.00212 \times 0.4}{0.00461}$$

$$= 1.092 + 0.184 = 1.276$$

Note the contribution of the ^{238}U to k_∞.

   b. Compute the diffusion length, material buckling, and the non-leakage probability for the core.

Material	$\sum_{tr}$	$\times$ Vol. Frac. =	net $\sum_{tr}$
PuO$_2$ + UO$_2$	0.18	0.30	0.054
Na	0.08	0.45	0.036
SS	0.25	0.25	0.0625
		1.00	0.1525

$$L^2 = D_f/\sum_a = \frac{1}{3\sum_{tr}\sum_a} = \frac{1}{3 \times 0.1525 \times 0.004613}$$

$$= 475 \text{ cm}^2$$

$$L = 21.8 \text{ cm}$$

$$B^2 = \frac{k_\infty - 1}{L^2} = \frac{1.276 - 1}{475} = 0.000580 \text{ cm}^{-2}$$

$$B = 0.0241 \text{ cm}^{-1}$$

$$P_{NL} = \frac{1}{1 + B^2L^2} = \frac{1}{1 + 0.00058 \times 475}$$

$$= 0.785$$

c. What would be the radius of a bare critical spherical core?

$$r = \frac{\pi}{B} - \frac{2}{3}\lambda_{tr} = 3.1416/0.0241 - \frac{2}{3} \times \frac{1}{0.1525}$$

$$= 131.2 - 4.4 = 126.8 \text{ cm}$$

FAST CORE BLANKET

The tendency for neutrons to leak from a fast reactor core makes it desirable to use a reflector, which is termed a *blanket*. This blanket contains fertile material so that, in addition to scattering neutrons back into the core proper, there will be conversion due to neutron absorption by the fertile nuclei. Also, there will be some neutron production because of fast fission in the fertile material. The effective use of a blanket contributes significantly to the ability of the reactor as a whole to breed more new fissile nuclei than are consumed. If this happens, the reactor is then a *breeder*.

The blanket can contain a higher fraction of fertile material than the sum of the fertile plus fissile material in the core proper, since there is less fission and less resultant heat generated. Because of the lower heat generation, less coolant is required and the fertile "fuel" elements can have a larger diameter, reducing the amount of cladding, as illustrated in Examples 7 & 8.

The blanket will have a subcritical infinite multiplication factor ($k_\infty < 1$) and in the diffusion equation the buckling will be negative. For steady state it is

$$k_{\infty r}\textstyle\sum_a^r\phi_r - (-D_r\nabla^2\phi_r) - \textstyle\sum_a^r\phi_r = 0 \tag{9.147}$$

$$\nabla^2\phi_r - \frac{(1 - k_{\infty r})\sum_a^r\phi_r}{D_r} = 0 \tag{9.148}$$

$$\nabla^2\phi_r - B_r^2\phi_r = 0 \tag{9.149}$$

Note that the subcritical B_r^2 is analogous to $1/L_r^2$ in the diffusion equation for a nonmultiplying thermal reflector (See Eq. [9.100]). Thus, the solution is identical if B_r is substituted for $1/L_r$.

$$\frac{D_c}{D_r}(1 - r_cB_c \cot B_cr_c) = B_rr_c \coth (B_rT) + 1 \tag{9.150}$$

When the diffusion constants are approximately equal for core and blanket the core radius becomes

$$r_c = \frac{\pi - \cot^{-1}(B_r/B_c)\coth(B_rT)}{B_c}$$ (9.151)

The reflector flux can be expressed as

$$\phi_r = \frac{Ce^{Br(r_c + T)}}{r}\sinh B_r(r - r_c - T)$$ (9.152)

Example 8. A 2-ft thick blanket is added to the spherical core of Example 7. The blanket is to contain 50 v/o $^{238}UO_2$, 35 v/o sodium, and 15 percent stainless steel cladding and structure.
a. Determine the reflector buckling.

Material	Σ_a	$\times$ Vol. Frac. =	Net Σ_a
$^{238}UO_2$	0.00815	0.50	0.00408
Na	4×10^{-5}	0.35	0.000014
SS	0.0015	0.15	0.000225
		1.00	0.004319 cm^{-1}

$$k_\infty = \frac{\eta_{238}\sum_a^{238}}{\sum_a^{\text{total}}} = \frac{0.4 \times 0.00408}{0.004319}$$

$$= 0.378$$

Material	Σ_{tr}	$\times$ Vol. Frac. =	Net Σ_{tr}
$^{238}UO_2$	0.18	0.50	0.090
Na	0.08	0.35	0.028
SS	0.25	0.15	0.0375
		1.00	0.1555 cm^{-1}

$$L_r^2 = \frac{1}{3\sum_{tr}\sum_a} = \frac{1}{3 \times 0.1555 \times 0.00432}$$

$$= 496 \text{ cm}^2$$

$$L_r = 22.3 \text{ cm}$$

$$B_r^2 = \frac{1 - k_\infty}{L_r^2} = \frac{1 - 0.378}{496} = 0.001253 \text{ cm}^{-2}$$

$$B_r = 0.0354 \text{ cm}^{-1}$$

b. What will be the critical radius of the core when surrounded by the blanket?

$$D_r = \frac{1}{3\sum_{tr}^r} = \frac{1}{3 \times 0.1555} = 2.14 \text{ cm}$$

$$D_c = \frac{1}{3\sum_{tr}^c} = \frac{1}{3 \times 0.1525} = 2.19 \text{ cm}$$

Therefore, D_r and D_c are approximately equal

$$r_c = \frac{\pi - \cot^{-1}((B_r/B_c)\coth TB_r)}{B_c}$$

$$= \frac{\pi - \cot^{-1}((0.0354/0.0241) \coth(2 \times 12 \times 2.54 + 4.3)(0.0354)}{0.0241}$$

$$= 105.9 \text{ cm}$$

The addition of the 2-ft blanket results in a reduction of 41.8 percent in the volume of core materials required to achieve criticality. In addition, a large fraction of the neutrons leaking from the core are captured by fertile nuclei in the blanket and are converted to fissile nuclei making a substantial contribution to the ability of the fast core to breed.

MULTIGROUP CALCULATIONS

To approach the actual situation where flux and cross sections are energy dependent, it is necessary to break the neutron population into numerous energy groups. Each group may gain neutrons by slowing down from higher energy groups and the higher energy groups will receive neutrons directly from fission. Neutrons are lost from a group by slowing down to the next lower group, by absorption (sometimes producing fission), or by leakage out of the core. For some of the fast groups absorption can be ignored, but in the epithermal and thermal regions it must be considered. For the thermal group there is no loss by slowing down. Proper cross sections must be used for each energy group.

The complexity of multigroup calculations demands the use of a digital computer to solve the complex array of simultaneous equations resulting from writing the diffusion equation for each group. The use of reflectors, blankets, and fuel loadings where either enrichment or lattice geometry varies will mean that separate equations must be written for each of the various regions for each group.

Computer codes are available for various combinations of fuel and moderator. Caution must be exercised that the code being used is correct for the calculation at hand. A code for a water moderated, UO_2 fueled core will be of little use if applied to a graphite-moderated, sodium-cooled core fueled with UC.

PROBLEMS

1. Compute the thermal fission factor for 4 percent enriched UC (uranium monocarbide).
2. Compute the thermal utilization factor for a core where there are 25 moles of heavy water per 1 mole of 4 percent enriched UC. What would be the value if light water replaced the heavy water?

3. Repeat Example 1, using natural uranium as the fuel.

4. Compute the infinite multiplication factor for a homogeneous mixture containing 10 moles of ^{232}Th and 500 moles of Be per 1 mole of ^{233}U.

5. A reactor lattice consists of 0.25 inch diameter UO_2 elements with 0.010 inch thick Zr clad spaced 1 inch on centers in a square lattice, as shown. The moderator is D_2O. Compute the infinite multiplication factor, k_∞. The fuel enrichment is 2 percent and the density of the D_2O of 0.77 gm/cm^3 at the average core temperature of 300°C.

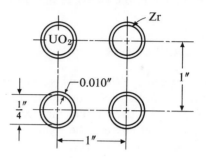

6. Using one-group theory for the lattice of Problem 5 determine
   (a) The material buckling,
   (b) The thickness of an infinite critical slab,
   (c) The diameter of a bare critical sphere,
   (d) The dimensions of a bare critical cube, and
   (e) The height of a critical core with a square base 4 feet on a side.

7. For the bare spherical core of Problem 6 the maximum flux is to be 10^{12} n/cm^2 sec. What power will be developed, Kw (th)?

8. Develop an expression similar to Eq. (9.93) for a bare critical cubic core. How many Kw (th) will be developed in the core of Problem 6(d) if the peak flux is 10^{12} n/cm^2 sec?

9. A spherical core having its lattice defined as in Problem 9.5 is to be reflected with heavy water. The peak flux is to be 10^{12} n/cm^2 sec.
   (a) Find the critical radius of the core when the extrapolated reflector thickness is equal to the thermal diffusion length for the D_2O. What power will it develop?
   (b) Determine the critical radius and the power developed if the reflector were infinitely thick.

10. For a critical infinite slab with an infinitely thick reflector develop an expression similar to Eq. (9.120) for the critical slab thickness.

11. A spherical shell reactor has been suggested to serve as an intense source of radiant thermal energy. Such a core fueled by a uniform dispersion of uranium carbide particles in a graphite matrix would operate as a thermal reactor. Use one-group theory to develop an expression for the critical extrapolated outer shell radius, assuming the inner radius is given. Also, determine an expression for the flux distribution in the shell.

For a core whose material buckling is equal to 0.0269 cm^{-1} and whose interior radius is 100 cm determine the outer extrapolated critical radius.

12. Using Fortran, write a program to solve Eq. (9.116) for a reflected spherical core using the lattice of Problem 5 and a graphite reflector. Plot the reflector savings versus reflector thickness.

13. An infinite slab is bare on one face and has an infinite reflector on the other face. Develop an expression for the critical thickness of the slab. Assume $D_r \approx D_c$.

14. For the semi-reflected slab of Problem 13 determine the core thickness if the core contains 200 moles of graphite moderator per mole of 5 percent enriched uranium. The reflector is graphite; how far from the bare face will the flux be maximum?

15. Compute the slowing down length and the migration length for the lattice described in Problem 5.

16. Using modified one-group theory and two-group theory, compute the radius of a bare critical sphere constructed with the lattice described in Problem 5.

17. A molten salt reactor core with 13 percent salt and 87 percent graphite by volume uses the salt described in Fig. 9.15 which has the following characteristics:

Thermal utilization factor = 0.744
Resonance escape probability = 0.651
Thermal fission factor = 2.275
Fast fission factor = 1.00
Macroscopic cross sections = cm^2/cm^3
    Thermal scatter = 0.4277
    Epithermal scatter = 0.4125
    Thermal transport = 0.405
    Epithermal transport = 0.390
    Absorption = 0.0065
    Fission = 0.0044
Collisions to thermalize = 108.6

Use one-group, modified one-group, and two-group theories to determine the radius and the height of a bare, critical, cylindrical core whose diameter is equal to its height.

18. Develop an expression for the power developed in a cylindrical core. Calculate the power developed by the bare, critical, cylindrical core of Problem 17 using one-group, modified one-group, and two-group theories. The peak thermal flux is to be 10^{14} n/cm^2 sec.

19. A liquid metal-cooled fast reactor is fueled with 20 percent enriched uranium dioxide which occupies 25 percent of the core volume, the remainder being 25 percent stainless steel and 50 percent sodium.
    Determine the infinite multiplication factor for the core. What would be the critical radius of a bare cylindrical core whose height is equal to its diameter?

20. Determine the peak flux in the previous core if it is to develop 1000 Mwt.

21. A spherical fast reactor core containing the same percentages of fuel, coolant, and stainless steel as the core for Problem 19 is to have a 50 cm

thick blanket. The blanket is to contain 50 percent ThO_2, 20 percent stainless steel, and 30 percent sodium.

Determine the critical core radius and the power developed in the core and blanket if the peak fast flux is 5×10^{14} n/cm² sec.

REFERENCES

1. Glasstone, S., and M. C. Edlund, *The Elements of Nuclear Reactor Theory.* Princeton, N. J.: D. Van Nostrand Co., 1952.

2. Glasstone, S., and A. Sesonske, *Nuclear Reactor Engineering.* Princeton, N. J.: D. Van Nostrand Co., 1963.

3. Murray, R. L., *Nuclear Reactor Physics.* Englewood Cliffs, N. J.: Prentice-Hall, Inc., 1957.

4. El-Wakil, M. M., *Nuclear Power Engineering.* New York: McGraw-Hill Book Co., Inc., 1962.

5. Stephenson, R., *Introduction to Nuclear Engineering.* New York: McGraw-Hill Book Co., Inc., 1954.

6. Hawley, J. P., *SNAP 10A Reactor Operation,* ASME Paper No. 65-WA/NE-6.

7. Soodak, H., *Reactor Handbook,* Vol. III, Physics. New York: Interscience Publishers, 1962.

8. Lamarsh, J. R., *Introduction to Nuclear Reactor Theory.* Reading, Mass.: Addison-Wesley Publishing Co., Inc., 1966.

9. Murray, R. L., *Introduction to Nuclear Engineering.* Englewood Cliffs, N. J.: Prentice-Hall, Inc., 1961.

10. King, C. D. G., *Nuclear Power Systems.* New York: Macmillan Co., 1964.

11. Almenas, K., "A Proposal for Using Nuclear Reactors as Thermal Radiation Sources," *Nuclear Technology* **10**, no. 1 (January, 1971), pp. 22-32.

Chapter 10

Transient Reactor
Behavior and Control

Previous chapters have dealt with reactors in which the flux (or neutron population) varies only with position. Perhaps as important as the steady state behavior is the behavior of the neutron population when it varies with time as well as position.

The change from steady state in reactor neutron population is referred to as reactivity change. Strictly speaking, the percent change in effective multiplication factor is the reactivity of a reactor. Any change in power level (up or down) is accompanied by a reactivity change. Reactivities are of two kinds:

(1) Temporary deliberate change in power level to a new steady value; and
(2) Accidental uncontrolled increase in power.

These reactivities can be compensated for by:

(1) Control devices;
(2) The reactor itself (self-regulating); and
(3) Safety devices.

NEUTRON LIFETIME

The total neutron lifetime, l, is the sum of the slowing down time, l_s, and the thermal lifetime, l_{th}. The slowing down time can be described as the time a neutron spends in slowing from fission to thermal energy, while the thermal lifetime is the time a neutron spends diffusing at thermal energies before absorption. Compared with the thermal lifetime in a thermal reactor, the slowing down time is short. Thus, the neutron lifetime is frequently taken equal to the thermal lifetime. This neutron lifetime is also called the generation time or the total cycle time. In equation form

$$l = l_{th} + l_s \approx l_{th} \tag{10.1}$$

For a core of infinite extent neutrons must diffuse until they are absorbed. The lifetime in an infinite core, $l_{th\infty}$, is found by dividing the absorption mean free path, λ_a, by the average neutron velocity, $\bar{v}$.

$$l_{th\infty} = \frac{\lambda_a}{\bar{v}} \tag{10.2}$$

If the reactor is finite only $(N \times P_{NL_{th}})$ neutrons remain in the core to contribute to the effective lifetime of the generation. $N(1 - P_{NL_{th}})$ neutrons leak out and make no contribution to the thermal lifetime. Thus, the effective lifetime will be shorter for a finite reactor.

$$Nl_{th} = Nl_{th\infty}P_{th} + N(1 - P_{th})0$$

$$l_{th} = l_{th\infty}P_{th} = \frac{l_{th\infty}}{1 + B^2L^2} \tag{10.3}$$

Substituting Eqs. (10.3) and (10.2) into (10.1)

$$l \approx \frac{1}{\sum_a \bar{v}(1 + B^2L^2)} \tag{10.4}$$

Table 10.1 compares thermal lifetimes and slowing down lifetimes for some common moderators. Notice that in each case the thermal lifetime is greater than the slowing down time. In a fast reactor, of course, there is no true slowing down time; the resulting neutron lifetime is about 10^{-7} seconds.

Example 1. Calculate the effective lifetime of a neutron in the reactor of Example 2 in Chapter 9 where

$$\frac{N_c}{N_u} = 200 \qquad\qquad L^2 = 68.2 \text{ cm}^2$$

$$B^2 = 0.00290 \text{ cm}^{-2} \qquad\qquad \sum_a = 0.0134 \text{ cm}^{-1}$$

$$\bar{v} = 2.482 \times 10^5 \text{ cm/sec}$$

Neglecting the effect of neutron slowing down time

$$l = \frac{1}{\sum_a \bar{v}(1 + B^2L^2)}$$

$$l = \frac{1}{0.0134(2.482 \times 10^5)(1 + 0.00290 \times 68.2)}$$

$$l = \frac{1}{0.0134(2.482 \times 10^5)(1.216)}$$

$$l = 2.50 \times 10^{-4} \text{ sec.}$$

This is much less than that for pure carbon. Comparison with Table 10.1 shows the effect on the lifetime of the increased neutron absorption in uranium.

TABLE 10.1

NEUTRON LIFETIMES IN SECONDS

	Slowing Down Time	Thermal Lifetime
C	1.5×10^{-4}	1.8×10^{-2}
H_2O	5.6×10^{-6}	2.1×10^{-4}
D_2O	4.3×10^{-5}	1.4×10^{-1}
Be	5.7×10^{-5}	3.7×10^{-3}

REACTIVITY

When a reactor is operating at steady state, as discussed in Chapter 9, the effective multiplication factor, k_{eff}, is unity. While the power is increasing or decreasing (a reactivity change) the multiplication factor differs from unity. This difference is referred to as the excess multiplication factor

$$\Delta k_{eff} = k_{eff} - 1 \qquad (10.5)$$

The reactivity, ρ, is the ratio of excess multiplication factor to effective multiplication factor

$$\rho = \frac{\Delta k_{eff}}{k_{eff}} = \frac{k_{eff} - 1}{k_{eff}} \qquad (10.6)$$

Under steady state conditions $\rho = 0$, and under normal power level changes near steady state $\rho \approx \Delta k_{eff}$. Reactivity has been given units of dollars (\$) and cents (¢) and inhours. More discussion of units will be encountered later. Since Δk_{eff} represents the ratio of the increase in number of neutrons from one generation to the next, then the total number of neutrons gained per generation equals $\phi \Delta k_{eff}$. The number of neutrons gained per unit time will be

$$\frac{d\phi}{dt} = \frac{\phi \Delta k_{eff}}{l} \qquad (10.7)$$

It is plain that the right side of (10.7) is the neutrons gained per generation divided by the total time per generation, or the number of neutrons gained per unit time.

Assuming Δk_{eff} is time independent and integrating

$$\phi = \phi_0 e^{\frac{\Delta k_{eff}}{l}t} \tag{10.8}$$

where ϕ_0 represents the initial or steady state neutron flux. Define the reactor period (or e folding time), T, as the time for the flux to change by a factor of e.

$$T = \frac{l}{\Delta k_{eff}} \tag{10.9}$$

$$\phi = \phi_0 e^{t/T} \tag{10.10}$$

For the reactor to be at steady state $\phi = \phi_0$ and, therefore, $T = \infty$. Reactor period is a very important concept and is one of the most responsive indicators of reactor conditions: all reactors employ an automatic safety system which will *scram* the reactor if the period gets too small. During power changes the period must be kept as large as possible to prevent dangerous power excursions. A period of less than 7 to 10 seconds represents a definitely dangerous condition.

Example 2. The neutron lifetime for a neutron produced by fission in a thermal reactor is about 10^{-3} sec. Using this value and a reactivity of $\frac{1}{2}$ of 1%, determine the power increase of a reactor in two seconds.

$$T = \frac{l}{\Delta k_{eff}}$$

We can use a value of $\Delta k_{eff} = 0.005$ since ρ will be very nearly equal to Δk_{eff}.

$$T = \frac{0.001}{0.005} = \frac{1}{5} \text{ seconds}$$

$$\frac{\phi}{\phi_i} = e^{5(2)} = 22{,}026$$

Since power is proportional to neutron flux the power would also increase to 20,000 times its original value. Any manmade structure would have a difficult time withstanding this power excursion! Of course, if the Δk_{eff} is decreased or the effective neutron lifetime increased, or both, the reactor period will be lengthened. This is the direction in which to strive for reactor control.

DELAYED NEUTRONS

Fortunately, not all neutrons occurring as a result of fission appear simultaneously. From observation, the neutrons appear in seven distinct groupings (see Table 10.2) according to their mean-lives from fission to absorption. The overwhelming majority (over 99%) are prompt neutrons. These are emitted directly from fission within about 10^{-13} seconds after fission begins. The remainder are the delayed neutrons, the result of neutron decay of some of the fission fragments. The decay of 55.72 second half-life ^{87}Br along one branch of its decay diagram (Fig. 10.1) involves β^- emission followed by the instantaneous emission of a

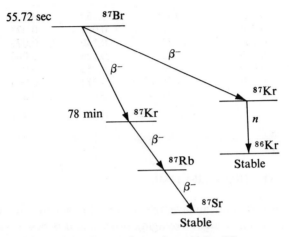

FIG. 10.1   *Energy decay diagram for ^{87}Br.*

neutron. Thus the half-life of the first decay group is characterized by that of the β^- decay of ^{87}Br. Similarly, for the second group, 22.72 seconds, ^{137}I decays by β^- emission followed by the ejection of a neutron.

$$^{137}\text{I} \xrightarrow{\ \beta^-\ } {}^{137}\text{Xe} \xrightarrow{\ n\ } {}^{136}\text{Xe}$$

Even though the delayed neutrons are a very small percentage of the total neutrons, they can have a significant effect on the reactivity because their mean lifetimes are long. Also, their energies are smaller than those of prompt neutrons (i.e., less fast leakage) and, therefore, they are more effective than an equal number of prompt neutrons. Table 10.2 presents the fraction of prompt $(1 - \beta)$ and delayed (β) neutrons for each of the three fissionable fuels. The groupings are not exact, but they represent the best available observations grouped into the most representative lifetimes.

TABLE 10.2

PROMPT AND DELAYED NEUTRON GROUPS FROM THERMAL FISSION

Group	Energy for ^{235}U Fission	Half-Life for ^{235}U Fission	Percentage of Total Neutrons from Fission		
i	(MeV)	(sec)	^{235}U (β_i)	^{233}U (β_i)	^{239}Pu (β_i)
0	~2	~10^{-3}	99.359	99.736	99.790
1	0.250	55.72	0.021	0.023	0.007
2	0.560	22.72	0.140	0.079	0.063
3	0.430	6.22	0.126	0.066	0.044
4	0.620	2.30	0.253	0.073	0.069
5	0.420	0.61	0.074	0.014	0.018
6		0.23	0.027	0.009	0.009
		$\sum\limits_{1}^{6} \beta_i =$	0.641	0.264	0.210

AVERAGE NEUTRON LIFETIME

We can now find an average lifetime for a neutron in a thermal reactor. This is a straight averaging process and is best done by means of an example.

Example 3. Find the average neutron lifetime, $\bar{l}$, of all neutrons in a ^{235}U reactor. Note that the mean lifetime of a delay group is the reciprocal of its decay constant.

$$\bar{l} = \frac{\sum\limits_{i=0}^{6} \beta_i l_{mi}}{\sum\limits_{i=0}^{6} \beta_i} \qquad \bar{l}_{mi} = \frac{1}{\lambda_i} = \frac{t_{1/2}}{0.693} \qquad \textbf{(10.11)}$$

i	β_i	l_{mi}	$\beta_i l_{mi}$
0	99.359	~10^{-3}	0.09936
1	0.021	80.65	1.694
2	0.140	32.79	4.591
3	0.126	9.01	1.135
4	0.253	3.32	0.840
5	0.074	0.88	0.065
6	0.027	0.33	0.009

$$\sum \beta_i = 100 \qquad \sum\limits_{i=0}^{6} \beta_i l_{mi} = 8.434$$

$$\bar{l} = \frac{8.43}{100} = 0.0843 \text{ second}$$

This shows that only 0.641 percent of the total neutrons have increased the effective generation time by a factor of approximately 84. This, of course, can effectively increase the reactor period by a like amount. Without the delayed neutrons control would indeed be difficult. Returning to Example 2, with an average lifetime of 0.0843 second for a ^{235}U fueled reactor, the period becomes

$$T = \frac{l}{\Delta k_{eff}} = \frac{0.0843}{0.005} = 16.86 \text{ seconds}$$

The resulting period, using l becomes the limiting value for very, very small reactivity increases. After two seconds the new flux level will be

$$\phi = \phi_0 e^{t/T} = \phi_0 e^{2/16.8} = 1.126\phi_0$$

EFFECT OF DELAYED NEUTRONS

Fig. 10.2 shows the effect of reactivity changes on the neutron flux. The dashed curve shows the relative neutron flux for a Δk_{eff} if there were no delayed neutrons present. It is merely a plot of Eq. (10.8). The curve

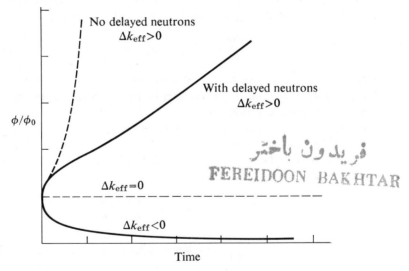

FIG. 10.2   *Effect of reactivity change on neutron flux in a critical reactor.*

labeled $\Delta k_{eff} > 0$, however, shows what actually happens when excess reactivity is introduced. At first the reactor behaves as if all neutrons are prompt because the delayed neutrons from the increased flux are not yet effective. After a few seconds the delayed neutrons appear and the rate of flux increase begins to level off. The flux is still increasing, but the number of delayed neutrons entering the reactor is still smaller than the number of neutrons being delayed. Therefore, the rate of increase of flux gradually decreases and approaches a constant value. The rate of flux increase finally approaches a value determined by what is called the stable reactor period. More will be said later concerning the stable period. When $\Delta k_{eff} < 0$ the rate of decrease of flux is very sharp at first. When the delayed neutrons appear they now tend to flatten out the curve. Since the flux is dying out, the short-lived delayed neutrons disappear completely and the curve approaches a slope whose value is determined by the longest-lived neutron group.

DIFFUSION EQUATION FOR A TRANSIENT REACTOR

In Chapter 9 the diffusion equation was developed and solved for various geometries. In a transient reactor we have exactly the same conditions and materials as in a critical reactor, except for the simplification that the neutron flux does not change with time. The equation governing the neutron flux will be (9.42) which is repeated here as (10.12).

$$\frac{\partial n}{\partial t} = D\nabla^2\phi - \phi\Sigma_a + S \tag{10.12}$$

where S represents some source of neutrons for the next fission. From the previous discussion it can be seen that the source, S, in a transient reactor will involve prompt and delayed neutrons. If we now restrict ourselves to reactors near steady (the region of most interest anyway) the shape of the flux distribution will stay the same, but the amplitude will rise or decrease. This means that the flux will not depend on geometry but on time. We can say, therefore

$$\nabla^2\phi \approx -B^2\phi \quad \text{and} \quad \frac{\partial n}{\partial t} = \frac{dn}{dt}$$

$$\frac{dn}{dt} = -DB^2\phi - \phi\Sigma_a + S \tag{10.13}$$

Fig. 10.3 illustrates the neutron cycle. $c_1, c_2, \ldots, c_6$ are the number of neutrons of each type per unit volume and $\lambda_1, \lambda_2, \ldots, \lambda_6$ are the decay constants. The neutrons which are left are available for slowing, leakage, absorption, and fission in the next cycle. This source can be divided into two parts, prompt, (S_p), and delayed, (S_d).

$$S = S_p + S_d \tag{10.14}$$

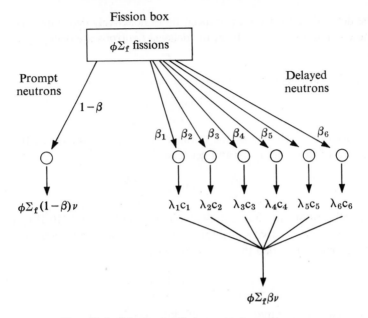

FIG. 10.3 *Neutron cycle in a transient reactor.*

The prompt source reaching thermal is that from the $1 - \beta$ fraction of prompt neutrons. In a manner similar to (9.41)

$$S_p = \phi \Sigma_a k_\infty P_f (1 - \beta) \tag{10.15}$$

The delayed source is made up of the remainder of neutrons which we have already divided into their six groups.

$$S_d = \sum_{i=1}^{6} C_i \lambda_i \tag{10.16}$$

where C_i = number of delayed neutrons in the i_{th} group actually reaching thermal energies = $p P_f c_i$. Substituting Eqs. (10.14), (10.15), and (10.16) into (10.13) gives

$$\frac{dn}{dt} = -\phi \Sigma_a \left[B^2 \frac{D}{\Sigma_a} + 1 \right] + \phi \Sigma_a k_\infty P_f (1 - \beta) + \sum_{1}^{6} C_i \lambda_i$$

$$\frac{dn}{dt} = -\frac{\phi \Sigma_a}{P_{th}} + \phi \Sigma_a k_\infty P_f (1 - \beta) + \sum_{1}^{6} C_i \lambda_i$$

$$\frac{dn}{dt} = \frac{\phi \Sigma_a}{P_{th}} [k_{eff}(1 - \beta) - 1] + \sum_{1}^{6} C_i \lambda_i \tag{10.17}$$

Combining Eqs. (8.22) and (10.4) with (10.17) yields

$$\frac{dn}{dt} = \frac{n}{l_{th}} [k_{eff}(1 - \beta) - 1] + \sum_{1}^{6} C_i \lambda_i \tag{10.18}$$

The delayed neutrons are produced by radioactively decaying precursors. These precursors and, in turn, the delayed neutrons are decaying at a rate

$$-\lambda_i C_i$$

while they are being produced (or generated) at a rate

$$\frac{k_{eff}\beta_i n}{l_{th}}$$

The net rate of change of the number of delayed neutrons is, therefore, the sum of those decaying and generating:

$$\frac{dC_i}{dt} = -\lambda_i C_i + \frac{k_{eff}\beta_i n}{l_{th}} \tag{10.19}$$

The solution of the seven simultaneous Eqs. (10.18) and (10.19) yields an expression for reactivity in terms of reactor period and neutron lifetime. This equation is called the *inhour equation*.

$$\rho = \frac{l}{k_{eff}T} + \sum_{1}^{6} \frac{\beta_i}{1 + \lambda_i T} \tag{10.20}$$

In (10.20) the thermal neutron lifetime has been replaced by the total neutron lifetime. A more accurate development and solution of (10.18) and (10.19) would yield this result. The first term of (10.20) refers to the prompt neutrons; the six succeeding terms apply to the delayed neutrons.

If (10.18) and (10.19) are solved for n, the number of neutrons per unit volume, the parameter T will also appear. This parameter has six negative values and one positive value. The negative values die out quickly, leaving the positive value to dominate. It is this positive number that is called the *stable reactor period* and is a result of the solutions to (10.18) and (10.19) which were plotted in Fig. 10.2. The slope of the curve is determined by the stable reactor period.

UNITS OF REACTIVITY

The *inhour* is the amount of reactivity that will make the stable reactor period one hour.

$$\rho \text{ (inhours)} = \frac{l}{3600 k_{eff}} + \sum_{1}^{6} \frac{\beta_i}{1 + 3600 \lambda_i} \tag{10.21}$$

A reactivity of one dollar ($) is an amount of reactivity equivalent to β. It follows that a cent is one-hundredth of a dollar.

Example 4. Find the amount of reactivity corresponding to one inhour for ^{235}U. What is this in units of dollars?

$$\rho = \frac{l}{3600k_{eff}} + \sum_{1}^{6} \frac{\beta_i}{1 + 3600\lambda_i}$$

Instead of using all six delayed neutron groups, combine the six groups into one group of average lifetime:

$$\rho = \frac{l}{3600k_{eff}} + \frac{\beta \bar{l}_d}{\bar{l}_d + 3600} \tag{10.22}$$

where $\bar{l}_d$ = average lifetime of delayed neutrons

$$\bar{l}_d = \frac{\sum_{1}^{6} \beta_i \bar{l}_{mi}}{\beta} = \frac{0.08335}{0.00641}$$

$$\bar{l}_d = 13.0 \text{ seconds}$$

$$\rho = \frac{10^{-3}}{3600} + \frac{0.00641(13)}{13 + 3600}$$

$$\rho = 0.0278 \times 10^{-5} + 2.306 \times 10^{-5}$$

$$\rho = 2.33 \times 10^{-5}$$

Therefore, one inhour is equivalent to 2.33×10^{-5} units of reactivity. This corresponds to

$$\$ = \frac{2.33 \times 10^{-5}}{0.00641} = \$0.00363$$

The inhour equation is frequently plotted graphically so that for a given reactivity the period can be determined. With the graph available, various parameters can be determined in terms of the reactivity added or taken away from the reactor. The resulting period is then available from the graph. Figs. 10.4 and 10.5 show a plot of the inhour equation. The reactivity used with these graphs would be evaluated in terms of such physical factors as control rod worth, temperature change, fuel depletion or addition, reflector adjustment or removal, moderator or coolant changes, and core size or shape changes.

LIMITING CASES OF Δk_{eff}

Suppose that Δk_{eff} and ρ are very very small ($\ll \beta$). The inhour equation (using one group of delayed neutrons) becomes

$$\frac{\Delta k_{eff}}{k_{eff}} = \frac{l + \beta \bar{l}_d}{T} \tag{10.23}$$

because T will be large compared with $\bar{l}_d$ in the denominator

$$\Delta k_{eff} = \frac{l}{T} \tag{10.24}$$

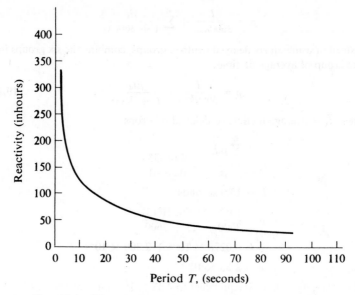

FIG. 10.4   *Plot of inhour equation on rectangular coordinates.*

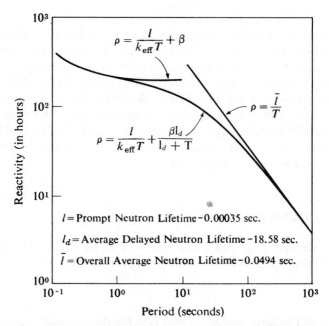

$$\rho = \frac{l}{k_{\text{eff}}\,T} + \beta$$

$$\rho = \frac{\bar{l}}{T}$$

$$\rho = \frac{l}{k_{\text{eff}}\,T} + \frac{\beta l_d}{l_d + T}$$

l = Prompt Neutron Lifetime – 0.00035 sec.

l_d = Average Delayed Neutron Lifetime – 18.58 sec.

$\bar{l}$ = Overall Average Neutron Lifetime – 0.0494 sec.

FIG. 10.5   *Plot of inhour equation on logarithmic coordinates for* ^{233}U
fueled reactor which is beryllium moderated with 1 mole ^{233}U *per 10 moles
Th and 500 moles Be.*

This shows that for very small reactivity all the delayed neutron emitters contribute to the increase of flux, and the period may be computed using the average lifetime of all the neutrons.

On the other hand if Δk_{eff} and ρ are large, the period will be small, and the inhour equation becomes

$$\frac{k_{eff} - 1}{k_{eff}} \approx \frac{l}{k_{eff}T} + \beta \tag{10.25}$$

$$T = \frac{l}{k_{eff} - 1 - \beta k_{eff}} = \frac{l}{k_{eff}(1 - \beta) - 1} \tag{10.26}$$

The prompt excess multiplication factor is sometimes defined as

$$\Delta k_{\text{exp}} = k_{eff}(1 - \beta) - 1 \tag{10.27}$$

Substituting, (10.26) becomes

$$T = \frac{l}{\Delta k_{\text{exp}}} \tag{10.28}$$

This shows that for large reactivity the $(1 - \beta)$ prompt neutrons govern the period, since the delayed neutrons cannot follow the reaction.

An interesting transition takes place when $\Delta k_{\text{exp}} = 0$. At this point

$$\Delta k_{\text{exp}} = k_{eff}(1 - \beta) - 1 = 0$$
$$\Delta k_{eff} = \beta k_{eff}$$
$$\rho = \beta$$

If this should be the case the reactor would be prompt-critical. This is a dangerous condition since the reactor is now critical on prompt neutrons alone. When $\rho < \beta$ the reactor is said to be delayed-critical; thus the delayed neutrons control the reactor. Needless to say a reactor should always be delayed-critical.

Example 5. A control rod is suddenly withdrawn from a water-moderated ^{235}U reactor. The period is seen to be 30 minutes. What is the reactivity in dollars? From Table 10.1 the thermal neutron lifetime of the water is seen to be 2.1×10^{-4} seconds. It can be assumed that a period of 30 minutes is long and that (10.24) applies.

$$\Delta k_{eff} = \frac{\bar{l}}{T}$$

For convenience let us use one group of delayed neutrons and the thermal neutron lifetime in the pure moderator.

$$\Delta k_{eff} = \frac{2.1 \times 10^{-4} + 0.00641(13.0)}{30(60)}$$

$$\rho \approx \Delta k_{eff} = 4.65 \times 10^{-5}$$

$$\$ = \frac{\rho}{\beta} = \frac{4.65 \times 10^{-5}}{0.00641}$$

$$\$ = 0.00724$$

NATURAL REACTIVITY CHANGES

In an operating reactor many reactivity changes occur as a result of physical or nuclear changes in the system. They take place over a relatively long period of time and result directly from reactor operation. These effects are due mainly to temperature changes, pressure changes, buildup of poisons, fuel depletion, and fuel buildup. To compensate for decreases in reactivity, excess reactivity ($\Delta\rho$) is built into reactors initially. Control rods are inserted far into the core and, as reactivity changes, their equilibrium position can be raised to balance the natural reactivity change. To simplify the solution to these reactivity changes it is usually assumed that either the reactivity changes almost instantaneously or that the reactivity changes so slowly that flux remains constant. Table 10.3 shows the expected change in reactivity for some

TABLE 10.3

FACTORS AFFECTING REACTIVITY

Factor	Effect
Temperature increase	Decrease
Pressure increase	Decrease
Steam formation	Decrease
Fission product accumulation	Decrease
Fuel depletion	Decrease
Fuel breeding	Increase

material factors in reactor operation. Succeeding paragraphs discuss these in more detail.

TEMPERATURE EFFECTS ON REACTIVITY

The temperature coefficient of reactivity (α) is made up of three parts:

(1) A nuclear temperature coefficient arising from a change in cross section with changing neutron temperature, $(\partial\rho/\partial T)_{N,B^2}$

(2) A density temperature coefficient arising from a change in material density N with changing temperature, $(\partial\rho/\partial T)_{\sigma,B^2}$

(3) A volume temperature coefficient arising from a change in geometric buckling when temperature changes. $(\partial\rho/\partial T)_{\sigma,N}$

The temperature coefficient of reactivity is then given by

$$\alpha = \frac{d\rho}{dT} = \left(\frac{\partial\rho}{\partial T}\right)_{N,B^2} + \left(\frac{\partial\rho}{\partial T}\right)_{\sigma,B^2} + \left(\frac{\partial\rho}{\partial T}\right)_{\sigma,N} \tag{10.29}$$

The temperature coefficient (α) should be (and is) negative for stable operation. A negative α means that as temperature increases, reactivity decreases, the fissioning rate ($\phi\sigma_f$) decreases, and the heat transfer decreases causing temperature to fall back toward its original value. In this case the reactor is said to be self-regulating.

Example 6. Let us develop an expression for the change in reactivity due to temperature variation at very nearly steady state. For a large reactor, Eqs. (9.2) and (9.140) give the effective multiplication factor

$$k_{eff} = \frac{k_\infty}{1 + (L_s^2 + L^2)B^2}$$

and Eq. (10.6) gives the reactivity

$$\rho = \frac{k_{eff} - 1}{k_{eff}}$$

Therefore

$$\rho = 1 - \frac{1/k_\infty}{1 + (L^2 + L_s^2)B^2} = 1 - \frac{1 + M^2B^2}{k_\infty} \tag{10.30}$$

In Eq. (10.30) L, L_s, and k_∞ are temperature dependent while B^2 is dependent on core volume which is, in turn, dependent on temperature.

The nuclear temperature coefficient $(\partial\rho/\partial T)_{N,B^2}$ will be dependent almost entirely on thermal diffusion length. If we assume that neutron cross sections follow the $1/v$ law then the absorption cross section is inversely proportional to the square root of the absolute temperature. Since the square of the thermal diffusion length, L^2, is also inversely proportional to the absorption cross section it will increase as the temperature increases. This increase in L also increases the neutron leakage. The result of this fairly large increase in L causes the reactivity, ρ, to decrease (Eq. 10.30), thereby making the nuclear temperature coefficient negative.

The buckling, B^2, is a geometrical quantity and has little effect on the nuclear temperature coefficient. The slowing down length, L_s, is inversely proportional to the scattering cross section. The scattering cross section is nearly independent of neutron energy, and therefore temperature has practically no effect on L_s.

Because of the characteristics of ϵ, p, f, and η temperature has relatively little effect on k_∞. Because of the definitions of ϵ and η they will not be affected by changes in temperature. Also, f will not be affected in a homogenous reactor. However, the thermal disadvantage factor will decrease somewhat with temperature increase, causing a slight increase in f in a heterogenous reactor. The resonance escape probability,

p, will decrease slightly with increase in temperature because of the increase in resonance absorption. This increase in resonance absorption arises chiefly through the Doppler effect. The Doppler effect means that the resonance peaks increase in width with increasing material temperatures. The phenomenon is analogous to frequency changes due to the relative motion of sources of sound. The decrease in p, however, is small and will tend to cancel any increase in f. The net effect on k_∞ due to increased temperature is, therefore, practically zero.

In determining $(\partial\rho/\partial T)_{N,B^2}$, the nuclear temperature coefficient, the partial reactivity with respect to the square of the thermal diffusion length is multiplied by the partial derivative of the square of the thermal diffusion length with respect to temperature.

$$\left(\frac{\partial\rho}{\partial T}\right)_{N,B^2} = \frac{\partial\rho}{\partial L^2} \times \frac{\partial L^2}{\partial T}$$

Letting σ'_a be a reference cross section at datum temperature T', the cross section may be expressed as a function of temperature, T.

$$\sigma_a = \sigma'_a \frac{T'^{1/2}}{T^{1/2}}$$

The square of the thermal diffusion length then becomes

$$L^2 = \frac{\lambda_{\mathrm{tr}} T^{1/2}}{3N\sigma'_a T'^{1/2}}$$

and

$$\frac{\partial L^2}{\partial T} = \frac{1}{2}\frac{\lambda_{\mathrm{tr}} T^{-1/2}}{3N\sigma'_a T'^{1/2}} \cdot \frac{T}{T}$$

$$= \frac{1}{2}\frac{\lambda_{\mathrm{tr}} T^{1/2}}{3N\sigma'_a T'^{1/2}} \cdot \frac{1}{T} = \frac{1}{2}\frac{L^2}{T}$$

Differentiating the reactivity with respect to the square of the thermal diffusion length gives

$$\frac{\partial\rho}{\partial L^2} = -\frac{B^2}{k_\infty}$$

and

$$\left(\frac{\partial\rho}{\partial T}\right)_{N,B^2} = -\frac{B^2 L^2}{2k_\infty T} \tag{10.31a}$$

The density temperature coefficient, $(\partial\rho/\partial T)_{\sigma,B^2}$, will be dependent on the change in nuclear density of reactor materials. An increase in reactor temperature will cause nuclear densities to decrease and also reduce the macroscopic cross sections. The mean free path, thermal diffusion length, and slowing down length will increase because they are inversely proportional to the density. Equation (10.30) then reveals that reactivity, ρ, will decrease, neutron leakage will increase, and density temperature coefficient will be negative. The effect of density changes on k_∞ will cancel one another, leaving k_∞ practically independent of temperature-caused density changes.

To establish the density temperature coefficient, $(\partial \rho / \partial T)_{\sigma, B^2}$, the partial derivative of reactivity with respect to the square of the migration length is multiplied by the partial of the square of the migration length with respect to temperature.

$$\left(\frac{\partial \rho}{\partial T}\right)_{\sigma, B^2} = \frac{\partial \rho}{\partial M^2} \cdot \frac{\partial M^2}{\partial T}$$

Differentiating (10.30) with respect to the square of the migration length

$$\frac{\partial \rho}{\partial M^2} = -\frac{B^2}{k_\infty}$$

Both L^2 and L_s^2 vary inversely as N^2

$$L^2 + L_s^2 = M^2 = \frac{1}{N^2}\left[\frac{1}{3\sigma_a \sigma_{tr_{th}}} + \frac{n}{3\sigma_{tr_f}^2}\right]$$

The number density of atoms in the core is inversely proportional to the specific volume of the core material. The specific volume is in turn proportional to the cube of the increase in linear dimension due to thermal expansion. Let N', v', and M' represent fixed values at the reference temperature T'. $\bar{\alpha}$ is the temperature coefficient of linear expansion of the core material.

$$\frac{v}{v'} = \left(\frac{N'}{N}\right) = [1 + \bar{\alpha}(T - T')]^3$$

$$M^2 = \left(\frac{N'}{N}\right)^2 M'^2 = [1 + \bar{\alpha}(T - T')]^6 M'^2$$

Differentiating with respect to temperature

$$\frac{\partial M^2}{\partial T} = 6[1 + \bar{\alpha}(T - T')]^5 M'^2 \bar{\alpha}$$

then

$$\left(\frac{\partial \rho}{\partial T}\right)_{\sigma, B^2} = -\frac{B^2}{k_\infty} 6[1 + \bar{\alpha}(T - T')]^5 \bar{\alpha} \cdot \frac{M^2}{[1 + \bar{\alpha}(T - T')]^6}$$

$$= \frac{-6B^2 M^2 \bar{\alpha}}{k_\infty[1 + \bar{\alpha}(T - T')]}$$

When the deviation from criticality is small

$$k_{eff} \cong 1 = \frac{k_\infty}{1 + B^2 M^2}$$

$$B^2 M^2 = (k_\infty - 1)$$

and for small temperature changes

$$[1 + \bar{\alpha}(T - T')] \cong 1$$

Then

$$\left(\frac{\partial \rho}{\partial T}\right)_{\sigma, B^2} = \frac{-6\bar{\alpha}(k_\infty - 1)}{k_\infty} \tag{10.31b}$$

The volume temperature coefficient, $(\partial \rho / \partial T)_{\sigma, N}$, depends only on the geometrical buckling. Buckling is inversely proportional to change in radius, and a volume increase due to temperature increase will decrease buckling. Equation (10.30) shows that reactivity will then increase. This will make the temperature coefficient positive.

To develop the volume temperature coefficient use the buckling of a spherical core. The resultant expression will be approximately correct for other compact core configurations. The radius of the sphere is a function of the extrapolated radius of the core

$$\frac{r_e}{r'_e} = 1 + \bar{\alpha}(T - T')$$

where r'_e is a reference radius at the base temperature T'. By developing $(\partial \rho / \partial T)_{\sigma, N}$ in a manner similar to that used for (10.31b) the volume temperature coefficient may be shown to be

$$\left(\frac{\partial \rho}{\partial T}\right)_{\sigma, N} = 2\bar{\alpha} \frac{(k_\infty - 1)}{k_\infty} \tag{10.31c}$$

Fortunately, the two negative coefficients usually more than overcome the one positive coefficient and leave the overall temperature coefficient of reactivity, α, negative. Table 10.4 summarizes the various contributions to temperature coefficient of reactivity.

The total temperature coefficient can be evaluated by summing the three partial coefficients

$$\frac{d\rho}{dT} = -\frac{B^2 L^2}{2k_\infty T} - 6\bar{\alpha} \frac{k_\infty - 1}{k_\infty} + 2\bar{\alpha} \frac{k_\infty - 1}{k_\infty} \tag{10.32}$$

where $\bar{\alpha}$ is a temperature coefficient of linear expansion.

A positive temperature coefficient would be very dangerous and care is taken to ensure that α is negative. In homogenous reactors the negative temperature coefficient is the largest, but heterogenous reactors with liquid coolants may also have large density variations providing large negative coefficients. Solid moderated gas-cooled reactors are not subject to density variations and have the smallest negative temperature coefficients. In a [235]U fueled fast reactor the temperature coefficient may be positive because the Doppler effect actually increases fission. To prevent this condition, the [235]U content is limited so that the [238]U contribution will maintain the temperature coefficient negative at operating temperature.

TABLE 10.4

TEMPERATURE EFFECTS ON REACTIVITY
FOR INCREASING TEMPERATURE

Parameter	Effect on Coefficient		
	Nuclear	Density	Volume
σ_s	←→	—	—
σ_a	↓	—	—
N	—	↓	—
$\sum_s$	←→	↓	—
$\sum_a$	↓	↓	—
L	↑	↑	—
L_s	←→	↑	—
λ	↑	↑	—
ϵ	←→	←→	—
η	←→	←→	—
p	↓	←→	—
f	↑ possibly	←→	—
k_∞	←→	←→	—
B	—	—	↓
Net effect	Negative	Negative	Positive

←→ Unchanged
↓ Decrease
↑ Increase

FISSION PRODUCT ACCUMULATION

Some of the fission products or their decay products are strong neutron absorbers. These poisons accumulate during reactor operation, causing a decrease in reactivity. Two fission decay products, ^{135}Xe and ^{149}Sm, exhibit extremely high absorption cross sections for thermal neutrons, 2.72×10^6 barns and 4.08×10^4 barns respectively. As a decay product ^{135}Xe has a 5.6 percent yield and a 0.3 percent yield as a direct fission fragment. ^{149}Sm has a 1.4 percent yield as a fission decay product. These absorbers, therefore, build up to significant amounts, and the neutrons they tend to absorb must be recognized. ^{135}Xe is a product in the decay chain

$$^{135}\text{Te} \xrightarrow[2m]{\beta} {}^{135}\text{I} \xrightarrow[6.7hr]{\beta} {}^{135}\text{Xe} \xrightarrow[9.2hr]{\beta} {}^{135}\text{Cs} \xrightarrow[3\times10^6yr.]{\beta} {}^{135}\text{Ba}$$

and ^{149}Sm is the stable product of the decay chain

$$^{149}\text{Nd} \xrightarrow[1.8hr]{\beta} {}^{149}\text{Pm} \xrightarrow[55hr]{\beta} {}^{149}\text{Sm}$$

In a steady state reactor secular equilibrium exists and the poisons will decay at the same rate they are produced. The primary effect of the poisons is reduction in thermal utilization. Three processes can exist which affect the rate of change of the poison nuclei. They are production, radioactive decay, and loss by absorption of neutrons. Table 10.5 indicates the rates at which these changes take place.

TABLE 10.5

RATES OF CHANGE OF POISON NUCLEI IN A REACTOR

Isotope	Production	Decay	Removal by Neutron Absorption
^{135}I	$\phi \sum_f y_{Te}$	$\lambda_I N_I$	$\phi N_I \sigma_{aI} \approx 0$
^{135}Xe	$\phi \sum_f y_{Xe}$ $\lambda_I N_I$	$\lambda_{Xe} N_{Xe}$	$\phi N_{Xe} \sigma_{aXe}$
^{135}Pm	$\phi \sum_f y_{Nd}$	$\lambda_{Pm} N_{Pm}$	
^{149}Sm	$\lambda_{Pm} N_{Pm}$		$\phi N_{Sm} \sigma_{aSm}$

When secular equilibrium exists, the production of an isotope must equal the loss of that isotope. From Table 10.5, for the chain including ^{135}Xe

$$\phi\sum_f y_{Te} + \phi\sum_f y_{Xe} + \lambda_I N_I = \lambda_I N_I + \lambda_{Xe} N_{Xe} + \phi N_{Xe} \sigma_{aXe}$$

$$N_{Xe} = \frac{\phi\sum_f (y_{Te} + y_{Xe})}{\lambda_{Xe} + \phi\sigma_{aXe}} \tag{10.33}$$

For the decay chain including ^{149}Sm

$$\phi\sum_f y_{Nd} + \lambda_{Pm} N_{Pm} = \lambda_{Pm} N_{Pm} + \phi N_{Sm} \sigma_{aSm} \tag{10.34}$$

$$N_{Sm} = \frac{\sum_f y_{Nd}}{\sigma_{aSm}} \tag{10.35}$$

Notice that the equilibrium concentration of ^{149}Sm is independent of neutron flux. To calculate the change in reactivity use Eq. (10.6)

$$\rho = \frac{k_{eff} - 1}{k_{eff}} = 1 - \frac{1}{k_{eff}}$$

$$\rho = 1 - \frac{1 + B^2 M^2}{k'_\infty} \tag{10.36}$$

where k'_∞ refers to the point where secular equilibrium exists. Considering that ρ varies mostly with k_∞ and differentiating without taking the limit

$$\frac{\Delta\rho}{\Delta k_\infty} = \frac{1 + M^2 B^2}{k_\infty'^2} \tag{10.37}$$

$$\Delta\rho = \frac{1 + M^2 B^2}{k_\infty'^2} \Delta k_\infty \tag{10.38}$$

Assuming that the change in k_∞ is due to a change in f

$$\Delta k_\infty = \eta\epsilon p\Delta f \tag{10.39}$$

$$\frac{\Delta k_\infty}{k_\infty'} = \frac{\Delta f}{f'} \tag{10.40}$$

where k_∞' and f' are evaluated at the point of secular equilibrium. Translating this to the original critical state

$$\frac{\Delta k_\infty}{k_\infty'} = \frac{\Delta f}{f'} = \frac{f' - f}{f'} \cdot \frac{f}{f} = -f\Delta\left(\frac{1}{f}\right) \tag{10.41}$$

where f refers to the original critical condition.

$$f = \frac{\sum_{au}}{\sum_{au} + \sum_{anf}}$$

$$\frac{1}{f} = 1 + \frac{\sum_{anf}}{\sum_{au}}$$

$$\Delta\left(\frac{1}{f}\right) = \frac{1}{\sum_{au}} \Delta(\sum_{anf}) \tag{10.42}$$

The only change in $\sum_{anf}$ is that due to poison; therefore

$$\Delta(\sum_{anf}) = \sum_{ap} \tag{10.43}$$

$$\Delta\left(\frac{1}{f}\right) = \frac{\sum_{ap}}{\sum_{au}} \tag{10.44}$$

substituting

$$\frac{\Delta k_\infty}{k_\infty'} = -f\frac{\sum_{ap}}{\sum_{au}} \tag{10.45}$$

substituting (10.45) into (10.38) and dropping the prime notation

$$\Delta\rho = -\frac{1 + M^2 B^2}{k_\infty} f\frac{\sum_{ap}}{\sum_{au}}$$

$$\Delta\rho = -\frac{f}{k_{eff}} \cdot \frac{\sum_{ap}}{\sum_{au}} \tag{10.46}$$

Equation (10.46) gives the change in ρ due to poison which produces a change in f. For ^{135}Xe

$$\sum_{ap} = \sum_{aXe} = N_{Xe}\sigma_{aXe} \tag{10.47}$$

$$\Delta\rho_{Xe} = -\frac{f}{k_{eff}} \frac{(y_{Te} + y_{Xe})\phi\sum_{fu}\sigma_{aXe}}{(\lambda_{Xe} + \phi\sigma_{aXe})\sum_{au}} \tag{10.48}$$

For ^{149}Sm

$$\Sigma_{ap} = N_{Sm}\sigma_{aSm}$$

$$\Delta\rho_{Sm} = -\frac{f}{k_{eff}}\frac{y_{Nd}\Sigma_{fu}}{\Sigma_{au}} \qquad (10.49)$$

Equations (10.48) and (10.49) give the change in reactivity at equilibrium concentration of poison.

Example 7. Find the equilibrium change in reactivity due to xenon and samarium buildup for a reactor fueled with 20 percent enriched uranium. The average neutron flux is 10^{13} n/sec-cm^2 and the thermal utilization factor is 0.87.

At thermal energies

$$\Sigma_{au} = N_u\sigma_{au} = \sigma_{a238}N_{238} + \sigma_{a235}N_{235}$$
$$= 2.71(0.80N_u) + 694(0.20N_u) = 140.97N_u$$
$$\Sigma_{fu} = N_u\sigma_f = \sigma_{f235}N_{235} = 582(0.20N_u) = 116.4N_u$$

$\sigma_{aXe} = 2.72 \times 10^6$ barns $\qquad \sigma_{aSm} = 4.08 \times 10^4$ barns

$\lambda_{Xe} = 2.1 \times 10^{-5}$ sec^{-1} $\qquad k_{eff} = 1$

$$\Delta\rho_{Xe} = -\frac{f(y_{Te} + y_{Xe})\phi\sigma_{aXe}\Sigma_{fu}}{(\lambda_{Xe} + \phi\sigma_{aXe})\Sigma_{au}}$$

$$\Delta\rho_{Xe} = -\frac{0.87(0.059)10^{13}(2.72 \times 10^6)(10^{-24})(116.4N_u)}{[2.1 \times 10^{-5} + 10^{13}(2.72 \times 10^6)(10^{-24})]140.97N_u}$$

$$\Delta\rho_{Xe} = -2.38 \text{ percent or } \frac{0.0238}{0.00641} = \$3.72$$

$$\Delta\rho_{Sm} = -\frac{0.87(0.014)(116.4N_u)}{140.97N_u}$$

$$\Delta\rho_{Sm} = -1.003 \text{ percent or } \frac{0.01003}{0.00641} = \$1.56$$

Notice that the change in reactivity due to samarium buildup is independent of flux.

FISSION PRODUCT POISONING AFTER SHUTDOWN

During steady state operation (and particularly for fluxes below 10^{15} n/sec cm^2) radioactive decay of xenon helps limit its equilibrium concentration. After reactor shutdown, however, the process is reversed. Now there are no neutrons to be absorbed by the xenon and because of its radioactive nature the xenon concentration builds up as iodine decays. This situation proceeds in a manner similar to transient equilibrium (Chapter 3) since the decay constant of the parent ^{135}I is slightly greater than that of the daughter ^{135}Xe. The increased negative reactivity to be overcome is referred to as *xenon override*, and it can rise to large values. Fig. 10.6 shows the effect of xenon poisoning on reactivity as a function of time after shutdown. If it is desired to start up a reactor shortly after shutdown a large excess reactivity must be built into the reactor to "override" the poisoning, otherwise, a day or more must elapse before

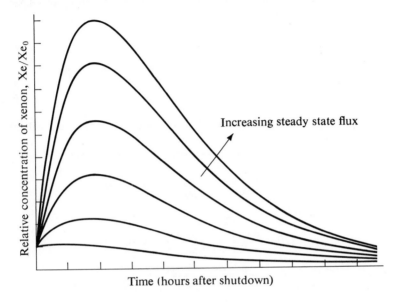

Increasing steady state flux

Time (hours after shutdown)

FIG. 10.6 *Effect of xenon poisoning on reactivity.*

the reactor can be restarted. This becomes particularly important in propulsion reactors. Of course, the reactor can be gradually shut down to reduce the equilibrium concentration before complete shutdown. The transient concentration after shutdown can be evaluated with the aid of Table 10.5.

$$\frac{dN_{Xe}}{dt} = \text{production} - \text{loss} \tag{10.50}$$

$$\frac{dN_{Xe}}{dt} = \lambda_I N_I - \lambda_{Xe} N_{Xe}$$

$$= \lambda_I (N_I)_0 e^{-\lambda_I t} - \lambda_{Xe} N_{Xe} \tag{10.51}$$

where the subscript 0 refers to the equilibrium concentration. Solving (10.51)

$$N_{Xe} = (N_{Xe})_0 e^{-\lambda_{Xe} t} + \frac{(N_I)_0 \lambda_I}{\lambda_{Xe} - \lambda_I} \left[e^{-\lambda_I t} - e^{-\lambda_{Xe} t} \right] \tag{10.52}$$

By combining (10.33), (10.46), and (10.52), an expression for the reactivity change as a function of time after shutdown can be obtained. Alternately, (10.50) could be evaluated for the time required to build up a specific concentration of xenon or some other poison.

Example 8. Determine the time for the reactor of Example 6 to reach its equilibrium concentration of ^{135}Xe. Assume that the concentration of xenon is zero at startup.

$$\frac{dN_{Xe}}{dt} = \text{production} - \text{loss}$$

$$= \phi \sum_f (y_{Te} + y_{Xe}) + \lambda_I N_I - \lambda_I N_I - \lambda_{Xe} N_{Xe} - \phi N_{Xc} \sigma_{aXe}$$

$$\frac{dN_{Xe}}{dt} = \phi \sum_f (y_{Te} + y_{Xe}) - N_{Xe}(\lambda_{Xe} + \phi \sigma_{aXe}) \qquad (10.53)$$

Integrating (10.53) and assuming $\sum_f$ does not vary significantly with time

$$\frac{dN_{Xe}}{dt} + (\lambda_{Xe} + \phi \sigma_{aXe}) N_{Xe} = \phi \sum_f (y_{Te} + y_{Xe})$$

$$N_{Xe} = \frac{\phi \sum_f (y_{Te} + y_{Xe})}{\lambda_{Xe} + \phi \sigma_{aXe}} + C e^{-(\lambda_{Xe} + \phi \sigma_{aXe})t}$$

at $t = 0$, $N_{Xe} = 0$

$$0 = \frac{\phi \sum_f (y_{Te} + y_{Xe})}{\lambda_{Xe} + \phi \sigma_{aXe}} + C$$

$$C = -\frac{\phi \sum_f (y_{Te} + y_{Xe})}{\lambda_{Xe} + \phi \sigma_{aXe}}$$

$$N_{Xe} = \frac{\phi \sum_f (y_{Te} + y_{Xe})}{\lambda_{Xe} + \phi \sigma_{aXe}} [1 - e^{-(\lambda_{Xe} + \phi \sigma_{aXe})t}]$$

If we assume that the time to reach equilibrium is essentially equal to the time to reach 99 percent of the equilibrium value

$$0.99 = 1 - e^{-(\lambda_{Xe} + \phi \sigma_a Xe)t}$$

$$0.01 = e^{-(21 \times 10^{-6} + 10^{13} \times 2.72 \times 10^{-18})}$$

$$0.01 = e^{-48.2 \times 10^{-6}t}$$

$$48.2 \times 10^{-6}t = 4.605$$

$$t = 0.956 \times 10^5 \text{ seconds or } 1.108 \text{ days}$$

Thus, the xenon builds up fairly slowly and concentration after shutdown will not become important if the reactor is operated for only short periods of time, say an hour or two.

FUEL DEPLETION

If in addition to its own fuel a reactor contains fertile material some new fuel will be produced as the original fuel is burned up. Reactors designed specifically to produce fissionable fuel are frequently called *breeder reactors*. In a reactor such as this, the amount of fissionable fuel produced is greater than the amount of fuel burnup, and the reactivity increases unless it is properly controlled. Even in a thermal ^{235}U reactor which contains ^{238}U there will be some conversion into ^{239}Pu according to the reaction

$$^{238}\text{U} + {}_0\text{n}^1 \rightarrow {}^{239}\text{U} \xrightarrow{\beta^-} {}^{239}\text{Np} \xrightarrow{\beta^-} {}^{239}\text{Pu}$$

This production of ^{239}Pu occurs for intermediate neutron energies as well as for thermal energies.

The *conversion ratio*, *CR*, is the number of fissionable nuclei produced per fissionable nucleus removed from the reactor by all processes.

The neutrons that are absorbed by ^{238}U during a cycle are absorbed either by resonance absorption or by thermal absorption. The conversion ratio, *CR*, is therefore the sum of these two factors.

RESONANCE ABSORPTION BY ^{238}U

The total number of fast neutrons produced per number of ^{235}U nuclei undergoing reactions is $\eta_{235}\epsilon$ where η_{235} is the number of neutrons produced per thermal neutron absorbed by ^{235}U.

A fraction, p, of neutrons will escape resonance absorption while slowing down, and a fraction, P_{NL_f}, of neutrons will not leak while slowing. Therefore, the number of neutrons absorbed by ^{238}U per number of thermal neutrons absorbed by ^{235}U nuclei is

$$\eta_{235}\epsilon(1 - p)P_{NL_f}$$

Since this is the number of neutrons absorbed by ^{238}U it is also the number of ^{239}Pu nuclei produced in the resonance region per ^{235}U nucleus removed.

THERMAL ABSORPTION BY ^{238}U

The number of thermal neutrons absorbed by ^{238}U nuclei per thermal neutron absorbed by ^{235}U is

$$\frac{\sum_{a238}}{\sum_{a235}}$$

This is also the number of ^{239}Pu nuclei produced at thermal per ^{235}U nucleus removed. Therefore, the conversion ratio is

$$CR = \eta_{235}\epsilon(1 - p)P_f + \frac{\sum_{a238}}{\sum_{a235}} \qquad (10.54)$$

REACTIVITY CHANGE IN A URANIUM REACTOR

Even though the change in reactivity due to a fuel change is a complicated matter, it can be evaluated from the change in effective multiplication factors. Considering only *one absorption* process

$$\frac{\text{number neutrons produced by new nuclei}}{\text{number neutrons produced by old nuclei}} = \frac{\sigma_{a\,\text{new}}\eta_{\text{new}}}{\sigma_{a\,\text{old}}\eta_{\text{old}}} \quad (10.55)$$

Equation (10.55) is equivalent to the ratio of new multiplication factor to original multiplication factor for *one absorption*. Since we must consider many absorption processes

$$\frac{\text{neutrons produced}}{\text{neutron used up}} = \frac{\text{nuclei produced}}{\text{neutron used up}}$$

$$\times \frac{\text{number neutrons produced by new nucleus}}{\text{number neutrons produced by old nucleus}}$$

$$\frac{\text{neutrons produced}}{\text{neutron used up}} = CR \times \frac{\sigma_{a\,\text{new}}\eta_{\text{new}}}{\sigma_{a\,\text{old}}\eta_{\text{old}}} \quad (10.56)$$

Equation (10.56) is equivalent to the ratio of new multiplication factor to ^{235}U nuclei removed by all processes. Considering now the change in multiplication factor due to depletion of ^{235}U

$$\frac{\Delta\rho}{^{235}\text{U removed}} = CR\frac{\sigma_{aPu}\eta_{Pu}}{\sigma_{a235}\eta_{235}} - 1$$

$$\Delta\rho = \left[CR\frac{\sigma_{aPu}\eta_{Pu}}{\sigma_{a235}\eta_{235}} - 1\right]R \quad (10.57)$$

where R = fraction of ^{235}U nuclei removed after a period of time t. It must be remembered that plutonium is not only produced by the conversion process but also is removed by absorption of neutrons. Equation (10.57) applies only to the reactivity change due to depletion of original fissionable fuel and does not include the reactivity change due to absorption of neutrons by plutonium.

The reactivity change, therefore, can be positive, negative, or zero. Except in the case of breeder reactors, the reactivity change is negative. This means that excess reactivity must be built into the reactor initially to compensate for the loss during the core lifetime.

The excess reactivity built into a reactor has been controlled with the Spectral Shift Control Reactor (SSCR). In the SSCR the reactivity was controlled by varying the concentration of D_2O-H_2O moderator. Since the slowing down power of the D_2O is much less than that of H_2O, a large concentration of D_2O effectively increases the critical mass of the reactor. As fuel is burned up and poisons decrease the reactivity, the concentration of D_2O was decreased by adding ordinary water. This increased the slowing down power of the moderator and reduced the critical mass. The D_2O concentration is periodically reduced throughout the life of the core. It is claimed that an SSCR has a longer core life than normal and that the reactor can be operated at full power all the time. Other advantages claimed were: higher average power since the reactor is operated with the control rods fully out; higher thermal efficiency; uniform fuel burnup; lower capital and fuel costs; and a larger conversion ratio.

Example 9. What is the theoretical conversion ratio for a natural uranium fueled reactor if the reactivity is to remain constant? Neglect any neutron losses such as poison or absorption by reactor structural materials.

$$\Delta\rho = 0 = \left[CR \frac{\sigma_{aPu}\eta_{Pu}}{\sigma_{a235}\eta_{235}} - 1 \right] R$$

$$CR_{\Delta\rho=0} = \frac{\sigma_{a235}\eta_{235}}{\sigma_{aPu}\eta_{Pu}}$$

$$\eta_{Pu} = \frac{\sum_{fPu}}{\sum_{aPu}} \nu_{Pu}$$

$$\eta_{Pu} = \frac{746}{1026} (2.90) = 2.11$$

$$\eta_{235} = \frac{\sum_{f235}}{\sum_{a235}} \nu_{235} = \frac{582}{694} (2.42)$$

$$\eta_{235} = 2.07$$

$$CR_{\Delta\rho=0} = \frac{694(2.07)}{1026(2.11)} = 0.664 \text{ or about } \frac{2}{3}$$

فریدون باختر

FEREIDOON BAKHTAR

REACTIVITY CHANGES IN FAST REACTORS

Small changes in reactivity can be introduced into a fast reactor in much the same fashion as into a thermal reactor. These allow power increases with long periods. The fast fission in ^{232}Th or ^{238}U causes the fraction of delayed neutrons to be slightly larger in a fast core than a thermal core. Table 10.6 shows delayed neutron fraction for various fissile and fertile species. Since the fraction of delayed neutrons from ^{232}Th and ^{238}U is so much greater than that from thermal reactor fuels a smaller reactivity change will give the same period (See Fig. 10.5).

The prompt neutron lifetime is the order of 10^{-7} sec for a fast reactor compared to 10^{-3} sec for a thermal core. This results in even a faster rate of increase in flux and power for a prompt critical excursion, making prompt criticality all the less desirable.

TABLE 10.6

DELAYED NEUTRON FRACTION (β) AND DELAYED NEUTRON
LIFETIMES ($\bar{l}_d$) FOR FAST AND THERMAL FISSION

Species	β_f	$\bar{l}_{d_f}$	β_{th}	$\bar{l}_{d_{th}}$
^{232}Th	0.022	10.02	—	—
^{233}U	0.0027	17.89	0.00264	18.58
^{235}U	0.0065	12.75	0.0064	13.14
^{238}U	0.0157	7.68	—	—
^{239}Pu	0.0021	14.63	0.0021	15.71
^{240}Pu	0.0026	13.12	—	—

Some of the reactivity changes discussed earlier in this chapter do not occur in fast reactors. Since there are no thermal neutrons, changes in temperature alone do not change the neutron spectrum. The ^{135}Xe and ^{149}Sm cross sections are fairly small for fast neutron energies so their effect can be neglected.

Three significant factors affecting reactivity changes of fast reactors are:

(1) Doppler effect
(2) Sodium void coefficient
(3) Fuel rod expansion

DOPPLER EFFECT

During a prompt critical power excursion in a fast reactor it is important to have an inherent mechanism for the rapid insertion of negative reactivity. There is no time for a mechanical scram system to operate. The Doppler effect may provide significant negative reactivity. As the temperature increases in the material through which neutrons are diffusing there tends to be a broadening of any resonance peaks. This is because the velocities of the target atoms can add to or subtract from the neutron velocity near the resonance region, broadening the resonance peak but keeping the area under the curve constant.

The net reactivity temperature coefficient depends to a large extent on opposite Doppler broadening of resonance peaks in the fissile and fertile fuel. Increasing temperature results in increased absorption in the fissile material (*positive coefficient*) and decreased absorption in the fertile material (*negative coefficient*). Therefore, there must be a limit to the ratio of fissile to fertile material in order to maintain a negative coefficient of reactivity in the fuel.

The important resonances involving the Doppler effect in fast reactors in the range of 0.5 Kev to 20 Kev are on the lower tail of a fast reactor spectrum. The softer the spectrum, the more neutrons there are in this low energy region and the larger the Doppler effect. A metal-fueled reactor has the hardest spectrum, followed by carbide fuels and then oxide fuels.

In a small metal-fueled reactor the Doppler effect is not significant but in reactors using a lot of sodium a significant number of neutrons reach the 0.5 Kev to 20 Kev range. This results in the negative tem-perature coefficient arising from the Doppler effect. Furthermore, it requires extremely accurate data to determine the lower energy neutron flux and the reactivity changes. The addition of BeO to large fast re-actors has been studied in some detail (Reference 8). The purpose of the BeO is to degrade the energy spectrum and thus enhance the negative Doppler coefficient. Table 10.7 shows two cores where Case B has

TABLE 10.7

COMPARISON OF HARD AND SOFT SPECTRUM CORES
FOR 1000-Mw(e) FAST OXIDE REACTORS

	Case A	Case B
Volume % BeO	0	8.3
UO_2–PuO_2	33.3	25
Steel	16.7	16.7
Sodium	50	50
Core Height	2.0 ft (0.610 m)	2.0 ft (0.610 m)
Core Diameter	11.8 ft (3.65 m)	13.7 ft (4.18 m)
Axial Blankets	1.25 ft (0.381 m)	1.25 ft (0.381 m)
Radial Blankets	1.0 ft (0.305 m)	1.0 ft (0.305 m)
Core Power, Mw(t)	2150	2150
Total Power, Mw(t)	2500	2500
Mean Energy of Power Spectrum (kev)	230	100
Fraction of Fissions Below 9 kev	0.12	0.28
Total Breeding Ratio	1.34	1.12
At. % (^{239}Pu + ^{241}Pu)	11.5	14.7
Doppler Coefficient $T(dk/dt)$	−0.006	−0.012
Δk for Sodium Loss From Core and Blankets[a]	+0.0070	−0.0051
Sodium Power Coefficient $\Delta k/1\% \Delta P$ at Full Power	+0.04¢	−0.03¢
Doppler Power Coefficient $\Delta k/1\% \Delta P$ at Full Power	−0.8¢	−1.8¢

[a] $\beta \approx 0.004$ for both Case A and Case B.

[From Hummel, H. H., and Okrent D., *Reactivity Coefficients in Large Fast Power Reactors*, American Nuclear Society, 1970] added 8.3 v/o BeO to soften the spectrum. Note the mean neutron energy is 0.23 MeV for the hard spectrum of Case A and 0.10 MeV for the soft spectrum of Case B. The Doppler coefficient is twice as big for Case B. Also Δk for sodium loss from core and blanket is -0.0051 compared to a positive value of 0.0070 for the hard spectrum. Fig. 10.7 shows the dynamic response to the addition of \$1.50 reactivity in 10 msec to the two cores. For Case A fuel failure would occur probably followed by boiling and expulsion of sodium from the core before the scram could act at 400 msec. The fuel in Case B will survive this reactivity insertion, the major difference being in the values of the Doppler coefficients. Note the magnitude and short duration of the power pulse in both cases.

The introduction of BeO into a reactor may prove difficult, practically, because the potential power generation of the reactor will be reduced due to the lower fuel volume.

The Doppler coefficient can cause a reverse effect in a cold sodium accident when the sodium temperature drops. This could occur with a large power reduction, not accompanied by a reduction in flow rate, or if a slug of cool sodium is pumped into a hot core unintentionally.

The Doppler coefficient is linked to the sodium void coefficient because of the hardening of the flux due to a void. This can reduce the Doppler coefficient by as much as a factor of two.

The use of ceramic fuels with their softer spectrum than metallic fuels does penalize the breeding gain and the doubling time in a fast

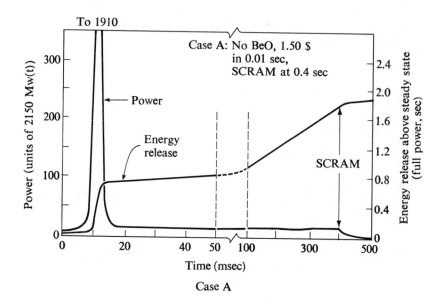

Case A

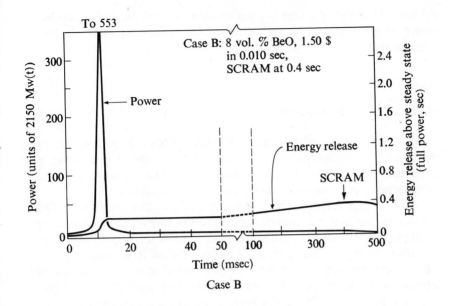

Case B

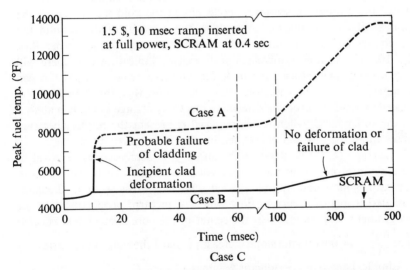

Case C

FIG. 10.7 *Comparison of responses hard (Case A) and soft (Case B) spectrum cores for 1000 MWe fast oxide reactors. $1.5 10 msec ramp inserted at full power. (From Hummel, H. H., and Okrent, D., Reactivity Coefficients in Large Fast Power Reactors, American Nuclear Society, 1970.)*

a) *Transient power and energy release (hard)*
b) *Transient power and energy release (soft)*
c) *Transient fuel temperatures for both cases*

reactor. However, the long burnup times make ceramic fuels desirable. Lower breeding gain along with the Doppler effect must share the economic penalty.

SODIUM VOID COEFFICIENT

Sodium coolant in the reactor expands as the reactor heats up or the number of sodium atoms decreases. This results in a decrease in the number of neutrons absorbed. While this is small in power reactors, changes resulting from other considerations are important.

One of the primary safety considerations in the design of a fast breeder system is that loss of part or all of the sodium will not result in a net positive increase in reactivity. Such a condition might result from a rupture in the sodium system, blockage of flow in coolant channels causing sodium vapor formation, or the introduction of a significant amount of entrained gas. Regardless of the cause, the effect is to produce a general hardening of the neutron spectrum because of the reduction of the number of scattering collisions in the void region due to the removal of coolant nuclei. Also, with the removal of the sodium the log energy decrement, ψ, is reduced contributing to the harder flux. Fig. 10.8 shows how η increases with energy, indicating that there will be more neutrons released per fission at higher average energies. It can be noted that the increase for ^{233}U is less than that for ^{235}U of ^{239}Pu. This effect tends to produce a negative reactivity change in fissile material. On the other hand, when fertile material is present the harder spectrum causes more fissions and consequently a positive reactivity change.

Leakage ($L^2 B^2$) is increased because Σ_s is decreased by removal of the sodium atoms from the voided volume. Thus, the transport mean free path is increased by the reduced scattering cross section. Leakage is related to neutron current flow which is, in turn, proportional to the flux gradient. A volume near the center of the core is much less affected since $\left.\dfrac{\partial \phi}{\partial \bar{y}}\right|_{r=0} = 0$ while the slope increases toward the outer boundaries, increasing leakage from peripheral volumes.

In small cores B^2 is large and the leakage overrides the positive reactivity effect of the hardened spectrum. In large power reactors this may not happen because B^2 is too small to allow the change in L^2 to have sufficient effect to override the positive effect of the harder spectrum. A local void at the center of a core tends to produce a positive contribution to reactivity due to the small neutron current flow at this location, but near the outer boundary of the core the effect would be negative.

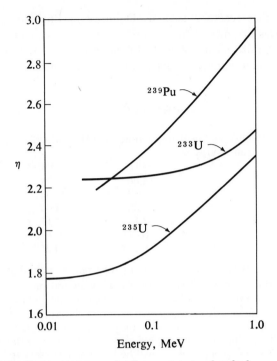

FIG. 10.8 *Fast neutrons emitted per neutron absorbed, η, vs. energy for ²³³U, ²³⁵U, and ²³⁹Pu.*

Overall then, the result in large reactors is to produce a positive coefficient of reactivity.

Positive void coefficients are of concern because the void might cause autocatalytic propagation through the whole core and a resulting loss of coolant flow accident could be even worse.

FUEL ROD EXPANSION

Lateral expansion of long fuel pins with temperature increase leads to a reduction in fuel density. This results in a leakage of neutrons and a decrease in reactivity. In reactors fueled with pellets it may be difficult to calculate this reactivity because in accident conditions fuel melt down could lead to an increase in reactivity.

In fast reactors control by means of neutron absorbing control rods may not be satisfactory because of their low rod section. However, in the Enrico Fermi fast breeder reactor, control rods using ¹⁰B have been used. The Fermi reactor uses 2 rods for control and 8 rods for shutting down. In other reactors, such as Dounray in England and EBR-II, fuel assemblies are moved in to increase reactivity and out to decrease reactivity. A third means of control is by moving the reflector in or out of the reactor in a manner similar to the fuel movement.

PROBLEMS

1. Compute the average neutron lifetime for ^{233}U and ^{239}Pu. Half-lives for delayed neutron groups are:

	^{233}U	^{239}Pu
1	55.00	54.28
2	20.57	23.04
3	5.00	5.60
4	2.13	2.13
5	0.615	0.618
6	0.277	0.257

2. In Problem 1 what will be the reactivity for a reactor period of one minute?

3. What is the reactivity in cents for a reactor period of 10 seconds and a prompt neutron lifetime of 2×10^{-4} seconds? The fuel is ^{235}U.

4. In shutting down a reactor $k_{eff} < 1$ and the delayed neutron contribution becomes effective at some time after the prompt neutrons have disappeared. Eventually the flux decreases with a period determined by the longest-lived delayed neutron group. What will be the time necessary to shut down a ^{235}U reactor if the average neutron flux goes from 1.75×10^{13} to 10^3 neutrons/cm^2 sec?

5. What is the reactivity (cents and inhours) of a carbon-moderated ^{235}U fueled reactor when the power is suddenly increased, resulting in a reactor period of 12 minutes?

6. Derive Eq. (10.31c).

7. A 75 percent enriched ^{235}U-H$_2$O moderated reactor has been operating at equilibrium for some time. The average neutron flux is 10^{14} n/cm^2-sec, and the moderator fuel ratio is 500 moles H$_2$O per mole uranium. Determine the reactivity change due to xenon and samarium.

8. Write a FORTRAN program to calculate the xenon concentration at any time after reactor shutdown.

9. Develop an electronic analog circuit to calculate the relative xenon buildup after reactor shutdown for various neutron fluxes. Is there a limiting value of flux for which no xenon buildup occurs? Neglect absorption cross section of ^{135}I.

10. A reactor is loaded with 25 kg of 3% enriched fuel. It operates continuously for one year at a power output of 10,000 kW. Determine the change in reactivity due to fuel consumption. The resonance escape probability is 0.677 and fast neutrons nonleakage probability is 0.973.

11. In starting up a reactor it is desired to reach full power in one minute. Full power is an increase by a factor of 10^4. What period is required?

12. Discuss the containment problem of a sodium-cooled fast reactor, especially the prevention of a sodium-air reaction.

13. A large PWR has $\sum_f = 0.005$ cm²/cm³ and is operating with a mean thermal flux of 3.5×10^{13} n/cm² sec. Assume a thermal utilization factor (based on ²³⁵U) equal to 0.87. The mean core temperature is 550°F. How much excess reactivity must the reactor have at shutdown to be able to override the maximum xenon buildup? How long after shutdown does the xenon reach its peak?

At the time of an unscheduled shutdown the reactor has $2 worth of excess reactivity. It takes 8 hours to correct the difficulty. Can the reactor be restarted immediately? If not, how long after the original shutdown must the operator wait to be able to go critical again?

14. A thermal reactor uses ²³⁹Pu as fuel and ²³²Th as the fertile material. If the resonance escape probability is 70% and the fast nonleakage probability is 95%, determine the conversion ratio. Assume there are 3 neutrons absorbed by Pu per neutron absorbed in thorium.

If the reactor produces 1500 Mwt for 10 months and is loaded with 2000 kg of Pu, determine the reactivity change due to plutonium consumption.

REFERENCES

1. *Proceedings of the Second United Nations International Conference on the Peaceful Uses of Atomic Energy*, vol. XI. Geneva: 1958.

2. Bonilla, C. F., ed., *Nuclear Engineering.* New York: McGraw-Hill Book Co., Inc., 1957.

3. Liverhant, S. E., *Elementary Introduction to Nuclear Reactor Physics.* New York: John Wiley and Sons, Inc., 1960.

4. Deuster, R. W., and Z. Levine, "Economics of Spectral Shift Control." *ASME Paper* 60-WA-335, 1960.

5. Glasstone, S., and A. Sesonske, *Nuclear Reactor Engineering.* New York: D. Van Nostrand Co., Inc., 1963.

6. El-Wakil, M. M., *Nuclear Power Engineering.* New York: McGraw-Hill Book Co., Inc., 1962.

7. *Reactor Handbook*, vol. II, USAEC, 1960.

8. Henley, J., and Lewins, J., ed., *Advances in Nuclear Science and Technology*, vol. 5. New York: Academic Press, 1969.

9. Hummel, H. H., and Okrent, D., *Reactivity Coefficients in Large Fast Power Reactors*, American Nuclear Society, 1970.

Chapter 11

Radiation Damage
and Reactor Materials
Problems

The interactions between radiation and matter can produce profound changes in the properties of a material. These may prove to be beneficial, as in the case of the strengthening in a thermal core of an austenitic stainless steel without serious loss in ductility, or they may court disaster, as illustrated by the sharp increase in the ductile-brittle transition temperature with low carbon structural steels.

To fully appreciate these changes one must take the basic approach of the solid state physicist who studies the interaction of a single type of radiation under carefully controlled conditions. This approach is gradually improving our understanding of the behavior of materials in a radiation field. However, many situations in a reactor are too complex to yield an answer by this fundamental approach. Thus, the engineering or phenomenological approach is used to give a specific answer to a particular problem, while it may shed little light on the understanding of the entire process.

RADIATION DAMAGE TO CRYSTALLINE SOLIDS

Crystalline materials have their atoms arranged in a well-defined lattice where each atom has a fixed rest position. Ideally, there should be no imperfections in the atomic arrangement; as a practical matter, however, imperfections exist due to the presence of impurities and alloying elements. Further irregularities can be introduced by plastic deformation. Any alteration in the regularity of the lattice will alter the properties of a material. Nuclear radiation tends to destroy order and alter properties by producing several types of defects.

(1) Vacancy-interstitial pairs are formed when energetic particles collide with atoms ejecting them from stable lattice sites. There may be a cascading effect because of a knocked-on atom having received sufficient energy to eject more atoms. These displaced atoms may finally lose their energy and occupy positions other than normal lattice sites, thus becoming interstitials. The presence of interstitials and vacancies make it more difficult for dislocations to move through the lattice, usually increasing the strength and reducing the ductility of a material.

　　These atom displacements which are produced in a reactor core are due primarily to the scattering of fast neutrons. The neutrons of 1 MeV energy and above have 90 percent of the total neutron energy and are responsible for the major amount of lattice disruption.

(2) Impurity atoms are produced by nuclear transmutations. Neutron capture in a reactor produces an isotope which, in turn, may be unstable and produce an entirely new atom as it decays. For example, ^{210}Po is produced in a reactor by irradiation of ^{209}Bi.

$$_{83}^{209}Bi + {}_0^1n \rightarrow {}_{83}^{210}Bi^* \longrightarrow {}_{84}^{210}Po^* + {}_{-1}^0e$$
$$\hookrightarrow {}_{82}^{206}Pb + {}_2^4\alpha \qquad (11.1)$$

The 138 day half-life ^{210}Po will produce 138 watts of heat energy per gram when freshly separated. This material was used as the heat source in the SNAP-3 project.

　　For most metallic materials long irradiations at high flux levels are necessary to produce significant property changes due to impurity buildup. However, a semiconductor such as germanium may have large changes in conductivity due to the gallium and arsenic atoms which are introduced as the activated Ge isotopes decay.

　　In stainless steels trace amounts of boron undergo an n,α reaction. The helium thus generated forms bubbles and leads to the deterioration of mechanical properties, as discussed more fully later in this chapter.

　　It should be noted that the production of impurities is largely due to the absorption of thermal neutrons which have much larger absorption cross sections than do fast neutrons.

(3) Replacement collisions occur when a moving interstitial ejects an atom from a lattice site and then lacks sufficient energy to leave itself. This is of particular interest in the study of the disordering of ordered solid solutions. It has little meaning if only a single type of atom is present in a lattice or if a solid solution has a random arrangement.

　　The beta prime phase in the Cu-Zn alloy system is an example of a body centered cubic structure with an ordered solid solution. Ag Cu_3 is a face-centered material with an ordered arrangement. Both these materials show increased amounts of order with low temperature irradiation.

(4) Spikes are caused by the intense local heating as knocked-on atoms and fission fragments energize particles along their track. This may occur as a high degree of excitation of the atoms without their leaving a stable lattice position (thermal spike) or as a shower of secondary displacements which drive interstitials into the surrounding lattice (displacement spike). In either case there is intense local heating with temperatures sometimes rising well above the melting point. If melting occurs the new lattice may form on the old lattice with new vacancies and interstitials replacing the original ones. Recrystallization and phase change may occur. The sudden cooling in a spike area for a steel will result in the local formation of hard brittle martensite.

A knock-on atom with an energy of 300 eV will have a range of 10–100 Å(2). Its energy is transferred to lattice vibrations. Considering this as a point source of heating, a region 30 Å in diameter would be heated to 1086°C in 5×10^{-12} seconds. After 20×10^{-12} seconds the heat-affected zone has expanded to 60 Å, but the mean temperature has dropped to 150°C. In like manner a 100 MeV fission fragment in uranium might produce a spike 4×10^4 Å long and 100 Å in diameter with temperatures reaching 4000°C. Localized melting, diffusion, and phase changes are all possible with such heating in the spike area.

(5) Ionization effects are caused by the passage through a material of gamma rays, or charged particles. This is particularly important with materials which have either ionic or covalent bonding. Materials such as insulators, dielectrics, plastics, lubricants, hydraulic fluids, and rubber are among those which are sensitive to ionization. Plastics with long chain-type molecules having varying amounts of crosslinking may have sharp changes in properties due to irradiation. Table 11.1 indicates that, in general, plastics suffer varying degrees of loss in unirradiated properties after exposure to high radiation fields. It is interesting to note that nylon begins to suffer degradation of its toughness at relatively low doses but suffers little loss in strength. The high density (linear) polyethylene, Marlex 50, loses both strength and ductility at relatively low doses.

In general, rubber will harden on irradiation. However, Butyl or Thiokol rubbers will soften or even become liquid with high radiation doses. Natural rubber will retain considerable flexibility on exposure to a gamma dose of 8.7×10^{10} ergs/gm. The exposure limit is usually considered to be 4×10^{10} ergs/gm for static applications and 5×10^9 ergs/gm for dynamic conditions. Radiation resistance of these elastomers is quite dependent on the conditions for curing and processing, curing agents, fillers, and antioxidants. Carbon black is often used as a filler and provides a degree of radiation resistance.

Those liquids to be used as lubricants or hydraulic fluids which have the aromatic ring type structure show an inherent radiation resistance. It is important that oils and greases be evaluated for their radiation resistance if they are to be applied in such an environment.

TABLE 11.1

EFFECT OF RADIATION ON THE MECHANICAL PROPERTIES OF PLASTICS*
IRRADIATED IN AIR AT 77°F

Key: A = 80% of initial value retained
B = 50–80% of initial value retained
C = 10–50% of initial value retained
D = <10% of initial value retained

Material	Property	Initial Value	Dose Rate megarads/hr	Thickness inch	Effect at Rad Dose				
					5×10^6	10^7	10^8	10^9	10^{10}
High Density (linear) Polyethylene-Marlex 50	Tensile Strength	4280 psi	1	0.002	A	D			
	Elongation	600%			D				B
Low Density (branched) Polyethylene-Alathon	Tensile Strength	1400 psi	2	0.19			B	A	B
	Elongation	250%				A	B	D	
	Notch Impact Str.	11.2 ft lb/in				A		D	
Nitrogen Containing Thermoplastic-Nylon	Tensile Strength	7600 psi	2	0.10	A	B	C	C	
	Elongation	62%			A	B	C	D	
	Notch Impact Str.	2.8 ft-lb/inch					C	D	A
Halogen Containing Thermoplastic-Teflon	Tensile Strength	3400 psi	1	0.14	B	C			
	Elongation	250%			C	D			
Thermoset-Cast Phenolic	Tensile Strength	11000 psi	2	0.18			A	B	D
	Elongation	2%					A	B	D
	Notch Impact Str.	0.53 ft lb/in					A	B	D
Thermoset-Cellulose Pulp-Filled Urea-Formaldehyde	Tensile Strength	7800 psi	2	0.125			A	C	D
	Elongation	0.5%					A	C	D
	Notch Impact Str.	0.31 ft lb/in						A	D

* Data abstracted from Bolt, R. O., and J. G. Carroll. *Radiation Effects on Organic Materials.* New York: Academic Press, 1963.

Metals with shared valence electrons which are relatively free to wander through the lattice are affected very little by ionization.

AMORPHOUS MATERIALS

An ideal amorphous material has no ordered structure and might be considered to have the maximum possible deviation from a crystalline state.   There are areas of limited order in all real amorphous substances. The major difference between amorphous solids and liquids is the difference in the time for ordered areas and disordered areas to interchange. For many liquids this time is 10^{-10} to 10^{-11} seconds, for glycerine it is 10^{-7} seconds, and for glass 10^{-1} seconds near the melting point, but 10^8 seconds at room temperature.

In a disordered array atomic displacements have little effect, but ionization can be very important.

NUMBER OF ATOM DISPLACEMENTS
PER NEUTRON SCATTERING COLLISION

When an energetic neutron strikes an atom it is necessary to transfer a minimum displacement energy, E_d, of approximately 25 ev to eject the struck atom from its lattice site.   The ejected atom is called a *primary knock-on* and it will travel through the lattice causing ionization, heating, and secondary displacements.   The maximum energy transfer, T_m, to the primary knock-on of mass A occurs when the neutron of energy E is backscattered ($\theta = 180°$).   It can be shown that

$$T_m = \frac{4AE}{(A + 1)^2} \tag{11.2}$$

We are particularly interested in determining the number of displacements which can be produced by each primary knock-on atom. The rate at which displacements occur, $\dot{n}_d$, can be given as

$$\dot{n}_d = N\phi(E)\sigma_d(E) \tag{11.3}$$

where N is the number density of target nuclei (atoms/cm³), $\phi(E)$ is the fast flux (n/cm² sec), and $\sigma_d(E)$ is the cross section for both primary and secondary displacements.   The latter is defined as

$$\sigma_d(E) = \int_{E_d}^{T_m} P(T)\nu(T)K(E, T) \, dT \tag{11.4}$$

where $P(T)$ is the probability that an atom receiving energy T is displaced, $K(E, T)$ is the differential cross section for the transfer of kinetic energy

T from a neutron of energy E, and $\nu(T)$ is the total number of displacements in a cascade originating from a primary recoil whose energy is T. The integration occurs between E_d, the displacement threshold energy and T_m, the maximum energy which can be transferred to a target atom by a neutron of energy E. At high energies the primary knock-on (ion) will lose energy primarily by ionization and excitation interactions as it passes through the lattice. As the knock-on loses energy it tends to pick up free electrons, effectively reducing its charge. As a result, the principal mechanism for energy losses progressively changes from one of ionization and excitation at high energies to one of elastic collisions with the lattice atoms at low energies. These elastic collisions produce secondary displacements. For simplification we will assume an ionization threshold energy ($E_i \approx 1000 \, A$) above which the primary knock-on causes only ionization and below which it produces only displacements. We will further assume that

(1)   There is a sharp displacement threshold

$$P(T) = 0 \quad \text{if} \quad T < E_d$$
$$P(T) = 1 \quad \text{if} \quad T \geq E_d$$

where P is the probability of displacement.

(2)   There is hard sphere scattering such that

$$K(E, T) = \sigma_s/T_m$$

(3)   The Kinchin-Pease Model may be used to define $\nu(T)$

$$\nu(T) = T/2E_d \quad \text{for} \quad T \leq E_i$$
$$\nu(T) = E_i/2E_d \quad \text{for} \quad T > E_i$$

Note the $2E_d$ in the denominator. Since it takes E_d to displace the atom originally in the site, another E_d will be required if the striking atom is to leave also.

Using the above assumption in Eq. 11.4

$$n_d = N\phi\sigma_s \left[\int_{E_d}^{E_i} \frac{T}{2E_dT_m} \, dT + \int_{E_i}^{T_m} \frac{E_i}{2E_dT_m} \, dT \right] \tag{11.5}$$

Dividing through by the rate of scattering interactions gives the number of displacements per scattering collision. Carrying out the integration yields

$$\frac{\dot{n}_d}{N\phi\sigma_s} = \frac{E_i^2 - E_d^2}{4E_dT_m} + \frac{E_iT_m - E_i^2}{2T_mE_d} \tag{11.6}$$

If $T_m < E_i$ the second integral is dropped and the upper limit on the first becomes T_m so that

$$\frac{\dot{n}_d}{N\phi\sigma_s} = \frac{T_m^2 - E_d^2}{4E_dT_m} \tag{11.7}$$

but, $E_d \ll T_m$, so

$$\frac{\dot{n}_d}{N\phi\sigma_s} = \frac{T_m}{4E_d} \tag{11.8}$$

Now if $T_m > E_i$, we must retain both terms and

$$\frac{\dot{n}_d}{N\phi\sigma_s} = \frac{E^2}{4E_dT_m} + \frac{2E_iT_m - 2E_i^2}{4T_mE_d}$$

$$= \frac{E_i}{4E_d}(2 - E_i/T_m) \tag{11.9}$$

Example 1.   a. Compare the maximum number of displacements per neutron scattering collision for 1 MeV neutrons in aluminum and zirconium. For aluminum

$$E_i = 1000A = 1000 \times 27 = 2.7 \times 10^4 \, \text{ev}$$

$$T_m = \frac{4AE}{(A + 1)^2} = \frac{4 \times 27 \times 10^6}{28 \times 28} = 13.8 \times 10^4 \, \text{ev}$$

In this case the maximum energy of the primary knock-on T_m, is greater than the ionization energy, E_i.

$$\frac{\dot{n}_d}{N\phi\sigma_s} = \frac{E_i}{4E_d}(2 - E_i/T_m)$$

$$= \frac{2.7 \times 10^4}{4 \times 25}(2 - 2.7 \times 10^4/13.8 \times 10^4)$$

$$= 488 \text{ displacements per scattering collision}$$

For zirconium

$$E_i = 1000 \times 91 = 9.1 \times 10^4 \, \text{ev}$$

$$T_m = \frac{4 \times 91 \times 10^6}{92 \times 92} = 4.32 \times 10^4 \, \text{ev} < E_i$$

$$\frac{\dot{n}_d}{N\phi\sigma_s} = \frac{T_m}{4E_d} = \frac{4.34 \times 10^4}{4 \times 25} = 435 \text{ displacements per scattering collision}$$

b. Determine the number of displacements per Zr atom per day predicted by the number of displacements per scattering collision. Assume a fast flux of 5×10^{15} n/cm² sec.

$$\frac{\dot{n}_d}{N} = \phi\sigma_s \, (\text{no. displ./target atom})$$

$$= 5 \times 10^{15} \, \text{n/cm}^2 \, \text{sec} \times 6.2 \times 10^{-24} \, \text{cm}^2/\text{Zr atom}$$
$$\times 435 \, \text{displ./scat. col.} \times (3600 \times 24) \, \text{sec/day}$$

$$= 1.17 \, \text{displ./day}$$

Note that in part (a) of this example, the number of displacements per scattering collision is the same order of magnitude for both zirconium and aluminum even though the atomic weights are quite different. This occurs because in aluminum most of the energy dissipation in the cascade is by ionization and we have not, in the model used, taken any of this as producing displacements. On the other hand, in zirconium we take no account of energy dissipation by ionization. On this basis the model probably underestimates the number of displacements in aluminum and overestimates the number in zirconium.

As to whether the calculations are more appropriate for Al or Zr one can argue either way. In Al the error in calculated displacements is greater because of the low ionization threshold discussed above. On the other hand, because ranges of knock-ons are greater in light elements (larger T_m) the cascade will be more spread out, displacements further apart, and there will be less tendency for mechanical relaxation of the displacement cascade. The above calculation estimating 1.7 displacements per Zr atom per day indicates the tremendous amount of disruption of the lattice structure caused by fast neutrons.

The model used tends to overestimate the number of displacements because of several significant omissions: replacement collisions as well as focusing and channeling effects have not been considered. Because of the directional nature of lattices, displaced atoms may travel preferentially in certain directions having only glancing collisions without removing struck atoms from stable lattices sites. Other limitations on using results of the calculations are that no consideration has been given to a thermal relaxation (mechanical relaxation and radiation annealing) and thermal recovery effects which will be discussed shortly.

TEMPERATURE AND MOBILITY EFFECTS

As temperatures increase, the vibration of atoms in the lattice increases, improving the probability that an interstitial atom might migrate to a vacancy and erase both defects. This ability of displaced atoms to diffuse in the lattice is known as mobility. The damage due to atom displacements may be healed either during or after irradiation if temperatures are high enough to allow the mobility necessary for atoms to migrate.

Fig. 11.1 shows in a schematic manner the way that fast neutrons in a reactor core introduce changes in mechanical properties of materials.

Atom displacements produce vacancies, interstitials, and spikes. The effect these displacements will have on properties will be determined by the amount of mobility introduced either during or after irradiation.

The data in Table 11.2 illustrate the effect of fast neutron irradiation

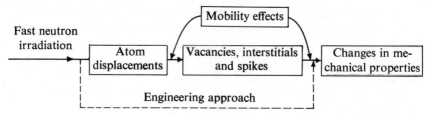

FIG. 11.1   *Radiation damage in solids due to fast neutron irradiation.*

TABLE 11.2

EFFECT OF FAST NEUTRON IRRADIATION
ON THE MECHANICAL PROPERTIES OF METALS

Material	Integrated Fast Flux, nvt	Radiation Temperature °F	Tensile Strength psi $\times 10^{-3}$	Yield Strength psi $\times 10^{-3}$	Elongation %
Austenitic SS	0	—	83.5	34.1	65
Type 304	1.2×10^{21}	212	104.5	91.6	42
Low Carbon	0	—	75	40	25
Steel	2×10^{19}	175	98	92	6
A-212 (0.2%C)	1×10^{20}	175	116	109	4
	2×10^{19}	560	102	76	9
	2×10^{19}	760	84	56	14
Aluminum	0	—	18	9.5	28.8
6061-0	1×10^{20}	150	37.3	25.6	22.4
Aluminum	0	—	45.0	38.5	17.5
6061-T6	1×10^{20}	150	50.6	44.4	16.2
Zircaloy-2	0	—	40	22.5	13
	1×10^{20}	280	45	40.5	4

on the properties of several structural alloys used in reactors. Aluminum is satisfactory at low temperatures in research reactors. As temperatures rise in power reactors zirconium becomes attractive to temperatures of 1000°F. For higher cladding temperatures stainless steel and other high-temperature alloys can be used despite cross sections which are much higher than those for aluminum and zirconium. In general, irradiation increases tensile strength and yield strength at the expense of ductility. The effects are much the same as those produced by cold work. Particularly with the face-centered cubic materials, such as 304 SS and 6061 Aluminum, the marked increase in yield strength with only modest loss in ductility can be considered as a distinct improvement in properties.

The data for 0.2 percent C steel show that at temperatures over 700°F there is a marked self-annealing effect during irradiation.   The temperature of the structural element during exposure to a fast neutron flux will determine the severity of the radiation induced damage.

INCREASE IN TRANSITION TEMPERATURE
FOR BCC METALS

An unhappy characteristic of body-centered cubic metals is their loss of toughness at reduced temperatures.   For ferritic steels this transition occurs between room temperature and $-100°F$, depending on the alloy content and melting practice used.   Fig. 11.2 shows results on hot

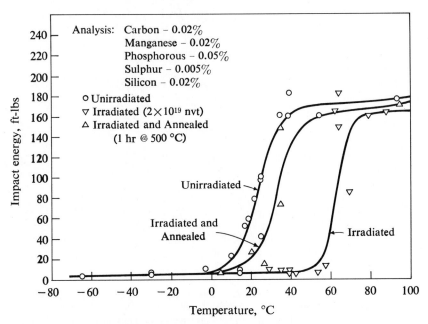

FIG. 11.2   *Radiation damage to Swedish iron.*

rolled Swedish iron, which illustrate this loss in impact absorption ability at reduced temperatures.

Irradiation to 2×10^{19} nvt raised the transition temperature by 60°C. Post-irradiation annealing at 500°C for one hour returned the transition temperature to within 10°C of its value in the unirradiated state.   These results indicate that the transition temperature can be raised in a ferritic iron alloy quite significantly (several hundred degrees in some cases) on exposure to a large integrated fast neutron flux.   It is also indicated that upon annealing the increased mobility allows much of the radiation damage to heal itself. Fig. 11.3 shows the increase in the nil ductility transition temperature for a representative group of low carbon steel alloys irradiated at temperatures below 450°F. Many current reactors have core vessel wall temperatures in the range of 400 to 550°F so that increase in the nil ductility transition temperature is of very real concern.

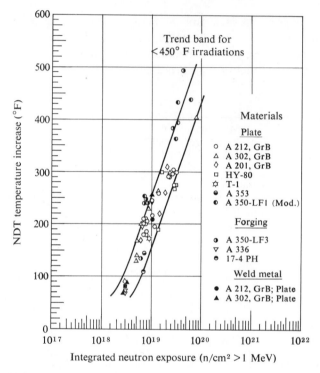

FIG. 11.3 *Increase in the NDT temperatures of steels resulting from irradiation at temperatures below 450°F.* [*From Simnad, M. T., and L. P. Zumwalt,* Materials and Fuels for High-Temperature Nuclear Energy Applications. *Cambridge, Mass.: M.I.T. Press, 1964.*]

Fig. 11.4 shows mechanical twinning in a ferrite crystal of the hot rolled Swedish iron, indicating that twinning was a mode of deformation as well as slip in this material.

For reasons of economics, the core vessels of large power reactors have been constructed of low carbon steels. The loss of ductility and increase in the transition temperature of these alloys is a serious concern to reactor designers. The use of steels that are vacuum melted or vacuum poured will reduce the original transition temperature of the steel. Also,

FIG. 11.4 *Mechanical twins near fracture in Charpy specimen of hot rolled Swedish iron. 200 X magnification.*

in many instances the core operating temperature is high enough to slow the rate at which radiation damage accumulates. Research is continuing in this area to improve our understanding of the changes that take place and to improve our ability to design safe pressure vessels for reactor cores.

STAINLESS STEELS IN FAST REACTORS

For stainless steel (see Table 11.2) exposed to a thermal reactor fluence of 10^{21} n/cm² sec the tensile properties show some increase in ultimate strength, an almost three-fold gain in the yield strength, and a drop of about 1/3 ductility. High temperature tests show a dramatic loss in strength and ductility. The damage is thought to be due largely to helium-filled bubbles where the gas has been produced by the n, α reaction of thermal neutrons with ^{10}B. Boron contents of the order of a few ten-thousandths of a percent are sufficient to produce the effects noted. The boron will burn out, however, after an exposure of about 10^{21} n/cm² sec and little further damage will be noted. Fig. 11.5 shows how for boron contents of 2 and 10 ppm the number of helium atoms formed reaches a plateau in less than 100 days at power.

Operation of fast reactors, such as EBR-II and Dounray, to fluences in excess of 2×10^{22} n/cm² sec indicates that significant amounts of

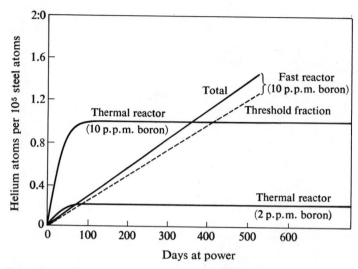

FIG. 11.5   *Helium production in fast and thermal fluxes.   Flux in the fast reactor* 2.5×10^{15} *n/cm² sec; flux in thermal reactor* 1.6×10^{14} *n/cm² sec.   [From Fraser et al.,* Nature 211 *(July 16, 1966), p. 291.]*

swelling occur in austenitic stainless steel cladding and structure.   These fast fluxes contain a significant number of neutrons at energies in excess of 3 MeV.   Above this energy level most materials will undergo an n, α reaction.   Thus, void formation is no longer dependent on boron.   The n, α reaction in boron will only occur at a rate approximately 1 percent of that in a thermal reactor.   Here, as shown in Fig. 11.5, the helium formation does not saturate, but is linear with time.   Further, the void formation is uniform throughout the steel, where in the thermal reactor it is limited to zones about precipitates where the boron may be concentrated.   The voids are larger than would be predicted by the amount of helium present.   This effect may be due to condensation of vacancies at sites where a few helium atoms have nucleated a bubble.

These voids can cause gross swelling of stainless steels where the volumetric change may amount to several percent for fluences in excess of 10^{22} n/cm².   As exposures at high burnups are ultimately expected to reach 10^{24} n/cm², this swelling must be accommodated in the design of a fast reactor core.   Correlation of available data has led to the development of an empirical equation (28) to predict the percent volume change for 304 stainless steel.

$$\Delta V/V = A(\phi t)^m + B \qquad \qquad (11.10)$$

where T = temperature in °C
ϕt = fluence $\times 10^{-22}$, $n \times 10^{-22}$/cm²

$$A = 2.65 \times 10^{-8}(T - 348)^3 - 1.54 \times 10^{-5}(T - 348)^2$$
$$+ 2.24 \times 10^{-3}(T - 348)$$
$$B = 0.2(1 - e^{-1.12\phi t})/(1 + e^{0.1(T - 480)})$$
$$m = 0.872 + 2.98 \times 10^{-3}T$$

Fig. 11.6 shows the temperature dependence of this volumetric change which peaks in the vicinity of 500°C. A fluence of 10^{23} n/cm² will produce a volume increase of 18 percent at 490°C. At 600° and the same fluence the increase has dropped to 4.8 percent.

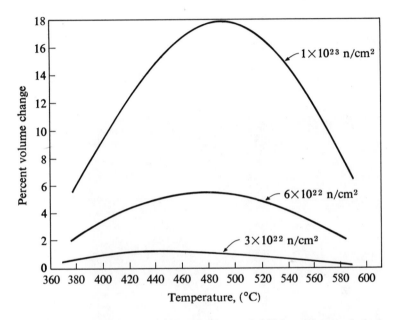

FIG. 11.6 *Swelling vs. temperature in annealed 304 stainless steel which has been irradiated to fast fluences of 3×10^{22}, 6×10^{22}, and 1×10^{23} n/cm². [Courtesy Hanford Engineering Development Laboratory USAEC, operated by the Westinghouse Hanford Company]*

The results from burst tests run on segments of EBR-II fuel-pin cladding taken at various core locations are shown in Table 11.3. Material taken from the plenum region where the fluence was low showed little change in properties. That below the midplane showed some radiation-induced hardening but still retained reasonable ductility, as indicated by the transgranular fracture shown in Fig. 11.7a. For those specimens above the midplane, which were irradiated at temperatures only about 50°C higher, there was a marked loss in both strength and

TABLE 11.3

FUEL-PIN CLADDING BURST TEST RESULTS

Operating Temperature (°C)	Fluence n/cm² (E > 0.1 MeV)	Failure Stress (psi)	Strain $\Delta D/D\%$	Specimen Location
475	1.2×10^{21}	59 090	18.4	Plenum
445	5.5×10^{21}	72 150	9.6	Below midplane
475	5.8×10^{21}	22 020	1.0	Above midplane
480	4.0×10^{21}	27 160	0.3	Above midplane
495	5.0×10^{21}	38 900	0.2	Above midplane
—	Control	56 960	19.2	—

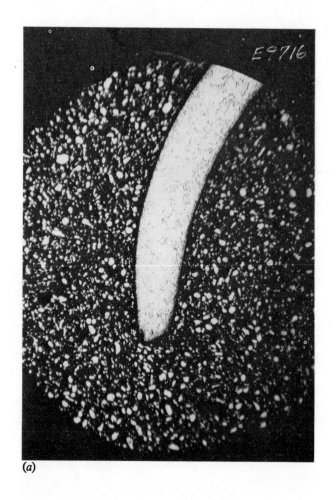

(a)

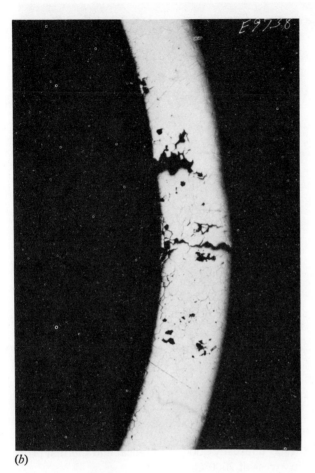

(b)

FIG. 11.7 *Typical transgranular and intergranular failures in irradiated stainless steel (a) below midplane of fuel, and (b) above midplane of fuel. [Courtesy WADCO Corp., subsidiary of Westinghouse Electric Corp.]*

ductility. The fractures became transgranular as is indicated by Fig. 11.7b. Fig. 11.8 shows how radiation-induced phase change has occurred in this cladding with the intergranular fracture. It contributes to the deterioration in the properties of the material.

GRAPHITE

Graphite is used effectively as a moderator and/or reflector in many sodium or gas-cooled reactors. Not only are its nuclear characteristics (i.e., log decrement, slowing down power and moderating ratio) very

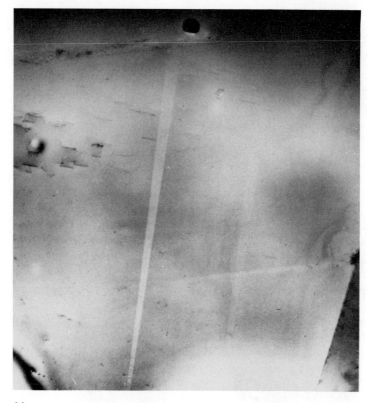

(a)

satisfactory, but it has unusually good mechanical and thermal properties at temperatures in excess of 2000°C.

The structure of graphite is hexagonal whereas the atoms in alternate planes are offset so that there is an ABABA stacking sequence. This is shown in Fig. 11.9. Only one-half of the atoms in the B plane lie directly over the atoms in the A plane. Bonding in the hexagonal planes is covalent, but in the c direction between planes weak Van der Waals bonding exists. Because some of the electrons are free to move in the layers, ionization has little effect. Because of the weak forces between layers, displaced atoms lodge between the planes and tend to force the layers apart, increasing the c distance.

A minimum energy of 25 eV is required for a neutron to dislodge a carbon atom from a stable lattice site. A 2 MeV fast neutron will displace an average of 60 carbon atoms from stable lattice sites before falling below the 25 eV energy level. These primary carbon atoms will displace

(b)

FIG. 11.8 *Fast-neutron irradiation-induced precipitation of $M_{23}C_6$ carbides in Type 316 stainless steel. (a) Unirradiated control sample, annealed 3050 hrs. at 480°C. (b) Sample irradiated in EBR-II at 480°C to 0.8×10^{22} n/cm^2 (>0.1 MeV). [Courtesy WADCO Corp., subsidiary of Westinghouse Electric Corp.]*

a total of about 20,000 secondary atoms for each fast neutron slowed down. As irradiation temperatures rise, more of these displaced atoms will be able to self-anneal by returning to stable lattice sites. Figure 11.10 indicates the increase in c spacing as a function of radiation exposure and irradiation temperature. Irradiation exposure above 300°C produces relatively little increase compared to irradiation at lower temperatures.

Graphite is usually produced by extrusion of a mixture of ground petroleum coke and a pitch binder, followed by baking at 800°C and graphitization at 2500 to 3000°C. During extrusion the coke particles are aligned in the direction of extrusion. This results in anisotropy in

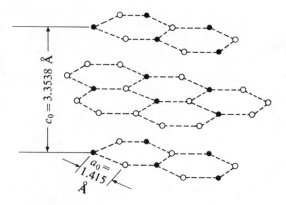

FIG. 11.9   *Atomic arrangement in crystalline graphite showing the ABABA type of stacking.*

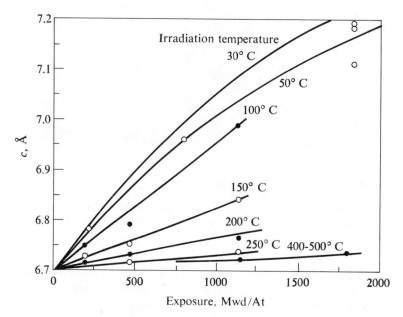

FIG. 11.10   *The expansion of* c *spacing at several irradiation temperatures.* (*From Nightingale, R. E., Yoshikawa, H. H., and Woodruff, E. M.,* Nuclear Graphite *New York, N. Y.: Academic Press, Inc., 1962, Chap. 9.*)

the final graphite.   The thermal conductivity parallel to the direction of extrusion of a graphite which was graphitized at 2800°C is 2.3 watt/cm°C, as compared to 1.4 watts/cm°C in the perpendicular direction.   Similarly, the electrical resistivity is 7×10^{-4} ohm-cm in the parallel direction and 9×10^{-4} ohm-cm in the c direction. The thermal conductivities are 4.0 watts/cm°C in the layer direction and 0.8 watt/cm°C perpendicular to the layer direction.

Irradiation produces gross dimensional changes in graphite. Below 300°C there will be significant expansion in a direction perpendicular to the extrusion direction and contraction in the parallel direction. Figure 11.11 shows the magnitude of these changes for three grades of graphite.

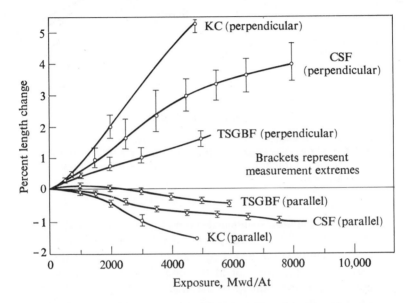

FIG. 11.11 *Radiation-induced dimensional changes in nuclear graphites at approximately 30°C. Note 1 Mwd/At = 0.87 × 10¹⁷ nvt, E > 0.18 MeV. (From Davidson, J. M., Woodruff, E. M., and Yoshikawa, H. H., "High Temperature Radiation Induced Contraction in Graphite," Proc. of the Fourth Conf. on Carbon, New York, N. Y.: Pergamon Press, 1960, p. 600.)*

Differences in the graphitization temperature and the character of the raw materials produce different amounts of anisotropy and crystallinity causing differing amounts of dimensional instability. Above 300°C irradiation can produce contraction both parallel and perpendicular to the extrusion axis, as is shown by Fig. 11.12. For long exposures over the lifetime of a reactor these dimensional changes can cause serious difficulty if they are not accounted for in reactor design.

Another problem with graphite irradiated at low temperatures is the accumulation of stored energy. On heating to a temperature high

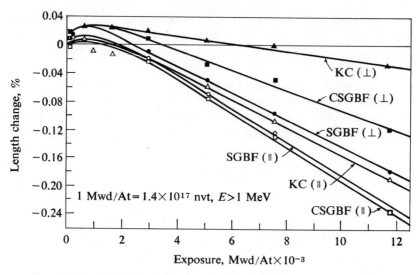

FIG. 11.12 *Dimensional changes in nuclear graphites irradiated at 400° to 500°C. (From Nightingale, R. E., Yoshikawa, H. H., and Woodruff, E. M.,* Nuclear Graphite. *New York, N. Y.: Academic Press, Inc., 1962, Chap. 9.)*

enough to allow the atoms sufficient mobility to return to a stable lattice site, this energy may be released, producing a further rise in temperature; this, if not carefully controlled, may lead to combustion of the carbon. In the early 1950s the operator at the English Windscale Reactor tried to anneal the radiation damage to the moderator graphite by raising the flux (and hence the core temperature) to a high enough level to release the stored energy in a controlled manner. Due to a faulty thermocouple, the flux level was raised too high. This unfortunate event taught the nuclear engineer what conventional power engineers had long known: carbon is a fine conventional fuel. The resultant fire released some fission products to the atmosphere, but the contamination of the sur- rounding countryside was less severe than had been anticipated. If irradiation occurs at high enough temperatures, displaced atoms have sufficient mobility to seek stable lattice sites and stored energy presents little problem. This is the case in high temperature gas cooled reactors moderated with graphite.

Pyrolytic graphite

Pyrolytic graphite is deposited on a substrate directly from a car- bonaceous vapor phase. Methane and natural gas are the most common media to provide the carbon. The crystallites of pyrolytic carbon have their layer planes parallel to the surface on which they are deposited. The good crystallite alignment can produce a density of 2.22 gm/cm³ which is close to the theoretical density. Most commercial graphite has a density around 1.8 gr/cm³ or less. The high density of PC makes it a desirable coating for carbide fuels because of its ability to contain fission fragments. One of the remarkable characteristics of this material is the anisotropy of its properties due to the nature of its structure. Electrical conductivity, thermal conductivity, and tensile strength are significantly greater in directions parallel to the *ab* basal planes than in the *c* direction, which is perpendicular to the basal planes. The tensile strength is about 10 times as great parallel to the basal planes as it is in the perpendicular *c* direction. The electrical conductivity is three orders of magnitude greater in the parallel direction than it is in the perpendicular direction. The temperature dependence of the thermal conductivity of the pyrolytic graphite both parallel and perpendicular to the basal planes is shown in Figs. 11.13 (a) and (b). When this material is used as a re-entry heat shield for a radioisotopic heat source (Ref. 26) this anisotropy of the thermal conductivity is very useful. The low conductivity in the *c* direction discourages heat flow through the shield. The large lateral

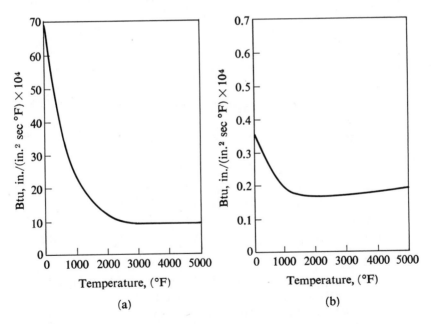

FIG. 11.13 *Thermal conductivity of pyrolytic graphite (a) parallel to the basal planes, and (b) perpendicular to the basal plane.* [*From Bramer et al.,* Nuc. Tech. 11, *no. 2 (June, 1971), p. 236.*]

conductivity transfers heat away from the stagnation point to reduce the maximum temperature due to aerodynamic heating.

NUCLEAR FUELS

Fissionable metals suffer from radiation damage in a manner similar to that encountered by structural alloys with the additional problems introduced by the high energy fission fragments and the heavy gases xenon and krypton which appear among the fission products. Each fission produces two fragments which share 167 MeV of kinetic energy in inverse proportion to their atomic masses. These will have a range on the order of several hundred angstroms as they produce their spikes. The gas formation produces eventual swelling of the fuel and may place the cladding under considerable pressure as well. There are several methods which may be used to cope with these problems, but first a consideration of the metallurgy of uranium, plutonium, and fertile thorium is in order.

Uranium

Domestic carnotite ore contains as little as 3 to 5 pounds per ton of U_3O_8. Leaching in H_2SO_4 and an ion exchange process result in relatively pure U_3O_8 which is reacted with hydrogen to produce UO_2.

$$U_3O_8 + 2H_2 \longrightarrow 3UO_2 + 2H_2O$$

The uranium dioxide is reacted with hydrofluoric acid to give the green salt of uranium.

$$UO_2 + 4HF \longrightarrow UF_4 + 2H_2O$$

If the uranium is to be converted to the metallic state directly it can be reduced with magnesium.

$$UF_4 + 2Mg \longrightarrow 2MgF_2 + U$$

The reaction is exothermic; because of the difference in densities of the liquid metal and molten slag separation takes place effectively.

When the uranium is to be enriched by the gaseous diffusion process the green salt must be first converted to uranium hexafluoride, a gas.

$$UF_4 + F_2 \longrightarrow UF_6$$

Isotopic separation is accomplished by the slightly different masses of ^{235}U and ^{238}U and their different diffusion rates to the top and bottom of a diffusion column. A multitude of stages in cascade is required for significant enrichment. Enrichments as high as 93 percent are available. The hexafluoride is reconverted to green salt by hydrogen.

$$UF_6 + H_2 \longrightarrow UF_4 + 2HF$$

Often the enriched uranium is reduced with calcium.

$$UF_4 + 2Ca \longrightarrow 2CaF_2 + U$$

Uranium exists with three separate crystal structures in the solid state (see Fig. 11.14). On solidification, the material exists as the γ phase

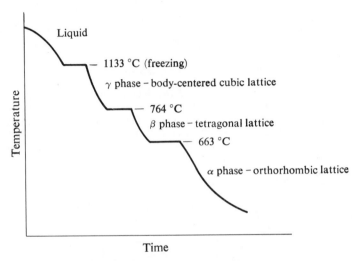

FIG. 11.14 *Cooling curve for unalloyed uranium.*

with a conventional body-centered cubic lattice. It is relatively soft at these temperatures and can be formed with relative ease, particularly by extrusion.

At 764°C it shifts to the β phase which has a complex tetragonal lattice with 30 atoms per unit cell. Fig. 11.15 shows the way in which alternate planes in the lattice have the atoms placed.

Alpha phase uranium with its unusual orthorhombic lattice will form when the metal cools below 663°C. The structure of α uranium is shown in Fig. 11.16.

This lattice structure has properties which are strongly anisotropic, as evidenced by the coefficient of thermal expansion. It is strongly positive in the a and c directions, while it is actually negative in the b direction. One can imagine the extension in the c direction straightening out the accordion pleating to reduce the b dimension.

When alpha uranium undergoes plastic deformation during a working process certain planes in each crystal will tend to rotate into the rolling direction, setting up preferred orientation. The character of the preferred orientation is dependent not only on the method of working,

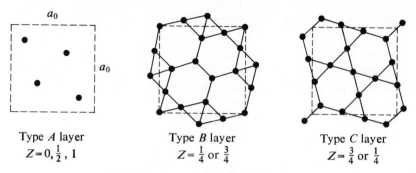

Type A layer
$Z = 0, \frac{1}{2}, 1$

Type B layer
$Z = \frac{1}{4}$ or $\frac{3}{4}$

Type C layer
$Z = \frac{3}{4}$ or $\frac{1}{4}$

Stacking arrangement, *AB AC AB AC*

FIG. 11.15 *(010) Projections of the Beta Uranium Structure. This phase with its complicated lattice tends to be stiffer than the adjacent alpha and gamma phases. Little effort has been made to work beta phase uranium.* [Holden, A. N., Physical Metallurgy of Uranium. *Reading, Mass.: Addison-Wesley Publishing Co., Inc., 1958; assigned to General Manager, U. S. Atomic Energy Commission.*]

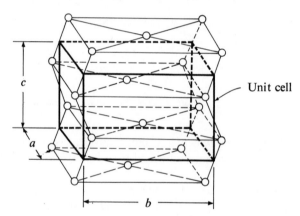

FIG. 11.16 *Structure of orthorhombic alpha phase uranium, its lattice dimensions and coefficient of thermal expansion.*

Lattice Direction		Lattice Dimension A	Coefficient of Thermal Expansion-in/in F (25–325°C)
a	100	2.852	26.5
b	010	5.865	−2.4
c	001	4.945	23.9

but also on the temperature at which the work is accomplished. Fig. 11.17 illustrates the difference in growth between two different types of alpha-deformed uranium with different working conditions and randomly oriented alpha uranium.

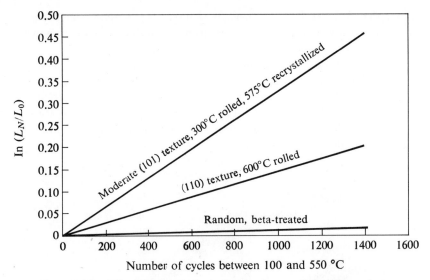

FIG. 11.17 *Effect of preferred orientation on growth of uranium during thermal cycling.* [*Holden, A. N.*, Physical Metallurgy of Uranium. *Reading, Mass.: Addison-Wesley Publishing Co., Inc.; assigned to General Manager, U. S. Atomic Energy Commission.*]

Growth is accounted for by the mechanism called thermal ratcheting. On heating above about 350°C, as adjacent crystals try to grow in different directions, the resultant stresses are relieved by grain boundary flow. On cooling, when the direction of motion would like to reverse, the lattice is too rigid to allow the accommodation. The net result is growth in the (010) direction.

Cold-worked alpha uranium retains its preferred orientation when annealed to allow recrystallization in the alpha region. Heating into the beta region, followed by quenching back to the alpha region, will produce random orientation of the alpha uranium. The treatment may be repeated for even better results.

In randomly oriented alpha uranium this growth due to thermal cycling will manifest itself by a roughening of the surface as some grains grow outward and others contract at the surface. This pimpling may be minimized by fine grain size. One of the disadvantages of gamma-worked uranium is its tendency towards coarse grain size with an attendant tendency to suffer from surface roughening.

When uranium is involved in the fission process the radiation damage produces growth in a manner somewhat like that due to thermal cycling if preferred orientation exists. One difference in irradiation growth is that individual crystals will undergo large changes in dimension where they will not do so on thermal cycling.   It is now felt that the generation of dislocation loops in alpha uranium accounts for its growth on irradiation.

As a heavy fission fragment is brought to rest in a displacement spike, a core of vacancies is surrounded by a shell of interstitials.   The interstitials form on (010) planes and the vacancies on (110) planes, producing growth in the *b* direction and shrinkage in the *a* direction (see Refs. 6 and 7).   Fig. 11.18 shows an extreme amount of growth that can occur under irradiation.

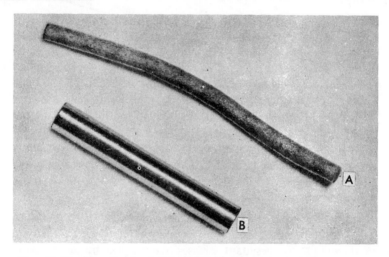

FIG. 11.18   *Growth of a highly textured uranium rod (a) due to irradiation compared with a dummy (b) the size of the original uranium rod.* [*Holden, A. N.*, Physical Metallurgy of Uranium.   *Reading, Mass.: Addison-Wesley Publishing Co., Inc.; assigned to General Manager, U S. Atomic Energy Commission.*]

As the burnup of uranium increases, the generation of xenon and krypton tends to cause swelling and gross distortion of the metal.   Not only are xenon and krypton isotopes stable end products of the decaying fission fragments, but they also provide some unstable isotopes which are merely an intermediate product in the decay chain.   One of the major challenges in alloying metallic uranium is the attainment of better dimensional stability under irradiation.   Fig. 11.19 shows the marked improvement which can be brought about by small additions of zirconium.

The strength of uranium generally decreases with increasing temperature from an ultimate tensile strength of 76,000 psia at 100°C to 5000 psia at the $\alpha - \beta$ transition temperature.   The beta uranium is somewhat stronger than the alpha at the transition temperature and the gamma

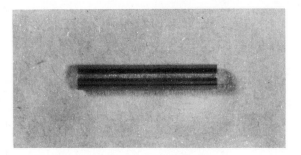

Before Irradiation

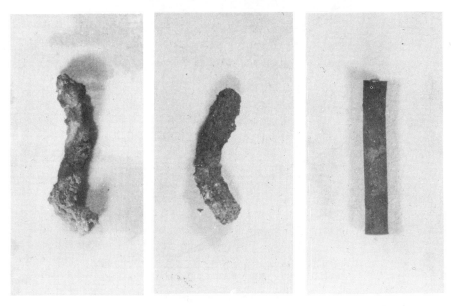

0 w/o Zr   0.52 w/o Zr   1.62 w/o Zr

FIG. 11.19   *Effect of zirconium additions on the stability of cast ura-nium irradiated to 0.6 a/o burnup.* [*Photograph Courtesy Argonne National Laboratory.*]

phase shows very little strength.   These changes are illustrated in Fig. 11.20.

The ductility of the uranium rises from about 15 percent at room temperature to 30 percent at 100°C.   Then it increases gradually to 35 percent at the $\alpha - \beta$ transition temperature and 37 percent at the upper extremity of the β region.   It is somewhat surprising that the two lower

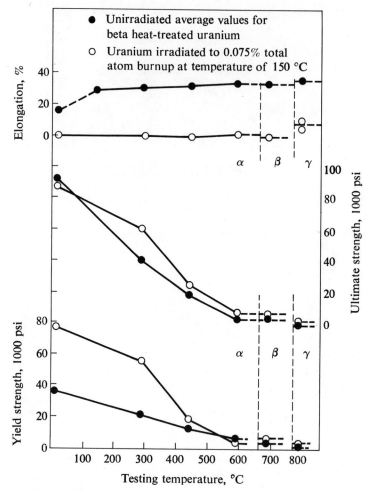

FIG. 11.20   *Effect of temperature on the properties of uranium, irradiated and unirradiated.*

temperature phases show this much ductility considering their complex lattice structures.

Fig. 11.21 illustrates the effect of irradiation on the room temperature properties of uranium. Burnups greater than 0.02 percent result in loss of ductility. The ultimate and yield strengths approach each other at 0.1 percent burnup.

The typical as-cast structures of alpha uranium are shown in Figs. 11.22a and 11.22b. The photomicrographs are taken of the same area with polarized light but with the stage rotated 45 degrees. Note that

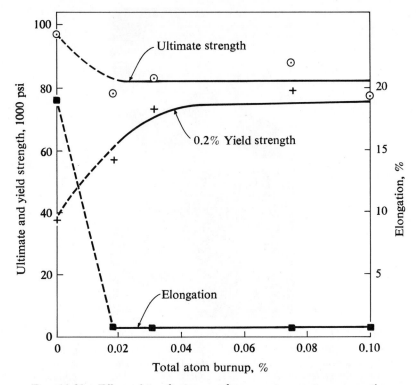

FIG. 11.21 *Effect of irradiation on the room temperature properties of uranium.*

some areas have shifted from dark to light and that the subgraining in the central area is much more evident on the left. As the stage is rotated each grain and subgrain will pass through a brilliant spectrum of colors, to which black and white photographs hardly do justice.

Fig. 11.23 shows a microstructure where recrystallization took place at 625°C after rolling at 400°C. Subgraining occurs during cooling where the anisotropic character of the shrinkage in neighboring crystals causes segments of the parent crystal to take on a slightly different orientation. This is encouraged by thermal cycling.

As fuel temperatures have continually risen with the development of larger power reactors, metallic uranium has become less and less attractive as a reactor fuel. Alloyed uranium, dispersion type fuels, liquid metal fuels, and ceramic fuels are some of the approaches to providing fuel elements less subject to gross dimensional change. These will be examined in some detail after a brief look at plutonium and thorium

(a)

(b)

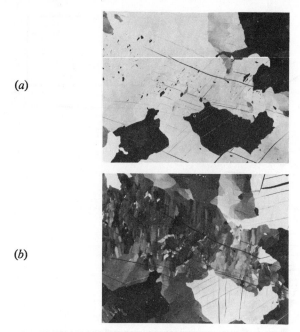

FIG. 11.22   *High purity cast uranium.   (a) as electropolished; polarized light.   (b) as electropolished; polarized light.   Note subgraining in large grain in center of field.   Stage rotated 45 degrees from position in (a). Subgraining less evident in large central grain.   Both 75 X before 80 percent reduction.   [From Wilkinson,* W. D., and W. F. Murphy, Nu*clear Reactor Metallurgy.   *Princeton, N. J.: D. Van Nostrand Co., Inc., 1958.*]

Plutonium

For all intents, plutonium is an artificial element produced by the transmutation of ^{238}U.   It does exist in uranium ore to the extent of five parts in a trillion, hardly enough to be commercially exciting.

Plutonium is exceedingly toxic.   The radioactivity concentration guides limit the maximum body concentration to 0.04 microcurie.   *All* handling must be done in glove boxes.   Fig. 11.24 shows part of the ANL Fuel Fabrication Facility.   Melting, casting, machining, rolling, and powder metallurgy operations are carried out entirely in glove boxes.

Fig. 11.25 shows the use of an analytical balance in one of the glove boxes at this ANL installation.

The use of metallic plutonium is complicated by its six allotropic forms.   These are summarized in Table 11.4.   The marked changes in density are accompanied by dimensional changes which are difficult to accommodate.   The δ and δ' phases have negative coefficients of thermal expansion.

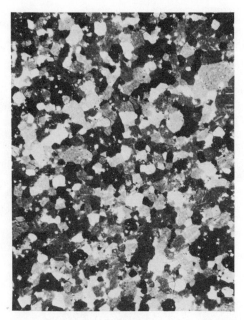

FIG. 11.23 *Recrystallized alpha uranium. Specimen rolled at 400°C, heated one hour at 625°C, furnace cooled. Electropolished; polarized light. 100X before 70 percent reduction.* [*From Wilkinson, W. D., and W. F. Murphy*, Nuclear Reactor Metallurgy. *Princeton, N. J.: D. Van Nostrand Co., Inc., 1958.*]

To be useful as a fuel, plutonium must be alloyed to provide a stable phase as a metal or a ceramic. It also may be used in a Pu-bearing liquid metal.

Thorium

Thorium is the most conventional of the three heavy metals being discussed. It solidifies at 1700°C with a body-centered cubic structure. At 1400°C it shifts to a face-centered cubic lattice which is stable to room temperature.

Thorium is alpha active and many of its daughter products are gamma as well as alpha emitters. ^{220}Rn which is sometimes called thoron, is a poisonous gas. It is undesirable to ingest thorium and one should guard against inhalation of ^{220}Rn.

The strength of thorium is quite dependent on the impurities and fabrication technique. Tensile strengths range from 20,000 to 40,000 psi with the yield strength being roughly 10,000 psi less. At 700°C cold-rolled thorium will have a yield strength of about 8000 psi, while powder

FIG. 11.24 *ANL Plutonium Fuel Fabrication Facility. Highly toxic plutonium fuels are fabricated within sealed glove boxes containing an inert atmosphere under negative pressure. By connecting these boxes with an enclosed conveyor system, material can be handled through all phases of fabrication while maintaining isolation from the outside environment.* [*Courtesy Argonne National Laboratory.*]

fabricated materials have a value of 5000 psi and cast thorium a value of only 2000 psi.

Recrystallization of severely cold-worked thorium will start at 500°C, but to be completed in two hours it requires a temperature of 750°C. Cold reductions of 90 percent are possible, but thorium tends to seize in swagging or drawing dies, making jacketing in a soft metal like copper quite desirable.

Alloyed Fuels

Although grain size and orientation in alpha uranium can be partially controlled through heat treatment, its degradation in physical properties and tendency to swell with large amounts of irradiation tend to make it unattractive for high output reactors. The multiple phase changes in plutonium tend to eliminate its use in the pure metallic state. The de-

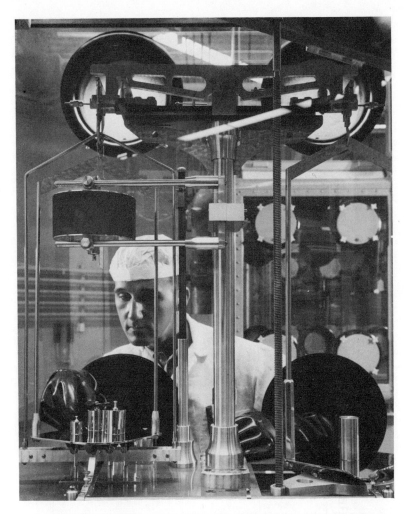

FIG. 11.25 *Weighing a Pu specimen in a glove box on a 1 kg balance in the weighing and inspection hood line at ANL's Plutonium Fuel Fabrication Facility.* [*Courtesy Argonne National Laboratory.*]

velopment of suitable alloys systems for fuels may attempt to accomplish a number of the following objectives:

(1) acquire a finer grain size;
(2) raise melting point to improve high temperature properties;
(3) lower melting point for ease of casting;
(4) improve corrosion resistance;
(5) eliminate or reduce growth due to anisotropy;
(6) reduce the tendency to swell;

TABLE 11.4

PHYSICAL PROPERTIES OF THE SIX PLUTONIUM ALLOTROPES

Phase	Crystal Lattice	Number of Atoms per Unit Cell	Transition Temperature to Next Higher Phase, °C	Density gm/cm³	Coefficient of Thermal Expansion μ in/in °C	Volume Change on Transition %
Alpha	Monoclinic	16	112	19.8	46.4	$\alpha \rightarrow \beta$ 8.9
Beta	Body-centered Monoclinic	34	185	17.65	38.4	$\beta \rightarrow \gamma$ 2.4
Gamma	Face-centered Orthorhombic	8	316	17.2	34.7 ($a = -19.7$) ($b = 39.5$) ($c = 83.4$)	$\gamma \rightarrow \delta$ 6.7
Delta	Face-centered Cubic	4	451	15.9	-8.8	$\delta \rightarrow \delta'$ -0.4
Delta Prime	Body-centered Tetragonal	2	480	16.0	-116 ($a = 305$) ($c = -659$)	$\delta' \rightarrow \epsilon$ -3.0
Epsilon	Body-centered Cubic	2	640	16.51	$+36.5$	

(7) improve working characteristics;
(8) dilution of fissionable material;
(9) produce a single phase which will be stable over the operating range of temperatures between start-up and full power; and
(10) neutron economy. The alloying elements should have small absorption cross sections.

Of the various fuel alloys the following types have had considerable development with varying degrees of success:

(1) Alpha phase uranium alloys. Small amounts of silicon, zirconium, or chromium all tend to produce a fine-grained alpha uranium which may be fabricated in a manner similar to that for pure uranium in the alpha region. Fig. 11.19 shows the effectiveness of Zr in controlling gross dimensional stability.

    An alloy with 5 w/o zirconium and 1.5 w/o niobium will have a somewhat distorted alpha structure after heat treating. It seems to be a supersaturated solid solution with improved corrosion resistance and radiation stability.

(2) Gamma uranium alloys. Alloys containing 10–20 percent Mo or Nb will operate in the gamma phase region. They show better dimensional stability and improved resistance to aqueous corrosion. Fig. 11.26 shows the phase diagram for the U–Nb system. Although an equilibrium condition at low temperatures would show an α plus γ mixture, all gamma may be retained by a rapid quench. These alloys may be susceptible to phase change during cold work.

    Alloys with 75–80 percent Nb and 15–25 percent U are all gamma in the solid state. These alloys are refractory in nature and are difficult to fabricate.

(3) Fissium alloys. Fissium is the alloy content found in irradiated fuel which is reprocessed by melting. Many of the fission products with high cross sections oxidize and go into the slag or volatilize. Those left behind will actually improve the characteristics of uranium. Often the major alloy constituents are added to uranium in an unradioactive state to simulate true fissium. This makes the alloy easier to use for research purposes because of its nonradioactive nature.

    In the EBR-2 Reactor the fuel is U–5 percent fissium whose composition is

U–95%	Rh–0.3%
Mo–2.5%	Ru–1.5%
Pd–0.5%	Zr–0.2%

Alloys of this type tend to have complex phase relationships but good radiation stability. They can be worked in the gamma region, but the most probable methods of fabrication will be by injection casting in remote reprocessing facilities. Sixteen-inch pins have been satisfactorily cast by this technique (see Ref. 3).

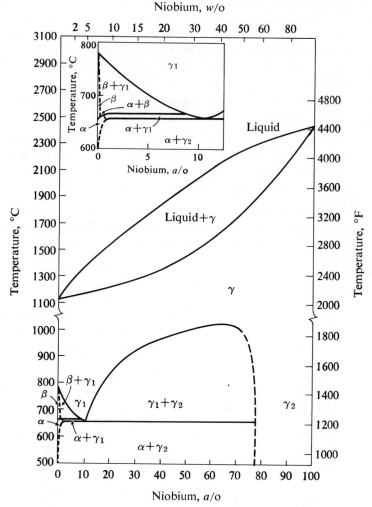

FIG. 11.26 *Uranium—niobium phase diagram* (*BMI-1000, June 1, 1955*).

(4) Ceramic fuels. Ceramic fuels are non-metallic oxides, carbides, nitrides, sulphides, etc., of U, Pu, or Th. They tend to be hard and brittle at low temperatures but have very high melting points. To date the most widely used ceramic fuel is uranium dioxide. Mixed oxides are also in use. Thoria and UO_2 elements are used in the Indian Point Reactor blanket elements and PuO_2—UO_2 combinations were used in the PRTR Reactor at Hanford.

Table 11.5 tabulates the densities and melting points for some of the uranium and plutonium ceramics.

TABLE 11.5

URANIUM AND PLUTONIUM CERAMICS

	Melting Point (°C)	Theoretical Density	Typical Density
UO_2	2750	10.97	10.5
PuO_2	2280	11.46	—
UC	2400	13.63	12.97
PuC	1654	13.6	—
UN	2630	14.32	13.52
PuN	>2500	14.2	—

The oxides, although less dense, show very good resistance to aqueous corrosion on exposure. This accounts for the wide use of UO_2 as a nuclear fuel in PWR and BWR power reactor cores. A cladding defect will not necessitate an unscheduled shutdown to remove the defective fuel assembly.

Fabrication and reprocessing of oxide fuels are relatively easy. Fabrication can be done by pressing and sintering powder into pellets with densities 92–97 percent of theoretical. The pellets are then slipped into a tube of clad material which is welded shut. Densities in the same range may be attained by vibrational compaction. Here loose powder is poured into the cladding tube which is then vibrated at its resonant frequency.

The thermal conductivity of UO_2 is not especially high. It is also sensitive to temperature and irradiation. Fig. 11.27 shows the thermal conductivity for various forms of UO_2 as a function of temperature. The temperatures at the center of a UO_2 fuel element may actually reach the melting point during startup or even at steady state operating temperatures, as evidenced by the columnar grains at the center of the fuel element in Fig. 11.28. The varied grain structure gives evidence of some of the structural changes which the element may undergo during irradiation. The resulting changes in physical properties are difficult to predict.

Carbides of uranium are very reactive in an aqueous environment and thus are ruled out for pressurized or boiling water applications. They are stable in sodium, and it is planned to use uranium carbide fuel for some sodium-cooled reactors. The fuel behaves well under irradiation, being dimensionally stable and anneals out much damage under high operating temperatures. Fig. 11.29 shows the microstructure of a carbide ceramic fuel with 5.75 percent C. Carbides which may be used in the dispersion type elements are discussed in the next section.

UO_2, PuO_2, and ThO_2 are all mutually soluble in all proportions, making the behavior and fabrication of mixed oxide fuels similar to that

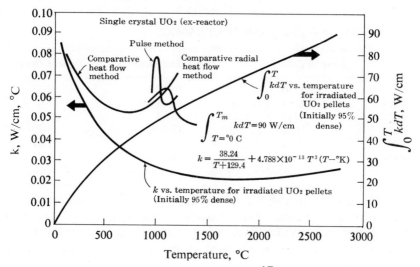

FIG. 11.27 *UO₂ Thermal Conductivity and $\int_0^T k\,dT$ versus Temperature.* [*From Pashos, T. J., et al., "Irradiation Behavior of Ceramic Fuels,"* Proceedings of the Third United Nations Conference on the Peaceful Uses of Atomic Energy, *Paper No. A/conf. 18/P/240, September, 1964.*]

for a single oxide. The $ThO_2 - PuO_2$ combination is an interesting one because during reprocessing the new fissionable ^{233}U produced can be easily separated by chemical means from the Pu and Th.

DISPERSION-TYPE ALLOYS

In a dispersion-type fuel a fissile phase is imbedded in a metallic or ceramic matrix. The fissile particles should be spaced far enough apart so that the areas damaged by fission fragments do not overlap and the matrix will retain its strength effectively, as shown by Fig. 11.30. The matrix often will have a better thermal conductivity than the fissile phase, tending to reduce the maximum temperatures in the fuel element. The retention of the mechanical properties of the matrix should assist in containing fission gases, allowing larger burnups without swelling. Table 11.6 shows some of the combinations which have been proposed for nuclear fuel elements.

Alloys of uranium with up to 45 w/o Al can be produced by inexpensive casting techniques and are then amenable to plastic deformation. Fig. 11.31 shows a phase diagram for this alloy system. There is a eutectic

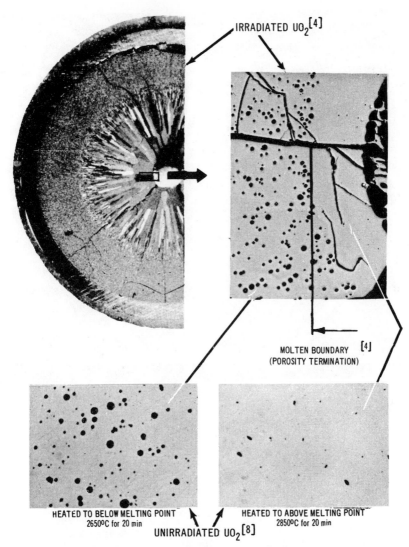

IRRADIATED UO$_2$[4]

MOLTEN BOUNDARY   [4]
(POROSITY TERMINATION)

HEATED TO BELOW MELTING POINT
2650°C for 20 min

HEATED TO ABOVE MELTING POINT
2850°C for 20 min

UNIRRADIATED UO$_2$[8]

FIG. 11.28 *Similarity of irradiated and unirradiated UO$_2$ microstructure above and below the melting point.* [*From Pashos, T. J., et al., "Irradiation Behavior of Ceramic Fuels,"* Proceedings of the Third United Nations Conference on the Peaceful Uses of Atomic Energy, *Paper No. A/conf. 28/P/240, September, 1964.*]

formed at 640°C between 13 w/o U and 87 w/o Al.   Fig. 11.32a shows an alloy with 10 w/o U where there are primary η phase grains (pure Al) in a matrix of UAl$_4$ $-$ η eutectic.   Fig. 11.32b shows a 15 w/o U alloy where the primary crystals are now UAl$_4$.   Alloys such as these may be

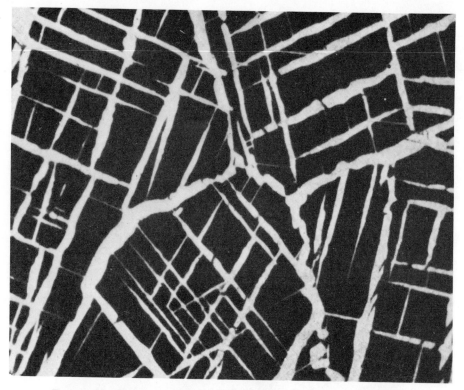

FIG. 11.29   *Uranium-carbon alloy (5.75%C).   Composed of 90% UC (dark) and 10% UC₂ (light Widmanstatten pattern).*   [*From Gray, R. J., et al.,* Metal Progress **74,** *1 (1958), p. 68.*]

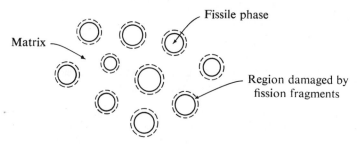

FIG. 11.30   *Dispersion-type alloy showing the region in the matrix which is damaged by fission fragments.*

hot-rolled with about a 3:1 reduction in thickness, cast clad in a 5 percent Si − 95 w/o Al alloy, followed by a final rolling to a fuel-plate thickness of less than 1/16 inch.   Fig. 11.33 shows the resultant structure.   Note the uniform dispersion of the UAl₄ in the Al matrix in the final fuel plate.

TABLE 11.6

EXAMPLES OF DISPERSION-TYPE FUEL SYSTEMS
(REF. 11)

Dispersed Phase	Matrix Phase
UO_2	Stainless Steel (austenitic and ferritic)., Fe, Nichrome, SiC-Si, Nb, Al, Zr, Zircaloy, Graphite, BeO, Al_2O_3, SiO_2
U	Mg, Th, Zr, Zircaloy, $ZrH_{1.65}$
UAl_4	Al
UZr_2	Zr, Zircaloy
UC	SS, Zr, Zircaloy
UN	SS, Zr
U_3Si	Zr
U_6Ni	Zr
U_2Ti	Zr
PuO_2	Mg, Al, Th, U, Zr, Fe, Graphite

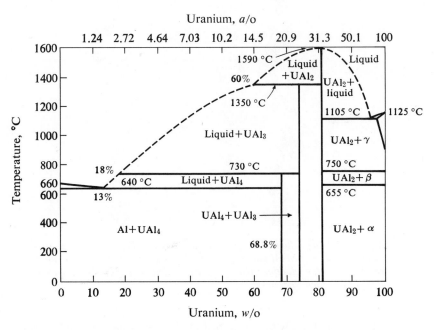

FIG. 11.31   *Uranium-aluminum phase diagram [TID-7502, April, 1955].*

 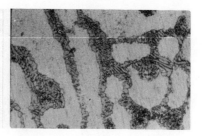

FIG. 11.32   *Cast uranium-aluminum alloys.   (a) shows a 10 w/o U hypoeutectic alloy where the primary crystals are nearly pure aluminum. (b) shows a 15 w/o U hypereutectic alloy where the primary crystals are UAl₄.*

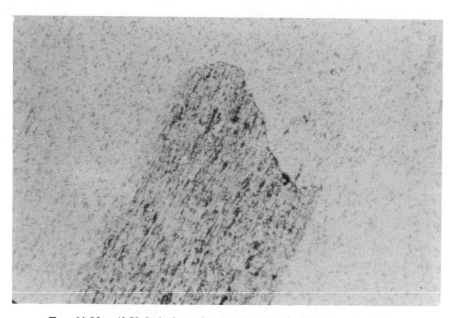

FIG. 11.33   *Al-U fuel plate showing the 10 w/o U fuel material surrounded by 5 w/o Si-Al cladding.   The fuel material is cast, hot-rolled, recast inside the cladding material, and rolled to a plate of approximately 1/16 inch thickness.*

Elements of this type were developed at the Argonne National Laboratory's International Institute of Nuclear Science and Engineering as being suitable for production and use in research reactors in underdeveloped nations.   The simplicity of the production methods used requires no heavy investment in special-purpose machinery.

An opposite extreme is the Nichrome — UO_2 type fuel element designed for the ill-fated Aircraft Nuclear Propulsion Project. Here approximately 40 w/o UO_2 is dispersed in a matrix of Nichrome (80 Ni — 20 Cr). Fig. 11.34 shows a fuel stage of this material. Ni, Cr, and UO_2 powders

FIG. 11.34 *Nichrome UO₂ fuel stage.* [*From Aitken, E. A., "Dispersion Fuel Elements." ASEE-AEC Summer Institute on Materials for Nuclear Reactors, Richland, Washington, 1962.*]

were blended in correct proportions, cold pressed, sintered, assembled with cover plates of Nb modified nichrome, hot pressed, rolled, edge seal brazed, rolled to ribbon, spot welded into an assembly, followed by a final brazing. The high temperature strength and oxidation resistance of these materials led to their use. The 100-hour creep data shown in Fig. 11.35 indicate the severe conditions under which these elements were intended to operate.

For even higher temperature service the fissile phase can be imbedded in a ceramic matrix. BeO, with up to 60 w/o UO_2, is an example of such

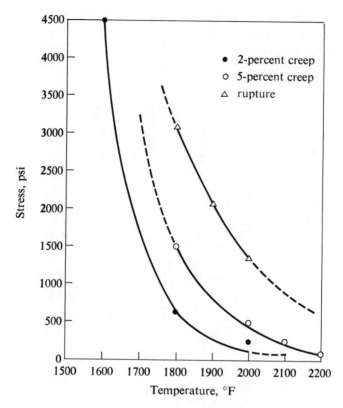

FIG. 11.35 *Plot of 2 percent and 5 percent deformation and rupture for 80 Ni − 20 Cr fuel ribbon in a 100-hour period. [From Aitken, E. A., "Dispersion Fuel Elements," Adv. Institute on Materials for Nuclear Reactors, Richland, Washington, August, 1962.]*

a material which could be called a fueled moderator. Tubular elements of this type open up the possibility of all-ceramic reactors.

Fuel elements for the Peach Bottom High-Temperature Gas-Cooled Reactor (HTGR) are pyrolytic carbon-coated (Th, U) C_2 particles in a graphite matrix. Fig. 11.36 shows the assembled elements. Fig. 11.37 shows an individual fuel compact. In this reactor, purge gas is passed through the grooves on the outside of the annular elements removing a substantial fraction of the escaping fission products. The uranium and thorium in the fuel compacts are in the form of carbides. The composition of the compacts is shown in Table 11.7.

The carbide particles are 100 to 400 microns in diameter coated with pyrolytic carbon 50 to 60 microns thick. The PC prevents contact of the carbides with atmospheric moisture which would lead to their rapid de-

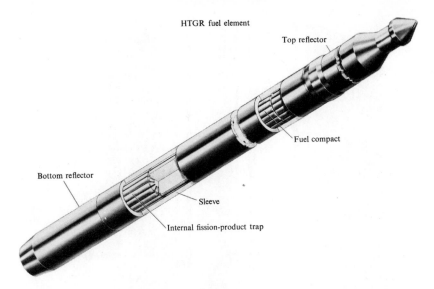

FIG. 11.36 *Peach Bottom HTGR Fuel Element.* [*From Goeddel, W. V.,* Nuc. Sci. and Eng., **20,** *201 (1964).*]

TABLE 11.7

HTGR FUEL COMPACT DATA (REF. 14)

Composition	
Uranium (93% enriched)	2.8 w/o
Thorium	16.1 w/o
Total Metal	18.9 w/o
Graphite	81.1 w/o
C: Th: U Atom Ratio	562:5.8:1
Temperature	
Maximum Fuel Compact Temperature	1340°C
Average Fuel Compact Temperature	980°C
Burnup (three-year core life at 80% Load Factor)	
Fissions/Original fissile atom	0.6
MW-days (t)/Met ton $^{235}U + ^{232}Th$	60,000
Fissions/cm^3	0.67×10^{20}

terioration.   It further helps contain fission fragments.   Fig. 11.38 shows PC coated (Th, U) C_2 particles.

Irradiation of these compacts at temperatures higher than antici-pated in HTGR operation produces what is known as the *amoeba effect.* When a temperature gradient exists across the carbide particle the UC_2 tends to migrate toward the higher temperature.   It appears to "eat" the

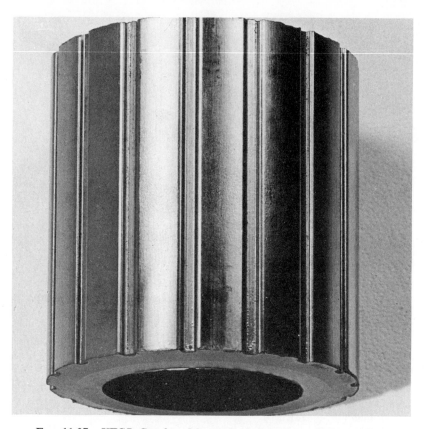

FIG. 11.37 *HTGR Graphite Matrix Fuel Compact. The compact is produced by hot pressing. The purge grooves are formed during the hot pressing process; no machining is required. [From Goeddel, W. V., Nuc. Sci. and Eng., 20, 206 (1964).]*

PC ahead of the particle and to precipitate carbon behind it, as shown by Fig. 11.39. The temperature gradient across this particle was estimated to be only 3°C. Both UC_2 and $(Th, U) C_2$ particles show the same type of attack.

Multilayered fuel-particle coatings have subsequently been developed to improve metallic fission-product retention and to reduce fission-gas release. An inner porous layer acts as a buffer from recoiling fission fragments and provides voids for fission-gas retention. An outer layer of pyrolytic carbon provides strength and retention of the noble fission gases. It is, however, less successful in stopping metallic fission products at high-temperature gas-cooled reactor temperatures. A layer of silicon

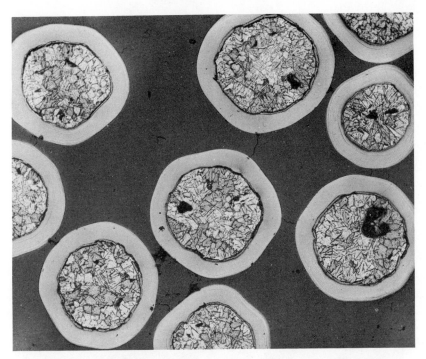

FIG. 11.38 *Photomicrograph of pyrolytic carbon coated (Th, U) C₂ particles. 75 X before 50 percent reduction. [From Goeddel, W. V., Nuc. Sci. and Eng., **20**, 206 (1964).]*

carbide may be deposited on the porous carbon layer before the outer layer of pyrolytic carbon is laid down. The SiC layer provides for better retention of the metallic fission products. Fig. 11.40 shows such a triple-coated UO_2 particle, both before and after irradiation to 4.6 percent burnup at 1250°C. The post-irradiation integrity of the SiC and pyrolytic carbon layers is evident. Improvement in the ability to retain fission gases has led to the abandonment of the purge-gas system used with the Peach Bottom HTGR.

The fuel being used in the 330 MWe Fort St. Vrain HTGR contains 100 micron UC_2 spheres and 400 micron spheres of Th_2, each type of particle using a four-layer coating. An extra layer of pyrocarbon is deposited between the porous carbon layer and the silicon carbide layer previously described. The particles are embedded in a carbonaceous binder and formed into rods 1/2 inch in diameter × 2 inches long. These rods are inserted in holes drilled in the hexagonal graphite moderator blocks. The whole assembly, which is 14 inches across flats and

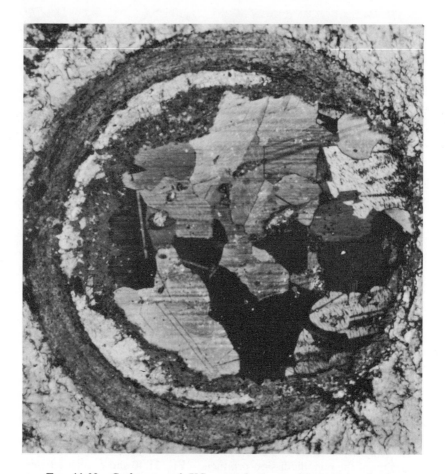

FIG. 11.39   *Carbon-coated UC$_2$ particle in graphite matrix showing "Amoeba Effect." Tested 150 hours in temperature range from 1780 to 1920°C. The carbide particle has migrated in the direction of increasing temperature. 200X before 27% enlargement. [Courtesy General Atomic, Division of General Dynamics Corporation.]*

31 inches long, forms a massive fuel element. Fig. 11.41 shows a fuel element and some of the quadruple-coated fuel particles. While the overall average burnup is expected to be 100,000 MWd/ton, in the fuel particles with their fully enriched uranium it will be 700,000 MWd/ton and in the fertile ThC$_2$ particles it will be only 40,000 MWd/ton. It is planned to replace 1/6 of the core at each annual refueling so that a fuel element going through the full cycle will reside in the core for six years, accounting for the large burnups.

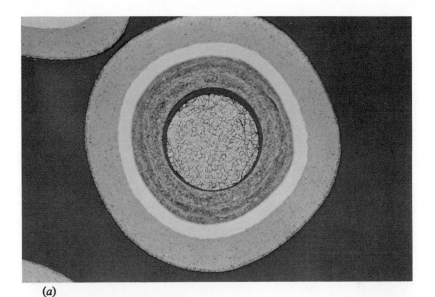

(a)

(b)

FIG. 11.40 *Triple-coated UO₂ fuel particle. The outer layer is dense pyrolytic carbon over a layer of silicon carbide surrounding the inner layer of porous carbon. (a) unirradiated, and (b) irradiated to 4.6 a/o burnup. Magnification 200X. [Courtesy Oak Ridge National Laboratory, operated by Union Carbide Corp. for U. S. Atomic Energy Commission.]*

FIG. 11.41 *Cross section of greatly magnified fuel particles with multilayered coatings* (above) *are bonded into fuel rods* (below) *which are inserted into a graphite block to form a single fuel element.* [*Courtesy Gulf General Atomic.*]

PROBLEMS

1. Show that the maximum energy which can be transferred by a neutron of energy E to a knock-on atom of mass A is

$$T_m(E) = 4AE/(A + 1)^2$$

2. Calculate the number of atom displacements per scattering collision in iron for neutrons with an energy of 1 MeV. If one considers a fast mono-energetic flux of 10^{15} n/cm² sec for neutrons at this energy, calculate the number of displacements per iron atom per day.

3. In a fusion reactor the D-T reaction produces a 14 MeV neutron. Niobium is being considered as the material for the fusion chamber wall. Compare the number of atom displacements per neutron scattering collision for a 14 MeV neutron with the number produced by a 1 MeV neutron. Comment on the probable radiation damage to the fusion chamber wall.

4. In Ref. 28 equations have been developed to fit experimental data on the percent swelling of solution treated Type 316 stainless steel at fluences above 10^{22} n/cm² ($E > 0.1$ MeV).

$$\Delta V/V = (\phi t/10^{22})^{N(T)} F(T)$$

where $N(T) = \dfrac{2 + 3 \exp{(0.05(T - 475))}}{1 + \exp{(0.05(T - 475))}}$

and $F(T) = \dfrac{\exp{(0.09(T - 340))}}{1 + \exp{(0.09(T - 340))}}$

$$\times \left\{ \frac{0.022}{1 + \exp{(0.05(T - 600))}} + \frac{0.06}{1 + \exp{(0.06(T - 460))}} \right\}$$

where ϕt = fluence, n/cm² ($E > 0.1$ MeV)
$\Delta V/V$ = swelling, %
T = temperature, °C

Write a computer program to plot the percent swelling vs. temperature between 300°C and 600°C for fluences of 3×10^{22}, 6×10^{22}, and 1×10^{23} n/cm². Compare the results to Fig. 11.6 for Type 304 stainless steel.

REFERENCES

1. Dienes, D. J., and D. H. Vineyard, *Radiation Effects in Solids*. New York: Interscience Publishers, 1957.

2. Holden, A. N., *Physical Metallurgy of Uranium*. Reading, Mass.: Addison-Wesley Publishing Co., Inc., 1958.

3. Wilkinson, W. D., *Uranium Metallurgy*, vols. I and II. New York: Interscience Publishers, 1962.

4. Wilkinson, W. D., and W. F. Murphy, *Nuclear Reactor Metallurgy*. Princeton, N. J.: D. Van Nostrand Co., Inc., 1958.

5. Strucken, E. F., "Anisotropic Growth in Metallic Uranium." ASEE-AEC Summer Institute on Materials for Nuclear Reactors, Richland, Washington, 1962.

6. Huntoon, R. T., "Properties of Uranium." ASEE-AEC Summer Institute on Materials for Nuclear Reactors, Richland, Washington, 1962.

7. Hudson, B., K. H. Westmacott, and J. J. Makin, *Dislocation Loops and Irradiation Growth in Alpha Uranium.* UKAEA Report AERE R 3752.

8. Kittel, J. H., "Uranium Alloys–Irradiation Behavior." ASEE-AEC Summer Institute on Materials for Nuclear Reactors, Richland, Washington, 1962.

9. Kaplan, G. E., "Metallurgy of Thorium." *International Conference on the Peaceful Uses of Atomic Energy*, vol. VIII (1955).

10. Kemper, R. S., "Irradiation Effects–Metallic Uranium, Physical and Mechanical Properties." ASEE-AEC Summer Institute on Materials for Nuclear Reactors, Richland, Washington, 1962.

11. Aitken, E. A., "Dispersion Fuel Elements." ASEE-AEC Summer Institute on Materials for Nuclear Reactors, Richland, Washington, 1962.

12. Bates, J. L., "Thermal Conductivity of UO_2 Improves at High Temperatures." *Nucleonics* **19,** 6 (June, 1961), pp. 83–87.

13. Walker, Jr., P. L., "Carbon—An Old But New Material." *American Scientist* **50,** 2 (June, 1962), pp. 259–93.

14. Simnad, M. T., and L. P. Zumwalt, *Materials and Fuels for High Temperature Nuclear Energy Applications.* Cambridge, Mass.: M. I. T. Press, 1964.

15. Foster, A. R., "Radiation Damage to Hot Rolled Swedish Iron." ANL Special Nuclear Studies Institute, 1960.

16. McDonell, W. R., "Kinetics of Structural Changes During Beta Transformation of Uranium." *Nucl. Sci. and Eng.* **12,** 3 (March, 1962), pp. 325–36.

17. Bolt, R. O., and J. G. Carroll, eds, *Radiation Effects on Organic Materials.* New York: Academic Press, 1963.

18. Blocher, J. M., et al., "Properties of Ceramic—Coated Nuclear—Fuel Particles." *Nucl. Sci. and Eng.* **20,** 2 (October, 1964), pp. 153–70.

19. Goeddel, W. V., "Development and Utilization of Pyrolytic-Carbon-Coated Carbide Fuel for the High-Temperature Gas-Cooled Reactor." *Nucl. Sci. and Eng.* **20,** 2 (October, 1964), pp. 201–18.

20. Gray, R. J., W. C. Thurber, and C. K. H. Du Bose, "Preparation of Arc-Melted Uranium Carbides." *Metal Progress* **74,** 1 (July, 1958), pp. 65–70.

21. Fraser, A. S., Birss, I. R., and C. Cawthorne, "High temperature Embrittlement of Stainless Steel Irradiated in Fast Fluxes." *Nature* **211,** 5046 (16 July, 1966), pp. 575–76.

22. Cawthorne, C., and E. J. Fulton, "Voids in Irradiated Stainless Steel," *Nature* **216,** 5115 (11 Nov. 1967), pp. 575–76.

23. Kaae, J. L., Stevens, D. W., and C. S. Luby, "Prediction of the Irradiation Performance of Coated Particle Fuels by Means of Stress-Analysis Models." *Nuc. Tech.* **10,** 1 (January, 1971), pp. 44–53.

24. Claudson, T. T., Baker, R. W., and R. L. Fish, "The Effects of Fast Flux

Irradiation on the Mechanical Properties and Dimensional Stability of Stainless Steel." *Nuc. Appl. & Tech.* **9,** 1 (July, 1970), pp. 10–23.

25. Reagan, P. E., Long, Jr., E. L., Morgan, J. G., and J. H. Coobs, "Irradiation Performance of Pyrolytic-Carbon- and Silicon-Carbide-Coated Fuel Particles." *Nuc. Appl. & Tech.* **8,** 5 (May, 1970), pp. 417–31.

26. Bramer, S. E., Lurie, H., and T. H. Smith, "Re-entry Protection for Radioisotope Heat Sources." *Nuc. Tech.* **11,** 2 (June, 1971), pp. 232–45.

27. Hamilton, C. J., "Heavy Metal Buildup in the HTGR." *A.N.S. Transactions,* **vol. 14,** no. 1 (June, 1971), p. 88.

28. Bates, J. F., and J. L. Straalsund, "A Compilation of Data and Representations of Irradiation-Induced Swelling of Solution-Treated Types of 304 and 316 Stainless Steel," Hanford Engineering Development Laboratory Report No. HEDL-TME 71-139, UC-25 (September, 1971).

Chapter 12

Nuclear Heat Transfer

Heat transfer in a reactor system involves many quite conventional problems. However, the presence of fission and intense radioactivity due to both fission fragment decay and to neutron activation of clad, structure, moderator, coolant, etc., causes intense heating. It is this heat which we wish to convert to a useful form of energy as effectively as possible. In Chapter 9 it was shown that the flux distribution was independent of power level. Consequently, the power extractable from a core is dependent on the magnitude of the heat transfer which can take place without damaging the reactor structure or the fuel elements.

HEAT TRANSFER FROM FUEL ELEMENTS

Consider a fuel plate as an infinite slab with heat flow in a transverse direction through the element. This assumes the problem is one-dimensional with temperature variation only in the transverse (x) direction. It is directly applicable for wide plates near the point of maximum temperature in the core where the axial temperature gradient is small.

The Fourier field equation, which describes the temperature distribution, can be written for a uniform value of k as

$$k\nabla^2 T + S = \rho c \frac{\partial T}{\partial t} \qquad (12.1)$$

where $\quad k =$ thermal conductivity, (Btu ft)/(hr ft^2 °F)
$T =$ temperature, °F
$S =$ source strength, Btu/(hr ft^3)
$\rho =$ density, ft^3/lb
$t =$ time, hrs.
$c =$ specific heat, Btu/(lb °F)

The first term in Eq. (12.1) represents the heat conduction from a unit volume of material. The second term represents the source strength (in this case due to fission, but it can also represent electrical resistance heating or heating due to dissipation of alpha, beta, or gamma radiation).

In the steady state condition, where $\partial T/\partial t = 0$, Eq. (12.1) reduces to

$$\nabla^2 T = -\frac{S}{k} \cdot \qquad (12.2)$$

If the temperature varies only in the x direction, Eq. (12.2) may be written

$$\frac{d^2 T}{dx^2} = -\frac{S}{k} \quad \text{(a constant per unit volume)} \qquad (12.3)$$

By integration of Eq. (12.3)

$$\frac{dT}{dx} = -\frac{Sx}{k} + C_1 \qquad (12.4)$$

A second integration gives

$$T = -\frac{Sx^2}{2k} + C_1 x + C_2 \qquad (12.5)$$

The boundary conditions will allow evaluation of the constants. If the surface temperatures on both sides of the fuel plate are equal, the temperature distribution is symmetrical. At the center of the plate $x = 0$, and $dT/dx = 0$. Therefore, $C_1 = 0$. Also, when $x = \pm w/2$, $T = T_s$, and the second constant of integration becomes

$$C_2 = T_s + \frac{Sw^2}{8k}$$

The temperature in the plate is then expressed as

$$T = -\frac{Sx^2}{2k} + T_s + \frac{Sw^2}{8k} \qquad (12.6a)$$

The maximum temperature in the fuel is then

$$T_{max} = T_s + \frac{Sw^2}{8k} \qquad (12.6b)$$

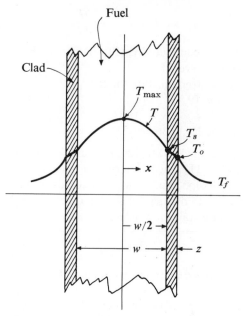

FIG. 12.1 *Temperature distribution in a plate type fuel element (treated as an infinite slab). Temperature drop through clad and convective film also shown.*

The fission induced heating can be expressed as

$S =$	180	$\times$	N	$\times$	σ_{fis}	$\times$	$\bar{\phi}$	$\times$	1	$\times 1.5465 \times 10^{-8}$
	$\dfrac{\text{mev}}{\text{fission}}$		$\dfrac{\text{fis nuclei}}{\text{cm}^3}$		$\dfrac{\text{cm}^2}{\text{fis nuclei}}$		$\dfrac{\text{neutrons}}{\text{cm}^2 \text{ sec}}$		$\dfrac{\text{fission}}{\text{neutron}}$	$\dfrac{\text{Btu sec cm}^3}{\text{mev hr ft}^3}$

$$= 2.7837 \times 10^{-6} \, N\sigma_{\text{fis}}\bar{\phi}(\text{Btu/ft}^3 \text{ hr}) \qquad (12.7)$$

The heat flux at the surface of the plate when $x = w/2$ is

$$\frac{q}{A} = -k\frac{dT}{dx} = \frac{Sw}{2} \qquad (12.8)$$

The same heat flux passes through the cladding of thickness z.

$$\frac{Sw}{2} = -\frac{k_{cl}(T_s - T_o)}{z} \qquad (12.9)$$

The fuel's surface temperature can be expressed as a function of the outer cladding surface temperature.

$$T_s = T_o + \frac{zSw}{2k_{cl}} \qquad (12.10)$$

Example 1. A fuel plate is fabricated from 0.125 inch thick 1.5 percent enriched uranium. The cladding is 0.010 inch 304 stainless steel. The average thermal neutron flux is 2.5×10^{14} n/cm² sec. The surface temperature of the clad is to be 600°F.

(1) What is the heat flux at the element surface?
(2) What is the temperature at the clad-fuel interface?
(3) What is the maximum temperature of the fuel?
(4) Does any of the fuel transform to beta phase uranium?

To evaluate the fission cross section of the fuel, estimate the approximate temperature to be 754°F (400°C).

$$\sigma_{\text{fis}} = 582 \sqrt{\frac{293}{400}} \frac{\sqrt{\pi}}{2} = 440 \text{ barns}$$

$$N_{235} = \frac{19 \times 6.024 \times 10^{23} \times 0.015}{238} = 7.21 \times 10^{20} \ (^{235}\text{U nuc/cm}^3)$$

$$S = 2.78 \times 10^{-6} \times 7.21 \times 10^{20} \times 440 \times 10^{-24} \times 2.5 \times 10^{14}$$

$$= 2.21 \times 10^8 \text{ Btu/ft}^3 \text{ hr}$$

The surface heat flux is then

$$\frac{q}{A} = \frac{Sw}{2} = \frac{2.21 \times 10^8 \times (0.125/12)}{2} = 1.155 \times 10^6 \text{ Btu/ft}^3 \text{ hr}$$

$$T_s = T_0 + \frac{zSw}{2k_{cl}}$$

$$= 600 + \frac{(0.010/12) \times 1.155 \times 10^6}{11}$$

$$= 600 + 88.0 = 688°F$$

$$T_{\max} = T_s + \frac{Sw^2}{8k}$$

$$= 688 + \frac{2.21 \times 10^8 (0.125/12)^2}{8 \times 18.8}$$

$$= 688 + 159$$

$$= 847°F$$

Since the alpha-beta transition temperature is 1234°F, phase change will cause no difficulty in this instance.

An even more common type of fuel element is the pin or rod. If the axial temperature gradient is ignored, the problem is one-dimensional in the radial direction. Fig. 12.2 shows a fuel pin with its cladding and temperature distribution. To solve this problem Eq. (12.1) must be converted to cylindrical coordinates. For steady state it reduces to

$$\frac{d^2T}{dr^2} + \frac{(1/r)\, dT}{dr} = -\frac{S}{k} \tag{12.11a}$$

Rearranging, Eq. (12.11a) can be written as

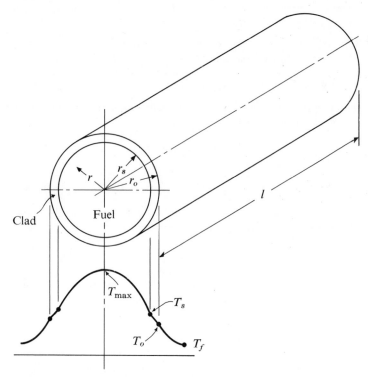

Fig. 12.2 *Cylindrical fuel pin with cladding showing temperature distribution in pin, clad, and convective film.*

$$r \frac{d^2T}{dr^2} + \frac{dT}{dr} = -\frac{Sr}{k} \tag{12.11b}$$

Note that

$$\frac{d}{dr}\left(r \frac{dT}{dr}\right) = r \frac{d^2T}{dr^2} + \frac{dT}{dr} \tag{12.12}$$

Substituting Eqs. (12.12) into (12.11b)

$$\frac{d}{dr}\left(r \frac{dT}{dr}\right) = -\frac{Sr}{k} \tag{12.13}$$

Integrating,

$$r \frac{dT}{dr} = -\frac{Sr^2}{2k} + C_1 \tag{12.14}$$

A second integration gives

$$T = -\frac{Sr^2}{4k} + C_1 \ln r + C_2 \tag{12.15}$$

For the cylinder of fuel the boundary conditions are:

(1) When $r = 0$, $dT/dr = 0$, because of symmetry,
(2) When $r = r_s$, $T = T_s$, at the fuel surface.

Therefore,

$$C_1 = 0$$

and

$$C_2 = \frac{T_s + Sr^2}{4k}$$

The temperature distribution in the element can then be expressed as

$$T = T_s + \frac{S}{4k}(r_s^2 - r^2) \qquad (12.16)$$

The temperature gradient in a radial direction is

$$\frac{dT}{dr} = -\frac{rS}{2k} \qquad (12.17)$$

The heat flux at the element surface is then

$$\frac{q}{A} = -k\left(\frac{dT}{dr}\right)_{r=r_s} = \frac{r_s S}{2} \qquad (12.18)$$

Example 2.   A fuel rod of UO_2 has a diameter of 0.375 inch and is clad with 0.010 inch 304 stainless steel.   The rod is to develop 5 kW per foot at the point under consideration.   The outside film coefficient is 1300 Btu/hr ft^2 °F and the boiling water has a temperature of 550°F.   Compute the temperature at the center of the rod and determine the heat flux at the fuel surface.

First determine the source strength.

$$S = \frac{3413 \text{ Btu/(hr kW)} \times 5 \text{ kW/ft}}{[\pi(0.375)^2/(4 \times 144)] \text{ ft}^3/\text{ft}} = 2.22 \times 10^7 \text{ Btu/ft}^3 \text{ hr}$$

The heat flux at the fuel surface is then evaluated.

$$\frac{q}{A} = \frac{r_s S}{2} = \frac{[3/(16 \times 12)]2.22 \times 10^7}{2}$$

$$= 0.173 \times 10^6 \text{ Btu/(hr ft}^2)$$

Because they are in series, the heat flowing from the fuel surface, the heat flowing through the clad, and the heat flowing into the fluid are all equal.   Let A_1 represent the area of the fuel surface, A_2 represent the mean area of the clad, and A_3 represent the outer clad surface area.

To find the temperature drop across the fluid film, the heat flow from the fuel is equated to the heat flow through the boiling film.

$$0.173 \times 10^6 \times A_1 = h_f A_3(T_o - T_f)$$

$$T_o - T_f = \frac{0.173 \times 10^6 A_1}{h_f \times A_3}$$

$$= \frac{0.173 \times 10^6 \times 0.187}{1300 \times 0.197} = 126°F$$

Thus, the outer clad temperature is

$$T_o = T_f + 126 = 550 + 126 = 676°F$$

For the clad, where the ratio of the outer diameter to the inner diameter is less than 1.5, it is acceptable to use the mean clad area and treat the heat flow as though the surface were plane. Equating the heat flow from the fuel to that through the clad

$$0.173 \times 10^6 A_1 = \frac{k_{cl} A_2 (T_s - T_o)}{r_0 - r_s}$$

$$T_s - T_0 = \frac{0.173 \times 10^6 (r_0 - r_s) A_1}{k_{cl} \times A_2}$$

$$= \frac{0.173 \times 10^6 (0.010/12)(0.187)}{11.0 \times 0.192}$$

$$= 12.8°F$$

The temperature of the clad-fuel interface is

$$T_s = T_o + 12.8 = 676 + 12.8 = 689°F$$

The peak fuel temperature is

$$T_{\max} = T_s + \frac{S r_o^2}{4k}$$

$$= 689 + \frac{2.22 \times 10^7 \times [3/(16 \times 12)]^2}{4 \times 1.85}$$

$$= 689 + 726 = 1415°F$$

The preceding example indicates the magnitude of the temperature which may exist at the center of a ceramic fuel element. Unfortunately, the thermal conductivity of UO_2 varies with both temperature and fuel burnup. Fig. 12.3 indicates the changes in the effective thermal conductivity of uranium dioxide after many startups. As the fuel suffers loss in conductivity, the temperature at the center of the elements may approach levels which can result in melting of some of the UO_2 at the centerline. The loss of conductivity occurs due to the microstructural changes and cracking during the heating and cooling cycles which the fuel must endure during its lifetime (See Fig. 11.28).

TEMPERATURE DISTRIBUTION ALONG A FUEL ROD IN A COOLING CHANNEL

Along the length of a fuel rod there is a variation in neutron flux. For a rectangular or cylindrical core this variation can be approximated

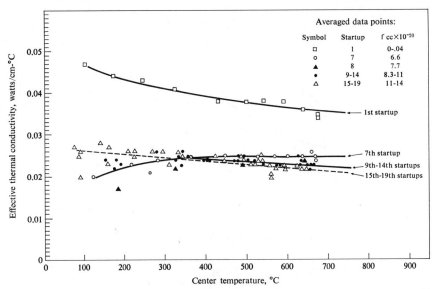

FIG. 12.3   *Effective thermal conductivity of UO$_2$ showing the effect of various numbers of startups (see Reference 1).*

by a cosine function.   In most real reactors a reflector will cause the flux to have an appreciable value at each end of the fuel element.   If the coolant flows in a channel parallel to the rod its temperature will increase in the direction of flow.   The point of maximum temperature in the fuel will then be displaced from the point of greatest flux (and hence, maximum energy release).

Fig. 12.4 shows the neutron flux variation along the fuel rod.   Note that the origin is at the midpoint of the rod, and that the ends of the rod are at $\pm l/2$, where l is the rod length. l_{ex} is the extrapolated pin length. The flux, ϕ, may be expressed as a function of position and the maximum flux, ϕ_m.

$$\phi = \phi_m \cos \frac{\pi x}{l_{ex}} \qquad (12.19)$$

The energy release rates are also position-dependent, being proportional to the neutron flux.

$$S = S_0 \cos \frac{\pi x}{l_{ex}} \qquad (12.20)$$

where S_o is the energy release rate at the point of maximum neutron flux.

Taking a point at a distance x from the origin and making an energy balance between the flowing fluid and the energy released in the differential length of rod dx gives

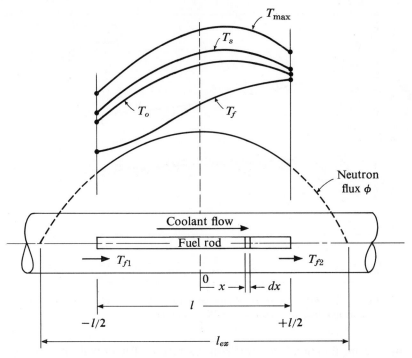

FIG. 12.4 *Temperature and flux (neutron) variation along a fuel rod located in a fuel channel with flow parallel to the fuel rod. T_{max} is the temperature of the fuel at the centerline of the fuel rod; T_s is the fuel-clad interface temperature; T_o is the temperature at the clad surface; and T_f is the coolant temperature.*

$$\dot{m}c_p \, dT_f = SA \, dx \tag{12.21}$$

where A is the cross sectional area of the pin and $\dot{m}$ is the coolant flow rate. c_p is the constant pressure specific heat of the coolant and dT_f is the temperature change of the coolant as it travels a distance dx. Note that it is assumed that the heat flow is entirely radial. The axial temperature gradient is small in comparison to the radial value; thus, axial heat flow is ignored without serious error.

When Eq. (12.20) is substituted into Eq. (12.21) and the equation is integrated over the length of the rod, a relation for the fluid temperature, T_f, at any position results.

$$\dot{m}c_p \int_{T_{f1}}^{T_f} dT_f = S_o A \int_{-l/2}^{x} \cos\frac{\pi x}{l_{ex}} \, dx \tag{12.22}$$

$$T_f = T_{f1} + \frac{AS_o l_{ex}}{\dot{m}c_p \pi}\left(\sin\frac{\pi x}{l_{ex}} + \sin\frac{\pi l}{2l_{ex}}\right) \tag{12.23}$$

The heat released in the elemental volume of the fuel rod flows from the fuel, through the cladding, into the coolant. The heat flow through the fluid film between the coolant and clad is equated to the heat release to give the outer cladding temperature, T_0.

$$S_o A \cos \frac{\pi x}{l_{ex}} \, dx = h_o(2\pi r_o)(T_o - T_f) \, dx \qquad (12.24)$$

Combining Eqs. (12.23) and (12.24) gives

$$T_o = T_{f1} + \frac{S_o A l_{ex}}{\dot{m} c_p \pi} \left(\sin \frac{\pi x}{l_{ex}} + \sin \frac{\pi l}{2l_{ex}} \right) + \frac{S_o A \cos (\pi x / l_{ex})}{2\pi r_o h_o} \qquad (12.25)$$

The slope of the outer clad temperature in a radial direction is

$$\frac{dT_o}{dx} = \frac{S_o A}{\dot{m} c_p} \cos \frac{\pi x}{l_{ex}} - \frac{S_o A}{2\pi r_o h_o} \sin \frac{\pi x}{l_{ex}} \qquad (12.26)$$

Equating the slope to zero determines an expression for the position of the point of maximum surface temperature of the clad, $x_{0\max}$.

$$x_{0\max} = \frac{l_{ex}}{\pi} \tan^{-1} \frac{2l_{ex} r_o h_o}{\dot{m} c_p} \qquad (12.27)$$

The temperature change across the cladding and the centerline temperature of the fuel can be determined by using the methods illustrated in Example 2 for the source strength at any given position. Problems of this type can be programmed conveniently for a digital computer (see Problem 8).

BURNOUT IN WATER-COOLED REACTORS

In both boiling water and pressurized water reactors the power producing capability is limited by the reactor's ability to transfer fission energy from the fuel elements to the coolant for transport from the core. In both types of reactor there is a variation in heat flux in the axial and radial directions due to neutron flux variation. Flow rates along elements may be variable, due to dimensional differences in the flow passages. These may be due to manufacturing variations or to orifices placed in the flow channels. The orifices adjust flow in the channels to have an equal enthalpy rise in each channel. In the BWR controlled phase change is intended, but in the PWR the water should remain liquid. In either case, film boiling that blankets the heat transfer surface with a layer of vapor must be prevented. Such a blanketing of the surface by vapor may result in "burnout." The very high temperatures produced in the cladding may produce rupture and release of fission products. At the point of maximum heating the heat flux must remain well below that required to cause burnout. The factor of safety, F_s, or burnout ratio, is the ratio of the burnout heat flux, $(q/A)_{BO}$ to the actual heat flux at a point in the flow channel.

$$F_s = \frac{(q/A)_{BO}}{(q/A)} \qquad (12.28)$$

BOILING

Pool Boiling (Natural-Convection Boiling)

Take a uniformly heated rod and immerse it in a pool of liquid at its saturation temperature, then increase the heat flux gradually. The flux (Btu/hr ft² °F) can be plotted, as shown in Fig. 12.5, versus the tem-

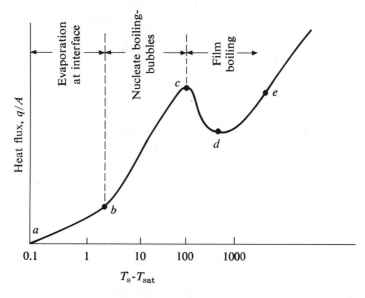

FIG. 12.5 *Pool boiling.*

perature differential between the rod surface temperature, T_s, and the liquid temperature, T_{sat}.

One can see that at very low heat fluxes from a to b there is only natural convection set up with evaporation at the liquid surface. Higher fluxes commence the formation of bubbles which leave the surface from favored nucleation sites and then collapse in the liquid. Somewhat higher fluxes from b to c result in the bubbles rising all the way to the surface. The agitation caused by the bubbles (they push the liquid back; it rushes in when they break away from the nucleation sites) produces high film coefficients. The bubble formation may become so intense, however, that the surface becomes blanketed with vapor and liquid cannot reach it. Thus, the ability to remove heat is reduced. This condition at c is known as the burnout point or the point of departure from nucleate boiling (DNB). The flux must be reduced to continue a smooth increase in ΔT. However, this is difficult with an electrically-heated rod or a fission-heated fuel element in a reactor. There will more likely be a large jump in ΔT from c to e, where stable film boiling will exist. In the range from c to d boiling is unstable and the temperature will jump to a new larger value if the flux increases even slightly. Beyond d the boiling is essentially all film boiling with radiation transporting the energy across the film. A temperature at the point e may be well above the melting point of the cladding material on a fuel rod; hence, burnout ensues.

For pool boiling the burnout flux can be evaluated from the Rohsenow and Griffith correlation (to be found in Reference 5).

$$\left(\frac{q}{A}\right)_{BO} = 143\, g^{1/4}\rho_v h_{fg}\left(\frac{\rho_l - \rho_v}{\rho_v}\right)^{0.6} \qquad (12.29)$$

where g = acceleration of gravity in G's
ρ_v = vapor density, lb/ft^3
ρ_l = liquid density, lb/ft^3
h_{fg} = latent heat of vaporization, Btu/lb

For pool boiling the burnout flux is independent of the material used for the surface, so long as it is reasonably smooth. Knurled or threaded surfaces will have a somewhat higher burnout flux.

Boiling with Forced Convection

When boiling occurs with forced convection the mass velocity, the geometry of the system, and any subcooling of the entering water complicate the correlation of burnout data.

Fig. 12.6 shows a schematic diagram of a burnout test where the tube is uniformly heated by electrical means. This simulates heating in the coolant passage of a reactor. If one picks a particular pressure, p, at the exit of the test channel, the only other variables remaining are the flow rate, the inlet temperature of the water, and the electrical input (which provides the heat flux in lieu of the fission heating in a reactor). For a given inlet temperature either the heat flux or the flow may be varied until burnout occurs. In general, with forced convection a higher heat flux is required to produce burnout than with pool boiling. This is

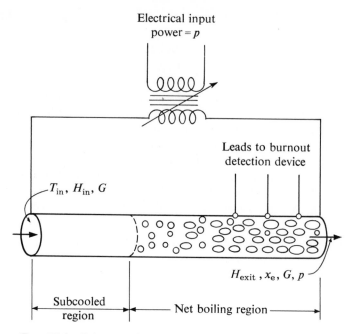

FIG. 12.6   *Schematic diagram of burnout test (Reference 11).*

because the forced convection sweeps away the bubbles as they are formed.

Fig. 12.7 shows typical results of tests run on a round test section using variable amounts of subcooling for the inlet water. Note that both increased flow and an increased degree of subcooling allow larger burnout fluxes. The utility of this set of curves is limited to the geometrical configuration tested. To successfully correlate data from many experiments of different geometry, Levedahl (Reference 12) proposed the steam energy flow (SEF) plot, where the burnout heat flux is plotted against steam energy flow (shown below in Fig. 12.8).

To understand the meaning of the term steam energy flow, equate the energy transmitted from the electrically heated surface of Fig. 12.6 to the enthalpy gain of the passing fluid.

$$\frac{q}{A} \pi DL = \frac{\pi D^2}{4} G(h_0 - h_{in}) \qquad (12.30)$$

where L = the section length from entrance to the point under consideration (often the exit), ft.

D = equivalent diameter of flow passage, ft. For a noncircular channel this is equal to four times the flow area divided by the heated perimeter.

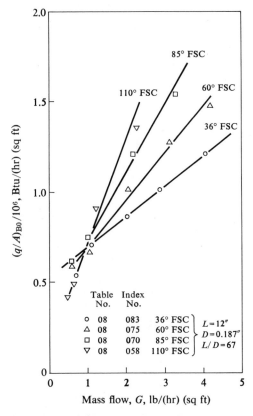

FIG. 12.7   *Plot of burnout heat flux versus mass flow for various amounts of subcooling of the inlet water.   Length of test section = 12 inches, tube diameter = 0.187 inch, L/D = 67, water pressure = 2000 psia. (Plotted in Reference 11 from data in Table 8 of Reference 14.)*

G = mass velocity, lb/hr ft.
h_o = enthalpy at distance L from inlet, Btu/lb.
h_{in} = inlet enthalpy, Btu/lb.

Solving for the heat flux, the expression may be written

$$\frac{q}{A} = \frac{D}{4L} \left[Gx_o h_{fg} + G(h_f - h_{in}) \right] \tag{12.31}$$

where h_o has been replaced by the enthalpy of the wet leaving steam which has a quality of $x_o(h_o = h_f + x_o h_{fg})$.   If one considers the enthalpy of saturated liquid as the datum point for SEF, the $G(h_{gn} - h_f)$ represents the energy of the entering subcooled liquid and $(Gx_o h_{fg})$ is the energy conveyed in the leaving steam.   For flow passing any point the SEF

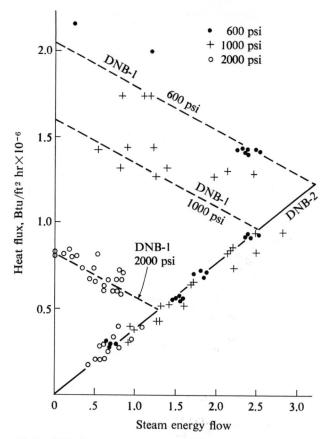

FIG. 12.8 *SEF plot showing two burnout regimes for uniformly heated channels (Reference 12).*

represents the departure of the enthalpy from the enthalpy of saturated liquid. For subcooled liquid its value is negative, while for wet or super-heated steam it will be positive. If the inlet condition of the water, the flow rate, and the heat flux along a uniformly heated rod are known, the exit quality can be computed.

Fig. 12.8 shows that the burnout points align themselves and indicate that there may be two modes of burnout. Lines for these are marked DNB-1 and DNB-2 (Departure from Nucleate Boiling). Burnout along the DNB-1 line represents failure due to the vapor release becoming so rapid as to blanket the surface. Points falling on the DNB-2 line represent burnout which occurs with accompanying hydrodynamic instability where there are pulsations in flow and pressure drop. DNB-2 data seem to be sensitive to orificing, surge volumes, and length of lines. It is very difficult for the designer to apply DNB-2 data as useful design information. Wiley (Reference 11) suggests that it signifies to the experimenter that he is generating ambiguous information which is difficult for the designer to utilize.

USE OF DNB-1 DATA IN DESIGN

In design it is important that the heat flux be kept safely below the burnout value indicated along the DNB-1 line. Fig. 12.9 shows an op-

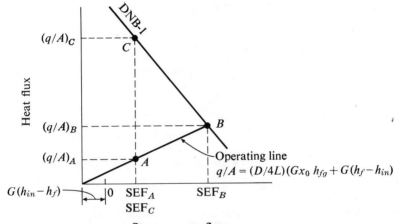

FIG. 12.9 *Steam energy flow plot showing an operating line and a DNB-1 line.*

erating line and a DNB-1 line on an SEF plot. The operating line represents the locus of points for a given mass velocity, G, as the heat flux is raised to burnout. There is some uncertainty as to whether the burnout ratio should be taken as the ratio of $(q/A)_B/(q/A)_A$ or $(q/A)_C/(q/A)_A$.

The heat flux burnout ratio is defined as

$$F_{S_1} = \frac{(q/A)_C}{(q/A)_A} \tag{12.32}$$

This has significance only if the DNB-1 line is determined solely by local conditions. The $(q/A)_C$ condition could not be reached for the flow rate used for the operating line AB.

A ratio which gives a better indication of the safety factor attainable with a given flow rate is called the power burnout ratio. It is defined as

$$F_{S_2} = \frac{(q/A)_B}{(q/A)_A} \qquad (12.33)$$

Fig. 12.10 shows the axial heat flux variation along a reactor fuel rod for two power levels, P and P'. The power level P represents the power such that the SEF at the exit represents the design point A of the previous Fig. 12.9. The power P' is a level such that burnout would occur at the exit, B, with the same flow rate as at A. At any other point A' the operating line will show burnout at B'. Depending on the shape of the

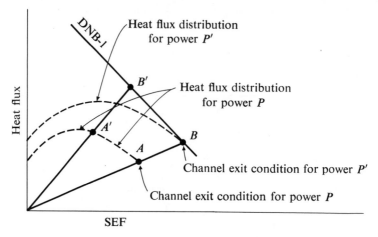

FIG. 12.10 *Nonuniform axial power distribution for reactor fuel rod operating at power levels P and P'. The power level P is the design power level and P' is a level such that burnout will occur at the channel exit.*

power distribution curve and the slope of the DNB-1 curve, it is possible for the power burnout ratio to reach unity initially at a point other than the channel exit. For a core with control rods inserted from the top the peak flux may be distorted with the peak heat flux closer to the inlet because of the rod insertion. At the end of the core life, when the rods are fully removed, the peak may move toward the exit because of the lesser poison buildup in the upper end of the core. In this region the flux was previously depressed. Fig. 12.11 shows a case where the burnout will occur at B'' for a power level P''.

Burnout fluxes can be evaluated from any one of several correlations. The Westinghouse equations (Reference 14) for 2000 psia water are useful for the design of pressurized water cores. The particular design equation (12.34) shown here incorporates a factor of 65 percent so that the burnout fluxes predicted will be well below the actual values of burnout flux. The design equation for round tubes is

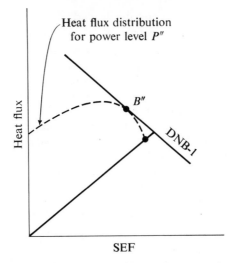

Fig. 12.11 *SEF plot showing outlet flux peak causing burnout to occur prior to exit.*

$$\frac{(q/A)_{BO}}{10^6} = 0.182 \left(\frac{h_{BO}}{10^3}\right)^{-2.5} \left(1 + \frac{G}{10^7}\right) e^{-0.0012\, L/D} \qquad (12.34)$$

The equation is valid over the following range of variables:

Pressure	$1850 \leq P \leq 2150$ psia
Enthalpy	$50 \leq h_{BO} \leq 1000$ Btu/lb
Mass velocity	$0.2 \times 10^6 \leq G \leq 8.0 \times 10^6$ lb/hr ft²
Length/Diameter	Data based on values $21 \leq L/D \leq 365$
	Entrapolation is possible.

The design burnout flux may be further reduced below the predicted value by the uncertainty factor, F_{S_1}. Reference 14 recommends a value of 1.1 to allow for lack of transient burnout and pressure drop data, plus another factor of 1.1 to allow for meager data on nonuniformly heated channels. These combine to give a total uncertainty of approximately $F_{S_1} = 1.2$.

NUCLEAR SUPERHEAT

The generation of saturated steam by both PWR and BWR reactors limits the attainable thermal efficiency. It also makes the large amounts of moisture formed during the expansion of the steam an aggravating problem. The design of reactors to accomplish boiling and superheating in the same core will permit attainment of better thermal efficiencies along with reduced moisture toward the end of the expansion, but it does present several other problems:

(1) The higher fuel and cladding temperatures associated with heat transfer to the superheated steam. This also may induce deposition of solids on the heat transfer surfaces in the superheat section;

(2) Maintaining the proper balance between power production in the boiling and the superheating sections of the core;

(3) Preventing excessive heat transfer from the superheated steam passages back to the cooler boiling water. This temperature differential will also cause some problems with differential expansion;

(4) The high concentration of radiolytically decomposed oxygen (30 ppm) precludes usage of most of the low neutron cross section materials for cladding and tubing in contact with the superheated steam. Cladding must operate at temperatures as high as 1250°F to produce 1000°F steam.

Fig. 12.12 shows the type of element used in the Puerto Rican Boiling

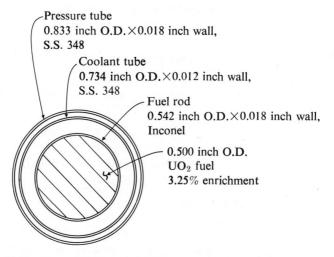

FIG. 12.12 *Cross section of BONUS superheater element.* [*From* Nuclear Reactor Technology, **6**, *No. 2, p. 76.*]

Nuclear Superheat Reactor (BONUS). Here the stainless steel pressure tube and the stainless steel coolant tube are separated by an insulating space. Steam flows between the coolant tube and the Inconel clad UO_2 fuel. The details of the core arrangement are shown in Fig. 12.13. The central region of the core provides the majority of the steam, while 6 percent of the steam is generated in the moderator surrounding the pressure tubes in the superheat region.

It is interesting to note the comparison of the heat transfer and power

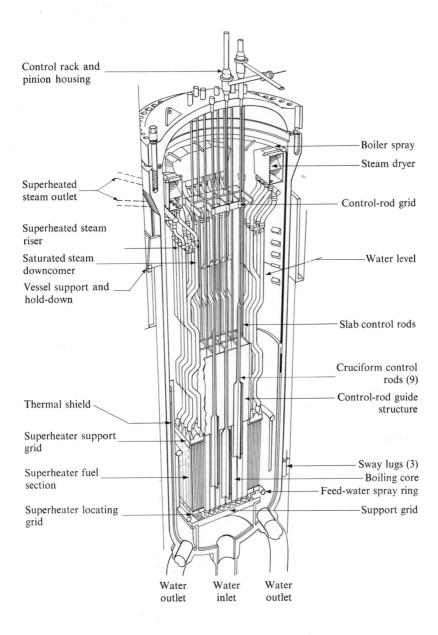

Control rack and
pinion housing

Boiler spray

Steam dryer

Superheated
steam outlet

Control-rod grid

Superheated steam
riser

Saturated steam
downcomer

Water level

Vessel support and
hold-down

Slab control rods

Cruciform control
rods (9)

Control-rod guide
structure

Thermal shield

Superheater support
grid

Superheater fuel
section

Sway lugs (3)

Boiling core

Feed-water spray ring

Superheater locating
grid

Support grid

Water
outlet

Water
inlet

Water
outlet

FIG. 12.13 *BONUS reactor, cross section of core vessel.* [*From* Nuclear Reactor Technology, **3**, *No. 4, p. 70.*]

density characteristics of the reactor core boiler region and the superheat region, as shown by Table 12.1. Because of the lower film coefficients

TABLE 12.1

PERFORMANCE DATA FOR THE BONUS REACTOR

	Boiler Region	Superheat Region
Volume of Active Region, liters	1126	1118
Net Heat Generation in Fuel, MWt	37.0	13.0
Heat Loss to Moderator due to γ and n heating, MWt	1.1	0.4
Thermal Insulation Heat Loss to Coolant, MWt	—	1.2
Net Heat Transfer to Coolant, MWt	35.9	11.4
Uranium Content of Region, tons	2.81	1.79
Fuel Enrichment, percent	1.85 and 0.71	3.5
Power Density of Region, KWt/liter	32.9	11.6
Average Specific Power, MWt per ton U	13.2	7.25
Average Heat Flux, Btu/(hr)(ft²)	102,000	65,000
Maximum Heat Flux, Btu/(hr)(ft²)	323,000	237,000
Steam Flow, lb/hr Core Region	142,770	
Moderator		9230
S. H. Passages		152,000

in the superheat region, the heat flux and the power density are significantly less.

Annular fuel elements are used in some of the designs intended for nuclear superheat. Fig. 12.14 shows such an element. The steam in the

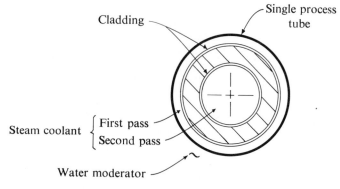

Fig. 12.14   *Advanced fuel element design for use in a superheating reactor.*   [*From* Nuclear Reactor Technology, **6**, *No. 2, p. 77.*]

TABLE 12.2

THERMAL CONDUCTIVITIES OF VARIOUS
NUCLEAR MATERIALS

Material	Melting Point °F	Density	Temperature °F	Conductivity Btu/hr-ft²-°F	Remarks
UO₂	5040	10.97	500	2.90	Unirradiated corrected to theoretical density
(Ref. 6)			1000	2.00	
			1500	1.85	
			2000	1.4	
			2500	1.3	
(Ref. 1)			500	1.45	Irradiated, 15–19 startups
			1000	1.27	
			1500	1.15	
UC	4200	12.97	500	13.02	Unirradiated
(Ref. 4)			1000	11.91	
			1500	11.73	
			2000	11.57	
Uranium	2066	19.0	100	15.8	Alpha phase
(Ref. 9)			500	17.2	Alpha phase
			1000	23.0	Alpha phase
		18.1	1300	26.6	Beta phase
		17.9	1500	29.2	Gamma phase
Beryllium	2330	1.8	77	128	
(Ref. 4)			200	82.2	
Aluminum	1220	2.7	32	117	
(Ref. 7)			212	119	
			392	124	
			572	133	
			752	144	
304 Stainless Steel	2550–2650	7.82	32	8.0	18 percent Cr − 8 percent Ni (Austenitic)
(Ref. 7)			212	9.4	
			572	10.9	
			932	12.4	
Zircaloy-2	3310	6.56	75	8.45	
(Ref. 8)			212	8.15	
			300	8.10	
			500	8.05	
			570	8.10	
Graphite Single Crystal	6680	2.2	77	230	Parallel
(Ref. 15)				40	Perpendicular to layer planes
Graphite Extruded	6680	1.8	77	132	Parallel to ext. dir.
(Ref. 15)				80	Perpendicular to ext. dir.
Pyrolytic Carbon	6680	2.2	77	172	Parallel to substrate
(Ref. 15)				17.2	Perpendicular to substrate surface

first pass loses some heat to the water moderator and its final temperature is produced in the second pass.

Fig. 12.15 shows a ring of superheating tubes embedded in a large

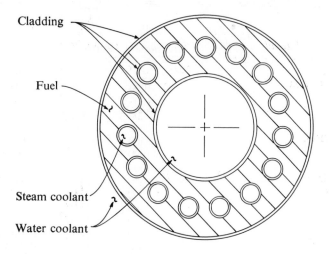

FIG. 12.15 *Advanced fuel element having superheated steam passages embedded in the annular fuel element.* [*From* Nuclear Reactor Technology, **6**, *No. 2, p. 77.*]

annular fuel element. There is water on both sides of the annulus. Such complex fuel elements can be fabricated effectively by vibrational compaction of UO_2 powder.

LIQUID METALS

In the cooling of fast reactors light water, heavy water, and organic liquids are unsatisfactory because of their moderating characteristics. Gases with their low atom density are possible coolants and studies are being made of helium and steam-cooled fast reactors. However, their thermal conductivity is poor. Liquid metals, on the other hand, have high thermal conductivities. Although their high melting temperatures present some problems, they enable the use of low pressures for liquid metal systems. Their high atomic weights give liquid metals poor moderating characteristics which, when coupled with the previous characteristics, make them desirable for use in fast reactors. Table 12.3 indicates some of the properties of liquid sodium, NaK (a eutectic mixture of sodium and potassium), lithium, and water. The liquid metals all have much better conductivities than water because of their free electrons

TABLE 12.3

PROPERTIES OF LIQUIDS

Substance	Temp. °F	Density lb/ft^3	Sp. Ht. Btu/lb°F	Viscosity $\times 10^3$ lb/ft sec	Th. Cond. Btu/hr ft°F
Na	200	58.0	0.33	0.47	49.8
	700	53.7	0.31	0.19	41.8
	1300	48.6	0.30	0.12	34.5
NaK	200	55	0.27	0.36	14.4
	700	51	0.25	0.16	15.8
	1300	47	0.25	0.10	16.7
Li	400	31.7	1.40	0.37	26.7
	700	30.7	1.20	—	23.4
	1300	28.8	—	—	~15
H$_2$O	200	60.1	1.00	0.205	0.394
(sat. liq.)	600	42.4	1.51	0.058	0.292

which transport the majority of their thermal energy in conduction. Sodium has by far the best conductivity and is the principal coolant for fast reactors.

This is not to say that sodium does not have some problems. It becomes radioactive due to neutron capture with ^{24}Na which is activated, being a β, γ emitter with a 15-hour half-life. Also sodium reacts with water violently. In order to prevent radioactive sodium contacting water in the event of a rupture in a steam generator a secondary sodium loop is used, where the radioactive Na transfers heat to the secondary sodium which in turn transports the energy to the steam generator. In addition, sodium reacts readily with oxygen. Oxygen contents below 30 ppm should be maintained and free surfaces should be covered with an inert gas such as helium or argon. Deposits of NaO$_2$ on heat transfer surfaces add a significant resistance to heat transfer and in extreme cases they may plug narrow heat transfer passages.

A number of heat transfer correlations have been made for liquid metals. Most involve the product of the Reynolds (Re) and Prandtl (Pr) numbers which is in turn dimensionless and known as the Peclet number.

$$Pe = RePr = \frac{DV\rho}{\mu} \cdot \frac{C_p\mu}{K} = \frac{DV\rho C_p}{K} \tag{12.35}$$

Note that the viscosity drops out, indicating that it has little bearing on liquid metal heat transfer.

For circular tubes with constant heat flux along the tube the Lyon-Martinelli correlation states the dimensionless Nusselt Number (Nu) is

$$Nu = \frac{hD}{k} = 7 + 0.025 \, Pe^{0.8} \tag{12.36}$$

If instead there is a uniform wall temperature, Seban and Shimazaki recommend

$$Nu = 5.0 + 0.025 \, Pe^{0.8} \tag{12.37}$$

For flow parallel to rod bundles a graphical correlation is given in Fig. 12.16 for fully developed turbulent flow and uniform heat flux.

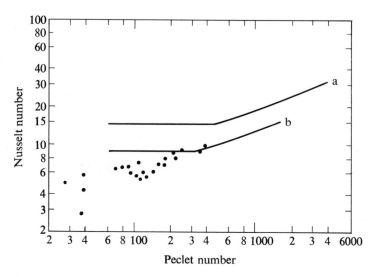

FIG. 12.16 *Heat transfer correlation for liquid metal flow parallel to rod bundles. For curve a $S/D = 1.5$ and for curve b $S/D = 1.2$. [From El-Wakil, M. M., Nuclear Heat Transport. Scranton, Pa.: International Textbook Co., Fig. 10.4, 1971, p. 269.]*

Curve a is for $S/D = 1.5$ and curve b is for $S/D = 1.2$. S is the distance between tubes and D is the tube O.D. The poor correlation of the experimental points at low Peclet numbers may be due to oxide contamination.

LMFBR STEAM GENERATOR

LMFBR heat transfer design is critical in both the primary and secondary sodium loops. The heat exchanger presenting the most serious design challenge is the steam generator, because of the extreme care that must be taken due to the reactivity of sodium and water. A number of designs are being developed. As a representative example we will discuss the bayonet-tube, split-bundle designed by Combustion Engineering, Inc.

Fig. 12.17 shows how the hot sodium enters the bottom of the superheater bundle in the center of the shell, passes upward through the superheater bundle, and then passes downward through the annular evaporator

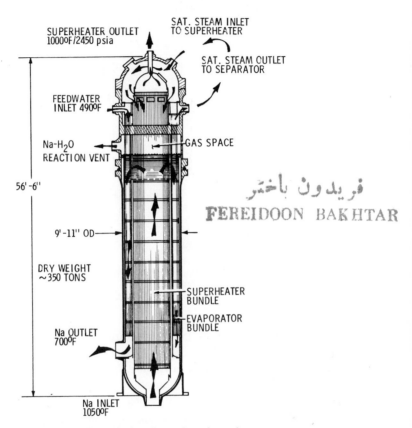

FIG. 12.17 *Bayonet-tube, split-bundle, sodium-heated steam generator.* [*Courtesy Combustion Engineering, Inc.* (*Sponsored by U. S. Atomic Energy Commission.*)]

bundle. Although not shown here, sodium from the reheater joins the sodium leaving the superheater bundle since these two streams will be at approximately the same temperature. Fig. 12.18 illustrates the internal flows within the steam generator shell. The feedwater enters the inner tube of the concentric evaporator bayonet tubes, passing to the bottom end before returning upward to boil. To prevent downward boiling the inner tube is double walled and open at the bottom, so that the stagnant

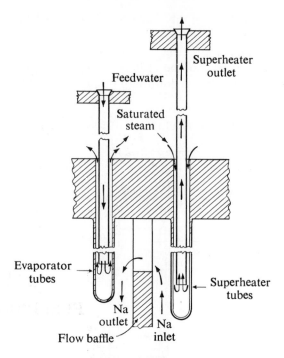

FIG. 12.18   *Schematic of internal flow in bayonet-tube, split-bundle, sodium-heated steam generator.* [*From Muenchow, H. O. and Armstrong, III, R. C., ASME Paper No. 71-NE-13 (1971).*]

fluid provides thermal insulation. The saturated steam leaves at the tube-sheet and passes through a steam separator and then returns to the outer annulus of the bayonet superheater tube. It flows downward being super-heated and flows upward inside another double-walled tube. The stagnant steam between the tube walls prevents excessive loss of superheat.

The system is designed to be operated on a once-through basis at full load and may use some recirculation at low loads, as shown in Fig. 12.19. The system is designed so that a 1000 MWe plant would operate with three loops, each having one of these 820 MWt sodium-heated steam generators. Table 12.4 indicates the conceptual design parameters. Particularly note that in the evaporator tubes there is a 7.5 foot length where film boiling is assumed to occur. Also, the mean temperature difference for this section is 207°F, compared to 123° in the nucleate boiling section.

Both evaporator and superheater bayonet tubes expand freely in an axial direction. Radial position of the tubes is maintained by crevice-free, egg-crate type tube supports. The egg crates are attached to a

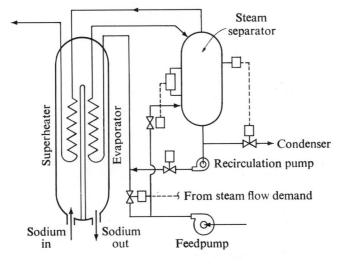

FIG. 12.19   *Schematic flow arrangement for LMFBR steam generator.* [*From Muenchow, H. O. and Armstrong, III, R. C., ASME Paper No. 71-NE-13 (1971).*]

polygonal flow baffle suspended by hanger rods from the tube sheet. This support expands axially with the bayonet tubes, resulting in little relative motion between them.

With this design concept only the superheater pressure tubing and the sodium inlet region of the shell operate at temperatures where creep properties govern the design stresses.   The sodium shell will be of 2 1/4 percent Cr, 1 percent Mo ferritic steel with a weld overlay of higher alloy ferritic composition to discourage carbon transfer.   The tubesheet, high pressure steam head, and superheater tubes will be 9–12 percent Cr ferritic steel.   If on the demonstration plants a superheat temperature somewhat lower than the 1050°F proposed for a full-scale 1000 MWe plant were used, a 9 percent Cr, 1 percent Mo could be used for the tubes.

To accommodate a massive sodium-water reaction a rupture disk set for approximately 50 psig will discharge reaction products into a gas-filled space above the sodium level and have them pass from there to a reaction-products separator.   For smaller leaks a vent line and relief valve will convey the reaction products to the separator.   There will also be provision to isolate and dump the steam/water side to prevent further reaction.   For leak detection in-sodium hydrogen or oxygen detectors are promising, but because of the massive size of the system, transport times may be excessive.   Acoustic detectors have the potential to eliminate the transport time delay, but they require further development before application to a commercial system.

TABLE 12.4

SUMMARY OF CONCEPTUAL DESIGN PARAMETERS
FOR BAYONET-TUBE, SPLIT-BUNDLE,
SODIUM-HEATED STEAM GENERATOR*

Thermal rating	= 820 MWt
Sodium flow rate	= 26.4 × 10⁶ lb/hr
Sodium inlet temperature	= 1050° F
Sodium outlet temperature	= 700° F
Steam flow rate	= 2.85 × 10⁶ lb/hr
Steam outlet temperature	= 1000° F
Steam outlet pressure	= 2,450 psia
Feedwater flow rate	= 2.85 × 10⁶ lb/hr
Feedwater temperature	= 490° F
Feedwater pressure	= 2,640 psia
Superheater heat transfer tube	= 1.125-in. O.D. × 0.835-in. I.D.
Superheater heat transfer rate	= 1.1 × 10⁹ Btu/hr
Superheater overall coefficient	= 515 Btu/hr ft² F
Superheater temperature difference	= 146°
Superheater heat transfer area	= 15,000 ft²
Superheater heated length	= 30 ft
Economizer-evaporator heat transfer tube	= 1.125-in. O.D. × 0.939-in. I.D.
Film boiling heat transfer rate	= 4.9 × 10⁸ Btu/hr
Film boiling overall coefficient	= 835 Btu/hr ft² F
Film boiling temperature difference	= 207°
Film boiling heat transfer area	= 2,950 ft²
Film boiling heated length	= 7.5 ft
Nucleate boiling heat transfer rate	= 4.8 × 10⁸ Btu/hr
Nucleate boiling overall coefficient	= 875 Btu/hr ft² F
Nucleate boiling temperature difference	= 123°
Nucleate boiling heat transfer area	= 4,660 ft²
Nucleate boiling heated length	= 11.5 ft
Economizer heat transfer rate	= 7.6 × 10⁸ Btu/hr
Economizer overall coefficient	= 725 Btu/hr ft² F
Economizer temperature difference	= 161°
Economizer heat transfer area	= 6,520 ft²
Economizer heated length	= 16 ft
Economizer evaporator bundle	= 67-in. dia.
Superheater bundle	= 106-in. O.D. × 78-in. I.D.
Sodium pressure loss	= 11.6 psi

* [From Muenchow, H. O. and Armstrong, III, R. C., ASME Paper No. 71-NE-13, 1971.]

PROBLEMS

1. If the fuel element used in Ex. 2 operates over a period of 18 reactor startups, estimate the maximum fuel temperature in the element. Use the

effective UO_2 conductivity shown in Fig. 12.3 for 800°C. Will the UO_2 at the center be molten?

2. A 3 percent enriched uranium fuel rod of $\frac{3}{4}$ inch diameter is clad with 0.025 inch of Zircaloy 2. The outer clad temperature is not to exceed 600°F. What is the highest thermal flux which will not allow any transition to beta phase uranium at the centerline of the fuel rod?

3. A fuel plate is fabricated with 0.060 inch 10 w/o U − 90 w/o Al alloy as the fuel clad with 0.015 inch aluminum of either side. Assume the conductivity of the fuel material is 100 Btu/hr ft² °F and that its density is 3.30 gm/cm³. The uranium is 5 percent enriched and the peak thermal neutron flux is 5.0×10^{14} neutrons/cm² sec. The film coefficient on the outside of the plate is 750 Btu/hr ft² F and the coolant temperature is 350°F:

(a) Determine the peak heat flux at the plate surface;
(b) Determine the kW produced per plate. They are 3 inches wide and 4 feet long with a truncated cosine neutron flux variation along the length of the plate. The peak neutron flux is four times the value at the end of the plate;
(c) At the point of peak flux determine the temperature of the outer clad surface and the temperature at the center of the fuel.

4. In the pebble bed reactor concept, spheres of uranium carbide (UC) are coated with graphite. For spherical fuel pellets develop the expression shown below for the temperature in the pellet, T, in terms of the temperature at the fuel-coating interface, T_s, the conductivity of the uranium carbide, k_f, and the rate of internal heat generation, S. The radius at any point is r and the outer radius is r_s.

$$T = T_s + \frac{S}{6k_f} (r_s^2 - r^2)$$

5. A fuel element of the type described in Problem 4 has a diameter of 0.875 inch for the UC and a graphite coating 0.125 inch thick. The material properties are as follows:

  Uranium Carbide
     Density = 13.0 gr/cm³
     Average Thermal Conductivity = 12.0 Btu/hr ft °F
  Graphite
     Density = 1.75 gr/cm³
     Average Thermal Conductivity = 50.0 Btu/hr ft °F
  Uranium
     Enrichment = 3%

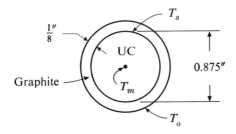

The temperature of the outer surface of the graphite is 1000°F. The thermal neutron flux is 10^{14} n/cm² sec. Assume an average UC temperature of 1540°F. Determine:

(a) The rate of internal heat generation, S(Btu/hr ft³);
(b) The temperature drop across the graphite; and
(c) The maximum temperature at the center of the sphere.

6. Fuel elements for the German Pebble Bed Reactor (AVR) are fueled graphite injection molded inside a 6 cm diameter sphere with a 1 cm wall thickness. If the fueled portion of the sphere has a rate of internal heat generation of 93.2 watts/cm³ and the surface temperature of the outer shell is 950°C, determine the peak temperature at the center of the fuel and the heat flux at the outer surface of the sphere.

Assume a mean conductivity for the fueled graphite of 0.145 w/cm C and a value for the graphite shell of 2.0 w/cm C.

7. The fuel pins for EBR-2 are 0.144 inch diameter by 14.22 inches long. The fuel is ^{238}U–^{235}U fissium alloy. The cladding is 304 stainless steel tube with 0.174 inch OD and 0.009 inch wall thickness. The intervening annulus of 0.006 inch is filled with sodium to give a good clad-core bond for heat transfer.

The fuel is to be discharged after 2 percent burnup. After 15 days the beta-gamma activity is releasing 0.2 watt/gram. Reprocessing by melt refining reduces the reactivity to one-third of the value after the cooling period. Assume that 75 percent of the energy is dissipated in the fuel and that the balance escapes to the surroundings.

If the elements lie horizontally in still air at 80°F, compute the maximum temperature at the center of the pin.

These pins are subsequently placed in a subassembly containing 91 elements in a hexagonal configuration which is about $2\frac{1}{4}$ inches across flats. Would you suggest forced cooling? Explain.

8. In a fuel assembly for a proposed 1000 mW(e) PWR water enters at 546°F. The fuel rods are 0.378 inch OD with 0.010 inch 304 SS cladding. The fuel is UO_2 pellets 0.358 inch diameter assembled in 13 foot long rods. Each rod has an equivalent hydraulic diameter of 0.563 inch for its unit cell. The average water velocity is 12.7 ft/sec.

Assume that the peak energy release rate is 10,000,000 Btu/hr ft³ and that this is 2.50 times the value at the rod ends.

It is desired to determine the temperature variation along the rod at the following points:

(a) In the fluid,
(b) At the outer clad surface,
(c) At the clad-fuel interface, and
(d) At the centerline of the fuel.

Write a FORTRAN program to give the desired temperature at positions one foot apart along the rod. Plot the results.

9. A boiling water pressure tube is to have a SEF of 2.0×10^6 Btu/hr. ft² operating at 800 psia with 400°F inlet water. If a heat flux burnout ratio of 1.30 is to be used, determine the quality of steam leaving the channel. Use Fig. 12.8 to determine $(q/A)_{BO}$. The channel is a 19-tube cluster of 0.625 inch OD rods in a 4 inch ID pressure tube which is 12 feet in length. Also estimate the power burnout ratio from the chart.

REFERENCES

1. Daniel, R. C., and I. Cohen, *In-Pile Effective Thermal Conductivity of Oxide Fuel Elements to High Fuel Depletions*, USAEC Report WAPD-246 (April, 1964).

2. Glasstone, S., and A. Sesonske, *Nuclear Reactor Engineering.* New York: D. Van Nostrand Co., Inc., 1963.

3. Sutherland, W. A., *Heat Transfer to Superheated Steam.* USAEC Report GEAP-4528 (May, 1963).

4. El-Wakil, M. M., *Nuclear Power Engineering.* New York: McGraw-Hill Book Co., Inc., 1962.

5. Rohsenow, W. M., and H. Y. Choi, *Heat, Mass, and Momentum Transfer.* Englewood Cliffs, N. J.: Prentice-Hall, Inc., 1961.

6. Hausner, H. H., and J. F. Schumar, *Nuclear Fuel Elements.* Reinhold Publishing Corporation, 1959.

7. Kreith, F., *Principles of Heat Transfer.* Scranton, Pa.: International Textbook Co., 1965.

8. Lustman, B., and F. Kerze, *Metallurgy of Zirconium.* New York: McGraw-Hill Book Co., Inc., 1955.

9. Holden, A. N., *Physical Metallurgy of Uranium.* Reading, Mass.: Addison-Wesley Publishing Co., Inc., 1958.

10. McAdams, W. H., *Heat Transmission.* New York: McGraw-Hill Book Co., Inc., 1954.

11. Wiley, John S., "Burnout Limits for Boiling Water Reactors," *Power Reactor Technology*, **7**, 1 (Winter 1963–64), pp. 14–26.

12. Levedahl, Wm. J., "Application of Steam Energy Flow to Reactor Design," *Transactions of the American Nuclear Society*, **5**, 1 (June, 1962), pp. 149–150.

13. Janssen, E. and J. A. Keriven, *Burnout Conditions for Nonuniformly Heated Rod in Annular Geometry, Water at 1000 psia.* USAEC Report GEAP 3755 (June, 1963).

14. DeBertoli, R. A., et al., *Forced Convection Heat Transfer Burnout Studies for Water in Rectangular Channels and Round Tubes at Pressures 500 psia.* USAEC Report WAPD-188 (October, 1958).

15. Walker, Jr., P. L., "Carbon—An Old but New Material," *American Scientist*, **50**, 2 (June, 1962), pp. 259–93.

16. *Nuclear Reactor Technology*, **3**, 4, pp. 68–74; **4**, 3, pp. 71–85; **6**, 2, pp. 75–80; **7**, 3, pp. 276–312.

17. Burkett, M. N., Eatherly, W. P., "Fueled-Graphite Elements for the German Pebble-Bed Reactor (AVR)," *High Temperature Nuclear Fuels* (A. N. Holden, ed.), New York, N. Y.: Gordon & Breach, 1966.

18. El-Wakil, M. M., *Nuclear Heat Transport.* Scranton, Pa.: International Textbook Co., 1971.

19. Muenchow, H. O., Armstrong, III, R. C., "A 1000-MWe LMFBR Steam Generator," ASME Paper No. 71-NE-13, 1971.

Chapter *13*

Nuclear Reactors

The previous chapters have dealt with various phases of reactor design, such as determination of critical size, reactor kinetics, heat transfer, and materials problems. This chapter will look at various types of reactors which are currently in use, under construction, or being planned for the future. While the list is far from complete, it will give the reader a reasonable view of the spectrum of reactor types useful for power generation.

A milestone was passed in 1966 when, for the first time, commitments for new nuclear generating capacity exceeded commitments to new fossilefired plant capacity. In 1966 installed domestic nuclear capacity accounted for roughly 1 percent of the total United States generating capability. Reactors planned for use by 1973 will account for 8 percent of the total in operation at that time. Fig. 13.1 shows long range AEC estimates of U. S. electric generating capacity. Note that nuclear generating capacity will account for an increasing fraction of the total. By the year 2000 a nuclear capacity of 750,000 MW will account for approximately 60 percent of the total. Estimating the capital cost for this equipment at \$180/kW gives about \$135 billion as the required cumulative investment in nuclear equipment by the year 2000.

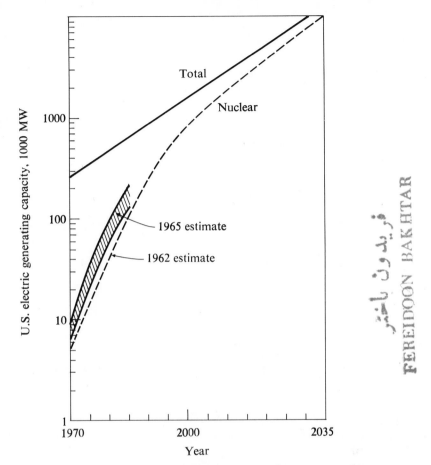

FIG. 13.1 *Long term nuclear power growth estimates.*

EFFECT OF SIZE ON PLANT COST

One of the most significant factors in the cost of nuclear power is plant size. Some costs increase more or less in proportion to size, while others are less sensitive to the rating of the plant. Overall there tends to be a decrease in unit cost in larger sizes.

For the large sized plants of the 70's an empirical equation has been proposed for the unit capital cost, C, in \$/KWe (Ref. 35).

$$C = \frac{4.45 \times 10^4}{(P/1000)^{0.8}} \pm 15\% \qquad (13.1)$$

where P is the net plant capacity in KWe. Fig. 13.2 shows how unit cost

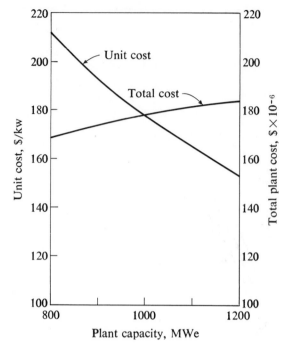

FIG. 13.2   *Effect of plant size on unit cost and total cost for light water reactors.*

drops from $212/KWe for an 800 MWe station to $153 for a 1200 MWe capacity while the total costs are $169.5 × 10⁶ and $180 × 10⁶, respectively.

Two pre-1960 plants, the Yankee Rowe Plant (PWR) and Dresden I (BWR), had design capabilities of 135 and 180 MWe, respectively. In the mid 60's the design capacity for Connecticut Yankee (PWR) was 462 MWe and Oyster Creek (BWR) was designed for 515 MWe. The reactors being completed between 1970 and 1975 have capacities between 800 and 1150 MWe, for example: Rancho Seco 1 (PWR)—800 MWe, Brown's Ferry 1, 2, and 3 (BWR's)—1064 MWe each, and Trojan 1 (PWR) —1153 MWe. These plants indicate the rather steady trend toward larger capacities. However, there was between 1967 and 1970 a jump in the predicted cost of an 800 to 900 MWe plant from $120/KWe to over $200/KWe. This was due to inflation, lengthened construction schedules and increased costs due to more stringent safety requirements with its associated costs of engineering and qualification testing of equipment. There has also been an increased contingency allowance in anticipation of design changes due to safety analyses made during construction.

FUEL BURNUP

Fuel burnup may be expressed as

(1) Megawatt days per metric ton of heavy metal, MWd/ton,
(2) Percent atom burnup, or
(3) Fissions per cm^3

Fuel is considered as atoms of the fertile or fissile isotopes of thorium, uranium or plutonium. Fuel material includes fuel plus any alloying elements. In (Th, UO_2) the thorium and uranium atoms is fuel, but the oxygen in this mixed oxide may be counted only as fuel material.

If all the atoms in a gram of ^{235}U could be fissioned, there would be an energy release of 0.949 MW-days of energy. This energy release is computed as follows:

$$\frac{6.024 \times 10^{23} \text{ (atoms } ^{235}U/\text{gm atom)}}{235 \text{ (gm}^{235}U/\text{gm atom)}} \times 200 \text{ (MeV}/^{235}U \text{ atom)}$$

$$\times \ 4.44 \times 10^{-23} \text{ (MW hrs/MeV)} \times \left(\frac{1}{24}\right) \text{ (days/hr)}$$

$$= 0.949 \text{ (MWd/gm } ^{235}U)$$

If all of the atoms in a ton of fuel were fissioned nearly a million MW days of energy would be produced. However, because of the buildup of fission products which reduces reactivity, the release of fission gases which contribute to pressure on the cladding, a tendency of the fuel to swell, and radiation damage to the cladding, the burnup is limited to a small fraction of the total number of heavy atoms. Early reactors using metallic fuels could tolerate burnups of only a few thousand MW days per ton. Ceramic fuels have raised this limit considerably and exposures of 30,000 MWd/ton are reasonable for oxide fuels. The fueled graphite for the HTGR is designed for exposures of 60,000 MWd/ton. Success of the proposed liquid metal fast breeder reactor is predicated on burnups of 100,000 MWd/ton. The natural UO_2 used in the Canadian heavy water moderated boiling light water reactors cannot undergo burnups over 10,000 MWd/ton due to its limited ^{235}U content.

Example 1. Fuel near the center of the CANDU–BLW reactor undergoes a burnup of 8500 MWd/ton. The thermal flux is 3×10^{14} n/cm^2 sec and the mean oxide temperature is 1000°C.

(a) Determine the atom % burnup.

$$\frac{8500 \, \dfrac{\text{MWd}}{\text{ton}} \times \dfrac{6.023 \times 10^{23}}{235} \, \dfrac{\text{atoms } ^{235}U}{\text{gm } ^{235}U}}{.949 \, \dfrac{\text{MWd} \times}{\text{gm } ^{235}U \text{ burned}} \, \dfrac{10^6 \, \text{gm fuel}}{\text{ton}} \, \dfrac{6.023 \times 10^{23}}{238} \, \dfrac{\text{atoms fuel}}{\text{gm fuel}}}$$

$$= .00907 \frac{\text{atoms } ^{235}\text{U}}{\text{atom fuel}}$$

Atom % burnup $= 0.907$

(b) How long will it take to achieve this burnup?

$$N_{235} = 10.5 \frac{\text{gm UO}_2}{\text{cm}^3} \times \frac{6.024 \times 10^{23} \frac{\text{molec UO}_2}{\text{gm mole UO}_2}}{270 \frac{\text{gm UO}_2}{\text{gm mole UO}_2}} \times .00714 \frac{\text{atoms } ^{235}\text{U}}{\text{molec UO}_2}$$

$$= 1.67 \times 10^{20} \frac{\text{atoms } ^{235}\text{U}}{\text{cm}^3}$$

$$\sigma_{\text{fis}} = 582 \frac{\sqrt{\pi}}{2} \sqrt{\frac{293}{1273}} = 250\text{b}$$

$$\frac{1}{10.5} \frac{\text{cm}^3}{\text{gm UO}_2} \times 10^6 \frac{\text{gm UO}_2}{\text{ton UO}_2} \times 1.67 \times 10^{20} \frac{\text{atoms } ^{235}\text{U}}{\text{cm}^3} \times 250$$

$$\times 10^{-24} \frac{\text{cm}^2}{\text{atom } ^{235}\text{U}} \times (\phi t) \frac{\text{n}}{\text{cm}^2} \times 200 \frac{\text{MeV}}{\text{n}} \times 4.44$$

$$\times 10^{-23} \frac{\text{MWhr}}{\text{MeV}} \times \frac{1\text{d}}{24 \text{ hr}} = 8500 \frac{\text{MWd}}{\text{ton}}$$

$$\phi t = 5.95 \times 10^{21} \frac{\text{n}}{\text{cm}^2} \text{ (thermal fluence)}$$

$$t = \frac{5.95 \times 10^{21} \frac{\text{n}}{\text{cm}^2}}{3 \times 10^{14} \frac{\text{n}}{\text{cm}^2 \text{ sec}} \times 3600 \times 24 \frac{\text{sec}}{\text{day}}} = 229.5 \text{ days}$$

A look at the answer for part a of the preceding example indicates that too simple an analysis has been used and that the burnup exceeds the ^{235}U content for natural uranium. However, the conversion of ^{238}U to ^{239}Pu and its subsequent fission accounts for a significant fraction of the 8500 MWd/ton.

NUCLEAR POWER COSTS

Nuclear power must compete with the conventional fossil fuels: coal, natural gas and oil. Within the nuclear industry there is intense rivalry among the manufacturers of various reactor types and fuel vendors as they vie for a share of the market. The following facts of economic life must be considered:

(1) nuclear plants require a greater capital investment than fossil stations and a substantial change in the differential is unlikely,

(2) operation and maintenance are but a small fraction of the total cost of power, and

(3) the fuel cycle costs are likely to be the most fruitful area for cost reduction.

The cost of electricity is the sum of annual fixed charges due to the initial investment in plant, operating and maintenance costs, and fuel costs.

The annual fixed charges include both direct and indirect costs. The direct costs include land, structures, reactor equipment, turbines and associated accessories, and electrical equipment. The indirect costs include administration, engineering and design, contingencies, interest during construction, etc. Table 13.1 shows these various costs as a

TABLE 13.1

CAPITAL INVESTMENT COST
FOR NUCLEAR POWER PLANTS*

	Peach Bottom 2	Brown's Ferry 1 & 2	Maine Yankee 2	Rancho Seco	Trojan 1
Land	0.1	0.3	0.4	0.4	0.4
Structures & Improvements	15.4	9.7	13.2	15.4	15.7
Reactor Plant Equipment	34.1	35.4	34.2	31.3	32.2
Turbogenerator Units	24.2	26.1	23.2	30.1	26.1
Accessory Drives	4.7	3.6	4.0	5.3	3.0
Misc. Power Plant Equip.	1.8	0.9	0.7	0.7	0.7
Total % Direct Costs	80.3	76.0	75.6	83.0	78.1
Engineering & Design	N.A.	4.6	N.A.	5.9	N.A.
Interest During Constr.	10.7	6.7	13.6	10.0	10.6
Other Indirect Costs	N.A.	12.7	N.A.	1.1	N.A.
Total % Indirect Costs	19.7	24.0	24.4	17.0	21.9
Type Reactor	BWR	BWR	PWR	PWR	PWR
Reactor Vendor	GE	GE	CE	B&W	W
Ultimate Rating, MWe	1115	1064	865	800	1153
Adjusted Unit Cost, $/kW (To July 1974 Operation)	169	166	187	181	160

* From *Reactor Technology*, **13**, No. 1, p. 16.

percentage of the total initial cost for some typical light water reactors. Note that the direct costs are about 80 percent of the total investment with the balance the indirect costs. Fig. 13.3 shows graphically how these costs are divided on the average for the reactors in Table 13.1. Note the large share for the reactor and the turbogenerators. Note also that

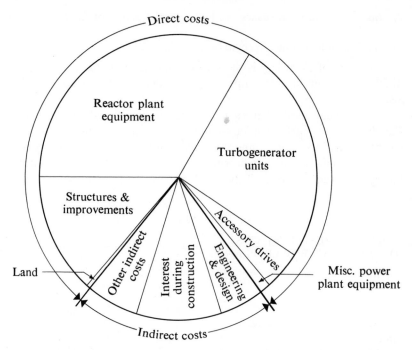

FIG. 13.3 *Typical division of capital costs for light water reactors.*

interest during construction amounts to roughly 10 percent and this is 14.5×10^6 for a plant such as Rancho Seco.

The annual fixed charge rate is taken as a percentage of the total capital investment. For private ownership this would amount to 14 to 16 percent, while for government ownership 7 to 8 percent is more appropriate. A 14 percent annual fixed charge might include:

Return on capital invested	6.00
30-Year depreciation	1.25
Interim replacements	0.50
Federal income taxes	2.25
Other taxes	3.80
Insurance (excluding liability)	.20
	14.00

For public ownership there is a lower return on invested capital and there are no taxes.

The operating cost is made up of payroll costs for operating, maintenance, supervisory personnel, liability insurance costs, and repair and maintenance materials. This cost is not expected to vary significantly between various reactor types.

The fuel cycle costs include ore cost, conversion and reprocessing of the fuel, fabrication of the fuel elements, shipping, and plutonium and uranium credits. Table 13.2 shows a PWR fuel cycle cost projection

TABLE 13.2

PWR FUEL CYCLE COST PROJECTION*
1,150 MWe
1975 Startup
80% Capacity Factor

	Fuel Cost (mills/KWh)			
	Consumption Costs	Financing Costs	Total	% of Costs
Fabrication (@ $70/kg U)	0.34	0.08	0.42	20
Uranium ore (@ $8/lb U₃O₈)	0.56	0.18	0.74	36
Conversion (@ $2.52/kg U) and reprocessing (@ $45/kg U)	0.62	0.16	0.78	37
Spent fuel shipping and reprocessing (@ $45/kg U)	0.19	−0.04	0.15	7
Plutonium (@ $7.50/gm Pu) and uranium credits	−0.35	0.08	−0.27	—
Totals	1.36	0.46	1.82	100

Notes: Consumption costs include interest during construction in the first core. Cost of money and interest during construction at 7%/yr and total fixed charge rate on non-depreciable capital at 14%/yr. The first three items include 4% sales tax.

* From Mason, E. A., *Nuclear News*, **14**, No. 2 (Feb. 1971), p. 36.

for a reactor startup in the mid 70's. A light water reactor with an 1125 MW rating requires 100 metric tons of uranium fuel worth $31 × 10⁶. The annual fuel cycle bill will be $14.7 × 10⁶/year of which $11 × 10⁶ is the cost of the materials and their processing, while $3.7 × 10⁶ is for financing. Here one can see there is a large incentive for fuel cycle improvements with their accompanying cost reduction. For a reactor whose fuel cycle costs average 1.63 mills/KWh at 70 percent load factor over a 30 year lifetime, the fuel cost will be 1.5 times the original capital investment (32).

The cost of electricity, e, in ϕ/KWh may be expressed as

$$e = 1000 \frac{\phi I + O + F}{E} \tag{13.2}$$

where ϕ = annual fixed charge rate, yr^{-1}
       I = capital investment for plant, $

O = operating expense, \$/yr

F = annual fuel cost, \$/yr

E = electrical energy produced, KWh(e)/yr.

The net annual power generation may be expressed as

$$E = 8760 \times \underset{\dfrac{hr}{yr}}{} \underset{\dfrac{KWh(e)\ actual}{KWh(e)\ rated}}{L} \times \underset{KW(e)\ rated}{P_r}$$

$$= 24 \times \underset{\dfrac{1}{1000}}{\dfrac{hr}{day}} \underset{\dfrac{ton}{KgU}}{1000} \times \underset{\dfrac{KW(t)}{MW(t)}}{1000} \times \underset{\dfrac{KW(e)}{KW(t)}}{\eta} \times \underset{\dfrac{MWd(t)}{ton}}{B} \times \underset{\dfrac{KgU}{yr}}{U}$$

$$E = 8760\,LP_r = 24\eta BU \tag{13.3}$$

where L = capacity or load factor, $\dfrac{KWh(e)\ actual}{KWh(e)\ rated}$

P_r = rated capacity of plant, KWh(e)

η = plant thermal efficiency, $\dfrac{KW(e)}{KW(t)}$

B = fuel burnup at discharge, $\dfrac{MWd(t)}{ton}$

U = nuclear fuel consumption, KgU fed to reactor/yr.

The annual fuel costs, F, is

$$F = C_f U \tag{13.4}$$

where C_f = total fuel cycle cost, \$/KgU fed to reactor.

Now Eq. (13.2) may be rewritten

$$e = \frac{1000}{8760L}\left[\phi\,\frac{I}{P_r} + \frac{O}{P_r}\right] + \frac{1000}{24}\left[\frac{C_f}{\eta B}\right] \tag{13.5}$$

Example 2. A 1000 MW LWR is expected to cost \$200,000,000. It will operate at a load factor of 80% with an annual fixed charge of 16%. The annual operating cost will be \$2.5 × 10⁶. Uranium cost is estimated at \$300/Kg. The predicted cycle efficiency is to be 31% and a burnup of 35,000 MWd/ton is expected. Calculate the cost of electricity.

$$e = \frac{1000}{8760 \times .8}\left[.16\left[\frac{200 \times 10^6}{10^6}\right] + \frac{2.5 \times 10^6}{10^6}\right] + \frac{1000 \times 300}{24 \times .31 \times 35000}$$

$$= 4.57 + .36 + 1.15 = 6.07 \text{ mills/KWh}$$

For a government operated plant the fixed charge might be 8%. The cost of electricity would then drop to

$$e = \frac{1000}{8760 \times .8} \left[.08 \times \frac{200 \times 10^6}{10^6} \right] + .37 + 1.15$$

$$= 3.80 \text{ mills/KWh}$$

Table 13.3 shows estimates for future power costs during the period

TABLE 13.3

ESTIMATES OF ENERGY COSTS FOR NUCLEAR PLANTS*

	1975	Potential (1980–2000)			
	LWR	LWR	HTGR	LMFBR	MSBR
	mills/KWh(e)				
Investment costs	4.0–4.8	3.0–3.6	2.7–3.3	3.2–3.8	3.0–3.6
Fuel costs	1.7–1.9	1.4–1.6	1.0–1.2	0.4–0.6	0.2–0.4
Operating and maintenance costs	0.3	0.3	0.3	0.3	0.5
Total energy costs	6.0–7.0	4.7–5.5	4.0–4.8	3.9–4.7	3.7–4.5

* From Mason, E. A., *Nuclear News*, **14**, No. 2 (Feb. 1971), p. 37.

from 1980 to 2000. Note that the HTGR, LMFBR, and MSBR all have potentially lower power costs than light water reactors. Note the overlap in the values predicted, which indicates any successful reactor type must achieve that success in the face of severe competition.

PRESSURIZED WATER REACTORS

In a pressurized water reactor (PWR) the fission energy released in the core increases the enthalpy of high pressure water ($\sim$2000 psia). This hot water generates steam at a lower pressure in the secondary loop of the system (see Fig. 13.4). The steam then produces power in a conventional turbine. Now it is condensed, and the feedwater is pumped back into the steam generator. Steam pressures in the secondary loop have increased from 600 psia to nearly 1000 psia as reactor plants have progressed (from Shippingsport which went critical in 1957 with a capacity of 60 MWe to Connecticut Yankee which went critical in 1967 with an initial power level of 490 MWe and sees a possibility of stretching this to 650 MWe with improved cores).

The primary pressure is maintained by electrical heaters in the pres-

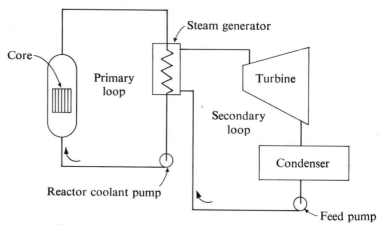

Fig. 13.4 *Simple pressurized water reactor system.*

surizer. Water in this tank is maintained at the saturation temperature corresponding to the desired pressure level.

The fact that no superheat is available means that considerable moisture will form during expansion through the turbines. Moisture separators between the high and low pressure turbine casings help to eliminate some of the problems due to excess moisture in the final stages of the expansion. This difficulty with moisture may be further alleviated by using live steam for reheating after the moisture separation. A system using reheating and several stages of regenerative feedwater heating is shown in Fig. 13.5. Notice that all of the primary working fluid stays inside the reactor containment.

The Connecticut Yankee Plant has a power cycle similar to that of Fig. 13.5. Water at 2150 psia is heated from 545°F to 583.5°F in the core. The primary coolant flow rate is 101.4×10^6 lbs/hour. When operating at 590 MWe a total of 7,600,000 lbs/hour is pumped to the four steam generators. At this power level steam is supplied to the throttle at 640 psia and one-fourth percent moisture. There is approximately a 50 psi pressure drop between the steam generator and the throttle. 24-inch lines from each steam generator lead to a 36-inch manifold and thence to the two turbine stop-trip valves via 30-inch diameter lines. The turbine is a tandem compound unit with the double flow high pressure casing, and has one impulse and seven reaction stages on each end. Two double flow low pressure casings have 10 reaction stages per end. The blade length for the final row of blades is 44 inches.

The reactor core contains 75,300 kg of uranium dioxide pellets. They are 0.600 inch long and 0.3835 inch in diameter. They are contained in stainless steel tubes with 0.422 inch OD and 0.0165 inch wall thickness.

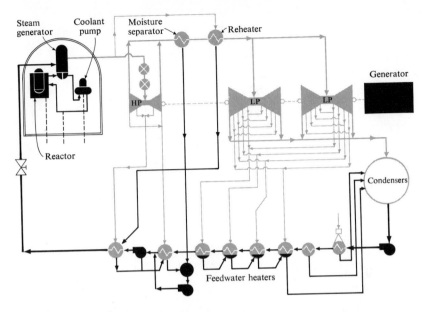

Steam generator

Coolant pump

Moisture separator

Reheater

Generator

HP

LP

LP

Reactor

Condensers

Feedwater heaters

FIG. 13.5 *Typical PWR plant arrangement for 400–600 MWe range.* [*Courtesy Westinghouse Electric Corporation.*]

The active fuel length in the tubes is 121.8 inches; the rods are arranged in a 15 by 15 array to form an assembly. There are 157 of these assemblies in the core. There are only 204 fuel rods per assembly with 20 of the remaining positions being available for control rods; one position is available as a central instrumentation sheath. The control rods are 85 percent Ag, 15 percent In, 5 percent Cd, clad with stainless steel. They have an OD of 0.44 inch.

The first core loading had three regions of varying enrichment, as shown by Fig. 13.6. The outermost 52 assemblies had a 3.67 percent enrichment, the intermediate region contained 52 assemblies with 3.24 percent ^{235}U, and the central region had a 3 percent enrichment. This variable enrichment tends to provide a flatter flux variation across the core. As refueling occurs the outer elements will move inward and new fuel will be added to Region III. The Region I fuel will be reprocessed. The division of power between the various fuel assemblies in the three regions is shown in Fig. 13.7. These figures are calculated for 15,900 MWd/ton burnup with the control rods withdrawn from the core. Under these conditions 36.1 percent of the power is developed in the central region, 36.4 percent in the intermediate region, and 27.4 percent in the outer region, indicating the effectiveness of the variable enrichment in equalizing the power generation across the core.

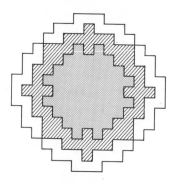

Region I (53 assemblies at 3.00 w/o U-235)

Region II (52 assemblies at 3.24 w/o U-235)

Region III (52 assemblies at 3.67 w/o U-235)

FIG. 13.6 *Region boundaries in the first cycle.* [*From Connecticut Yankee Atomic Power Company, Facility Description and Safety Analysis, Vol. I, Report No. NYO-3250-5.*]

1.06	1.06	1.06	1.07	1.12	1.13	1.06	.77
1.06	1.06	1.06	1.07	1.09	1.12	1.05	.65
1.06	1.06	1.07	1.08	1.12	1.09	.89	
1.07	1.07	1.08	1.12	1.10	1.03	.66	
1.12	1.09	1.12	1.10	.99	.72		
1.13	1.12	1.09	1.03	.72			
1.06	1.05	.89	.66				
.77	.65						

Location of power peak $F_{\Delta H} = 1.41$

Burnup = 15,900 MWD/MTU
No control rods

Region	Power fraction
Center	.362
Intermediate	.364
Outer	.274

FIG. 13.7 *Assembly to average power distribution.* [*From Connecticut Yankee Atomic Power Company*, Facility Description and Safety Analysis, *Vol. I, Report No. NYO-3250-5.*]

Reactivity is controlled by both control rods and by the injection of boric acid into the core (chemical shim). The use of boron as a uniformly distributed poison promotes a more uniform flux distribution by requiring less control rod insertion. The cold core with no power and no Xe or Sm buildup has an effective multiplication factor of 1.28. When the core is hot at full power with equilibrium Xe and Sm buildup the effective multiplication factor drops to 1.163. Initially a boron concentration of 2470 ppm will give a shutdown margin of nine percent with the control rods fully inserted. At full power with equilibrium xenon and samarium the boron concentration will be reduced to 1800 ppm. As the fuel burnup proceeds, the boron concentration will be gradually reduced to zero. The control rod worth is designed to be 0.0642 at the beginning of core life: at the end of core life this will have increased to 0.0732.

Improvements in core design have permitted marked increases in the water temperature leaving the reactor core. One factor in this improvement is the reduction of the enthalpy rise hot channel factor. This is the ratio of the enthalpy rise of the water in the hottest channel to the enthalpy rise in the average channel. In 1960 this factor was 3.6. It decreased to a value of 1.8 at the end of 1966. Further reduction to 1.6 is anticipated. This permits higher water temperatures in the core with a corresponding improvement in the thermal efficiency of the steam cycle and power costs. Fig. 13.8 shows the water temperature variation, as it passes through the core, for 1960 technology, the technology of the mid-1960s and for "near future" technology. Power costs for the original Yankee Atomic Electric Plant at Rowe, Massachusetts, have been reduced to 7–8 mills per KW hour with more recent cores. The Connecticut Yankee Atomic Power Plant produces power at close to 5 mills per KW hour. This reflects the improvements due to larger size, lower hot channel factors, and the higher pressures and temperatures possible in the steam cycle.

BOILING WATER REACTORS

The boiling water reactor (BWR) generates steam directly within the reactor core. This steam is used as the working fluid for the associated power cycle. Saturated steam is typically produced at a pressure of 1000 psia (545°F).

BWR Fuel Assembly Design

Fig. 13.9 shows a schematic diagram of a BWR fuel assembly and Fig. 13.10 is a schematic drawing of a fuel rod. The rods are assembled in a 7 × 7 array, each assembly being contained in a can-like fuel channel with the fuel rods being spaced and supported between upper and lower

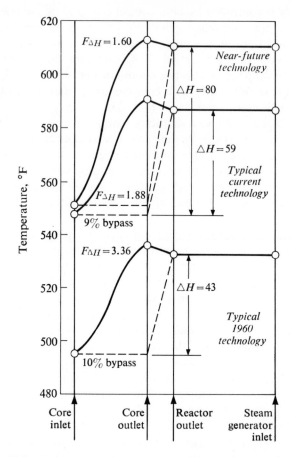

FIG. 13.8 *Pressurized water reactor core performance advancements since construction of the 1960 plant.* [*Courtesy Westinghouse Electric Corporation.*]

tie plates. Eight of the rods are threaded into the bottom support plate and are bolted down to the upper support plate to provide a structural tie for the assembly which allows it to be inserted into or removed from the core by the upper tie plate handle. The remaining rods have end plugs which fit into holes in the support plates.

The assemblies are arranged roughly in a right cylinder inside the core vessel. Flow enters at the bottom of each assembly through a nose piece and passes upward between the fuel rods.

Control is provided by cruciform control blades. Within the cruciform sheath boron carbide powder is contained in $\frac{1}{4}''$ SS tubes. With fresh fuel supplementary reactivity control may be provided by boron bearing stainless steel curtains inserted between the fuel assemblies.

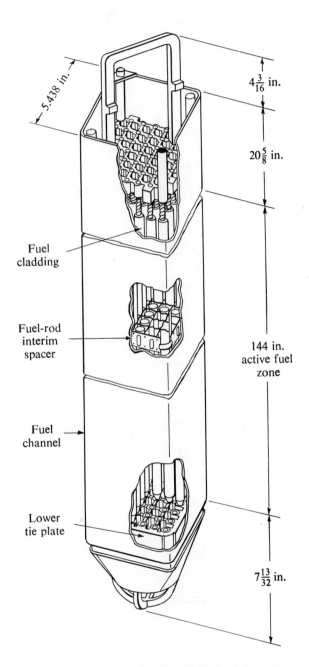

FIG. 13.9 *BWR fuel assembly schematic.* (*From* Reactor Technology **14,** *No. 1, p. 69.*)

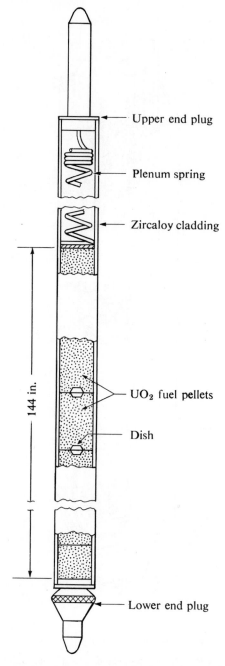

FIG. 13.10 *BWR fuel rod.* (*From* Reactor Technology, **14,** *No. 1,* p. 72.)

Also certain fuel rods may contain gadolinia as a burnable poison. When the ^{10}B is consumed in the curtains, they are removed from the core, but the gadolinia bearing rods remain as ordinary fuel rods once the high absorption cross section gadolinium isotopes have disappeared.

As the control blade is withdrawn, water in the vacated space provides more effective neutron moderation and tends to cause local flux peaking. Observe in Fig. 13.11 that four different enrichments are used in each assembly to offset the tendency for this flux peaking.

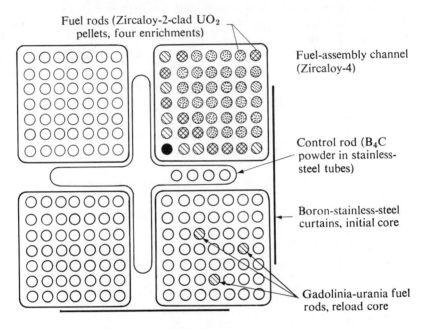

FIG. 13.11   *BWR fuel module consisting of four fuel assemblies surrounding a cruciform control blade.* (*From* Reactor Technology, **14**, *No. 1, p. 71.*)

The low enrichment UO_2 fuel is typically in the form of $\sim 1/2$ inch diameter pressed and sintered pellets stacked in a 12 foot column contained by free standing Zircally-2 cladding. The cladding is 0.563″ OD with a 32 mill wall thickness capable of withstanding the external pressure of 1000 psia without collapsing against the fuel pellets. Above the fuel a plenum having a volume 8 to 11 percent of the fuel volume is provided. This plenum accommodates helium backfill plus such gaseous fission products as may be released during operation. The fuel pellets in the high flux regions near the center of the rod are dished to accommodate radiation induced swelling. Pellets near the top and bottom are undished, as no energy will be released in a volume containing no uranium. An initial diametral gap of 0.012″ is allowed between pellets and clad to accommodate radial swelling.

Fuel rod failure occurs when cladding perforation or rupture allows release of fission gases to occur. During reactor transients fuel damage may occur because of

(1) Local overheating due to insufficient cooling or
(2) Excessive strain due to relative pellet/cladding expansion.

Fuel damage due to local overheating has been defined as occurring at the onset of film boiling. However, it is not expected to occur until well into the film boiling regime. A partial flow blockage could cause this type of failure.

Any value of plastic strain under 1 percent is defined as insufficient to cause damage due to excessive strain during a transient. A linear heat generation rate (LHGR) of 28 kW/ft will produce this strain in fresh fuel, compared to 22 kW/ft required after a local exposure of 40,000 MWd/ton. Note that a LHGR of 21.5 kW/ft produces incipient melting in the UO_2. Current design practice limits the maximum LHGR to 18.5 kW/ft.

At any one time less than 1 percent of the fuel rods in a core should experience this peak LHGR. The long term average LHGR for the element which sees this peak generation rate is only 7 to 12 kW/ft. The local design peak exposure for these pellets is 45,000 MWd/ton with a 30,000 MWd/ton maximum assembly exposure. The core residence time for a fuel assembly is four to six years.

SINGLE-CYCLE BWR

In the single-cycle BWR all the steam generation occurs within the core vessel. Small plants (under 100 MWe) may use natural circulation, but the larger units use forced circulation. Fig. 13.12 shows the power loop for a single-cycle plant. The 500/600 MWe Nine Mile Point Station built by the Niagara Mohawk Power Corporation, the 520/620 MWe Oyster Creek Unit No. 1 of the Jersey Power and Light Company, the 714 MWe Dresden 2 Plant of Commonwealth Edison, and TVA's three 1064 MWe BWR's at Brown's Ferry are all single-cycle plants.

Orifices at the base of each fuel assembly control the coolant flow to the individual fuel assemblies. Steam with a quality of approximately 9 percent is generated as the water flows upward along the fuel rods. It is separated from the water in the steam separators and dryers in the top of the core vessel, as shown in Fig. 13.13. Unevaporated water is recircu-

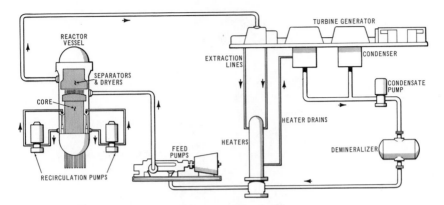

FIG. 13.12   *BWR single-cycle power loop.*   [*Courtesy General Electric Company.*]

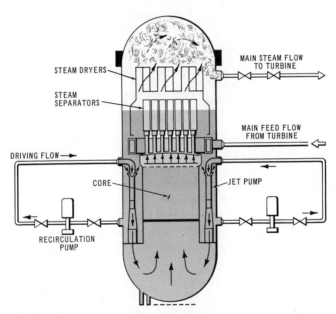

FIG. 13.13   *BWR jet pump system.*   [*Courtesy General Electric Company.*]

lated between the core shroud and the core vessel.   The recirculation system uses two jet pumps to augment the tendency of natural circulation in producing downcomer flow.   A more detailed sketch of the reactor internals is shown in Fig. 13.14.

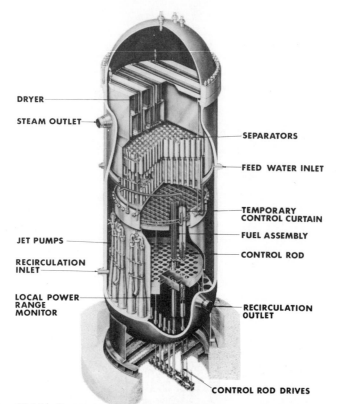

FIG. 13.14 *Reactor vessel, forced circulation single-cycle BWR.* [*Courtesy General Electric Company.*]

Control of single-cycle BWR's may be accomplished by either of the modes shown in Fig. 13.15. Part (a) shows the turbine slaved to the reactor. Pressure is held at the desired level by an initial pressure regulator. The turbine governor then adjusts the position of the control rods to change the reactivity of the core and the amount of steam being generated. A change in the power level of 25 to 30 percent may also be attained by modulating the recirculation flow through the core without any control rod motion being required. To raise the power level, the flow rate through the core is increased, reducing the void fraction and increasing reactivity. This in turn raises the thermal output. The increased power output will stabilize when the temporary excess of reactivity is balanced by an increased void fraction. To reduce the power level the recirculation flow rate is reduced.

When the reactor is slaved to the turbine Fig. 13.15(b), the turbine governor controls the turbine admission valves. A change in flow results in a change in reactivity and produces a change in pressure. Either

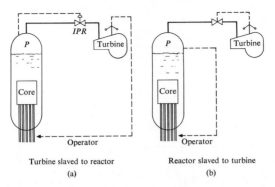

FIG. 13.15   *Basic modes of BWR control; (a) turbine slaved to reactor, and (b) reactor slaved to turbine.* [*Courtesy General Electric Company.*]

manual or automatic repositioning of the control rods will return the pressure to the desired level.   Since reactivity is sensitive to pressure changes (reduced void fraction accompanying a pressure increase will enhance the effectiveness of the moderator), this method of control is not popular.

DUAL-CYCLE BWR

In the dual-cycle BWR (Fig. 13.16) only about half the steam is generated in the core at the higher pressure.   On its way back to the core the recirculated water is subcooled by generating steam at a lower pressure.   The 180 MWe Dresden 1 Station of the Commonwealth Edison Company uses this cycle and generates primary steam at 1000 psia and secondary steam at 520 psia for maximum flow (this rises to 950 psia at minimum flow).   High pressure steam is admitted to the first stage of the turbine and secondary steam is admitted at the ninth stage.   Some of the operating conditions are shown for the cycle in Table 13.4.

A very interesting characteristic of this system is its ability to respond to load changes without requiring any motion of the control rods.   This is accomplished by allowing the turbine governor to regulate the admission of secondary steam to the turbine.   The increased flow of secondary steam creates more subcooling in the recirculation line.   The cooler water entering the core reduces the void fraction somewhat, increasing the effectiveness of the water as a moderator.   This, in turn, raises the reactivity of the core, causing it to be slightly supercritical.   The output rises until the void fraction increases sufficiently to reduce the effective multiplication factor to unity.   The increased output tends to raise the

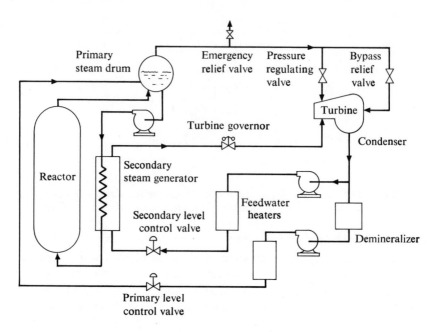

Fig. 13.16 *BWR dual-cycle flow diagram.* [*Courtesy General Electric Company.*]

TABLE 13.4

DRESDEN 1 RATED OPERATING CONDITIONS

Power Level	630 MWth
	180 MWe
Recirculation Flow*	25×10^6 lb/hr
Primary Steam Flow	1.4×10^6 lb/hr
Secondary Steam Flow	1.2×10^6 lb/hr
Inlet Core Subcooling	53 Btu/lb
Average Core Exit Quality	5%
Peak Heat Flux (at overpower)**	350,000 Btu/(hr)(ft²)
Minimum Burnout Ratio (at overpower)	2.1
Maximum Void Fraction at Hot	
Channel Exit (at overpower)	65%
Thermal Efficiency	
Test Value at Rated Power	29.75%
Test Value at 60% Power	29.45%

* During system tests recirculation was measured at 27.1×10^6 lbs/hr.
** Core loading of 452 fuel assemblies having a peaking factor of 3.64.

primary steam pressure and open the primary admission valves wider. Reduced load demands reverse this sequence. Fig. 13.17 shows the relation between primary and secondary steam flows for the Dresden 1 Station for various fixed control rod settings. Load changes of 40 percent may be accommodated with a particular control rod setting.

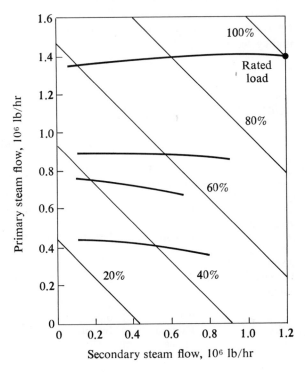

FIG. 13.17   *Dresden 1 dual-cycle BWR control characteristics.*   [*Courtesy General Electric Company.*]

COMPARISON OF DUAL AND SINGLE CYCLE BWR'S

The dual cycle has the advantage of inherent load-following capability by regulation of secondary steam flow to the turbine. This is being matched by the single cycle units with the advent of flow control applied to the core recirculation rate. The dual cycle has the ability to produce more power from a given size of core vessel because of the generation of the secondary steam outside the core proper. This may be a distinct advantage for siting conditions where transportation of a large core vessel is a serious problem.

The simplicity of the single cycle allows a lower capital investment for piping, heat exchangers, pumps, etc. It also has a somewhat better thermal efficiency because of the direct generation of all steam at the maximum cycle temperature. The loss in availability as heat is transferred from the recirculated water to the secondary steam costs the cycle about 1 percent on its thermal efficiency at rated load. A study of comparable cycles working between 1000 psia and $1\frac{1}{2}$ inches Hg gave an efficiency of 30.9 percent for the single cycle plant, as compared to 29.7 percent for the dual cycle.

TABLE 13.5

DESIGN PROGRESS-BWR TECHNOLOGY*

Characteristics	Dresden 1* (1955)[a]	Dresden 2* (1965)[a]	Brown's Ferry 1 (1966)[a]
Power rating MWe (net)	200	714	1080
Type reactor	Dual cycle	Single cycle	Single cycle
Systems and Hardware			
Containment	Dry sphere	Pressure suppression	Pressure suppression
Secondary steam generators	4	0	0
Recirculation loops	4	2 (jet pumps)	2 (jet pumps)
Number of fuel bundles	488	724	764
Control rods	80	177[b]	185
Rods/MWe	0.4	0.25	0.171
Steam separation	External steam drum	Internal	Internal
Power Density			
Core average, kWt/liter	28	37[b]	51
Refueling time, days	33	15–20	—
Fuel exposure, MWd/ton	8000	15/20,000[c]	19/25,000
Plant heat rate, Btu/kW-hr	11,200	10,710	10,380

    a   Year of commitment
    b   Based on initial rating of 714 MWe (net)
    c   Equilibrium core is 20,000 MWd/ton

* Elliott, V. A., "Boiling Water Reactor," *Mechanical Engineering*, **89**, 1 (January, 1967), pp. 19–26.

Table 13.5 shows an interesting comparison of the Dresden 1 & 2, and Brown's Ferry plants which indicates the progress in BWR design in the period between 1955 and 1966.

GAS-COOLED REACTORS

Gas cooling for a reactor core will allow substantially higher temperatures for the working fluid than is possible when water is the cooling medium. Carbon dioxide was used in the European Magnox Reactors, but as cycle temperatures have risen helium has come into favor. It is inert with respect to materials of construction and ^{4}He has no neutron absorption (there is .00013 percent ^{3}He which undergoes an (n, p) reaction to form tritium). The majority of gas cooled plants built thus far generate steam at conditions equivalent to modern fossil practice, but the German KSH Plant, described later in this chapter, uses the helium directly in a gas turbine cycle.

The High Temperature Gas-Cooled Reactor in the United States started with the 40 MWe prototype at Peach Bottom, Pa. which went critical in 1966. This has been followed by a 330 MWe which itself is a step toward units as large as 1100 MWe. It is this 330 MWe Fort St. Vrain plant which will be described in some detail.

The plant is graphite moderated, helium cooled, and fueled with coated microspheres of thorium and fully enriched uranium embedded in a carbonaceous binder. The hexagonal fuel element which was described in Chapter 11 and shown in Fig. 11.40 contains 210 fuel cavities and 100 coolant passages. These fueled graphite blocks are stacked in columns which are arranged 7 columns to each of 37 refueling regions. Fig. 13.18 shows the stacking of the fuel elements in a segment of the core. There are 2 B_4C control rods for each of the refueling regions and the He flow is orificed to each region to attain a uniform discharge temperature for the hot helium. In the helium circuit the core heats helium from 760° to 1430°F.

Fig. 13.19 shows a schematic diagram for the plant power cycle. Hot helium passes from the core down to two steam generators each containing 6 modules. The modules are once through steam generators producing superheated steam at 2400 psia and 1000°F. The internal piping for one of these modules is shown in Fig. 13.20. After expansion through the high pressure turbine steam returns to the reheat section of the steam generator modules via single stage turbines driving the 4 helium circulators for the core. After reheat to 1000°F steam at 600 psia passes to an intermediate turbine and then through a double flow low pressure turbine before being condensed. The condensate passes through three low pressure feedwater heaters, a deaerating heater and two high pressure heaters before returning to the economizer section of the steam generator modules at 403°F.

The entire primary circuit consisting of core, steam generator modules and helium circulators is contained in a Prestressed Concrete Reactor

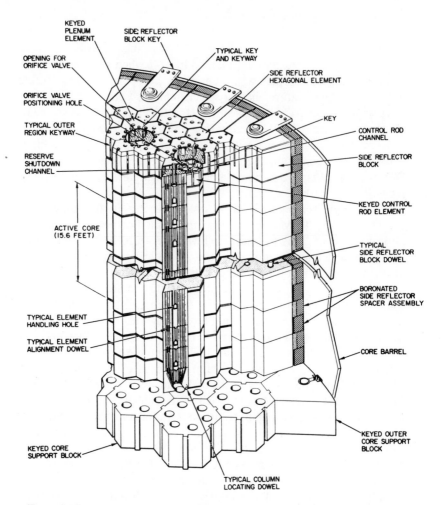

FIG. 13.18 *Core elevation arrangement for Fort St. Vrain HTGR.* (*Courtesy Gulf General Atomic Company.*)

Vessel (PCRV) which is more or less a hexagonal prism, 61 feet across flats and 106 feet high. A cutaway of the PCRV is shown in Fig. 13.21. The internal cavity has an internal diameter of 31 feet and an internal height of 75 feet. The upper and lower heads have a nominal thickness of 15 feet. The vessel provides not only containment of the 700 psia helium, but also radiological shielding. Steel tendons pass through tubes in the concrete and when properly tensioned they will place the concrete under enough compression to more than offset the tensile stress due to the internal helium pressure. The arrangement of the reactor within the

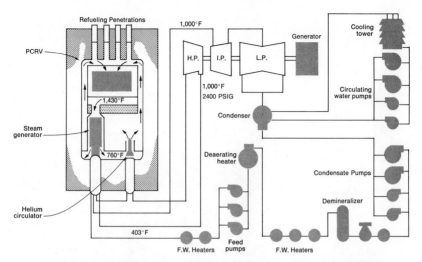

FIG. 13.19 *HTGR power plant flow schematic. (Courtesy Gulf General Atomic Company.)*

PCRV is shown in Fig. 13.22.   Penetrations in the top head provide for refueling and control rod drives.

Control over the plant output is by a reactor-follow-turbine system. The governor on the turbine controls steam flow.   It is then desired to maintain the steam pressure and temperature at the throttle and the reheat steam temperature.   The steam pressure at the throttle is maintained by variation of feedwater flow, the throttle steam temperature is controlled by variation of helium flow and the reheat steam temperature is controlled by variation of control rod position in the core.

The ^{235}U-^{232}Th-^{233}U fuel cycle being employed is an interesting one. As burnup continues an increasing fraction of the fission occurs in the ^{233}U which has been bred from the fertile thorium.   Since the value of η for ^{233}U is higher than that for ^{235}U this helps the conversion ratio which is expected to be 0.62 for the equilibrium core.   In the all ceramic core there is no structural metal with its parasitic capture of neutrons and the coolant has virtually no absorption.   If sufficient ^{233}U becomes available for the fissile UC_2 microspheres, a higher conversion ratio should be possible.

DIRECT CYCLE GAS TURBINE CYCLES

A parallel development to the Fort St. Vrain HTGR is the 25 MW(e) KSH direct cycle reactor being built in Germany.   As shown in

FIG. 13.20 *One of twelve steam generator modules for the Fort St.
Vrain HTGR. (Courtesy Gulf General Atomic Company.)*

Fig. 13.23, the helium passes directly to a gas turbine without a transfer
of energy to a secondary working medium. The system incorporates
three stage compression with intercooling, a regenerative heat exchanger
to return enthalpy from the turbine exhaust gas to the high pressure
helium prior to its entry into the core of the reactor. A precooler rejects
heat to cooling water before the gas from the regenerator enters first
compression stage. It is of interest to note that this plant matches an
existing reactor type to a new power cycle, rather than matching a new
reactor concept with an existing power system, as is usually the case.

This system can utilize the high temperatures developed in a gas
cooled core and produce good thermal efficiencies. The simplicity of
the direct cycle should reduce the capital costs for such plants. There

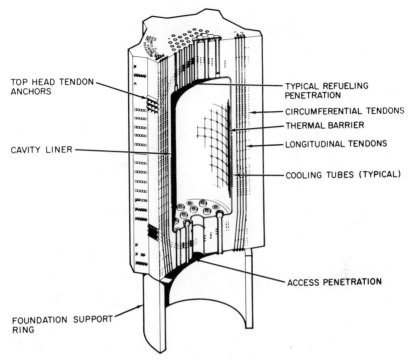

TOP HEAD TENDON
ANCHORS

TYPICAL REFUELING
PENETRATION

CIRCUMFERENTIAL TENDONS

THERMAL BARRIER

LONGITUDINAL TENDONS

CAVITY LINER

COOLING TUBES (TYPICAL)

ACCESS PENETRATION

FOUNDATION SUPPORT
RING

FIG. 13.21   *Cutaway view of Prestressed Concrete Reactor Vessel (PCRV).   (Courtesy Gulf General Atomic Company.)*

will be no steam circuit and steam generators, as at Peach Bottom and Fort St. Vrain.   The elevated temperatures for heat rejection offer the possibility of process heating and also for atmospheric heat rejection to avoid thermal pollution of a river or other body of water used as a heat sink.   In this regard the high thermal efficiencies of the plant tend to reduce its heat rejection for a given electrical output.

The fact that the primary fluid circulates through the system means there may be problems with radiation during operation and maintenance, but these are not insurmountable.   Operation of this system at less than half load will be rather inefficient.   Load may be varied between 50 and 100 percent by adding or removing helium to the flow system.   Pressure ratios and temperatures around the circuit, as well as the cycle efficiency are little affected by the addition or subtraction of helium.   At loads less than 50 percent it is necessary to bypass some of the hot gas from the reactor around the turbine through valve V1 shown on Fig. 13.23.   As this gas is much hotter than the turbine exhaust it is necessary to also bypass some gas through valve V2 around the regenerator to keep the reactor inlet temperature constant.   Reactor power required for 50 per-

REACTOR ARRANGEMENT

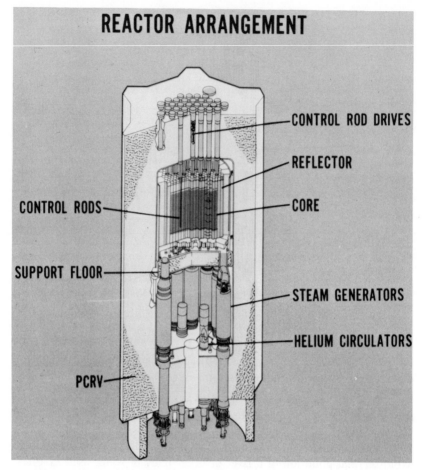

CONTROL ROD DRIVES

REFLECTOR

CONTROL RODS

CORE

SUPPORT FLOOR

STEAM GENERATORS

HELIUM CIRCULATORS

PCRV

FIG. 13.22 *Arrangement of Fort St. Vrain Reactor within PCRV. (Courtesy Gulf General Atomic Company.)*

cent electrical output is 51 percent of full reactor power when the reduction is by inventory depletion, but it is 92 percent when the reduction is accomplished with bypass control.

Serious consideration is being given to gas cooling for fast reactors. The direct cycle offers much in the way of capital cost reduction as the double energy interchange of the sodium cooled fast reactor systems is eliminated. Studies have also been made on a sodium cooled fast reactor coupled to a CO_2 gas turbine cycle for power generation. Carbon dioxide does not react violently with sodium, as does water. Therefore, the cycle is simplified by eliminating the double energy exchange used with sodium-steam power systems.

The choice of working fluid for a gas-cooled reactor must consider

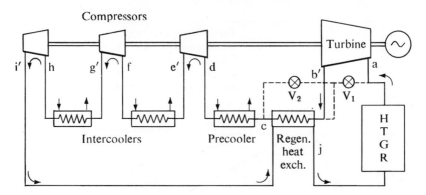

FIG. 13.23 *The KSH 25 MW(e) power cycle.*

the questions of neutron activation, required pressure levels, cost, and the properties of the gas as they affect the cycle performance. The early Magnox reactors in England and France, as well as their successors, the advanced gas-cooled reactors, use carbon dioxide as the coolant. The high temperature gas-cooled reactors are using helium. Figs. 13.24 and 13.25 show how work per pound and thermal efficiencies vary with the ratio

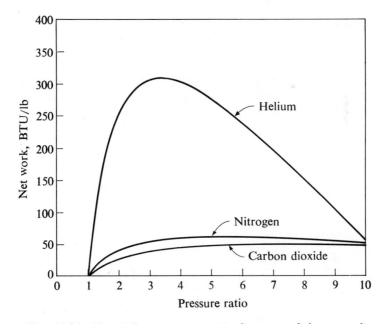

FIG. 13.24 *Net work vs. pressure ratio for gas cooled reactor direct cycle.*

Compressor Eff. = 80%
Turbine Eff. = 85%

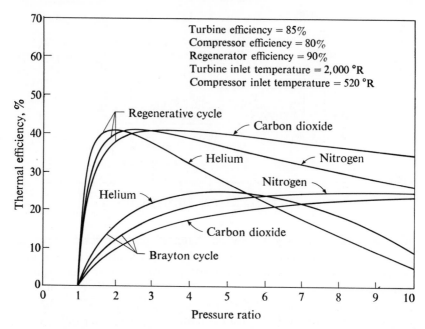

Fig. 13.25 *Effect of pressure ratio on thermal efficiency for gas turbine cycles with and without a regenerator for three working fluids (He, N_2, and CO_2).*

of high side to low side pressure in gas turbine cycles either with or without a heat exchanger for three different working fluids. The choice of helium, nitrogen, and carbon dioxide gives a considerable range of properties which are summarized in Table 13.6.

TABLE 13.6

PROPERTIES OF WORKING FLUIDS USED
IN GAS-COOLED REACTOR COMPARISONS

Gas	Mol. Wt.	k	C_p Btu/lb R
He	4.003	1.66	1.25
N_2	28.016	1.4	0.248
CO_2	44.01	1.285	0.203

Carbon dioxide was chosen for the earlier gas-cooled reactors because of its availability at low cost, its inertness in contact with materials used in the reactor system, and lack of serious activation problems. However, as temperatures increase, dissociation becomes somewhat of a problem. Helium, being inert, monatomic and having no neutron absorption cross section is attractive at high temperatures. It should be noted on Fig. 13.24 that the maximum work per pound for helium occurs at a much lower pressure ratio than CO_2. The nitrogen was chosen as an inert diatomic gas with properties intermediate between the other two.

For an ideal Brayton cycle, the thermal efficiency will continuously increase with pressure ratio. However, when the turbine and compressor efficiencies are considered, and fixed values of turbine and compressor inlet temperatures are used, the efficiency will eventually peak. In Fig. 13.25 this is evident only for the helium, but will eventually occur for the N_2 and CO_2 as well. If a regenerator is incorporated into the ideal cycle with given values of turbine and compressor inlet temperatures the highest efficiency occurs at a pressure ratio of one. The incorporation of efficiencies for the turbine, compressor and regenerator makes the efficiency drop to zero at a pressure ratio of unity, but the efficiency peaks at pressure ratios much lower and at values much higher than for the Brayton cycle with comparable efficiencies for the turbine and compressor. For helium the regenerative cycle efficiency peaks at a pressure ratio of 2.0 and the work per pound peaks at a pressure ratio of 3.25. In the KSH plant, although the cycle is somewhat more complex, the ratio of turbine inlet pressure to exhaust pressure is 2.54 which indicates a design compromise between maximum work and efficiency. Note that the Brayton cycle peaked at an efficiency just under 25 percent at a pressure ratio of 4.75 for the cycle conditions studied compared with 41 percent with the regenerator. The advantage of the regenerator is evident. To attain high thermal efficiencies a large regenerator is required. Some recent studies indicate, if the desired thermal efficiency is reduced somewhat to 30 or 35 percent rather than striving for the 40 to 50 percent which is attainable, the savings in regenerator investment may produce minimum power cost.

HEAVY WATER MODERATED-LIGHT WATER COOLED REACTOR

The Canadian approach to nuclear power couples Canada's supply of uranium ore and abundant hydroelectric power which may be used for heavy water production. The 250 MWe Gentilly Station which went on line in 1971 is natural uranium fueled, light water cooled, and heavy water moderated. The station is shown in Fig. 13.26.

FIG. 13.26   *The 250 MWe Gentilly Nuclear Power Station near Trois Rivieres, Quebec. It is the world's first plant to use natural uranium as fuel and light water as the coolant. The station produced its first electricity early in Feb. 1971. (Courtesy Atomic Energy of Canada Limited.)*

Light water boils in pressure tubes, entering at 920 psia, leaving at 805 psia, and arriving at the turbine at 750 psia and 511°F. A simplified flow diagram for the system is shown in Fig. 13.27. Reactor coolant pumps force the water through 308 vertical coolant channels with the wet steam with 16 percent quality in the present design passing to two steam drums for steam separation before delivery to the high pressure turbine. Between the high and low pressure turbines there are moisture separators and live steam reheaters similar to those described previously for the PWR. The steam cycle also uses seven stages of feedwater heating and attains a thermal efficiency of 34.45 percent.

The high pressure steam is confined to the Zircaloy-4 pressure tubes so the heavy water moderator is contained in a low pressure callandria vessel. The moderator is cool and is separated from the pressure tubes by an annular gas gap between the pressure tube and the callandria tubes. The temperature of the callandria tubes is only 140°F which means neutrons will be slowed to velocities lower than if the moderator were at the temperature of the boiling light water. Thus, the effective fission cross

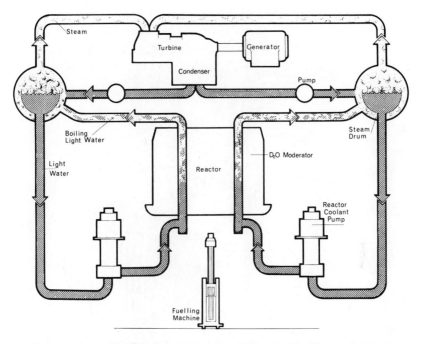

FIG. 13.27 *Simplified flow diagram for Gentilly Nuclear Power Station.* (*Courtesy Atomic Energy of Canada Limited.*)

section of the fuel is larger. Another advantage is that the callandria does not have to stand the high pressures of the working fluid. A picture of the reactor assembly is shown in Fig. 13.28. The region containing the pressure tubes and fuel is surrounded by a heavy water reflector. This is in turn surrounded by a dump annulus. Helium under pressure prevents water flow through a dump port into the annulus and then the dump tank. During a scram, pressure equalization between the helium and the space over the moderator allows the D_2O to be dumped and the reactor to shut down.

The fuel rod bundles shown in Fig. 13.29 are 19.5″ long and contain 18 fuel elements arranged around a central tie rod. The 0.78 inch O.D. rods contain natural UO_2 pellets inside 59 mil Zircaloy-4 cladding. The tie rod joins a string of ten bundles. Refuelling occurs with the reactor on-line when a string of elements is removed and a new set of elements is inserted in the vertical pressure tube from the bottom. The out of core string may have spent bundles removed and replaced by new ones.

The core uses a two zone system of refueling which contributes with

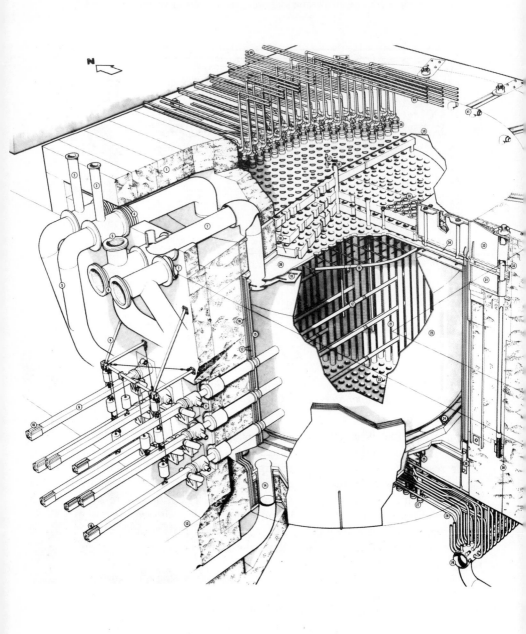

FIG. 13.28 *Reactor assembly for the heavy water moderated-light water cooled Gentilly Reactor.* (*Courtesy Atomic Energy of Canada Limited.*)

1 *Helium pipe penetration shield*
2 *Pressure relief riser*
3 *Helium vent lines*
4 *Bellows*
5 *Vacuum rupture disc*
6 *Outward bursting rupture disc*
7 *Helium balance lines*
8 *Booster drive support frame*
9 *Booster mechanism*
10 *Booster drive*
11 *Moderator inlet, booster cooling*
12 *Booster flow tube*
13 *Grating floor elevation 59' 6"*
14 *Moderator dump lines*
15 *Calandria vessel shell*
16 *Thermal shield vessel shell*
17 *Radial shields*
18 *Upper axial shield slabs*
19 *Spray cooling piping*
20 *Calandria upper tube sheet*
21 *Calandria tubes*
22 *Calandria lower tube sheet*
23 *Reflector boundary shell*
24 *Annular dump port*
25 *Lower axial shields*
26 *Calandria support link*
27 *Lower ending fitting*
28 *Heat transport system inlet feeders*
29 *Heat transport system inlet heads*
30 *Biological shield*
31 *Embedded bearing stool*
32 *Main anchor bolts*
33 *Cantilever beam*
34 *Annular shield slab*
35 *Coolant seal plates*
36 *Control absorber assembly*
37 *Flux monitor*
38 *Upper end fitting*
39 *Thermal shield vessel upper tube sheet*
40 *Outlet feeders*
41 *Helium purge lines*

فریدون باختر

FEREIDOON BAKHTAR

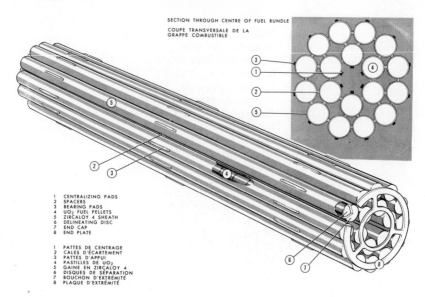

SECTION THROUGH CENTRE OF FUEL BUNDLE
COUPE TRANSVERSALE DE LA GRAPPE COMBUSTIBLE

1 CENTRALIZING PADS
2 SPACERS
3 BEARING PADS
4 UO₂ FUEL PELLETS
5 ZIRCALOY 4 SHEATH
6 DELINEATING DISC
7 END CAP
8 END PLATE

1 PATTES DE CENTRAGE
2 CALES D'ÉCARTEMENT
3 PATTES D'APPUI
4 PASTILLES DE UO₂
5 GAINE EN ZIRCALOY 4
6 DISQUES DE SÉPARATION
7 BOUCHON D'EXTRÉMITÉ
8 PLAQUE D'EXTRÉMITÉ

FIG. 13.29 *Eighteen element fuel bundle for Gentilly Reactor.* (*Courtesy Atomic Energy of Canada Limited.*)

the reflector to flux flattening in the core. The central zone irradiates fuel to a burnup of 10,220 MWd/ton and the outer zone goes only to 7372 MWd/ton. The central zone produces 23 percent of the power and the outer zone produces 77 percent. The ratio of the radial average to peak power is 0.79.

Control is attained through "shimming" with horizontal booster (control) rods and variation of the coolant flow rate. Long term reactivity changes are also compensated by neutron absorbers in the moderator. For rapid shutdown the moderator may be dumped, as indicated previously.

This reactor system hopes to develop low cost power due to

(1) The neutron economy because of the heavy water moderator and the use of Zircalloy-4 as the major structural metal in the core,
(2) The use of natural uranium as a low cost "throw away" fuel,
(3) The replacement of the heavy walled core vessel of the usual light water reactor by the lighter callandria, and
(4) Greater availability due to on-line refueling.

MSBR: A THERMAL BREEDER REACTOR

The Molten Salt Breeder Reactor concept depends on molten fluoride salts containing $^7LiF_2$, BeF_2, ThF_4 and $^{233}UF_4$ being pumped through a graphite moderated core where heat released by fission will raise the salt temperature to 700°C (~1300°F). The heated salt then passes through an intermediate heat exchanger where its enthalpy is reduced by transfer of heat to a secondary salt, sodium fluoroborate, which in turn may transfer the energy to steam which can be generated at modern fossil conditions (say 3500 psia and 1000°F).

Initially a two salt system was favored with a salt containing only fissile UF_4 and no fertile ThF_4. The blanket salt would contain only ThF_4 and no UF_4. Some of the blanket salt would also circulate through the core in separate passageways cut in the moderator blocks. The fuel salt would pass up through graphite fuel tubes, as shown in Fig. 13.30. The fertile salt in the central core region would enhance the conversion of thorium to uranium-233.

The two fluid concept appeared to offer a simple fuel reprocessing scheme as shown in Fig. 13.31. The fuel salt would be fluorinated to

TABLE 13.6

TYPICAL MSBR SALT COMPOSITIONS AND PROPERTIES

| | Two Fluid Core | | Single Fluid Core | Secondary Salt |
	Fuel Salt	Blanket Salt		
Composition, mole %				
$^7LiF_2$	68.75	71.0	71.6	—
BeF_2	31.0	0	16.0	—
UF_4 (fissile)	0.25	0	0.4	—
ThF_4	0	29.0	12.0	—
$NaBF_4$	—	—	—	92.0
NaF_2	—	—	—	8.0
Liquidus Temp., F	840	1050	930	725
Density, lb/ft³			205 (@ 1300F)	117 (@ 988F)
Molecular Wt.	46.3	121.3	64	104
Viscosity, lb/hr ft			16.4 (@ 1300F)	2.5 (@ 900F)
Sp. Heat, Btu/lb F			0.32	0.34
Th. Cond., Btu/hr ft F			0.75	0.27

convert the UF_4 to UF_6 (a gas), allowing the separation of the uranium. The remaining salt could then have the carrier fluorides separated from the fission products by vacuum distillation. The blanket salt would only be fluorinated to remove the bred uranium, since there would be few fission products if the uranium content were kept low. As indicated previously, the graphite fuel tubes would keep the two salt streams from

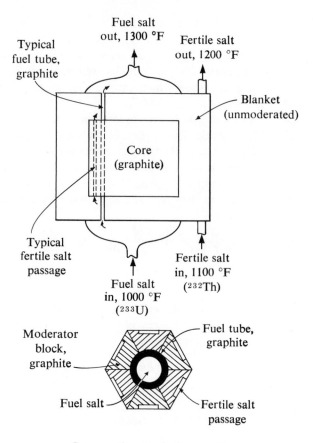

Cross section, typical core cell

FIG. 13.30   *MSBR-I conceptual design for a thermal, two-stream reactor core.* [*From Bauman, H. F., and P. R. Kasten,* Nuclear Applications, **2,** *4 (1966).*]

mixing.   A breeding ratio of 1.07 to 1.08 was predicted for such a system with low fuel costs and small fuel inventories.

As data were accumulated on the dimensional instability of graphite under long term irradiation, it raised the question as to the ability of the graphite piping to stand up under large fluences.   This concern led to the consideration of a single-salt, two-region core with an easily replaceable graphite assembly in the core.   The blanket region in the single-salt core is obtained by increasing the salt fraction from 13 percent to 35–40 percent.   This will make k_∞ for the blanket region less than 1.0.   Fig. 9.15 shows how, as the salt content is increased, the decrease in modera-

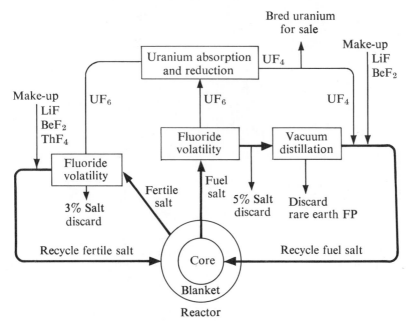

FIG. 13.31 *MSBR fuel processing flow diagram.* [*From Bauman, H. F., and P. R. Kasten, op. cit.*]

tion reduces the resonance escape probability. The thermal utilization factor improves as the salt fraction becomes larger and there is less parasitic neutron capture by the graphite. As the other two terms in the four factor equation do not change, k_∞ will peak at approximately 4 percent salt content and drop below unity at just over 18 percent salt. In a single-salt core the reflector region having a 37 percent salt content will have a subcritical k_∞ of 0.392 and the core region with a 13 percent salt fraction will have $k_\infty = 1.034$. Fig. 13.32 shows a schematic diagram of a single-fluid two-region MSBR.

To effect breeding ^{233}Pa with its 27.4 day half life must be held up outside the core so it can decay to ^{233}U. With ^{233}Pa's $\sigma_a = 43$b neutron capture in the core would produce ^{234}Pa which decays to ^{234}U which is not thermally fissionable. It also reduces the thermal utilization factor and in turn k_∞ and the excess reactivity of the core. A liquid to liquid extraction process shows promise for removal of Pa and U from the molten salts. The Pa is then trapped in salt in a decay tank and the U may be transferred back to the carrier salt by electrolysis for return to the reactor.

Also essential to breeding will be the reduction of ^{135}Xe by a factor

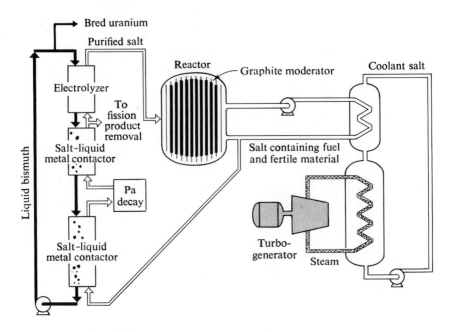

FIG. 13.32 *Schematic flow diagram for a single-salt two-region molten salt breeder reactor. (From Rosenthal, M. W., Kasten, P. R., Briggs, R. B.*, Nuclear Applications & Technology (*now* Nuclear Technology), **8,** *No. 2 (Feb., 1970), p. 110.)*

of 10. This gaseous fission poison has an absorption cross section of 2.72×10^6b. Much of the reduction is accomplished by sparging with helium (bubbling helium through the molten salt). Also there must be a marked reduction in the porosity of the graphite used in the core. This will prevent a significant quantity of ^{135}Xe from diffusing into the pores. It will be necessary to reduce the porosity below 10^{-8} cm²/sec. Impregnating the graphite surfaces with pyrolytic carbon shows promise, but more development and irradiation testing are required to produce the required characteristics in reactor sized graphite blocks.

Capital costs for the MSBR are expected to be comparable to those of LWR's, as shown in Table 13.3. There is an increased cost for remote maintenance due to the circulation of fission products through the primary loop, the fuel reprocessing facilities, and the off gas system. Offsetting this, the cost of a turbo-generator unit is reduced by 17×10^6 for a 1000 MWe plant due to the high thermal efficiency achieved in the steam cycle.

It is the fuel cycle cost which is expected to provide the major cost reduction for this system. Table 13.7 shows a cost breakdown for a single-fluid MSBR. Note that the cost of graphite is a significant item. Using

TABLE 13.7*

FUEL CYCLE COST BREAKDOWN FOR A
SINGLE-FLUID MOLTEN-SALT BREEDER REACTOR**

	Mills/kWh
Fissile inventory	0.26
Thorium inventory	0.01
Carrier salt inventory	0.04
Thorium and carrier salt makeup	0.05
Processing plant fixed charges and operating cost	0.30
Credit for sale of bred material	−0.09
Graphite replacement cost (4-year interval)	0.10
Net fuel cycle cost	0.67

* (*From Rosenthal, M. W., Kasten, P. R., & Briggs, R. B.*, Nuclear Applications & Technology (*now* Nuclear Technology), **8**, *No. 2 (Feb. 1970)*, *p. 111*.)
** At 10% per year inventory charge on material, 13.7% per-year fixed charge rate on processing plant, $13/g ^{233}U, $11.2/g ^{235}U, $12/kg ThO$_2$, $120/kg ^{7}Li, $26/kg carrier salt (including ^{7}Li).

the Th-^{233}U fuel cycle, only thorium makeup is required and there is a credit for the bred uranium which is available for sale.

On balance the inherent safety characteristics of this system appear to be an asset. On the negative side the accumulation of fission products in the primary system, the reprocessing plant, the off gas system, and fuel storage tanks dictate provisions for containment and removal of decay heat under all circumstances. Positively, however, the system has a number of virtues:

(1) the operating conditions of the salt at low pressures and at temperatures more than 1000°F below the boiling temperature,
(2) the ability to drain the salt to tanks with redundant cooling systems,
(3) continuous fission product removal reduces the need for excess reactivity, and
(4) the molten salt has an inherent negative temperature coefficient of reactivity associated with heating.

Table 13.8 indicates some of the principal characteristics expected of a one-fluid two-region MSBR. The high outlet temperature of salt leaving the core (1300°F) will permit the generation of supercritical steam to produce a cycle thermal efficiency of 44 percent. A breeding ratio of 1.05–1.07 is predicted along with a doubling time of 15–25 years. Design studies look forward to the construction of such a reactor during the coming decade.

TABLE 13.8*

CHARACTERISTICS OF ONE-FLUID, TWO-REGION MOLTEN-SALT BREEDER REACTORS

Fuel-fertile salt, mole%	72 ^{7}LiF, 16 BeF$_2$, 12 ThF$_4$, 0.3 UF$_4$
	Melting point, 930°F
Moderator	Graphite (bare)
Salt volume fractions, %	Core, 13; blanket, 40
Core temperatures, °F	Inlet, 1050; outlet, 1300
Reactor power, MW(e)	1000–2000
Steam system	3500 psia, 1000°F, 44% net cycle efficiency
Breeding ratio	1.05–1.07
Specific fissile fuel inventory,[a] kg/MW(e)	1.0–1.5
Doubling time (compound interest),[a] year	15–25
Fuel cycle cost,[a] mills/kWh (including graphite replacement)	0.6–0.7

[a] The lower values are associated with the higher reactor powers.
* (*From Rosenthal, M. W., Kasten, P. R., Briggs, R. B.*, Nuclear Applications & Technology (*now* Nuclear Technology), **8**, *No. 2 (Feb. 1970), p. 111.*)

FAST REACTORS

Fast reactors use no moderator to promote the slowing down of fission neutrons. There is, however, some degradation of neutron energies, with the result that the median energy for the neutron spectrum might lie between 0.1 and 0.5 MeV. This energy loss occurs mainly due to inelastic scattering collisions with atoms of the coolant, structural materials and the fuel material. The coolant for fast reactors is usually sodium, which has excellent heat transfer characteristics. The fuel is enriched uranium or plutonium surrounded by a blanket region containing thorium, natural uranium, or depleted uranium.

The neutron spectrum for a particular reactor is affected by the core size and the combination of materials used. Oxide or carbide fuels will cause a shift of the spectrum to lower energies because of the moderating effect of the oxygen or carbon which is present. Fig. 13.33 shows the spectra calculated for the EBR-I, EBR-II, and PBR reactors. EBR-I was a 1 MW, 6 liter, fast core reactor which used highly enriched uranium, NaK coolant, and stainless steel cladding. EBR-II has a 50 liter core fueled by 50 percent enriched uranium, having sodium as the coolant, and stainless steel for cladding. The Power Breeder Reactor (PBR) has an 800 liter core, fueled by 15 to 20 percent enriched uranium or of a Pu-U^{238} fuel with an output greater than 600 MWth.

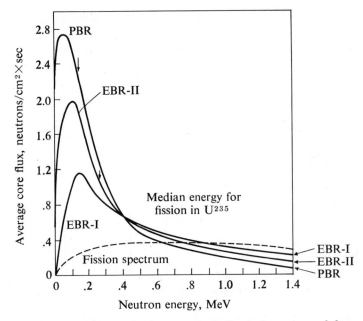

FIG. 13.33 *Comparison of neutron spectra for various sizes of fast reactors.* [*From Okrent, D., R. Avery, and H. H. Hummel, "A Survey of the Theoretical and Experimental Aspects of Fast Reactor Physics,"* Proceedings of the Second United Nations International Conference on the Peaceful Uses of Atomic Energy, *Vol. V, 1955, p. 347.*]

Experimental Breeder Reactor

EBR-II will be used as an example of a successful fast reactor. It produces 62.5 MWth and 20 MWe (gross). Fig. 13.34 shows a schematic diagram for the reactor. Primary sodium circulates through the core, leaving at 880°F. It transfers heat to a secondary sodium coolant loop, which in turn generates steam at 1250 psig and 837°F. The secondary coolant loop prevents the possibility of radioactive sodium coming in contact with water in the steam generator. Note in the diagram that the entire core and primary heat exchanger, along with the sodium circulating pumps, are immersed in molten sodium. This protects the core against large temperature fluctuations due to low power demand or changed conditions in the secondary loop. It also insures against loss of sodium in the core except for the possibility of a rupture in the 8000 gallon tank.

The EBR-II reactor vessel assembly is shown in Fig. 13.35 and a core fuel assembly is shown in Fig. 13.36. The 91 fuel pins are 14.22 inches long and 0.144 inch in diameter. They are located in the central section of the 92-inch assembly. The initial fuel was 49 percent ^{235}U, 46 percent

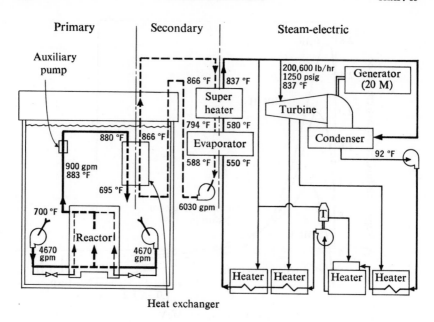

Fig. 13.34 *Simplified flow diagram of the EBR-II power system.* [*From McLain, S., and J. H. Martens,* Reactor Handbook, *Vol. IV, Engineering. New York: Interscience Publishers, 1964.*]

[238]U, and 5 percent fissium. Subsequent loadings will contain up to 20 percent plutonium. The pyrometallurgical reprocessing facilities are adjacent to the reactor, giving a simple reprocessing cycle (see Chapter 11). Above and below the fuel section are 18 rods of depleted uranium which form the upper and lower blankets. These are 0.316 inch in diameter. Surrounding the 61 core assemblies are 12 control assemblies which essentially move fuel in and out of the core to change the sodium to fuel ratio and provide the reactivity of the core. Around the core are inner and outer blanket assemblies of 19 rods, each containing depleted uranium. As neutrons leak from the core proper, many of them are absorbed in the fertile [238]U; this produces plutonium.

Full sodium flow takes place through the core and the inner blanket assemblies, while a reduced flow occurs in the outer blanket. Note that at full power 85.6 percent of the heat is generated in the core, 9.8 percent in the inner blanket, 2.4 percent in the upper and lower blankets, and 2.2 percent in the outer blanket.

As in the thermal reactors, control of fast reactors is dependent upon the delayed neutron fraction. The smaller delayed neutron fraction for [233]U and [239]Pu means that particular attention must be paid to design of the control system when these fuels are used. Prompt neutron lifetimes

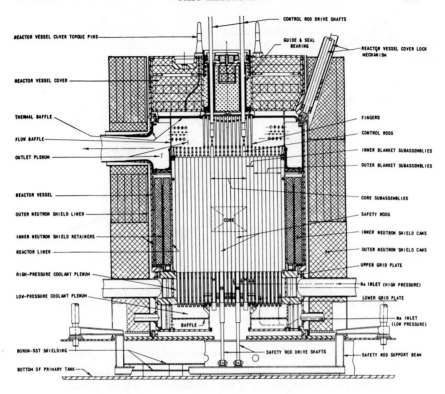

FIG. 13.35 *EBR-II Reactor Vessel Assembly.* [*From McLain, S., and J. H. Martens,* Reactor Handbook, *Vol. IV, Engineering, New York: Interscience Publishers, 1964.*]

are about 10^{-8} seconds for fast reactors, as opposed to 10^{-3} seconds for thermal reactors, which makes prompt criticality even more undesirable for fast reactors. Control may be effected, as in EBR-II, by movement of fuel in or out of the core, by movement of part of the reflector or by conventional control rods. At the higher neutron energies found in a fast reactor core the common thermal neutron poisons do not have very large absorption cross sections.

The sodium presents problems due to its induced radioactivity, its flammability, and its reactivity with water. Operation of components such as pumps, which are completely immersed in molten sodium, is a further problem. Sodium does, however, have excellent heat transfer characteristics. Heat fluxes as high as 929,000 Btu/(hr)(ft²) occur in the core.

The high power density of fast reactor cores (kW per liter) means that particular care must be taken with design. Connected with this is the

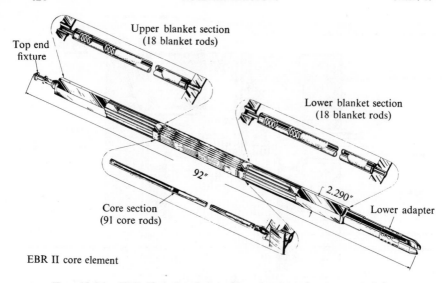

EBR II core element

FIG. 13.36 *EBR-II fuel subassembly, showing the upper and lower blanket sections and core section containing 91 enriched fuel elements.* [*Courtesy Argonne National Laboratory.*]

necessity for providing adequate shutdown cooling and emergency cooling. The high power density also leads to concern that in a power excursion meltdown of the fuel might cause the formation of a critical mass.

Fast Breeder Demonstration Plant

The next step enroute to full scale commercial fast breeder reactors will be the construction of one or more fast breeder demonstration plants during the mid-seventies, looking forward to the introduction of full scale plants by 1980. These plants must show reliability and availability superior to current plants in order to be economically viable. Several manufacturers are designing demonstration plants which, if funded and successfully operated, should lead to 1000 MWe or larger fast breeders.

Typical of these designs is the 500 MWe Atomics International fast breeder reactor, which is shown in Fig. 13.37. This plant utilizes a loop type system where each of the primary elements is located in a separate vault within the containment structure. This contrasts with the pot system where all of the primary elements are submerged in molten sodium in a single vessel, as in EBR-II and the French Phenix Reactors. As there is no clear capital cost or safety advantage of one system over the other, Atomics International felt the mechanical and thermal decoupling of the primary units will allow easier maintenance and also permit changes in the system to be accomplished more simply.

The power cycle is similar to that shown in Fig. 13.35 for EBR-II,

FIG. 13.37 *500 MWe Atomics International LMFBR Demonstration Plant. Reactor is shown in center foreground with the steam generators located in the front of the turbine hall. Note the size of the natural draft cooling tower at the right.* (*Courtesy Atomics International*)

except that the steam pressure is 2400 psig, steam temperature is 900°F at the throttle valve and after the reheater, which has been added between the high and low pressure turbines. Note that the steam temperatures at the throttle and after reheat are about 100°F lower than the 1000°F usually associated with modern fossil stations. Also this plant will use only 4 feedwater heaters instead of the 6 to 8 used with fossil fuels. The low fuel cycle costs change the overall balance between efficiency and capital cost with efficiency becoming less important. Also the reduced temperatures lessen the problems with creep and should improve reliability.

Fig. 13.38 shows the reactor assembly. The cylindrical core has an active diameter of 44 inches and a height of 70 inches. It contains 133 hexagonal fuel assemblies, each containing 271 fuel rods with an outside diameter of 0.27 inches. Axial and radial blanket regions surround the active core. The mixed oxide (UO_2 and PuO_2) fuel is fabricated into pellets of 85 percent theoretical density. The lower than usual density allows improved fission gas retention within the pellets. Eighteen motor driven control rods penetrate the core from the top.

Heat is transported from the core in two parallel heat transfer circuits, each having a primary and a secondary sodium loop. The primary loops are common to the reactor, but the secondaries are not interconnected. The steam generators are of modular design, there being 5 evaporator modules, 2 superheater modules, and 2 reheater modules

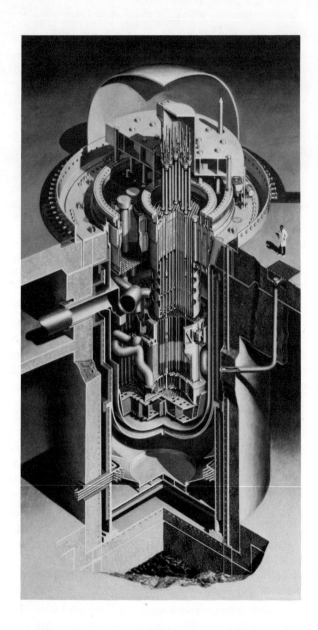

FIG. 13.38   *Cutaway view of LMFBR Reactor (Courtesy Atomics International).*

per loop. The evaporator and superheater modules are identical, but the reheater modules require larger tubes because of the reduced steam pressure.

For this system a fuel burnup of 75,000 MWd/ton is expected with a breeding ratio of 1.25 to 1.30 and a doubling time of 15 years. Sodium will leave the core at 1060°F and return at 760°F.

Extrapolation to a 1000 MWe size will require a modest increase in reactor vessel diameter from 24 to 29 feet, 256 fuel assemblies instead of 133, and four heat transfer loops instead of two. The steam generator modules will be identical with those in the demonstration plant. It is expected that the initial full sized fast breeders should show an economic advantage of 0.2 to 0.3 mill per KWhr over contemporary light water reactors. Advanced designs might improve this advantage to 0.5 to 0.6 mill per KWhr.

THERMAL DISCHARGES

Although power plants have always discharged significant amounts of heat to their surroundings, the problem has become more serious with the advent of nuclear plants for several reasons.

(1) The size of plants has jumped to be in excess of 1000 MWe. The size of fossile units has kept pace, but the capability to produce these large capacities developed during the 1960's.

(2) The efficiency of light water nuclear plants is lower (30 to 33%) than that of modern fossile units (40 to 42%) due to the use of lower pressure saturated steam in the nuclear units. For the same electrical output the less efficient plant will reject more heat to its heat sink.

(3) Fossile plants discharge 10% or more of their heat directly up the stack to the atmosphere, where the entire heat rejection load must be born by the condenser in a nuclear plant.

Adequate provision must be made to handle the rejected heat without adversely affecting ecological conditions in the vicinity of the plant. For a 1000 MWe plant Fig. 13.39 shows the massive cooling water flow rates (gallons per minute) required for both an LWR and an LMFBR (or HTGR) where the efficiencies are assumed to be 33.3 percent and 40 percent respectively. The advantage of using an LMFBR or HTGR, where the higher peak temperatures permit greater thermal efficiency, is evident. There is 25 percent less heat rejection for the more efficient plant. If both plants were designed for a 20°F temperature rise for the condenser cooling water, the LWR would require 684,000 gpm while the LMFBR would require only 512,000 gpm. If the LMFBR used a flow of 684,000 gpm its cooling water would rise only 15°F.

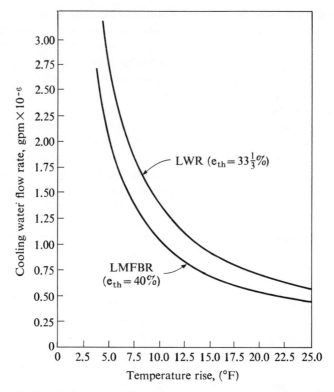

Fig. 13.39 *Cooling water flow rates vs. temperature rise for an LWR and an LMFBR each having an output of 1000 MWe.*

As greater flows are used the impact on aquatic life is lessened, but the size and cost of cooling equipment (condensers, pumps, piping, etc.) increases rapidly. On the other hand reduced flows will raise temperatures to the point where there may be ecological damage done to aquatic life if direct discharge to a water body is permitted. Ecological surveys must be made early in the planning at any plant site in order to know how best to handle the discharge of waste heat to the surroundings. In the case of the Merriman study for the Connecticut Yankee Plant, (41) data were accumulated for three years prior to plant operation in order to provide a comparative base for subsequent observations.

Accumulating meaningful biological data is a tedious and painstaking process, complicated by the diversity of aquatic animal and plant life to be studied, each with its own responses to a change in its environmental conditions. For fish the temperatures which induce optimum growth vary with the species; for brook trout it is 59°F, for northern pike it is 70°F, and the optimum for large mouth bass is 81°F. Thus, a temperature producing optimum growth for northern pike will be lethal to brook trout and suboptimal for large mouth bass. Also to be considered are the temperatures and temperature changes which may trigger the reproductive process. No two sites will have identical conditions and each must be very carefully surveyed to be sure no serious ecological damage will be caused. If such damage does occur, the thermal discharge may truly be called thermal pollution.

Here it might be noted that there may be beneficial effects of the warm discharge from a power plant. There have been numerous reports of improved sports fishing at the outfall of many plants in the fall, winter, and spring months. The warm discharge from nuclear plants is being considered to stimulate oyster production in Long Island Sound, to increase the growth rate of lobsters in Maine, and for shrimp aquaculture in Florida. District heating and cooling using low level heat have been studied and experiments are underway using warm water for the irrigation of crops. In many areas streams have been impounded to create ponds or lakes for heat dissipation. These almost invariably support a sizeable fish population and provide other recreational opportunities.

Careful attention must be given to the means chosen for rejection of heat from a large power station, giving attention to technical feasibility, economics, and its social and ecological impact. There are several schemes which may be considered for dissipation of waste heat.

1) Mixing Followed by Remote and Gradual Dissipation

A typical temperature rise for cooling water passing through a condenser is 18°F, but for a particular site the maximum allowable temperature rise at discharge may be 5°F. For the 1000 MW LWR discussed previously this would require 2.73×10^6 gpm instead of 0.754×10^6 gpm. Rather than building a bigger condenser to accommodate this flow, it is simpler to bypass the extra two million gallons per minute and allow it to mix with the condenser effluent prior to discharge. Alternatively the discharge system may employ diffusers to promote mixing of the effluent with the passing current within a limited mixing zone to achieve the desired 5°F temperature rise. Because of the small temperature differential between the water and the atmosphere, a rather large surface area will be required to return the water to ambient conditions.

2) Rapid Local Dissipation Using Open Water Bodies

Here the natural buoyance of the heated water allows it to rise to the surface and exchange heat more rapidly with the atmosphere due to its higher temperature. Both sensible and latent heat transfer are more rapid. A study (32) indicates that only half as much area is required to return heated water to within 1°F of ambient when an 18°F temperature rise is allowed instead of a 5°F rise. With proper outfall design the warmed water will spread over the surface area, having little effect on the aquatic life more than a few feet below the surface. Either natural or man made water bodies will require an appropriate mixing and dissipation zone in which the majority of the heat dissipation may take place. Beyond this zone temperature standards can be applied.

3) Seasonal Heat Storage in Water Bodies for Dissipation in Cool Weather

Some bodies of water have considerable temperature stratification during the summer months. If volumes of water are sufficient, cool water may be drawn from the lower levels, discharged from the condenser at temperatures well below the surface temperature, and returned to the body of water. This returned water will tend to seek a level underneath the warm surface layer and remain there until fall. When its temperature becomes greater than that of the surface water, it will rise and belatedly transfer its stored energy to the atmosphere. During the cooler seasons the heated water cools promptly at the surface.

4) Wet Cooling Towers and Spray Ponds

In some locations the size of the water body available or the ecological circumstances demand a water temperature unattainable by any of the previous methods. Evaporative cooling by wet cooling towers or spray ponds may then provide an appropriate solution. The spray pond is more or less a cross between the cooling tower and the cooling pond where a limited surface area in contact with the atmosphere is increased by water sprays. In the cooling tower (see Fig. 13.40) water is pumped to spray nozzles atop a latticework of redwood slats. The water droplets are interrupted by the latticework and the water is held up as it runs down the slats, reforms new drops, lands on another slat, etc., until it reaches the bottom of the tower. All the while sensible heat transfer between the water and air is taking place due to temperature difference and mass transfer (evaporation) takes place due to the difference in vapor pressure between that for saturated water at the surface of the water droplets or films and that of the water vapor in the air flowing upward counter to the water. Air flow may be due to natural convection where the heated air is less dense than the ambient air. These are huge hyperbolic structures, some having a base diameter in excess of 300 feet and a height of 450 feet or more (see Fig. 13.41). Induced draft fans may be used in much smaller towers to increase the air flow, but they do add the cost of the fan and the power to operate it. For nuclear plants the natural draft tower costs $10 to $14 per KW and the wet mechanical draft tower costs

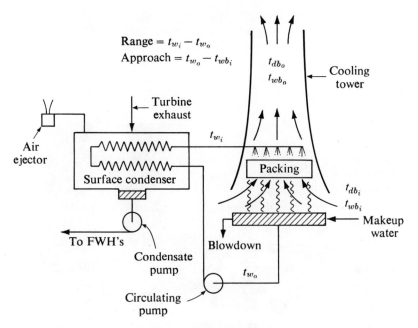

FIG. 13.40 *Wet cooling tower using natural draft and a closed cooling water system.*

$7 to $10 per KW (34). At $10 per KW for a 1000 MW plant this amounts to $10,000,000.

The cooled water from the tower may be recirculated in a closed system or it may operate as an open system with the cooled water being returned to the body of water being used as the coolant source. It is well to remember that the order of 5 percent of the water flow is required for evaporation and blow down. In the winter months the evaporative loss may produce fog and icing conditions in the vicinity of the plant. Often where insufficient river flows dictate the use of cooling towers during the warm months of the year, it may be more appropriate to use once through cooling during the cold weather to prevent fog and icing.

In a wet cooling tower the drop in water temperature as it falls through the tower is called the range. The difference between the leaving water temperature and the inlet wet bulb temperature is the approach. If a tower were to have an infinitely large water-to-air heat transfer surface area the temperature of the leaving water, t_{wo}, would approach the wet bulb temperature of the air, t_{wb} and the approach would be zero. The ability of the wet cooling tower to approach the wet bulb temperature rather than the dry bulb temperature gives it a distinct advantage over

FIG. 13.41 *Natural draft cooling towers at Rancho Seco #1 shown during construction.* (*Courtesy Sacramento Municipal Utility District.*)

the air cooled condenser or dry cooling tower where the outlet water temperature must approach the inlet dry bulb temperature of the cooling air.

5) *Dry Cooling Tower*

Where water supplies are insufficient for a wet cooling tower the only alternative becomes a dry cooling tower.

The German GEA system is essentially an air cooled condenser where a fan forces air to flow across the finned condenser tubes which are located within the tower. This system has been applied in Europe to units as large as 120 MW, but because of the size of the pipes required to convey the exhaust steam to the cooling coils of the condenser it is doubtful that this system will be effective for large nuclear stations.

The Heller system, however, is not so limited. It is shown in Figure

13.42. Here a jet or spray type condenser is used at the turbine exhaust. In this closed system the cooling water and condensate mix as the cool water returning from the dry cooling tower sprays into the exhaust steam causing condensation and a rise in temperature of the cooling water toward the saturation temperature at the condensing pressure. Feedwater is pumped toward the reactor through the feedwater heaters while the circulating pump returns the cooling water to the tower. The cooling tower may use either natural draft or induced draft (as shown in Fig. 13.42). A steam driven air ejector helps maintain the vacuum by removing air and other noncondensible gases. The main circulating pump maintains the water in the tower at a positive pressure to prevent air

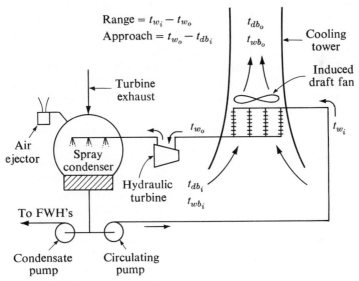

Range $= t_{w_i} - t_{w_o}$

Approach $= t_{w_o} - t_{db_i}$

t_{db_o}

t_{wb_o}

Cooling tower

Induced draft fan

Turbine exhaust

Air ejector

Spray condenser

t_{w_o}

t_{w_i}

Hydraulic turbine

t_{db_i}

t_{wb_i}

To FWH's

Condensate pump

Circulating pump

FIG. 13.42 *Dry cooling tower using the Heller system with induced draft.*

leakage into the system. Some of the pump work may be recovered by a hydraulic turbine after the water leaves the tower on the way to the jet sprays in the condenser.

Condensing pressure and temperatures using a dry cooling tower will tend to be significantly higher and more variable than for a wet tower or a once through system. To accommodate the higher pressures, perhaps as high as 10 in. Hg compared to the usual values of $1\frac{1}{2}$ to 3 in. Hg, a smaller last stage annulus area will be required in the low pressure turbine. During the cooler months when lower pressures are possible this will penalize the turbine performance somewhat. Because of the more variable performance from this type of system it is important that economics be studied from the point of view of the unit being integrated into the system, rather than as a base loaded unit.

A dry cooling tower imposes a severe economic penalty on a nuclear plant with the cost estimated at $35 to $45 per KW (34). This cost is about the same as that for the turbine-generator or the cost of the reactor. If the cost were taken as $40 per KW, it would mean an investment of $40,000,000 for a 1000 MW plant. As more plants are built and suitable sites become scarcer dry cooling towers may be the only answer.

LOSS OF COOLANT ACCIDENTS

One of the principal concerns in any reactor safety analysis is the ability of the system to cope with a loss of coolant accident (LOCA). This is assumed to occur by the rupture of one of the lines leading to or from the core vessel, allowing the coolant to be discharged into the containment. In such an accident it is imperative that fission products be prevented from leaking from the containment in any significant quantity. Probably the worst of these are the iodine isotopes because of their volatility and bodily uptake with concentration in the thyroid.

Fig. 13.43 shows a schematic diagram of a spray system used with a PWR to provide emergency cooling and control of fission products, particularly the iodine. The decay heat pump floods the core with borated water to insure subcriticality and to provide for decay heat removal.

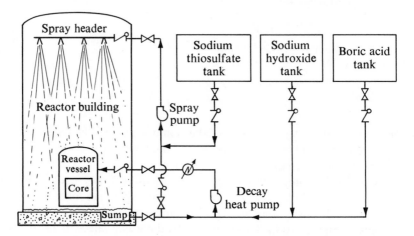

Fig. 13.43 *Schematic diagram of reactor building spray system.* (*From Bishop, W. N. and Nitti, D. A.*, Reactor Technology, **10,** *No. 4* (*April, 1971*), *p. 451.*)

Also sodium hydroxide is added to control the pH. It must be high enough to encourage molecular iodine absorption and low enough to discourage corrosion (7 < pH < 10). Sodium thiosulfate may be added to remove methyliodide. As can be seen in Figure 13.43, once the borated water and NaOH tanks have been emptied both the spray pumps and the decay heat pumps will recirculate the water from a sump in the reactor building with the sodium thiosulfate reaching the core at this time. In the B&W system the sump will attain an accumulated dose of 10^8 rads in 30 days and 2×10^8 rads in 180 days, primarily from the absorbed iodine. Activity in the containment atmosphere will be primarily due to noble gases. Zircaloy-4, inconels, and stainless steels are not seriously corroded by these solutions. The use of aluminum and copper is restricted because of corrosion when immersed in the spray solution.

Loss of coolant accidents pose an even more serious problem in LMFBR's for several reasons:

(1) The specific power (KW/liter) is approximately ten times that in an LWR. Thus, the temperature rise will be much more rapid during a loss of coolant accident.

(2) Cladding temperatures are higher (1100–1300°F) compared to LWR's (600–700°F). To compound this the melting temperature for stainless cladding proposed for fast reactors has a lower melting temperature than the Zircaloy used in many LWR's.

(3) With loss of coolant and melting of fuel it is doubtful the LWR could achieve a critical array, but in the LMFBR loss of coolant and melting or rearrangement of the fuel may achieve a supercritical configuration. A molten critical mass of fuel might melt through the containment and keep going downward (the China syndrome).

(4) Release of iodine would be serious, as in the LWR, but the large plutonium inventory in the core presents an even greater hazard due to its toxicity. Thus, the LMFBR may require larger exclusion areas and low-population zones.

The pool concept used in EBR-II has its core, primary pumps, primary piping, and intermediate heat exchangers submerged in molten sodium. There are no subsurface penetrations of the tank wall. A second tank or a minimum volume vault may surround the primary tank to contain the sodium in the unlikely event of a primary tank rupture. It will contain the sodium at a level sufficient to keep the core covered. Dip tubes should stop at a high enough level to prevent siphoning liquid sodium from the core. Natural circulation is limited and some forced circulation may be required. A G. E. design study has indicated that natural circulation may be sufficient. It is proposed that in the event of a core meltdown with the burnthrough of a critical mass that the accident could be contained. Dilution by a sacrificial barrier, such as concrete, and the enlargement of the molten pool would provide both a temperature reduction and tend to reduce reactivity to a subcritical configuration followed by solidification.

The loop-type LMFBR has an advantage in that greater heads are available to encourage natural circulation. However, a secondary containment must surround all components of the primary system. A LOCA may require positive action with respect to pump operation, valve closure, etc., to prevent serious consequences.

If sodium loss can be prevented, it appears that reliable emergency core cooling will be possible for LMFBR's.

PUMPED STORAGE

Pumped storage plants are being constructed in order to have large nuclear power stations base loaded continually and at the same time to give a utility system a readily available large block of peaking power. During off peak hours a pump-turbine operates as a motor driven pump. Water is discharged to an upper reservoir and stored until peaking power is required. During that part of the day when peak load occurs on the system flow is reversed and water flows back to the lower reservoir. The pump-turbine now functions as a turbine driving an electric generator to provide the peaking power.

The Northfield Mountain Pumped Storage Project on the Connecticut River at Northfield, Mass. is an excellent example of such a plant. Here four Francis type pump-turbines deliver water against a head, depending on the difference in reservoir levels, of 730–825 feet. When generating the net operating heads are 720–825 feet. Each machine has a nominal capacity of 250 MW, giving the plant a total output of 1000 MW.

The massive size of the project is indicated by the dimensions of the powerhouse cavern which contains the machinery. It is 328 feet long by 70 feet wide by 120 feet high. It is reached through an access tunnel which is 26 ft by 26 ft and 2450 ft long. The pressure shaft carrying the water from the upper reservoir down to the turbine is 31 ft in diameter and 850 ft long, while the tailrace tunnel out to the river is a 33 ft diameter horseshoe 5200 ft long.

At this site and in the adjacent State Forest in excess of $4,000,000 are being spent by Northeast Utilities and the state and federal governments in a joint development of new recreational facilities. Included are boat launching areas, facilities for fishing, swimming, and camping, as well as trails for hiking, snowmobiling, and horseback riding. With a growing population increased recreational opportunities are equally as important as power if we are to achieve an increased quality of life.

DUAL PURPOSE POWER-DESALINATION REACTORS

Large reactors designed with the dual objectives of developing low cost electrical power and inexpensive fresh water from sea water are attractive in areas where adequate fresh water supplies are not readily available from natural sources. An 1800 MWe-150 million gallon per day dual purpose plant has been proposed for the Metropolitan Water District, just south of Long Beach, California. Fig. 13.44 shows the proposed plant on the 40 acre man-made Bolsa Island. Fig. 13.45 shows the arrangement of the two reactors with three turbine generator sets. Two of the units run condensing in the conventional manner, while the third low pressure turbine exhausts at a back pressure to the brine heaters of the desalting plant.

A multistage flash desalting plant was chosen because it should produce fresh water at the least cost and because this concept was the most highly developed at the time of selection. A flow diagram for the MWD plant is shown in Fig. 13.46. Enthalpy from the exhaust of the back pressure turbine is transferred to the brine in the brine heaters, warming the liquid from 235°F to 250°F. The brine then passes through 49 stages of the heat recovery section, a small fraction of the warm liquid being evaporated in each section. This flashed vapor is condensed on the tubes carrying the recycled brine in the opposite direction to the brine heater. The fresh condensate flows successively through all 53 stages, being cooled as it flows from stage to stage and leaving with a final temperature of 78°F. In the last four stages raw sea water provides the cooling before it enters the atmospheric degassing tank where sulphuric acid is added for scale control. It then discharges into the brine sump where the majority of the brine is recycled to the heat recovery section. Some acid is dumped through the brine blow-down.

The water plant will have a performance ratio of 10.6 pounds product water per 1000 Btu of steam. The fresh water cost is estimated at 27¢ per 1000 gallons delivered at the filtration plant. At this price one can fill a bathtub to overflowing for 2¢.

In the studies made for this MWD Dual Purpose Plant comparison was made of power and water costs for nuclear fuel as opposed to a gas-oil fired plant. The water costs were 26.5¢ per 1000 gallons for nuclear fuel and 33¢ per 1000 gallons for the fossil fired plant. Electrical costs were 3.05 mills per kW hr for nuclear fuel and 4.05 mills for fossil fuel. This clearly illustrates the advantage for nuclear power for this large dual purpose plant.

Although the Bolsa Island Dual Purpose Plant has not been funded, it is still under consideration. A more recent study on a "Nuplex" Center for Puerto Rico is an even more ambitious proposal. It would

FIG. 13.44 *Bolsa Island Dual-Purpose Plant.* [*From Homer, W. A., and H. T. Holtom, Combination Nuclear Power and Desalting Plant, Engineering and Economic Feasibility Study, AMU-ANL 5th Annual Student-Faculty Conference, August, 1966.*]

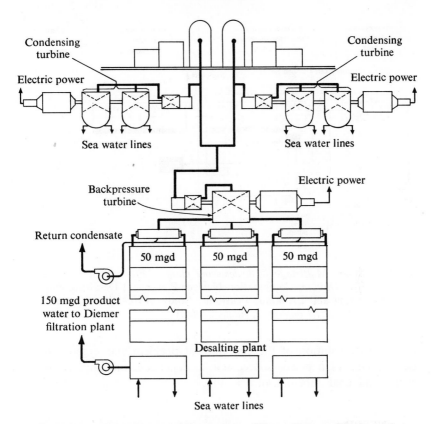

FIG. 13.45 *Dual-purpose plant concept.* [*From Homer, W. A., and H. T. Holtom,* **Combination Nuclear Power and Desalting Plant, Engineering and Economic Feasibility Study,** *AMU-ANL 5th Annual Student-Faculty Conference, August, 1966.*]

be a 650×10^6 multipurpose nuclear-industrial complex which would include a 540 MWe nuclear plant producing electricity and 20 million gallons per day of fresh water from a desalination plant. Electricity and water would be supplied to various petro-chemical industries and possibly an aluminum plant in the complex.

FUSION REACTORS

With experimental work on the containment of plasmas proceeding in a hopeful manner much attention is being given to other aspects of the development of fusion power such as engineering, environmental problems, and economics. This is a measure of the newfound confidence in

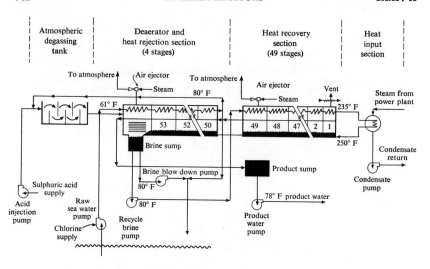

FIG. 13.46 *Multistage flash desalting plant.* [*From Homer, W. A., and H. T. Holtom,* Combination Nuclear Power and Desalting Plant, Engineering and Economic Feasibility Study, *AMU-ANL 5th Annual Student-Faculty Conference, August, 1966.*]

the ultimate solution of the containment problem and urgency for the development of a power source not so dependent on limited resources such as oil, coal, thorium, or uranium.

ENGINEERING

The probable fuel choice for the first reactors will be deuterium and tritium, which when joined by fusion produce 17.6 MeV shared as 14.1 MeV by a neutron and 3.5 MeV by an alpha particle. It will be burned in a closed torroidal system with the neutrons escaping from the plasma through a vacuum wall into a coolant surrounded by more coolant and moderator, neutron shielding, and finally the coils of a superconducting magnet. Fig. 13.47 shows a conceptual drawing of such a Molten Lithium Fusion Breeder Reactor (MLFBR) less containment domes and hot cells for handling. The inset shows the blanket cross-section.

The most severe radiation damage problem occurs in the vacuum chamber wall where a flux the order of 3.7×10^{15} neutrons per cm^2 sec with an energy of 14 MeV passes through the wall. Here the problem occurs at the boundary of the plasma where in a fission reactor both fuel and structure occupy the volume where neutrons are produced. In the fusion reactor the designer has control over the surface area to volume ratio.

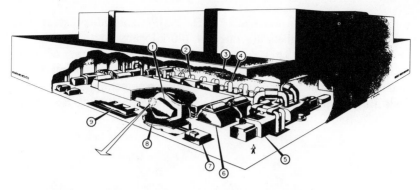

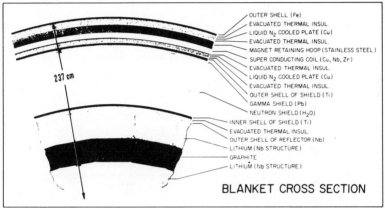

OUTER SHELL (Fe)
EVACUATED THERMAL INSUL.
LIQUID N_2 COOLED PLATE (Cu)
EVACUATED THERMAL INSUL.
MAGNET RETAINING HOOP (STAINLESS STEEL)
SUPER CONDUCTING COIL (Cu, Nb, Zr)
EVACUATED THERMAL INSUL.
LIQUID N_2 COOLED PLATE (Cu)
EVACUATED THERMAL INSUL.
OUTER SHELL OF SHIELD (Ti)
GAMMA SHIELD (Pb)
NEUTRON SHIELD (H_2O)
INNER SHELL OF SHIELD (Ti)
EVACUATED THERMAL INSUL.
OUTER SHELL OF REFLECTOR (Nb)
LITHIUM (Nb STRUCTURE)
GRAPHITE
LITHIUM (Nb STRUCTURE)

237 cm

BLANKET CROSS SECTION

1　PLASMA

2　VESSEL VACUUM SYSTEM

3　BLDG. SERVICE AND MAINTENANCE AREA

4　CRYOGENIC SYSTEMS

5　STEAM TURBINES AND GENERATORS

6　POTASSIUM TURBINES AND
　　HEAT EXCHANGERS

7　TRITIUM REMOVAL SYSTEM

8　FUSION REACTOR

9　INJECTOR POWER SUPPLY

FIG. 13.47　*Conceptual drawing of a fusion power plant with the blanket cross section shown in the inset.*　(*From Postma, H.,* Nuclear News, **14,** *4 (1971).*)

Fig. 13.48 shows the size of a 5000 MWt torroidal reactor. The superconducting magnets are rated at 100 kilogauss at the coils, would cost approximately $200 $\times$ 10^6, and store 10^5 megajoules of energy which require six hours to charge or discharge in a non-catastrophic manner due to their inductance. The superconducting Nb$_3$ Sn·Nb Ti coils must be maintained superconducting at 4°K by boiling He.

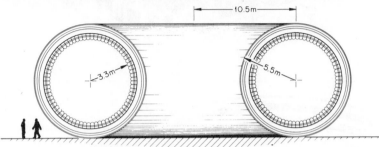

FIG. 13.48   *Torroidal fusion reactor for a 5000 MWt plant.* (*From Postma, H.*, Nuclear News, **14,** *4* (*1971*).)

The deuterium required for fuel is available from seawater and is almost inexhaustible, but the tritium must be bred from ^{6}Li (*n, α*)*t* and ^{7}Li (*n, αn'*)*t* reactions where the former reaction has a 1/*v* cross section below 0.3 MeV and the latter has a threshold of 2.8 MeV. The ^{6}Li reaction produces about 2/3 of the tritium where the balance is from ^{7}Li. Steiner has shown that with the ORNL blanket design (see Fig. 13.49) that a breeding ratio of 1.33 is possible using Li as the coolant and Nb as the structural material. Breeding would be required during the initial phases of an expanding fusion economy, but once equilibrium is established the breeding ratio may be reduced.

The heat developed in the coolant is transported from the core to a lithium-potassium heat exchanger where the potassium boils and acts as the topping fluid in a binary steam cycle having possible thermal efficiencies as great as 58 percent. The tritium will diffuse into the potassium cycle where it must be trapped out and kept from either leaking or getting into the steam cycle. One challenge is to keep the radioactive tritium from leakage less than .0001 percent per day.

ENVIRONMENTAL CONCERNS

There are three principal environmental concerns with fusion reactors:

(1)   high neutron flux and activation of the structure;
(2)   creation, separation, and confinement of tritium, and
(3)   waste disposal.

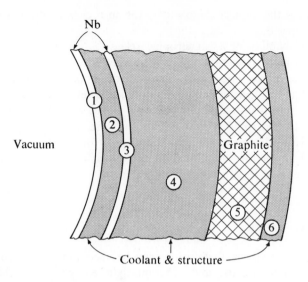

FIG. 13.49 *The standard configuration of the ORNL blanket designs.*

Region no.	Description of region	Thickness (cm)	Composition
1	First wall	0.5	Nb
2	Coolant & structure	3.0	94% Li or Flibe 6% Nb
3	Second wall	0.5	Nb
4	Coolant & structure	60.0	94% Li 6% Nb
5	Moderator− reflector	30.0	Graphite
6	Coolant & structure	6.0	94% Li 6% Nb

Activity due to the flux of approximately 4×10^{15} n/cm² sec for 14 MeV fusion neutrons will amount to a decay power of ∼0.2 percent (10 MWt) and a decay time of 35 days. This is not bad when compared to LMFBR where the activity might be 10^{10} curies with a decay time of 13.6 years.

Note the modular design in Fig. 13.47 which is intended to make replacements simpler. Molybdenum and vanadium are being considered as alternate materials. The vanadium is attractive as it will have only 1/10 the after heat and 1/1000 the waste disposal problem as Nb.

The major environmental problem will be tritium containment. Under normal operations the inplant radioactivity must be less than

30 percent of the natural radioactivity (36 m rem/yr) with leakage kept below 10^{-6} per day.

The probability of a catastrophic release is small with the relative hazards considerably less than for a fission reactor.

At some future time if all power were developed by fusion (6×10^6 MWe) with a 10^{-6} leakage rate, there would be a release of 4×10^7 Ci/yr. If assumed, mixed with air and water on a global scale there would be an activity of 10^{-6} μCi/cm^3 which is 1/500 the dose from natural radiation.

The waste disposal problems will depend on the structure and its lifetime which in turn is related to activation and radiation damage. Also tritium must be kept away from water.

FUSION BY LASER

It has been shown that fusion may be accomplished by an intense beam of monochromatic and coherent light energy from a laser. A neodymium glass laser with suitable amplification can produce, when focused, a power density of 10^{17} watts per cm^2. Fig. 13.50 shows how a single pulse may be extracted from a train of pulses and be shaped. The shaping permits the low power leading edge to vaporize the fuel droplet prior to the heating of the main pulse which induces fusion. The energy release will far exceed that required to drive the laser and to recycle and condense (or freeze) the unused fuel along with any bred tritium.

Some concepts would try to restrain the plasma by a magnetic field. However, it has been shown that fusion can be induced in a plasma expanding freely in a vacuum.

The laser pulse must be absorbed in the expanding plasma (inverse bremsstrahlung) where the absorbed energy is transferred to electrons. The electrons then transfer energy to the heavier positive ions present in the expanding plasma, which takes the order of 10^{-11} sec. Also the pulse must not exceed the time for the plasma to expand to the point where it is too dilute to absorb the radiation (a few nanoseconds). Thus a pulse with a duration of 10^{-10} sec will be bracketed by these two times. Fig. 13.51 shows how a pulse of laser energy is absorbed in an expanding plasma.

One fusion reactor concept for central station power has been proposed by workers at the Oak Ridge National Laboratory. It is shown in Fig. 13.52. In this concept frozen pellets of deuterium-tritium are injected into a vacuum in the vortex of a swirling pool of molten lithium. A pulse of laser energy ignites the pellet at the midplane, releasing fusion energy. The blast energy is attenuated in the lithium by gas bubbles introduced through the ring at the bottom of the pressure vessel. Also

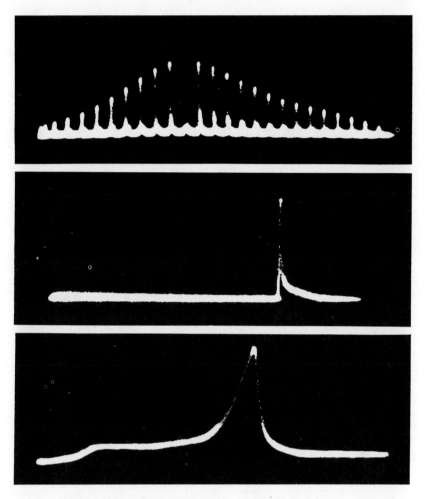

FIG. 13.50 *Tailoring of a laser pulse. Upper trace shows a train of laser pulses with one pulse removed. The extracted pulse (center) is shown after amplification. The pulse is then shaped (bottom) with a leading edge to vaporize the fuel prior to heating by the main pulse to produce fusion. (By permission Laboratory for Laser Energetics, University of Rochester.)*

the primary shock wave travels up the long jagged injection port where the irregular profile will break the normal shock into many oblique waves to cause the attenuation.

The energy is transported by the lithium to a heat exchanger to provide a heat source for a thermal cycle. A conventional steam cycle might attain a 40 percent efficiency, but if a potassium-steam binary cycle were

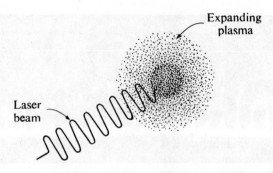

FIG. 13.51   *Absorption of a laser pulse by an expanding plasma.   The amplitude of the oscillating electric field decreases rapidly as it is absorbed in the surface layer of the plasma.*

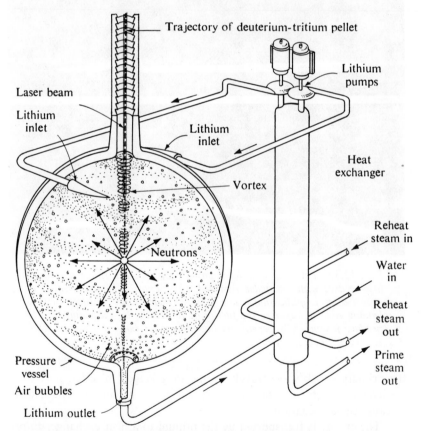

FIG. 13.52   *Proposed fusion reactor where fusion takes place in an expanding laser heated plasma.* (From "Fusion by Laser" by M. J. Lubin and A. P. Fraas. *Scientific American,* Volume 224, **No. 6** (June 1971). Copyright © 1971 by Scientific American, Inc. All rights reserved.)

used with an 1800°F peak lithium temperature, the efficiency could reach 58 percent.

It has been estimated that the pressure vessel for a unit with a 40 percent efficient steam cycle and a 60,000 KW output would cost $10/KW. The balance of the capital cost for the steam cycle should be equivalent to a conventional plant. The equipment for fuel recovery and pellet fabrication would be a small fraction of the total cost. A fuel cost of 3¢ per 10^6 Btu can be compared to 40¢ per 10^6 Btu for fossil fuel and 15¢ per 10^6 Btu for nuclear fuels. Thus, if the development problems can be overcome, this type of fusion reactor appears very attractive from an economic point of view.

FUSION-FISSION SYMBIOSIS

In a hybrid fusion-fission system, fusion neutrons would be used to breed plutonium from ^{238}U or ^{233}U from thorium. The fusion reactor blanket would contain a subcritical amount of fertile material and breed fissionable material for a thermal fission reactor. A fissile doubling time of five years might be possible in a hybrid system with the fuel being burned in a molten salt converter.

For the future there will be a multitude of challenges which must be faced by the engineer, whether it is in the development of advanced fission reactors, fusion reactors, or, as suggested above, a combination of the two.

PROBLEMS

1. A dual cycle BWR generates 1.4×10^6 lb/hr dry saturated steam at 1000 psia. 25×10^6 lb/hr of saturated water is recycled through the secondary steam generator to produce 1.2×10^6 lb/hr secondary steam at 580 psia. Condensation takes place at 2-1/2″ Hg. The efficiency of each section of the turbine is 80 percent and all pumps are 60 percent efficient. Steam is bled from the turbine at 300 psia and 50 psia to closed feedwater heaters located in both the primary and secondary feed lines (see sketch below). Water leaving both high temperature heaters is at 400°F and is heated to 250°F in the low temperature heaters. All condensate from the heaters is trapped back to the condenser.

    The primary feed pump discharges water at 1030 psia and there is a 10 psia pressure drop through each heater and also a 10 psia drop between the last heater and the steam separator. The secondary feed pump discharges at 610 psia and there are pressure losses of 10 psia through each feedwater heater and the secondary steam generator. The recirculation pump discharges at 1050 psia and there is a 25 psia pressure drop in the high pressure side of the secondary steam generator.

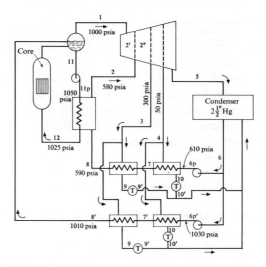

Determine:

(1) The enthalpy at all points in the cycle. Also, sketch the cycle neatly on the TS diagram.

(2) The total amount of steam extracted at each bleed pressure.

(3) The thermal efficiency of the cycle.

(4) The annual fuel cost if the plant operates for 12 months at the design load. Energy costs are estimated at 20¢ per 10^6 Btu.

2. HTGR fuel contains 10 moles of ThC_2 per mole of 93 percent enriched UC_2. The core contains 150 kg of uranium. The fuel exposure is to be 70,000 MWd/ton.

(1) What is the total weight of fuel material in the core loading?

(2) What fraction of the heavy atoms is ^{235}U?

(3) Assuming that all fissions involved ^{235}U, what weight of ^{235}U would be fissioned? Considering that some fissile atoms are consumed by non-fission captures, compute the weight of ^{235}U burned up.

(4) What percentage of the original fissile atoms is consumed?

3. The Peach Bottom HTGR net station heat rate is 9800 Btu/kW hr and the net electrical output is 40 MWe. Water enters the steam generator at 425°F and leaves as superheated steam at 1450 psia and 1000°F. The helium enters the reactor at 660°F and leaves at 1380°F. Compute the flow rates required for the helium and the steam. If the fuel cost is 19¢ per 10^6 Btu, compute the fuel cost for one full year of full power operation.

4. A pressurized water reactor (PWR) passes 100×10^6 lbs of 2000 psia water through the core per hour. The temperature of the water increases from 540°F to 585°F. In the steam generator the high pressure water transfers heat to generate steam at 800 psia. This steam expands to 80 psia in the high pressure turbine. Moisture is separated and live steam reheat increases the steam temperature to 500°F before it enters the low pressure casing. In the low pressure turbine the steam expands to 10 psia where a fraction is bled to a closed feed-water heater. Expansion continues to the

condenser pressure of 2" Hg. The separated moisture is drained to an open feed-water heater. The condensate from the reheater is also trapped back to this same OFWH. The closed FWH has a 10°F terminal temperature difference. Each segment of the turbine expansion is 80 percent efficient and the pumps are 60 percent efficient.

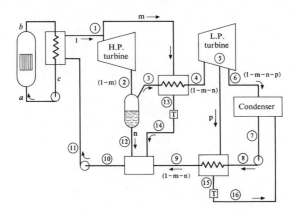

(1) Sketch the cycle on the TS plane.
(2) How many pounds of steam per hour must be generated?
(3) How many MWe can be produced if the turbines drive a 92 percent efficient generator?
(4) What is the thermal efficiency of the cycle?

5. An 150 million gallon per day water plant uses the arrangement of equipment shown below. The following operating conditions exist.
   Sea water inlet temperature, 60°F
   Temperature of sea water leaving the heat rejection system, 72°F
   Temperature of brine leaving the heat rejection system, 72°F
   Temperature of brine leaving the heat recovery system at brine heater, 220°F
   Temperature of brine leaving the brine heater, 235°F
   Temperature of product water, 78°F
   Sea water, 525,000 gpm
   Makeup brine, 2 × condensate
   Steam from back pressure turbine, 30 psia and 85 percent quality

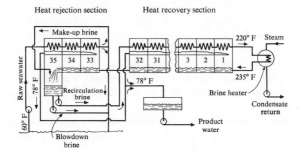

Determine the following:

(1) The steam flow from the back pressure turbine (lbs/hr).

(2) The plant performance (lbs water produced per pound of steam).

(3) The temperature of the brine as it flows from the heat recovery section to the heat rejection section.

6. An HTGR is to be coupled to a gas turbine in a direct cycle, as shown in Fig. 13.23. The helium flow rate is 320,000 lbs/hr. Gas enters the turbine at 1346°F and 367 psia. It is discharged at 842°F and 144 psia. The regenerative heat exchanger cools the gas to 220°F. At the inlet to the first stage of the 3 stage compressor the pressure is 140 psia and the temperature is 60°F. After each stage of compression the temperature is 150°F and intercooling returns the temperature to 60°F at the inlet of the second and third stages. The discharge pressure from the third stage is 375 psia.

Assume equal pressure ratios in each stage of the compressor and that the pressure drop through the intercoolers may be neglected.

(1) List the pressure and temperature at each point in the cycle.

(2) What is the reactor power (MWt)?

(3) What is the net cycle output (MWe)?

(4) If the fuel cost is 17¢ per 10^6 Btu, how much will fuel cost to operate the plant at full load for one year? What will be the fuel cost in mills/KWhr?

(5) What is the plant thermal efficiency and heat rate if the generator efficiency is 97%?

(6) What would be the fuel cost in mills/KWhr for a plant with a single stage compressor having the same efficiency as each stage in the 3 stage machine and the same regenerator efficiency?

REFERENCES

1. Gast, P. F., *Nuclear Power Growth and Uranium Supplies*. 5th AMU-ANL Faculty Student Conference (August, 1966).

2. Graham, R. H., *30-Year Fuel Cycle Price Forecast*. G. E. BWR Seminar (October 25–29, 1964).

3. *Power Reactor Technology*, **3**, No. 2 (March, 1960), pp. 1–12.

4. Rosenthal, M. W., and others, *A Comparative Evaluation of Advanced Converters*. ORNL-3686, (January, 1965).

5. Glasstone, S., and Sesonske, A. *Nuclear Reactor Engineering*. New York: D. Van Nostrand Company, Inc., 1963.

6. El-Wakil, M. M., *Nuclear Power Engineering*. New York: McGraw-Hill Book Company, Inc., 1962.

7. "Advances in Thermal Performance of Nuclear Reactor Cores," Westinghouse R and D Letter (December, 1966).

8. Connecticut Yankee Atomic Power Company, *Facilities Description and Safety Analysis*, Vols. I and II. Topical Report No. NYO-3250-5.

9. Connecticut Yankee Atomic Power Company, *Annual Report*, July 1965–June 1966. Topical Report No. NYO-3250-8 (October, 1966).

10. Elliott, V. A., "Boiling Water Reactor," *Mechanical Engineering*, **89**, No. 1 (January, 1966), pp. 19–26.

11. Parrish, J. R., Roy, G. M., and Bailey, F. G., "Nuclear Power Plant of T.V.A. at Brown's Ferry, Background and Description," American Power Conference, Chicago, Ill. (April 25–27, 1967).

12. Bray, A. P., *Operating and Control Characteristics of a BWR.* G. E. BWR Seminar (October, 25–29, 1964).

13. Hoyt, H. K., *Operation and Performance of the Dresden Nuclear Power Station.* 24th Annual Meeting of the American Power Conference (March, 1962).

14. Williamson, H. E., Ditmore, D. C., "Current BWR Fuel Design Experience," *Reactor Technology*, **14**, 1 (Spring 1971).

15. Steigelman, W., "The Outlook for Nuclear Power-Station Capital Costs," *Reactor Technology*, **13**, 1 (Winter 69–70).

16. Edison Elec. Inst., "Report on the EEI Reactor Assessment Panel," Edison Elec. Inst., New York, 1970.

17. Mason, E. A., "An Over-all View of the Nuclear Fuel Cycle," *Nuclear News*, **14**, 2 (Feb. 1971), pp. 35–38.

18. Fraas, A. P., *A Potassium-Steam Binary Vapor Cycle for a Molten Salt Reactor Power Plant.* ASME Paper No. 66-GT/CLC-5 (1966).

19. Zinn, W. H., and Dietrich, J. R., "Peach Bottom Reactor," *Power Reactor Technology*, **5**, No. 3 (June, 1962), pp. 61–65.

20. Philadelphia Electric Co., Application of Philadelphia Electric Co. for Construction Permit and Class 104 License, Part B, *Preliminary Hazards Summary Report*, Vol. I, *Plant Description and Safeguards Analysis.* Report NP-9115 (July, 1960).

21. Bechtel Corp., *Engineering and Economic Feasibility Study for a Combination Nuclear Power and Desalting Plant Summary.* Vol. III. TID-22330 (January, 1966).

22. Holtom, H. T., and Galstaum, L. S., *Study of 150 MGD Desalted Water-Power Plant for Southern California.* 1st International Symposium on Water Desalination, SWD/92 (October, 1965).

23. Othmer, D. F., *Technology of Water Desalination.* U. N. Pub. 64. II. B. 5, Annex A, 1964.

24. Holtom, H. T., *Integration of a Nuclear Power-Desalting Plant into the Metropolitan Water District System.* 5th Annual AMU-ANL Faculty Student Conference (August, 1966).

25. Homer, W. A., *Combination Nuclear Power and Desalting Plant: Engineering and Economic Feasibility Study.* 5th Annual AMU-ANL Faculty Student Conference (August, 1966).

26. Meneghetti, D., *Introductory Fast Reactor Physics Analysis*, ANL-6809 (1963).

27. McLain, S., and Martens, J. H., *Reactor Handbook.* Vol. IV, Engineering. New York: Interscience Publishers, 1964.

28. Stoker, D. J., Balent, R., "Design of the Atomics International Fast Breeder Demonstration Plant," ASME Paper No. 71-NE-16 (1971).

29. Langley, Jr., R. A., "Evolution of the LMFBR Plant Design for Reliability and Availability," ASME Paper No. 71-NE-3 (1971).

30. Bauman, H. F., and Kasten, P. R., "Fuel Cycle Analysis of Molten Salt Breeder Reactors." *Nuclear Applications*, **2**, No. 4 (August, 1966).

31. Post, R. G., and Seale, R. L., *Water Production Using Nuclear Energy.* The University of Arizona Press, 1966.

32. Lee, W. S., "Environmental Effects of Thermal Discharges-Technological Elements," Effects of Thermal Discharges (ASME Symposium), 1970.

33. Mount, D. I., "Environmental Effects of Thermal Discharges-Ecological Elements," Effects of Thermal Discharges (ASME Symposium), 1970.

34. Leung, P., Moore, R. E., "Thermal Cycle Arrangements for Power Plants Employing Dry Cooling Towers," ASME Paper No. 70-PWR-6 (1970).

35. Beall, Jr., S. E., "Uses of Waste Heat," ASME Paper No. 70-WA/Ener (1970).

36. Postma, H., "Engineering and Environmental Aspects of Fusion Power Reactors," *Nuclear News*, **14**, 4 (Apr. 1971), pp. 57-62.

37. Steiner, D., "The Nuclear Performance of Fusion Reactor Blankets," *Nuclear Applications & Technology*, **9**, 1 (July, 1970), pp. 83-92.

38. Rose, D. J., "Engineering Feasibility of Controlled Fusion—A Review," *Nuclear Fusion*, **9**, 3 (Oct. 1969), pp. 183-203.

39. Gough, W. C., Eastlund, B. J., "The Prospects of Fusion Power," *Scientific American*, **224**, 2 (Feb. 1971), pp. 50-67.

40. Lubin, M. J., Fraas, A. P., "Fusion by Laser," *Scientific American*, **224**, 6 (June, 1971), pp. 21-33.

41. Merriman, D., et al., "The Connecticut River Investigation, 1965-72," A series of semiannual reports submitted to the Water Resources. Commission of the state of Connecticut.

42. Katterhenry, A. A., "Gas Turbine Power Plants," *Reactor Technology*, **13**, 1 (Winter 1969-1970), pp. 7-13.

43. Böhm, E., Ehret, A., Geppert, H., Hauck, W., Küper, K. D., "The 25 MW Schleswig-Holstein Nuclear Power Plant (Greesthacht II)," *Kerntechnik*, 11(2), Feb. 1969, pp. 69-76.

44. Taygun, F. and Frutschi, H. U., "Conventional and Nuclear Gas Turbines for Combined Power and Heat Production," ASME Paper No. 70-GT-22, 1970.

45. Bammert, K., et al., "Performance of High-Temperature Reactor and Helium Turbine, *Kerntechnik*, 11(2), Feb. 1969, pp. 77ff.

46. Dalle Donne, M., et al., "High Temperature Gas Cooling for Fast Breeders," *Kerntechnik*, 11(2), Feb. 1969, pp. 99ff.

47. Bishop, W. N. and Nitti, D. A., "Stability of Thiosulphate Spray Solutions," *Nuclear Technology*, **10**, No. 4 (April, 1971), pp. 449-453.

48. Gallagher, J. L., Green, L. D., and Marchese, R. T., *Nuclear Technology*, **10**, No. 4 (April, 1971), pp. 406-411.

49. Charak, I., "The Emergency Core Cooling Problem in LMFBR's," *Reactor Technology*, **13**, No. 3 (Summer 1970), pp. 280-309.

50. Hesson, J. C., "Retaining Fast Reactor Fuel Debris in the Secondary Containment," *A.N.S. Transactions*, **14**, No. 1 (June, 1971), pp. 294-295.

51. Rosenthal, M. W., Kasten, P. R., & Briggs, R. B., "Molten-Salt Reactors—History, Status, & Potential," *Nuclear Applications & Technology*, **8**, No. 2 (Feb. 1970), pp. 107-117.

52. McCoy, E. E., et al., "New Developments in Materials for Molten-Salt

Reactors," *Nuclear Applications & Technology*, **8,** No. 2 (Feb. 1970), pp. 156–169.

53. Whatley, E. E., et al., "Engineering Development of the MSBR Fuel Cycle," *Nuclear Applications & Technology*, **8,** No. 2 (Feb. 1970), pp. 170–179.

54. Scott, D., Eatherly, W. P., "Graphite and Xenon Behavior and Their Influence on Molten-Salt Reactor Design," *Nuclear Applications & Technology*, **8,** No. 2 (Feb. 1970), pp. 179–189.

55. Bettis, E. S., and Robertson, R. C., "The Design and Performance Features of a Single-Fluid Molten-Salt Reactor," *Nuclear Applications & Technology*, **8,** No. 2 (Feb. 1970), pp. 190–207.

56. Perry, A. M., and Bauman, H. F., "Reactor Physics and Fuel Cycle Analysis," *Nuclear Applications & Technology*, **8,** No. 2 (Feb. 1970), pp. 208–219.

Nuclear Data for Various Elements and Isotopes

Atomic No. Z	Element or Isotope	Abundance %	Atomic Mass Weight u	Density gm/cm³	Half-Life	Absorption at 0.025eV	Scattering Thermal	Scattering Epithermal
1	H	~100	1.00797			0.332	38	20.4
	^{1}H	~100	1.007825			0.332	38	20.4
	^{2}H (D)	0.0151	2.01410			0.00046	7	3.4
	^{3}H (T)	—	3.01605		12.6y			
2	He		4.0026			0.007	0.8	0.83
	^{3}He	0.00013	3.01603			5500	0.8	
	^{4}He	~100	4.00260			0	0.8	
3	Li		6.939	0.53		70	1.4	0.9
	^{6}Li	7.52	6.01513			945(n, α)		
	^{7}Li	92.48	7.01601			0.033		
	^{8}Li	—			0.845s			
4	^{8}Be	—	8.00531		~3 × 10^{-16}s			
	^{9}Be	100	9.01219	1.82		0.010	7	6.11
5	B		10.811	2.54		755	4	3.7
	^{10}B	19.8	10.01294			3813(n, α)		
	^{11}B	80.2	11.00931			<50 × 10^{-3}		
	^{12}B	—			0.019s			
6	C		12.01115	2.22		0.0034	4.8	4.66
	^{12}C	98.89	12.00000					
	^{13}C	1.11	13.00335			0.0005		
	^{14}C	—			5570y			
7	N		14.0067			1.88	10	9.9
	^{13}N	—			10m			
	^{14}N	99.63	14.00307			1.75		
	^{15}N	0.37	15.00011					
	^{16}N	—			7.4s			
8	O		15.9994			0.00019	4.2	3.75
	^{16}O	99.759	15.99491					
	^{17}O	0.037	16.99914					
	^{18}O	0.204	17.99916					
	^{19}O	—			29s			
9	^{19}F	100	18.99840			0.010	3.9	3.6
11	^{23}Na	100	22.98977	0.971		0.53	4.0	3.1
	^{24}Na	—			15.05h			
12	Mg		24.312	1.74		0.063	3.6	3.4
	^{24}Mg	78.60	23.98504			0.034		
	^{25}Mg	10.11	24.98584			0.280		

Nuclear Data for Various Elements and Isotopes

Atomic No. Z	Element or Isotope	Abundance %	Atomic Mass Weight u	Density gm/cm³	Half-Life	Absorption at 0.025eV	Scattering Thermal	Epithermal
	^{26}Mg	11.29	25.98259			0.050		
	^{27}Mg	—			9.45m			
13	^{27}Al	100	26.9815	2.70		0.230	1.4	1.4
	^{28}Al	—			2.3m			
14	Si		28.086	2.4		0.16	1.7	2.2
	^{28}Si	92.27	27.97693			0.080		
	^{29}Si	4.68	28.97649			0.280		
	^{30}Si	3.05	29.97376			0.40		
	^{31}Si	—			2.62y			
15	^{31}P	100	30.97376	2.34		0.20	5	3.4
17	^{37}Cl	24.47	36.96590			56		
18	^{37}Ar	—	36.96678		35.1d			
19	K	—	39.102	0.87		2.07	2.5	2.1
22	Ti		47.90	4.5		5.8	4	4.2
23	V		50.942	6.0		4.5	5.0	
24	Cr		51.996	6.92		3.1	3.0	3.9
	^{53}Cr	9.55	52.9407			1.82		
25	^{55}Mn	100	54.9381	7.2		13.2	2.3	1.9
	^{56}Mn	—			2.58h			
26	Fe		55.847	7.87		2.62	11	11.4
	^{54}Fe	5.84	53.9396			2.3		
	^{55}Fe	—			2.6y			
	^{56}Fe	91.68	55.9349			2.7		
	^{57}Fe	2.17	56.9354			2.5		
	^{58}Fe	0.31	57.9333			1.2		
	^{59}Fe	—			45d			
	^{58}Co	—			71.3d	1.9×10^3		
27	^{59}Co	100	58.9332	8.71		18 & 19	7	5.8
	^{60}Co	—			10.5m & 5.24y			
28	Ni		58.71	8.9		4.8	17.5	17.4
29	Cu		63.54	8.96		3.77	7.2	7.7
	^{63}Cu	69.1	62.9298			4.6		
	^{64}Cu	—			12.9h			
	^{65}Cu	30.9	64.9278			2.2		
	^{66}Cu	—			5.1m			
37	^{87}Rb	27.85			4.7×10^{10}y	0.12		
40	Zr		91.22	6.44		0.180	8	6.2

Nuclear Data for Various Elements and Isotopes

Atomic No. Z	Element or Isotope	Abundance %	Atomic Mass Weight u	Density gm/cm³	Half-Life	Absorption at 0.025eV	Scattering Thermal	Scattering Epithermal
41	^{93}Nb	100	92.90638	8.57		1.15	5	6.5
	^{94}Nb	—			6.6m			
42	Mo		95.911	10.22		2.7	7	6
47	Ag		107.870	10.50		63	6	6.4
	^{107}Ag	51.35	106.9051			31		
	^{108}Ag	—			2.3m			
	^{109}Ag	48.65	108.9047			87		
	^{110}Ag	—			24s			
48	Cd		112.40	8.64		2450	7	
49	In		114.82	7.28		196	2.2	
	^{113}In	4.2	112.9043					
	^{114}In	—			72s & 49d			
	^{115}In	95.77	114.9039		6×10^{14}y	50 and 150		
	^{116}In	—			14s and 54m			
54	Xe		131.30			35	4.3	
	^{135}Xe	—			9.2h	2.72×10^6		
	^{136}Xe	8.87	135.9072			0.15		
62	Sm		150.35	7.7		5600		
	^{149}Sm	13.84	148.9169			40,800		
64	Gd		157.25	7.94		46,000		
	^{155}Gd	14.73	154.9226			61,000		
	^{157}Gd	15.68	156.9239			240,000		
79	^{197}Au	100	196.9666	19.3		98.8	9.3	
	^{198}Au	—			2.7d	26,000		
82	Pb		207.19	11.35		0.170	11	11.3
	^{204}Pb	1.5	203.9731		1.4×10^{17}y	0.8		
	^{205}Pb	—			3×10^7y			
	^{206}Pb	23.6	205.9745			0.025		
	^{207}Pb	22.6	206.9759			0.70		
	^{208}Pb	52.3	207.9766			0.03		
	^{209}Pb	—	208.9810		3.3h			
83	^{209}Bi	100	208.9804	9.8		0.019 & 0.015	9	9.28
	^{210}Bi	—			2.6×10^6y & 50d			
	^{211}Bi	—			2.15m			
84	^{210}Po	—	209.9829		138d			
	^{213}Po	—	212.9928		4μs			
88	^{226}Ra	—	226.0254		1620y	20		

Nuclear Data for Various Elements and Isotopes

Atomic No. Z	Element or Isotope	Abun- dance %	Atomic Mass Weight u	Density gm/cm³	Half-Life	Absorp- tion at 0.025eV	Scattering Ther- mal	Epi- ther- mal
90	^{230}Th	—	230.0331		7.6×10^4y			
	^{232}Th	100	232.0382	11.5	1.45×10^{10}y	7.56	12.5	12.5
	^{233}Th	—			22.1m			
91	^{233}Pa	—			27.4d	43		
92	U		238.03	19.0		7.68	8.3	
	^{233}U		233.0395		1.62×10^5y	530(n, f) 46(n, γ)		
	^{234}U	0.0057	234.0409		2.5×10^5y	105		
	^{235}U	0.714	235.0439		7.1×10^8y	582(n, f) 112(n, γ)	10	
	^{236}U	—	236.0457		2.39×10^7y	7		
	^{237}U	—			6.75d			
	^{238}U	99.28	238.0508		4.51×10^9y	2.71	8.3	
	^{239}U	—			23.5m	14(n, f)		
93	^{239}Np	—			2.35d			
	^{238}Pu	—	238.04958		87.8y			
94	^{239}Pu	—	239.0522	19.6	24,360y	746(n, f) 280(n, γ)	9.6	
	^{240}Pu	—	240.0540		6760y	<0.1(n, f) 295(n, γ)		
	^{241}Pu	—			15y	1025(n, f) 375(n, γ)		
	^{242}Pu	—	242.0587		3.79×10^5y	<0.2(n, f) 30(n, γ)		
95	^{241}Am	—	241.0567		433y	710(n, γ) 3(n, f)		
96	^{242}Cm	—	242.0588		163d	25(n, γ) <5(n, f)		
	^{244}Cm	—	244.0628		18.1y	~13(n, γ) 1(n, f)		
98	^{252}Cf	—	252.08		2.65y(α) 85.5y(s. fis.)	20(n, γ)		

APPENDIX B

Various Convenient Constants

Proton Rest Mass	1.007277 u
Neutron Rest Mass	1.008665 u
Electron Rest Mass	0.000548597 u
Avagadro's Number	6.02252×10^{23} molecules/gm mole (atoms/gm atom)
Rydberg Constant (infinite)	109,737.309 cm^{-1}
Boltzman's Constant	1.38054×10^{-16} erg K^{-1}
	8.617065×10^{-5} eV K^{-1}
Speed of Light	2.997925×10^{10} cm/sec
Planck's Constant	6.6252×10^{-27} erg sec
	4.1355×10^{-15} eV sec

APPENDIX C

Useful Conversion Factors

1 u	1.660438×10^{-24} gm
	931.482 MeV
1 Curie	3.7×10^{10} disintegrations/sec
1 esu	1 gm$^{1/2}$ cm$^{3/2}$/sec
1 Coulomb	2.998×10^{9} esu
1 erg	1 gm cm^2/sec^2
	0.6242×10^6 MeV
1 eV	1.60210×10^{-12} erg
	1.517×10^{-22} Btu
	4.44×10^{-26} kW hr
1 fission	$\sim$200 MeV (total)
	8.9×10^{-18} kW hr (total)
	$\sim$180 MeV (in fuel)
1 Joule	10^7 ergs
1 hp	2545 Btu/hr
	0.7457 kW
	550 ft lb/sec
1 unit electronic charge	4.80×10^{-10} esu
1 Watt	1 Joule/sec
	3.4 Btu/hr

Table of Radioisotopes

Isotope	Half-Life	Type Decay	Most Predominant Energy (ies) MeV
$_0^1$n	12.8m	β^-	0.78
$_1^3$H	12.6y	β^-	0.18
$_3^8$Li	0.845s	β^-	13
		2α	3.2(total)
$_4^8$Be	$<1.4 \times 10^{-16}$s	2α	0.047(each)
$_6^{14}$C	5568y	β^-	0.155
$_7^{13}$N	10m	β^+	1.24
$_{11}^{22}$Na	2.6y	β^+, γ	0.542, 1.28
$_{11}^{24}$Na	15hr	$\beta^-, \gamma_1-\gamma_2$	1.39, 1.37–2.75
$_{13}^{28}$Al	2.27m	β^-, γ	2.86, 1.78
$_{15}^{32}$P	14.3d	β^-	1 707
$_{19}^{40}$K	1.2×10^9y	β^-	1.33(89%)
		EC, γ	1.46(11%)
$_{20}^{47}$Ca	4.8d	β^-, γ	0.66, 1.3
$_{21}^{47}$Sc	3.43d	β^-, γ	0.439, 0.160(60%)
		β^-	0.60 (40%)
$_{23}^{48}$V	16.0d	EC, β^+, γ_1, γ_2	0.69, 0.986, 1.314
$_{23}^{53}$V	2.0m	β^-, γ	2.50, 1.00
$_{26}^{55}$Fe	2.6y	EC	
$_{26}^{59}$Fe	45d	β^-, γ	0.460, 1.10(54%)
			0.270, 1.29(46%)
$_{27}^{60}$Co	5.24y	$\beta^-, \gamma_1, \gamma_2$	0.302, 1.33, 1.17
$_{29}^{64}$Cu	12.9h	EC, γ	1.34 (42%)
		β^-	0.571 (39%)
		β^+	0.657 (19%)
$_{29}^{66}$Cu	5.1m	β^-	2.63 (91%)
		β^-, γ	1.5, 1.04(9%)
$_{30}^{65}$Zn	245d	EC	(55%)
		EC, γ	1.12(45%)
$_{36}^{85}$Kr	10.3y	β^-	0.695 (98.5%)
		β^-, γ	0.15, 0.54(0.65%)
$_{38}^{90}$Sr	27.7y	β^-	0.545
$_{39}^{90}$Y	64.2h	β^-	2.26
$_{47}^{108}$Ag	2.3m	β^-	1.77(97%)
		EC, γ	0.45(1.5%)
$_{47}^{110}$Ag	24s	β^-	2.82 (40%)
		β^-, γ	2.24, 0.66(60%)

Table of Radioisotopes

Isotope	Half-Life	Type Decay	Most Predominant Energy (ies) MeV
$_{49}^{116}$In	13s	β^-	3.29
$_{53}^{131}$I	8.08d	β^-, γ	0.608, 0.364(87.2%)
		β^-, γ	0.335, 0.638(9.3%)
$_{53}^{137}$I	22s	β^-	(94%)
		$\beta^-,$ n	0.56(6%)
$_{54}^{135}$Xe	9.23h	β^-, γ	0.51, 0.250(97%)
$_{54}^{137}$Xe	3.9m	β^-	3.5
$_{55}^{132}$Cs	7.1d	EC, γ	0.67
$_{55}^{137}$Cs	30y	β^-, γ	0.51, 0.66(92%)
		β^-	1.17 (8%)
$_{56}^{133}$Ba	7.2y	EC, γ	0.320, 0.081
$_{56}^{140}$Ba	12.8d	β^-, γ	1.021, 0.16–0.03(60%)
		β^-, γ	0.48, 0.54–0.03 (30%)
$_{57}^{140}$La	40h	$\beta^-, \gamma_1-\gamma_2-\gamma_3$	1.32, 0.33–0.49–1.60(70%)
		$\beta^-, \gamma_1-\gamma_2$	1.67, 0.49–1.60 (20%)
$_{58}^{144}$Ce	285d	β^-	0.309
$_{61}^{147}$Pm	2.6y	β^-	0.223
$_{77}^{192}$Ir	74.4d	EC, β^-, γ	0.66, 11 at different energies
$_{80}^{197}$Hg	65h	EC, γ	0.077
$_{82}^{214}$Pb	26.8m	β^-, γ	0.67, 0.295–0.352
$_{83}^{213}$Bi	47m	β^-	1.39 (98%)
		β^-, γ	0.959, 0.434(2%)
		α	5.86
$_{84}^{208}$Po	2.93y	α	5.108
$_{84}^{210}$Po	138d	α	5.30
$_{84}^{213}$Po	4.2×10^{-6}s	α	8.34
$_{88}^{226}$Ra	1622y	α	4.78 (94%)
		α, γ	4.77, 0.186(5.7%)
$_{90}^{231}$Th	25.6h	β^-, γ	0.308, 0.084 (44%)
		β^-, γ	0.094, 0.058, 0.026(45%)
$_{92}^{233}$U	1.62×10^5y	α	4.823
$_{92}^{234}$U	2.48×10^5y	α	4.76 (73%)
	s. f. 2×10^{16}y	α, γ	4.72, 0.05(27%)
$_{92}^{235}$U	7.1×10^8y	α	4.40 (83%)
	s. f. 1.9×10^{17}y		
$_{92}^{238}$U	4.51×10^9y	α	4.195(77%)
	s. f. 8×10^{18}y	α, γ	4.18, 0.048(23%)

Table of Radioisotopes

Isotope	Half-Life	Type Decay	Most Predominant Energy (ies) MeV
$_{92}^{239}$U	23.5m	β^-, γ	1.2, 0.73
$_{93}^{238}$Np	2.1d	β^-, γ	1.272, 0.044(47%)
		β^-, γ	0.258, 1.03 (53%)
$_{94}^{238}$Pu	89.6y	α	5.49 (72%)
	s. f. 3.8×10^{10}y	α, γ	5.45, 0.044(28%)
$_{95}^{241}$Am	458y	α, γ	5.477, 0.060
$_{96}^{242}$Cm	35y	α	6.11 (73.7%)
		α, γ	6.07, 0.044 (26.3%)
$_{96}^{244}$Cm	17.9y	α	5.801 (76.7%)
	s. f. 1.4×10^7y	α, γ	5.759, 0.043 (23.3%)
$_{98}^{252}$Cf	2.65y(97%)	α	6.12(82%)
	s. f. 85y(3%)		6.08(15%)
$_{98}^{254}$Cf	s. f. 60.5d	n	
		γ	
$_{97}^{247}$Bk	1.4×10^3y	α, γ	5.68(37%)
			5.52(58%)
$_{99}^{253}$Es	20.5d	α, β	6.64, .017, .027
$_{100}^{257}$Fm	80d	α	6.53(94%)
	s. f. 100y		
$_{101}^{257}$Md	3h	EC, α	7.25(97%), 7.08(3%)

Note: Beta energies are the maximum energies.
    s. f. = spontaneous fission

Properties of Materials for Oxide Fueled Fast Reactors

Material	σ_{fis}	σ_a	Σ_{fis}	Σ_a	η	Σ_{tr}
B (natural)		0.54		0.058**		
^{10}B		2.73		0.30**		
C		0				
O		0.001				
Na		0.0016		4×10^{-5}		0.08
Fe		0.010		0.00085		0.25
SS				0.0015		0.25
^{232}Th	0.014	0.40	0.00815*	0.0091*	0.076	0.18*
^{233}U	2.1	3.5	0.0489*	0.0815*	2.31	0.18*
^{235}U	1.3	2.71	0.0480*	0.0630*	1.93	0.18*
^{238}U	0.048	0.35	0.00112*	0.00815*	0.4	0.18*
^{239}Pu	1.8	2.36	0.0458*	0.060*	2.4	0.18*
^{240}Pu	0.5	0.72	0.0128*	0.0184*	1.315	0.18*
^{241}Pu	2.5	2.51	0.051*	0.064*	2.72	0.18*
^{242}Pu	0.35	0.71	0.0089*	0.0181*	1.4	0.18*

* As oxide
** As carbide

Answers to
Selected Problems

CHAPTER 2

1. (a) 6.02×10^{22} atoms Al/cm³
   (b) 3.91×10^{15} atoms O^{17}/cm³
   (c) 5.12×10^{22} atoms Al/cm³
3. 1.96×10^9 cm/sec. It is nonrelativistic.
5.

v/c	KE_e (MeV)	KE_D (MeV)
0.1	.00258	9.445
0.5	.0792	290.5
0.9	.6627	2430
0.999	10.94	40,118

8. $E = -3920$ eV
   $\lambda = 3.165$ Å
10. $\lambda_{min} = 0.1293$ Å
    $E_{21} = -55.9$ kev, $\lambda_{21} = 0.2219$ Å
    $E_{31} = -66.3$ kev, $\lambda_{31} = 0.1872$ Å

CHAPTER 3

2. $v/c = 0.93$
4. $t = 1600$ years

6. $t = 4.59 \times 10^9 y$
8. $wt = 0.64$ gr $^{210}P_o$
10. $t = 5.64$ days
    $N_1/N_{10} = 0.435,$ $N_2/N_{10} = 0.305,$ $N_3/N_{10} = 0.260$
12. $t_{max} = 5.654d$
    at t_{max} $N_{Ba}/N_0 = 0.73625,$ $N_{La}/N_0 = 0.09635,$ $N_{ce}/N_0 = 0.16741$

CHAPTER 4

2. 11.95 MeV per alpha
4. $Q_{(r,n)} = 1.66$ MeV
    $v_\alpha = 1.576 \times 10^8$ cm/sec
6. $KE_\gamma = 2.226$ MeV, $V_D = 3.555 \times 10^7$ cm/sec
    $KE_D = 1.319$ KeV
9. $Q = 4.79$ MeV
12. $^{40}_{20}Ca + ^{16}_{8}O \rightarrow ^{56}_{28}Ni^* \rightarrow ^{53}_{27}Co + 2^1_0n + ^1_1p$
    $^{54}_{26}Fe + ^1_1p \rightarrow ^{55}_{27}Co^* \rightarrow ^{53}_{27}Co + 2^1_0n$

CHAPTER 5

1. Aluminum — 0.00141 cm
    Lead — 0.000760 cm
3. $\mu m = 0.0595$ cm^2/gm
    $x_{1/2} = 1.03$ cm
5. 35.6 percent
7. 4 volts
10. 101 ± 11 cpm

CHAPTER 6

2. 11.4 hrs at 1 cm
4. 3.58 mrem/hr
6. 244 mrem
8. 400 mrem
10. 1.265×10^{-1} micro curies/cm^3

CHAPTER 7

3. 127 gm/sec
5. 2225 yrs

7. $T_H = 453°K$
   $\eta_{th} = 5.9$ percent
9. 0.615 gm

CHAPTER 8

1. (a) 1.66 n/cm² sec
   (b) 9.76 × 10⁴ n/cm² sec
3. (a) $v_p = 3587$ m/sec
   (b) $v = 4070$ m/sec
   (c) $KE_{mp} = 0.0333$ eV
5. (a)   3.68 × 10⁸ μci (2 hr)
         7.02 × 10⁴ μci (2 days)
        17.55 × 10⁴ μci (2 months)
   (b)   5.4 × 10⁴ μci
7. 6.32 × 10⁻² curies
9. $\dot{T}_1 = 0.996$ Ci/day due to ¹⁰B(n, 2α)T
   $\dot{T}_2 = 3.00$ ci/day due to ¹⁰B(n, α) ⁷Li(n, αn)T
   $\dot{T} = 4.00$ ci/day
11. (a) $\xi = 0.174$
    (b) $MSDP = 0.110$
    (c) $n = 97$ collisions
    (d) $MR = 315$
    (e) $\alpha_{Be} = 0.64$, $(E/E_0)_{\theta=90} = 0.82$

CHAPTER 9

1. $\eta = 1.86$ fast n's emitted/thermal n abs in fuel
3. $k_\infty = 0.776$
5. $k_\infty = 1.202$
7. $P = 94.5$ kW(th)
10. $x_g = (2/B) \arctan (D_r/D_c BL_r)$
13. $x_g = \pi/B - (\arctan L_r B)/B - 0.71\lambda_{tr}$
15. $L_s = 17.25$ cm
    $M = 19.58$ cm
17.

	1 Grp.	Mod 1 Grp.	2 Grp.
r_g	99.8	170.5	172.5
h_g	199.5	341.1	344.9

19. $k_\infty = 1.295$
    $r_g = 106$ cm

CHAPTER 10

1. $U^{233} - 0.049$ sec
    $Pu^{239} - 0.033$ sec
3. $0.565
5. 5.95 inhours
7. Sm $= -0.720\%$,   Xe $= -2.8\%$
10. $0.144
14. CR $= 0.934$
    $\Delta\rho = \$-49.34$

CHAPTER 11

1. $T_m = \dfrac{4AE}{(A+1)^2}$
3. 10,880 displ./collision with 14 MeV neutron
    433 displ./collision with 1 MeV neutron

CHAPTER 12

1. $T_{max} = 1804°F$
3. (a) $(q/A)_{max} = 5.98 \times 10^4$ Btu/hr ft^2
    (b) $P = 6.63$ kW
    (c) $T_0 = T_s = T_{max} = 430°F$
5. (a) $S = 7.38$ Btu/in^3 sec
    (b) $\Delta T_{cl} = 116°F$
    (c) $T_{max} = 1966°F$
6. $T_m = 1401$ C
    $(q/A)_0 = 27.61$ w/cm^2 (87,200 Btu/hr ft^2)
9. $x_e = 0.381$
    $F_{S_2} = 1.22$

CHAPTER 13

1. 0.535×10^6 lb/hr bled at 300 psia
    0.459×10^6 lb/hr bled at 50 psia
    $e_{th} = 0.294$
    $FC = \$3,700,000/yr$
3. $m_{H_2O} = 362,000$ lb/hr
    $m_{He} = 435,000$ lb/hr

$FC = \$650{,}000/\text{yr}$

5. (a) 1.072×10^5 lbs stm/min
    (b) 8.06 lb fresh water/lb steam
    (c) 88.6°F

Index

(NOTE: Elements written as ^{238}U, are indexed as Uranium^{238}.)